UTOPIAS
AND UTOPIAN THOUGHT

THE DAEDALUS LIBRARY

Each of these volumes is available as a Beacon Press Paperback.

A New Europe? Edited by Stephen R. Graubard
The Professions in America, Edited by Kenneth S. Lynn
The Woman in America, Edited by Robert Jay Lifton
Science and Culture, Edited by Gerald Holton
Utopias and Utopian Thought, Edited by Frank E. Manuel
The Contemporary University: U.S.A., Edited by Robert S. Morison
The Negro American, Edited by Talcott Parsons and Kenneth B. Clark
Creativity and Learning, Edited by Jerome Kagan
Religion in America, Edited by William G. McLoughlin and Robert N. Bellah
Toward the Year 2000, Edited by Daniel Bell
Fiction in Several Languages, Edited by Henri Peyre
Color and Race, Edited by John Hope Franklin
Students in Revolt, Edited by Seymour Martin Lipset and Philip G. Altbach
America's Changing Environment, Edited by Roger Revelle and Hans H. Landsberg

UTOPIAS
AND UTOPIAN THOUGHT

EDITED BY FRANK E. MANUEL

BEACON PRESS BOSTON

First published as a Beacon Paperback in 1967 by arrangement with Houghton Mifflin Company

Beacon Press books are published under the auspices of the Unitarian Universalist Association

Published simultaneously in Canada by Saunders of Toronto, Ltd.

With the exception of the Introduction by Frank E. Manuel, "Paradise and Utopia" by Mircea Eliade, "Utopia and Cultural Renewal" by Frederik L. Polak, and "Critique and Justification of Utopia" by Paul Tillich, the essays in this book first appeared in the Spring 1965 issue of *Dædalus*, the Journal of the American Academy of Arts and Sciences.

Printed in the United States of America

International Standard Book Number: 0–8070–1579–2

Second printing, July 1971

CONTENTS

vii FRANK E. MANUEL
Introduction

I. The Historical Dimension

3 LEWIS MUMFORD
Utopia, The City and The Machine

25 NORTHROP FRYE
Varieties of Literary Utopias

50 CRANE BRINTON
Utopia and Democracy

69 FRANK E. MANUEL
Toward a Psychological History of Utopias

II. Utopia Is Dead

101 JUDITH SHKLAR
The Political Theory of Utopia: From Melancholy to Nostalgia

116 ADAM ULAM
Socialism and Utopia

III. Limitations on Utopia

137 PAUL B. SEARS
Utopia and the Living Landscape

150 JOHN MAYNARD SMITH
Eugenics and Utopia

169 JOHN R. PIERCE
Communications Technology and the Future

IV. Utopia as Practice

183 MAREN LOCKWOOD
The Experimental Utopia in America

201 FRANÇOIS BLOCH-LAINÉ
The Utility of Utopias for Reformers

219 BERTRAND DE JOUVENEL
Utopia for Practical Purposes

V. Utopia the Eternal Human

239 GEORGE KATEB
Utopia and the Good Life

260 MIRCEA ELIADE
Paradise and Utopia: Mythical Geography and Eschatology

281 FREDERIK L. POLAK
Utopia and Cultural Renewal

296 PAUL TILLICH
Critique and Justification of Utopia

310 Notes on Contributors

313 Index

FRANK E. MANUEL

Introduction

In Western culture visions of the ideal society have generally assumed either of two primary forms. One has been descriptive, a dramatic narrative portrayal of a way of life that was so intrinsically good and fulfilled so many profound longings that it would win immediate, almost instinctive, approbation. The other model has been more rationalistic: the underlying principles of an optimum society are expounded and argued either by the author directly or by several interlocutors.

The distinction is as old as Plato. In the opening of the *Timaeus* Socrates voiced his vague dissatisfaction with mere discourse about the framework of an ideal city as it had emerged in the *Republic:*

> I may compare my feeling to something of this kind: suppose, for instance, that on seeing beautiful creatures, whether works of art or actually alive but in repose, a man should be moved with desire to behold them in motion and vigorously engaged in some such exercise as seemed suitable to their physique; well, that is the very feeling I have regarding the State we have described.[1]

Unfortunately, the Platonic dialogue in which Critias, in response to the challenge, undertakes to "imitate" an ideal state "in action"—the depiction of the real life of those perfect primeval Athenians who defeated the Atlantans—is only a truncated fragment. It was not until some nineteen centuries later that Thomas More finally realized the Socratic wish in his *Utopia.* In the title of the present volume this differentiation between utopia and utopian thought has been preserved, and we have provided for the inclusion of both modes of expression, albeit our colleague Bertrand de Jouvenel, for good and sufficient reasons of his own, would drive abstract philosophers who debate rather than describe from the society of true utopians. Neither utopian form is of course ever, or rarely ever, found in a simon-pure state, since the living portrait rests on a set of implicit psychological assumptions about the nature of man, and the discursive exposition of utopian principles resorts to frequent illustration.

There have been many attempts to divide the inchoate body of utopias into polar types: the soft and the hard, the static and the dynamic, the sensate and the spiritual, the aristocratic and the plebeian, the utopia of escape and the utopia of realization, the collectivist and individualistic utopias. Such typologies all have their uses, and their very multiplicity suggests that utopian types can be as varied as life itself. The "speaking picture"—to borrow Sir Philip Sydney's fortunate name for utopia—may resurrect a good historical society that has been in ages past and should be again. It may idealize or romanticize an existing polity, even one's own, project the vision far into space—to a distant island, a mountain-top, a hidden valley, another planet, into the bowels of the earth—or in time, into a future epoch. The vision may be born of a mere wish, often a rather hopeless wish; or, at the other extreme, its actualization may be accepted on faith as inevitable in some historical or religious sense, in which event the separation of plain foretelling from dream becomes problematic. In a few exceptional instances the vision turns out to be essentially a playful exercise. Though Northrop Frye's essay on the "Varieties of Literary Utopias" would insist on the divorcement of the pastoral from the classically utopian, which in his judgment is a "city-dominated society," he is well aware that the pastoral element has insinuated itself into utopian thinking. The flood of eighteenth-century nature-utopias, both exotic and domestic, amply bears out his interpretation.

In the religious West, one is confronted with the question as to whether paradise is an ideal society. If one does not enclose oneself within terrestrial limits, then religious heaven, a rather selective society, has as much claim to the epithet utopian as those visions that soar to other planetary abodes beyond our tiny sphere. The heavenly city has relentlessly possessed the Western mind, though reasonable men might differ over the appropriateness of its intrusion into our secular deliberations. Surely Mircea Eliade and the late Paul Tillich would have objected to the neglect of the religious utopia, and we would have been the poorer without their participation in our volume.

I

Like the utopias themselves, the analytic study of utopia has also had a long tradition going back to the Greeks. The conviction that certain "ideal states" demanded critical examination was first expressed by Aristotle in Book II of the *Politics,* where he entered the lists against states "designed by the theorists" and seriatim took on Plato, Phaleas of Chalcedon, and Hippodamus of Miletus. If we forego a laborious tracing of Aristotle's successors among the Church Fathers and the Schoolmen and restrict ourselves to relatively modern times, the earliest academic treatment of utopian thought is probably a still-born Latin dissertation published in Cologne in 1704 by the hapless Henricus ab Ahlefeld, whose fame has been obscured by cataloguers attributing his work to Georg Pasch, the professor who approved the thesis.[2] It was not until Louis Reybaud's *Études sur les réformateurs ou socialistes moderne,* crowned by the Academy of Moral and Political Sciences in 1841, that the *utopies sociales,* which he considered subversive, received fulsome consideration. Simultaneously, on the other side of the Rhine, Robert von Mohl drafted a list of some twenty-five utopias from Plato down, baptized them *Die Staatsromane,* and bravely proposed to incorporate them into political science.[3] When Marx in the *Communist Manifesto* and Engels in the *Anti-Dühring* set forth distinctions between what they called utopian socialism and their own special brand of scientific socialism, utopia became an intellectual problem in the world revolutionary movement.[4] They conceived of their doctrine dialectically, as at once an outgrowth of utopian thought and its contradiction, which in effect condemned the utopias as outdated and historically superseded fantasy.

Although utopianism had a few champions—one of them was our contributor Lewis Mumford, who in 1923 wrote the appreciative *Story of Utopias, Ideal Commonwealths and Social Myths*—to most observers it seemed a corpse by the 1920's and 1930's. The nails were hammered into the coffin with resounding blows struck by Marxists at one end and by Fascist theorists at the other. The latter group, deriving in this respect from Georges Sorel, with grandiloquent rhetoric stressed the contrast between their own creative myths that were "dynamic realities," expressions of authentic desires, and the utopias, which they dismissed as mere rationalistic constructs. For a whole galaxy of mid-twentieth-century thinkers utopia was still a *Schimpfwort*. Ortega y Gasset labeled it outrightly "the fallacious." Karl Popper has been more verbose on the subject, though no less contemptuous.

But somehow the utopian way of thinking and feeling, with its origins in the great historical visions of the golden age, of paradise, and of the firebringer Prometheus, sustained by both Judaic and Christian eschatology, and embodied in hundreds of works in all European societies since the late fifteenth century, would not stay buried. Though dystopian novels of the post-World-War-II period sold more copies than any utopia in human memory with the possible exception of Bellamy's *Looking Backward*, within the past decade, and not only among the committed, the word utopian is beginning to be divested of an overtone of derision. Aldous Huxley, author of the popular dystopian *Brave New World* (1932), lived to write a utopia, *Island* (1962).

II

In the critical and historical study of utopia, a growing number of works have been making a strenuous effort to grasp its inner meaning as a human phenomenon rather than to sit in pontifical judgment of approval or condemnation. Karl Mannheim's redefinition in his own private language of the very idea of utopia in *Ideology and Utopia: An Introduction to the Sociology of Knowledge* (1929),[5] while it hardly won universal acceptance among sociologists and political scientists, was a point of departure for a whole school of thought and in its day was hailed as the outline of "a new discipline which promises to give new and more profound understanding of social life."[6] Reviewing this work after more than thirty years, Judith N. Shklar is rather severe on Mannheim's division of all political theory of the past into two classes, the utopian and the ideological. While most of us would agree with her contention that "it is . . . more than questionable whether the vast variety of Europe's intellectual past can be squeezed into this Manichaean strait-jacket," we might not accept her strictures against his motivation.

In the period after the Second World War, two French thinkers, both of whom died prematurely, devoted themselves to a fresh consideration of the whole problem of utopia. Raymond Ruyer's *L'Utopie et les utopies* (1950) delineated the "utopian mentality" in psychological terms and identified what he called *le mode utopique*, "a mental exercise on lateral possibilities."[7] Georges Duveau's construction of a full-scale sociology of the utopia was left incomplete, but his posthumously assembled essays constitute a serious attempt at a rehabilitation of the "realistic" eighteenth- and nineteenth-century utopias as worthy guides for the world of tomorrow, in preference to Hegelian-Marxist historical determinism.[8]

Even more ambitious undertakings on the conceptual level during the same period were the writings of Ernst Bloch and Frederik Lodewijk Polak. Bloch, a philosopher who has recently moved from East to West Germany, first propounded his ideas in *Geist der Utopie* back in 1918, a work aimed at infusing positive meaning into the idea of utopia; the large-scale elaboration of his concept of the *Noch-Nicht-Seins* with its provocative amalgam of Marxism and imaginative flights of fancy did not come until the 1940's and 1950's with the publication of his three-volume chef d'oeuvre *Das Prinzip Hoffnung.*[9] Polak, whose *The Image of the Future* has enjoyed the patronage of the Council of Europe, is represented in our collection, where he speaks for himself in an essay entitled "Utopia and Cultural Renewal".[10]

Finally, in Roger Mucchielli's *Le Mythe de la cité idéale* (1961) we have perhaps the most recent sign of a tendency to take utopia seriously as an enduring manifestation of the human spirit:

> The ideal cities have seemed to us to be other than simple imaginary portraits reducible to socio-cultural, historical, or psychological factors. Beyond these influences—which are to be sure not negligible—they are attempts with a common purport: to express the pure relationship of man to humanity in the form of a social order which, at its boundaries, loses the character of a political solution and reveals its meta-empirical character.[11]

We may not necessarily accept Mucchielli's rather complex typology of ideal cities, of which utopia, one of five basic forms, is "the myth, awakened by a personal revolt against the human condition in general in the shape of existing circumstances, which meets the obstacle of impotence and evokes in the imagination an *other* or a nowhere, where all obstacles are removed."[12] But it is easy to join him in his rather pointed critique both of Ruyer's psychological reductionism in isolating a utopian mentality and of sundry exclusive historico-sociological interpretations.

For myself, I have become convinced that utopian fantasies are amenable to interpretation on as many different levels as are ordinary dreams. If utopias be classified by the style of their furniture, sociological and historical, by their concrete equipment, and the style is related to a contemporary social reality, the utopia can be read as expressive of specific social conflicts which it presumes to resolve. Since most epochs in Western society have been turbulent, it becomes virtually self-evident that they have produced utopias of one sort or another which reflect their economic dislocations and social upheavals. To announce in tones of dramatic revelation that a utopia mirrors the misery of the working classes or the squeeze of the lesser nobility caught between the peasants and the royal power is to say something, but not enough. Similarly there may be some validity to Arnold Toynbee's historical emphasis upon one aspect of utopia as a symptom of the downward stage of the cycle of civilizations, when he writes:

> As for the Utopias, they are static *ex hypothesi*. For these works are always programmes of action masquerading in the disguise of imaginary descriptive sociology and the action which they are intended to evoke is nearly always the "pegging" at a certain level of an actual society which has entered on a decline that must end in a fall unless the downward movement can be artificially arrested.[13]

Such historical and sociological observations, however, apply only to certain types of utopia to the derogation of the genuinely novelty-bearing power of others.

In an age when individual psychological analysis flourishes in the marketplace, one is prone to turn from the fantasy itself to the fantast. His illusory world must serve some purpose in his psychic economy, and the interpreter seeks to ferret out the hidden drives behind each element of his imaginary society. For many utopians the data are richly available; for others we know nothing but an author's name—perhaps a nom de plume at that. But the paucity of materials does not discourage the convinced believer in the paramountcy of his psychological techniques: he can reconstruct a personality on the basis of the psychological revelations in the fantasy and then successfully interpret the fantasy in terms of its creator. An ideal visionary type, the perfect utopian, would probably both hate his father and come from a disinherited class. A bit of schizophrenia, a dose of megalomania, obsessiveness, and compulsiveness fit neatly into the stereotype. But the utopian personality that is more than a bibliographical item must be endowed with genius and stirred by a creative passion. The great utopias are not marked with the scars of their authors. If there are wounds they lie well concealed, as was More's hair-shirted and lacerated body beneath the inky cloak of the Holbein portrait.

The utopian has often been disregarded as a fool, or feared as a dangerous madman, the contagion of whose fancies could lead his followers to destruction, particularly if the fantast proceeded to act out his vision. When sixteenth-century enthusiasts—to summon a remote example—not only called the staid German city of Münster "Jerusalem," but proclaimed its independence and invited the wretched of the earth to partake of the delights of its primitive communism and sexual freedom, they brought death to the credulous at the hands of the Bishop's invading armies, who refused to accept the reality of the Anabaptist dream.

Many utopias, on the other hand, have been acted out without such carnage—witness the rich nineteenth-century experience with utopian communities which Maren Lockwood describes for us with special reference to Oneida. As she indicates, most of these communities had altered their character or disappeared by the end of the century and only a few isolated specimens of a once luxuriant growth remain. Though the chapter seems closed, their full collective story has not yet been told, despite the availability of individual accounts. When these communities find their proper historian, who comes not to mock but rather to understand, the image of the utopian and his ideal society may be significantly amended. Surely the social sciences have much to learn from these unconventional experiences.

III

Along with major theoretical works on the nature of utopianism, international conferences among the learned from various parts of the world bear witness to the liveliness of our problem. In 1956 the subject was discussed at a Symposium in Paris of the International Institute of Philosophy. While the organizers of the Royaumont assembly of 1961 on *Quel avenir attend l'homme?* would bridle at their inclusion under the rubric utopian, the papers presented by French, English, and Eastern European philosophers and scientists, though they initially set out to do nothing but predict, often ended up wishing.[14] We shall have occasion to contrast the spirit of their colloquium with ours. In 1963 Eranos conducted a conference under the title *Vom Sinn der Utopie* which explored another facet of utopian thought, its profound psychological and religious roots.[15] "Paradise and Utopia: Mythical Geography and Eschatology" by Mircea Eliade is a translation of the essay he presented at that meeting. Current interest in utopia has spilled over into a variety of historical studies involving international cooperative effort. A colloquium took place at Brussels in April 1961 on *Les Utopies à la Renaissance;*[16] a similar international study has treated *Edward Bellamy Abroad;*[17] and conversations were held in Ivrea, Italy, on *Un viaggio alle "isole Utopia."*[18] Thus the Dædalus Planning Conferences on Utopia in 1964–1965 were themselves testimony to the growing preoccupation with the subject. And the enduring concern of the American Academy of Arts and Sciences with a form of prediction—which some of us, at least, cannot entirely disentangle from utopian hope—is manifest in its recent establishment of a Committee on the Year 2000.

It remains for us to assess in the pages of this introduction where the present inquiry stands both in the study of utopia as a historical experience and in the evaluation of the significance of contemporary utopias.

In 1809 letters were exchanged between one Hippolyte Azaïs and Henri Saint-Simon in the course of which these two French utopians explored the possibilities of meeting somewhere in order to argue their rival systems to the point of agreement. Unfortunately, the confrontation never occurred. Utopians have, at least in the past, tended to be relatively isolated men—even when they were activists—and it is not recorded that any two utopians have ever compromised their visions. Similarly, it was not to be expected that the critical analysts of utopias and utopian thought gathered from a variety of disciplines at the *Dædalus* Conference should have many points of agreement among them, let alone uniformity of presentation. In fact, when a participant remarked that the one thing he could say with certainty about the future was that it would not be the same as the present, he probably uttered the only affirmation that enjoyed universal assent. Thus there was agreement on the minimal point that most utopias dealt with that which had not yet been experienced, what Ernst Bloch called the *Noch-Nicht-Erfahrung,* but beyond that, fundamental differences obtruded—about the nature of utopia, about its worth as an expression of man, and about its future prospects. How much further could divergence go? At moments the preliminary conference was marked by a controlled Kilkenny spirit.

There was an early consensus that we had better not embark upon any attempt to achieve a common definition of the term utopia. If we were to pass beyond the function of the lexicographers, each man would have to wrestle with his own individual conception. As a rule we were wise with Nietzsche, who taught that only that which had no history could be defined. After all, the immortals of the French Academy have substantially changed the meaning of utopia from one edition of their dictionary to another, and will doubtless do so again at some remote point in time when they reach the letter "u" in their new revision. Those of us who found it necessary to set some bounds to the amorphous concept of utopia generally resorted to a historical presentation, which allowed for the multifarious varieties of utopian experience. Others let the past bury its own utopias and boldly undertook to formulate what was the next utopian mission viewed from the vantage point of the here and now. The collection should probably be subtitled, in the Baylian manner, a "historical and critical" study, for the bona fide utopians among us are in a minority. There is another limitation to this collection: the representation is exclusively from the Atlantic community, which may account for its undisguised provinciality. The utopian traditions of China and the Muslim world perforce stand neglected; the Western tradition has been difficult enough to assimilate.

Since there are no utopians in this issue who speak with tongues in the romantic manner, it is a rather academic document revealing various degrees of tolerance toward the phenomenon. Despite the intense individualism of the participants, in general three groupings may be identified: those who praise utopian thought as a significant expression of man, those who unequivocally condemn it as wrong-headed and stupid or perverse, and those who remain in a state of ambivalence about the utopian thinkers. There are the yea-sayers and the nay-sayers, and the middle-of-the roaders, who seem to be saying yea and nay at the same time. This is generally a fairly polite collection; you will not find here anything like Pareto's castigation of the utopian spirit, though one or two pieces do approach his level of, shall we say, vigor.

IV

George Kateb poses the utopian question fitting for our age: granted a world of leisure and abundance (an assumption which he makes far more casually than scientists like Paul B. Sears), what shall be the dominant tone of life in a modern utopia worthy of man? After a critical review of the rival ideals of sensate pleasure, play, and political action as developed by older moral thinkers such as Schiller and Mill and by our contemporaries Herbert Marcuse and Hannah Arendt, he concludes with a declaration of his own, a reassertion of the traditional values of the contemplative life as the supreme goal, though with a difference: his utopian ideal manages to encompass in a harmonious whole all the other common goals while still safeguarding the supremacy of the higher pleasures of the mind. When Northrop Frye touches upon the same theme, his summation is markedly less Platonic than Kateb's. "New utopias," he believes, "would have to derive their form from the shifting and dissolving movement of society that is gradually replacing the fixed locations of life. They would not be rational cities evolved by a philosopher's dialectic: they would be rooted in the body as well as in the mind, in the unconscious as well as the conscious, in forests and deserts as well as in highways and buildings, in bed as well as in the symposium."

In flagrant contradiction of this faith in the prospect of a new utopia, two of our contributors assure us that we are finally being rid of this utopian nonsense, and none too soon at that. In her spirited journey through the whole range of the political theory of utopia, Judith Shklar impresses upon us the "realization that the disintegration of nineteenth-century ideology has not made it possible simply to return to classical-critical theory, of which utopia was a part." Adam Ulam adopts as the main focus of his attack the role of utopianism in nineteenth-century European socialist thought and he concludes with a sense of relief: "Perhaps we have reached a moratorium, if not indeed the end of utopias, and perhaps this is not an altogether bad thing." The emerging nations clamor for the concrete realities of automobiles and washing machines, he reminds us, not utopian visions.

To all this Crane Brinton, skeptical as always, has entered a cautious demurrer. The democratic utopian drive, which for him lies at the core of the American utopia, may, he concedes, no longer enjoy the active support of the intellectuals as a class, but he is far from certain that all of them have definitively abandoned the ship. "There may be among the intellectuals today a revival, as among some of them there was always a survival, of the utopian spirit . . . Perhaps the next cultural generation will work its way out of alienation . . . into a new flowering of all the arts, into a new great culture shared with the many." And Lewis Mumford, after describing in rather tragic terms the corruption of the original sacred utopia of the ancient city through the organization of the power machine, is still open to the prospect that we may today be approaching a far more fertile area than that of the classical utopia, "the realm embracing potentiality as an aspect of all natural existence, 'foreplans of action' . . . as a dynamic attribute of living organisms, and design as a necessary constituent of rational human development." In this expectation he seems to join that whole group of contemporary European thinkers who make his point the very heart of their new definition of utopia, a position that would be acceptable to as solidly "scientific" a philosopher as Ernst Mach, who once called utopia a "mental experiment."

The contributions of the three physical scientists in our group are warnings against the hubris of technological and scientific utopias which might be prone to forget the limitations still imposed upon us by physical and human nature. Both Paul B. Sears and John Maynard Smith raise the ominous specter of the population explosion and its disastrous consequences for any utopian vision. Sears admonishes us that man is part of a great system of life and environment and that this ecosystem cannot be disrupted without grave consequences for his existence. He dwells on the dangers of overcrowding, insisting on the problems of water and food and the increasing degree of uniformity that congestion enforces. His concern for a state of dynamic equilibrium in nature leads him to examine the growing modern city with horror—"a sprawling monster, devouring space regardless of its best potential and without regard to amenities far more elemental than those of any utopian dream." Sears is no dogmatic anti-utopian, but he has established certain absolute prerequisites for dealing with the living landscape in any society which those who glibly prate of "freedom from necessity" will neglect only to our common peril. His rather balanced position contrasts sharply with the undiluted optimism of a Soviet scientist like Nicolai Semenov in his paper prepared for the Royaumont Conference and the sanguine predictions of English Marxists like Bernal. At Royaumont a whole group of participants depicted Teilhardism and Marxism as advancing hand-in-hand into the dawn of a brilliant future. In our group neither Marx nor Teilhard won the same accolades.

In a temper similar to Sears's, the zoologist John Maynard Smith presents the possibilities of the recent revolutionary discoveries in eugenics, but then spells out the many dilemmas which these present to any utopian who would conclude too hastily that we are well on our way to the perfection of the human species. His paper inevitably evokes a comparison with that Baconian visionary of the modern scientific utopia, the Marquis de Condorcet, in his *Fragment sur l'Atlantide* and the commentary on the "Tenth Epoch" of his own *Esquisse d'un tableau historique des progrès de l'esprit humain.* Whereas Condorcet quickly extrapolated a prodigious multiplication of geniuses in the world from the mere fact of wider literacy, John Maynard Smith is not so sure that it will be easy to increase human intelligence significantly, even after our new eugenic discoveries. The scientific tools, so to speak, will be available: "It will be surprising if direct gene transformation does not become possible in man and higher animals during the next hundred years." But the implementation of this knowledge for social ends becomes another matter. And while our eighteenth-century *philosophe* dreamed of infinite perfectibility (through the transmission of acquired characteristics as well as through genetic control), our modern scientist is far less confident: "Experience shows that if intense artificial selection for a single character is continued for a number of generations, the genetic response, although rapid at first, tends to slow down and even to stop." In contrast to Condorcet's utopia of inevitable longevity, Maynard Smith is again rather skeptical: "It is not at present possible to say whether we shall ever be able to produce a large increase in human life expectancy, even though we can already ensure that a large proportion of people survive to old age."

Our third scientific representative takes the position that technology in and of itself points neither to a utopian nor to a dystopian future. Almost two centuries ago, Herder had arrived at a similar conclusion. Technology is a neutral force capable of great good and great evil. John Pierce can be eloquent in conjuring up the delights which the new technology of communications provides for people separated by distance who need and love each other—though he may forget Freud's rather acid remark in *Civilization and Its Discontents* that without technology they would not likely be apart in the first place. But Pierce also sees another side to the picture; faced by growing nationalism in underdeveloped nations and their steady fall behind well-integrated industrial economies, he ends with an open query as to "whether a prosperous technological civilization can indefinitely survive" this nationalism.

By all odds the most optimistic contributors to this academic volume are the French. These visitors from the Old World seem to redress the balance of the New—a world that came into being as utopia finally discovered, as Eliade shows, but one whose intellectuals now have doubts about the prospects of heaven on earth. The two contemporary activist utopians who joined us from France and who would, I think, proudly accept this title, are a far cry from the older French utopians who were possessed by the demon of the absolute. They consider themselves practical utopians, and in their daily lives, through participation in contemporary French studies on planning, they do more than merely preach. François Bloch-Lainé writes in an entirely different key—I did not say higher or lower—from a young American professor like Kateb. "Serious utopianism," he tells us, "deals with things as they are: the nature of man, who is neither angel nor beast—this excludes utopias founded on angelic natures in a universe where everyone would always be good and pure—and the nature of the material world, a hard world where the easy life will not arrive tomorrow—which also excludes utopias characterized by such an abundance of material goods that everyone might soon be satisfied without threatening his neighbor." Bloch-Lainé's middle-of-the road utopia for reformers is based on the reasoned reconciliation of polar needs and desires in man: of the autonomy or independence of human elements and the effective functioning of the whole; of present welfare and future welfare; of man's rival ways of self-fulfillment in education, work, and leisure. And after he confronts a "flexible dream with probable reality" he arrives at a logical compromise that is "both a hypothesis and a conviction." He prophesies that "the future will be a period of technocracy tempered by democracy."

Bertrand de Jouvenel would go so far in his quest of the pragmatic utopia as to deny the very designation of utopia "to any exposition of a 'New Model' of Society which is bereft of pictures concerning daily life." Philosophical utopian discussions leave him cold, and he would dismiss one whole Western tradition because of the inherent ambiguity of its abstract formulations. Not all of us would agree with his limitation of the concept, but few writers since Plato himself have expressed the need for concrete utopian description so cogently. In his "Utopia for Practical Purposes" de Jouvenel would have us descend from the high a priori argument about the meaning of felicity to seek the causes of happiness and unhappiness in the existential reality of our ordinary routine and proceed to "plan for the good day." "This is where I am, if you will," he challenges our philosophers of eudaemonism, "utopian in the vulgar sense of the word: I feel convinced that if we put our mind to it, we can transform the daily existence of man. Putting our mind to it means that we must begin to consider our man's day in all its aspects instead of proceeding analytically as we tend to do."

Bloch-Lainé and de Jouvenel are "realistic utopians." They have the same pervasive distrust of the rationalist ideologists of happiness as did Charles Fourier in the nineteenth century. I for one was glad to see de Jouvenel invoke that much-maligned genius, who had such deep insight into the problems of love and labor.

Finally we have representatives of that group of contemporary thinkers who assert that in science, religion, and political action some form of utopia is antecedent to every important human adventure. The interpretation of Western man's utopian experience, they feel, may have to pass into a metahistorical realm, to the understandable annoyance of common-sense positivists. Along with Mucchielli and Bloch, three of our writers—Polak, Tillich, and Eliade—have been prepared to grapple with this other utopian dimension. All are united in a belief that man cannot live as a full human being without utopian visions, though each of them conceives of the character and nature of these visions in different terms.

Polak feels that at this critical moment of his history man has virtually exhausted his treasury of inherited utopian images and stands naked and unprepared to meet the extraordinary requirements of the new automated society, which will be more radically different from the present than the present is from the pre-industrial epoch. The forethought of constructive images is an absolute necessity lest we be overwhelmed by chaos. The problem of a society without work must be faced, and totally new "images of the future," different from the traditional ones, will have to be created. "It does not seem very probable, in the context of our cultural evolution, that there will be a mass revival of eschatological images of the future. A counterthrust against modern anti-utopian thought, though difficult, is not impossible. A positive future-consciousness is an absolutely indispensable antidote against the mind-poisoning negativism and threatening ideologies now undermining the foundations of Western culture."

The late Paul Tillich is represented here by the last of a group of lectures published in Berlin in 1951. After having previously laid down the fundamental premise that being human means having a utopia, he goes on to place utopia in a total historical context, arriving at a "Critique and Justification of Utopia." Those who know his work will recognize the hand of the master in this presentation first of the positivity of utopia and then of its negativity, with a resolution in a final affirmation of the transcendence of utopia. The subject afforded Tillich an opportunity to express his innermost feelings about the relationship of the religious ideal and political potentiality as he had experienced their contradictions in his own spiritual life, from the period after the German debacle of World War I through the aftermath of World War II. In this moving personal document the late theologian first speaks in praise of utopia:

Where no anticipating utopia opens up possibilities we find a stagnant, sterile present—we find a situation in which not only individual but also cultural realization of human possibilities is inhibited and cannot win through to fulfillment. The present, for men who have no utopia, is inevitably constricting; and, similarly, cultures which have no utopia remain imprisoned in the present and quickly fall back into the past, for the present can be fully alive only in tension between past and future. This is the fruitfulness of utopia—its ability to open up possibilities.

In the second turn of the dialectic, his statement of the negativity of utopia, he formulates again his objections to a certain form of liberal Protestantism as well as to a whole generation of former believers in particular utopias such as the Russian one, who in their disillusionment reacted with bitter violence against the very idea of utopia itself and became *"fanatics against their own past."* For Tillich, the "unfruitfulness of utopia is that it describes impossibilities as real possibilities—and fails to see them for what they are, impossibilities, or as oscillation between possibility and impossibility. In so doing, utopia succumbs to pure wishful thinking which, to be sure, has to do with the real (in that it is projected out of and onto real processes) but not with what is essentially human."

Tillich finds the solution to the problem of utopia in the reciprocal participation of what he calls the two "orders," one an order living on a horizontal plane, the order of finitudes, the other the vertical order of the Kingdom of God that cannot be described.

A Kingdom of God that is not involved in historical events, in utopian actualization in time, is not the Kingdom of God at all but at best only a mystical annihilation of everything that can be "Kingdom"—namely, richness, fullness, manifoldness, individuality. And, similarly, a Kingdom of God that is nothing but the historical process produces a utopia of endless progress or convulsive revolution whose catastrophic collapse eventuates in metaphysical disillusionment.

Mircea Eliade, writing as a historian of religion, takes cognizance of the diverse economic, sociological, and historical interpretations of prophetic and messianic movements, and he is far from denying the significance of these contingent explanations of human behavior, especially in times of crisis. But he also highlights certain persistent and universal utopian beliefs which can endure for centuries without social crises as a provocation. The experience of the Tupi-Guaranis of Brazil and their century-long search for the Lost Paradise he cites as a primitive parallel to the central Judeo-Christian tradition, and he finds a further counterpart in the contemporary personal quest of intellectuals in the United States and Latin America for their "primordial history." "This desire to return to one's beginnings . . . ," he writes, "also denotes the desire to start out again, the nostalgia to relive the beatitude and the creative exaltation of the 'beginnings'; in short, the nostalgia for the earthly paradise that the ancestors of the American nations had crossed the Atlantic to find." He holds the eschatological and paradisiacal elements in the colonization of North America to be one of the factors that give rise to the popular American optimism and cult of youth and novelty. In his paper the current scholarly interest in millenarian movements and utopias appears as no passing fad, but "one of the characteristic traits of contemporary Western thought."

The study of the problem of utopia has only begun. Its historical, sociological, and psychological depths have not yet been fathomed and evaluated. Its political and religious meaning is open to controversy. The term utopia is still ambiguous; its positive or pejorative connotations vary sharply, depending upon who utters the word and the intonation of his voice. Are utopian solutions misleading signposts in the darkness that can bring us to disaster? Do they divert energies along tortuous irrelevant bypaths from issues that are or at least seem to be solvable in immediate practical terms? Or is the utopian fantasy an enduring need and a stimulant of the creative human spirit?

This volume, which suggests many different answers, owes a great deal to an American Academy planning committee, under the chairmanship of Stephen R. Graubard, editor of *Dædalus,* which assisted in formulating the questions that seemed paramount in this field, proceeded to set the guidelines for our inquiry, read early drafts of the papers, and then met in a formal conference to discuss them. We are grateful to those who were able to help in these several respects. Sincere thanks go to Stanley Cavell, Peter J. Caws, Karl Deutsch, Erik Erikson, Alexander Gerschenkron, Louis Hartz, Jack H. Hexter, Hudson Hoagland, Gerald Holton, Everett C. Hughes, William Letwin, T. H. Marshall, Henry A. Murray, Richard

E. Pipes, Don K. Price, David Riesman, Walter A. Rosenblith, Krister Stendahl, Morton White, and Dennis H. Wrong.

This study was made possible by a generous grant from the Carnegie Corporation. The American Academy of Arts and Sciences, conscious of the encouragement offered by this foundation to so many of its activities, feels a very special gratitude for the assistance which it has received.

REFERENCES

1. *Plato,* with an English translation by R. G. Bury, VII (Cambridge, Mass., and London: Harvard University Press, 1961), p. 23.

2. Henricus ab Ahlefeld, *Disputatio philosophica de fictis rebus publicis* (Cologne, 1704).

3. Robert von Mohl, "Ein Beitrag zur Literaturgeschichte der Staatswissenschaften," *Tübingen Zeitschrift für die gesamte Staatswissenschaft,* Band 2 (1845).

4. What appeared as Friedrich Engels, *Die Entwicklung des Sozialismus von der Utopie zur Wissenschaft* (Zurich: Hottingen, 1882), was put together from three chapters of *Herrn E. Dührings Umwälzung der Wissenschaft* (Leipzig, 1878). This excerpt had first appeared in a French translation as *Socialisme utopique et scientifique* (Paris, 1880).

5. Karl Mannheim, *Ideology and Utopia: An Introduction to the Sociology of Knowledge,* was originally published in German in 1929; an expanded version, translated into English by Louis Wirth and Edward A. Shils, first appeared in 1936.

6. Karl Mannheim, *Ideology and Utopia* (New York and London: Harcourt Brace, 1952), preface by Louis Wirth, p. xxxi.

7. Raymond Ruyer, *L'Utopie et les utopies* (Paris: Presses universitaires de France, 1950), p. 9.

8. Georges Duveau, *Sociologie de l'utopie et autres "essais," ouvrage posthume,* introduction by André Canivez (Paris: Presses universitaires de France, 1961).

9. Ernst Bloch, *Geist der Utopie* (Munich and Leipzig: Duncker & Humboldt, 1918); *Freiheit und Ordnung: Abriss der Sozial-utopien* (New York: Aurora Verlag, 1946); *Das Prinzip Hoffnung* (Berlin: Aufbau Verlag, 1954), 3 vols.

10. Frederik Lodewijk Polak, *De Toekomst is verleden tijd: cultur-futuristische Verkenningen* (Utrecht: De Haan, 1955); *The Image of the Future* (Leyden and Dobbs Ferry, N. Y.: Oceana Publications, 1961).

11. Roger Mucchielli, *Le Mythe de la cité idéale* (Paris: Presses universitaires de France, 1961), pp. 7–8.

12. *Ibid.*, p. 170.

13. Arnold Toynbee, *A Study of History,* Somervell edition (Oxford: Oxford University Press, 1947), pp. 182–183.

14. Rencontre internationale de Royaumont, May 17–20, 1961, *Quel avenir attend l'homme?* (Paris: Presses Universitaires de France, 1961).

15. *Vom Sinn der Utopie, Eranos Jahrbuch 1963* (Zurich: Rhein-Verlag, 1964).

16. Université de Bruxelles, *Travaux de l'institut pour l'étude de la renaissance et de l'humanisme, Les Utopies à la Renaissance* (Brussels and Paris: Presses universitaires de Bruxelles and Presses universitaires de France, 1963).

17. Sylvia E. Bowman, *et al., Edward Bellamy Abroad: An American Prophet's Influence,* preface by Maurice Le Breton (New York: Twayne Publishers, 1962).

18. Ugo Fedeli, *Un viaggio alle "isole Utopia,"* conversazioni tenute in Ivrea al Centro culturale Olivetti, gennaio-febbraio 1958 (Ivrea? 1958?).

UTOPIAS
AND UTOPIAN THOUGHT

I

THE HISTORICAL DIMENSION

LEWIS MUMFORD

Utopia, The City and The Machine

The fact that utopias from Plato to Bellamy have been visualized largely in terms of the city would seem to have a simple historical explanation. The first utopias we know were fabricated in Greece; and in spite of their repeated efforts at confederation, the Greeks were never able to conceive of a human commonwealth except in the concrete form of a city. Even Alexander had learned this lesson so well that at least part of the energies that might have gone into wider or more rapid conquests went into the building of cities. Once this tradition was established, later writers, beginning with Thomas More, found it easy to follow, all the more so because the city had the advantage of mirroring the complexities of society within a frame that respected the human scale.

Now, there is no doubt that utopian thinking was deeply influenced by Greek thought; moreover, as I shall try to show, this mode of thinking, precisely because it respected certain human capacities that the scientific method deliberately ignores, may still serve as a useful corrective for a positivism that has no place for the potential, the purposeful, or the ideal. But when one digs deeper into the utopian tradition, one finds that its foundations are buried in a much older past than that of Greece; and the question that finally arises is not, "Why are cities so often the locus of utopia?" but, "Why did so many of the characteristic institutions of utopia first come to light in the ancient city?"

Though I have long been a student of both utopias and cities, only in recent years have sufficient data come to light to suggest to me that the concept of utopia is not a Hellenic speculative fantasy, but a derivation from an historic event: that indeed the first utopia was the city itself. If I can establish this relationship, more than one insight should flow from it: not least an explanation of the authoritarian nature of so many utopias.

I

But first let us look at utopia through the eyes of the Greeks. Strangely enough, though Plato approaches the domain of utopia in four of his dialogues, the one that had the greatest influence, the *Republic,* is the utopia that is most lacking in any concrete image of the city, except in the provision that it should be limited in numbers in order to maintain its integrity and unity.

In Plato's reaction against the democratic Athenian polis, the model that seduced him was that of Sparta: a state whose population was dispersed in villages. In the *Republic,* Plato retained many of the institutions of the ancient city and sought to give them an ideal dimension; and this in itself will throw an oblique light upon both the ancient city and the post-Platonic literature of utopias. But it is only in the *Laws* that Plato came down from the heights sufficiently to give a few details, all too few, of the actual physical characteristics of the city that would incorporate his moral and legal controls.

There is no need to go into Plato's meager descriptions of the city: most of the details of the urban environment in the *Laws* are drawn from actual cities, though in his glowing description of Atlantis his imagination seems to conjure up the bolder Hellenistic town planning of the Third Century B.C. What we must rather take note of in Plato are those singular limitations that his admirers—and I am still one of them—too charitably overlooked until our own day, when we suddenly found ourselves confronted by a magnified and modernized version of the kind of totalitarian state that Plato had depicted. Bertrand Russell had first made this discovery on his visit to Soviet Russia in the early nineteen-twenties, almost two decades before Richard Crossman and others pointed out that Plato's Republic, far from being a desirable model, was the prototype of the fascist state, even though neither Hitler nor Mussolini nor yet Stalin exactly qualified for the title of Philosopher-King.

In the Second Book of the *Republic,* it is true, Plato came near to describing the normative society of Hesiod's Golden Age: essentially the pre-urban community of the Neolithic cultivator, in which even the wolf and the lion, as the Sumerian poem put it, were not dangerous, and all the members of the community shared in its goods and its gods—in which there was no ruling class to exploit the villagers, no compulsion to work for a surplus the local community was not allowed to consume, no taste for idle luxury, no jealous claim to private property, no exorbitant desire for power, no institutional war. Though scholars have long contemptuously dismissed the "myth of the Golden Age," it is their scholarship, rather than the myth, that must now be questioned.

Such a society had indeed come into existence at the end of the last Ice Age, if not before, when the long process of domestication had come to a head in the establishment of small, stable communities, with an abundant and varied food supply: communities whose capacity to produce a surplus of storable grain gave security and adequate nurture to the young. This rise in vitality was enhanced by vivid biological insight and intensified sexual activities, to which the multiplication of erotic symbols bears witness, no less than a success unsurpassed in any later culture in the selection and breeding of plants and cattle. Plato recognized the humane qualities of these simpler communities: so it is significant that he made no attempt to recapture them at a higher level. (Was the institution of common meals for male citizens, as still practiced in Crete and Sparta, perhaps an exception?) Apart from this possibility, Plato's ideal community begins at the point where the early Golden Age comes to an end: with absolute rulership, totalitarian coercion, the permanent division of labor, and constant readiness for war all duly accepted in the name of justice and wisdom. So central was war to his whole conception of an ideal community that in the *Timaeus*, when Socrates confesses a desire to behold his static Republic in action, he asks for an account of how she waged "a struggle against her neighbors."

Everyone is familiar with the foundation stones of the *Republic*. The city that Plato pictures is a self-contained unit; and to ensure this self-sufficiency it must have enough land to feed its inhabitants and make it independent of any other community: autarchy. The population of this community is divided into three great classes: husbandmen and craftsmen, military "protectors," and a special caste of "guardians." The last have turned out to be the usual controllers and conditioners of most ideal commonwealths, either at their inception or in their daily government: Plato had rationalized kingship.

Once selected, the members of each of these classes must keep their own vocation and strictly mind their own business, taking orders from those above and not answering back. To make sure of perfect obedience, no "dangerous thoughts" or disturbing emotions must be permitted: hence a strict censorship that extends even to music. To ensure docility, the guardians do not hesitate to feed the community with lies: they form, in fact, an archetypal Central Intelligence Agency within a Platonic Pentagon. Plato's only radical innovation in the *Republic* is the rational control of human breeding through communal marriage. Though delayed, this practice came to fruition briefly in the Oneida Community, and today insistently haunts the dreams of more than one geneticist.

But note that the constitution and daily discipline of Plato's ideal commonwealth converge to a single end: fitness for making war. Nietzsche's observation that war is the health of the state applies in all its fullness to Plato's Republic, for only in war is such stringent authority and coercion temporarily tolerable. Let us remember this characteristic, for with one emphasis or another we shall find it in both the ancient city and in the literary myths of utopia. Even Bellamy's mechanized "nation in overalls," conscripted for twenty years labor service, is under the same discipline as a nation in arms.

If one thinks of Plato's scheme as a contribution to an ideal future, one must wonder whether justice, temperance, courage, and wisdom had ever before been addressed to such a contradictory "ideal" outcome. What Plato had actually accomplished was not to overcome the disabilities that threatened the Greek commonwealth of his day, but to establish a seemingly philosophic basis for the historic institutions that had in fact arrested human development. Though Plato was a lover of Hellenic society, he never thought it worth while to ask how the manifold values of the society that had brought both him and Socrates into existence could be preserved and developed: at most, he was honest enough to admit in the *Laws* that good men could still be found in "bad"—that is, unplatonic—societies.

What Plato did, I shall try to demonstrate, was to rationalize and perfect the institutions that had come into existence as an ideal pattern long before, with the founding of the ancient city. He purposed to create a structure that, unlike the actual city in history, would be immune to challenge from within and to destruction from without. Plato knew too little history to realize where his imagination was leading him: but in turning his back on contemporary Athens he actually retreated even further back than Sparta, though he had to wait more than two thousand years before the development of a scientific technology would make his singularly inhumane ideals realizable.

One other attribute of Plato's utopia must be noted for it was not merely transmitted to later utopias, but now threatens, paradoxically, to be the final consummation of our supposedly dynamic society. To fulfill its ideal, Plato makes his Republic immune to change: once formed, the pattern of order remains static, as in the insect societies to which it bears a close resemblance. Change, as he pictured it in the *Timaeus,* occurred as a catastrophic intrusion of natural forces. From the first, a kind of mechanical rigidity afflicts all utopias. On the most generous interpretation, this is due to the tendency of the mind, or at least of language, noted by Bergson, to fix and geometrize all forms of motion and organic change: to arrest life in order to understand it, to kill the organism in order to control it, to combat that ceaseless process of self-transformation which lies at the very origin of species.

All ideal models have this same life-arresting, if not life-denying, property: hence nothing could be more fatal to human society than to achieve its ideals. But fortunately nothing is less likely to happen, since, as Walt Whitman observed, it is provided in the nature of things that from every consummation will spring conditions that make it necessary to pass beyond it—a better statement than Marxian dialectic supplies. An ideal pattern is the ideological equivalent of a physical container: it keeps extraneous change within the bounds of human purpose. With the aid of ideals, a community may select, among a multitude of possibilities, those which are consonant with its own nature or that promise to further human development. This corresponds to the role of the entelechy in Aristotle's biology. But note that a society like our own, committed to change as its principal ideal value, may suffer arrest and fixation through its inexorable dynamism and kaleidoscopic novelty no less than a traditional society does through its rigidity.

II

Though it is Plato's influence that first comes to mind when we think of later utopias, it is Aristotle who considers more definitely the actual structure of an ideal city; in fact, one may say that the concept of utopia pervades every page of the *Politics.* For Aristotle, as for any other Greek, the constitutional structure of a polity had a physical counterpart in the city; for it was in the city that men came together not only to survive military attack or to become wealthy in trade but to live the best life possible. But Aristotle's utopian bias went beyond this; for he constantly compares the actual cities whose constitutions he had studied so carefully with their ideal possible forms. Politics for him was the "science of the possible," in a quite different sense from the way that phrase is now used by those who would cover up their mediocre expectations or their weak tactics by succumbing, without any counter-effort, to probability.

Just as every living organism, for Aristotle, had the archetypal form of its species, whose fulfillment governed the whole process of growth and transformation, so the state, too, had an archetypal form; and one kind of city could be compared with another not just in terms of power, but in terms of ideal value for human development. On one hand, Aristotle considered the polis as a fact of nature, since man was a political animal who could not live alone unless he were either a brute or a god. But it was equally true that the polis was a human artifact; its inherited constitution and its physical structure could be criticized and modified by reason. In short, the polis was potentially a work of art. As with any work of art, the medium and the artist's capability limited the expression; but human evaluation, human intention, entered into its actual design. Not dissatisfaction over the shortcomings or failures of the existing polis so much as confidence in the possibility of improvement sustained Aristotle's rational interest in utopias.

The distinction that More, an inveterate punster, made when he chose the word utopia, as an ambiguous midterm between outopia, no place, and eutopia, the good place, applies equally to the difference between Plato's and Aristotle's conceptions. Plato's Republic was in Cloudcuckooland: and after his disastrous experience in Syracuse, he could hardly hope to find it anywhere else. But Aristotle, even when in the Seventh Book of the *Politics* he outlines the requirements for an ideal city cut to his own pattern, still has his feet on the earth: he does not hesitate to retain many traditional characteristics, even such accidental ones as the narrow, crooked streets which might help confuse and impede an invading army.

In every actual situation, then, Aristotle saw one or more ideal possibilities that arose out of the nature of the community and its relations with other communities, as well as out of the constitution of the groups and classes and vocations within the polis. His purpose, he declares clearly in the first sentence of the Second Book, "is to consider what form of political community is the best of all for those who are most able to realize their ideal of life." Perhaps one should underline this statement, for in it Aristotle expressed one of the permanent contributions of the utopian mode of thought: the perception that ideals themselves belong to the natural history of man the political animal. It is on these terms that he devotes this chapter to a criticism of Socrates as interpreted by Plato and then goes on to examine other utopias, such as those of Phaleas and Hippodamus.

The association of the potential and the ideal with the rational and the necessary was an essential attribute of Hellenic thought, which took reason itself to be the definitive central characteristic of man: it was only in the social disintegration of the Third Century B.C. that this faith in reason gave way to a superstitious belief in chance as the ultimate god of human destiny. But when one examines Aristotle's exposition of the ideal city, one is again struck, as one is with Plato, by how restricted these original Greek ideals were. Neither Aristotle nor Plato nor even Hippodamus could conceive a society that overpassed the bounds of the city: none of them could embrace a multi-national or poly-cultured community, even if centered in the city; nor could they admit, even as a remote ideal, the possibility of breaking down permanent class divisions or doing away with the institution of war. It was easier for these Greek utopians to conceive of abolishing marriage or private property than of ridding utopia of slavery, class domination, and war.

In this brief review of Greek utopian thought one becomes conscious of limitations that were monotonously repeated in later utopian writers. Even the humane More, though tolerant and magnanimous on the subject of religious convictions, accepted slavery and war; and the very first act of King Utopus, when he invaded the land of Utopia, was to put his soldiers and the conquered inhabitants to work digging a broad canal that turns the territory into an island and cuts it off from the mainland.

Isolation, stratification, fixation, regimentation, standardization, militarization—one or more of these attributes enter into the conception of the utopian city, as expounded by the Greeks. And these same features remain, in open or disguised form, even in the supposedly more democratic utopias of the nineteenth century, such as Bellamy's *Looking Backward*. In the end, utopia merges into the dystopia of the twentieth century; and one suddenly realizes that the distance between the positive ideal and the negative one was never so great as the advocates or admirers of utopia had professed.

III

So far I have discussed utopian literature in relation to the concept of the city, as if utopia were a wholly imaginary place, and as if the classic utopian writers, with the exception of Aristotle, were formulating a prescription for a quite unrealizable mode of life, one that could be achieved only under exceptional conditions or in a remote future.

In this light, every utopia, down to those of H. G. Wells, presents a real puzzle. How could the human imagination, supposedly liberated from the constraints of actual life, be so impoverished? And this limitation is all the stranger in Fourth Century Greece, for the Hellenic polis had in fact emancipated itself from many of the disabilities of the power-driven oriental monarchies. How is it that even the Greeks could visualize so few alternatives to customary life? And why did so many evils, long acknowledged if uncorrected, remain in every utopia, in return for its poor show of promised goods? Where did all the compulsion and regimentation that mark these supposedly ideal commonwealths come from?

One can give more than one plausible answer to these questions. Perhaps the one that would be least palatable to our present science-oriented generation is that the abstract intelligence, operating with its own conceptual apparatus, in its own self-restricted field, is actually a coercive instrument: an arrogant fragment of the full human personality, determined to make the world over in its own oversimplified terms, willfully rejecting interests and values incompatible with its own assumptions, and thereby depriving itself of any of the cooperative and generative functions of life—feeling, emotion, playfulness, exuberance, free fantasy—in short, the liberating sources of unpredictable and uncontrollable creativity.

Compared with even the simplest manifestations of spontaneous life within the teeming environment of nature, every utopia is, almost by definition, a sterile desert, unfit for human occupation. The sugared concept of scientific control, which B. F. Skinner insinuates into his *Walden Two,* is another name for arrested development.

But there is another possible answer to these questions; and this is that the series of written utopias that came to light in Hellenic Greece were actually the belated reflections, or ideological residues, of a remote but genuine phenomenon: the archetypal ancient city. That this utopia in fact once existed can now be actually demonstrated: its real benefits, its ideal pretensions and hallucinations, and its harsh coercive discipline were transmitted, even after its negative features had become more conspicuous and formidable, to later urban communities. But in utopian literature the ancient city left, as it were, an after-image of its "ideal" form on the human mind.

Curiously, Plato himself, though seemingly as an afterthought, took pains to give his utopia this historic foundation; for, in the *Timaeus* and the *Critias,* he describes the city and the Island Empire of Atlantis in ideal terms that might well have applied to Pharaonic Egypt or Minoan Crete, even going so far as to give the Atlantean landscape, with its abundant natural resources, an ideal dimension that was lacking in the austere background of the *Republic.* As for antediluvian Athens, the supposedly historic community that conquered Atlantis nine thousand years before Solon's time, it was "by coincidence" a magnified embodiment of the ideal commonwealth pictured in the *Republic.* Later, in the *Laws,* he draws repeatedly on the historic institutions of Sparta and Crete, again closely linking his ideal future with a historic past.

While the motive for Plato's severely authoritarian utopia was doubtless his aristocratic dissatisfaction with demagogic Athenian politics which he considered responsible for the successive defeats that began with the Peloponnesian War, it is perhaps significant that his ideological withdrawal was coupled with a return to an earlier actuality which underwrote his ideals. That this idealized image came via the Egyptian priesthood at Sais, a country Plato as well as Solon had visited, provides at least a plausible thread of connection between the historic city in its originally divine dimensions and the more secular ideal commonwealths of a later period. Who can say, then, that it was only the problems of contemporary Athens and not also the actual achievements of the historic city that prompted Plato's excursions into utopia?

Though at first reading this explanation may seem far-fetched, I propose now to indicate the data mainly from Egypt and Mesopotamia that make this historic hypothesis plausible. For it is at the very beginning of urban civilization that one encounters not only the archetypal form of the city as utopia but also another coordinate utopian institution essential to any system of communal regimentation: the machine. In that archaic constellation the notion of a world completely under scientific and technological control, the dominant utopian fantasy of our present age, first becomes evident. My purpose is to show that at this early stage the historic explanation and the philosophic one come together. If we understand why the earliest utopia miscarried, we shall perhaps have an insight into the dangers our present civilization faces; for history is the sternest critic of utopias.

IV

This reference to the archetypal city that greets us a little before the beginning of recorded history as "utopia" is no idle figure of speech. To make this clear, let me first paint a composite picture of the city as Egyptian, Mesopotamian, and later records reveal it to us. First of all, the city is the creation of a king (Menes, Minos, Theseus), acting in the name of a god. The king's first act, the very key to his authority and potency, is the erection of a temple within a heavily walled sacred enclosure. And the construction of another wall to enclose the subservient community turns the whole area into a sacred place: a city.

Without this strong religious underpinning, the king's magic powers would have been lacking and his military prowess would have crumbled. Roland Martin's observations about the later Aegean cities, that the city is "un fait du prince," is precisely what distinguishes this new collective artifact from earlier urban structures.

By effecting a coalition between military power and religious myth, under conditions I first attempted to outline in the symposium published as *City Invincible* (Carl Kraeling, editor), the hunter-chieftain of the later Neolithic economy transformed himself into a king; and kingship established a mode of government and a way of life radically different from that of the proto-historic village community, as described, from the Sumerian records, by Thorkild Jacobsen. In this new constitution, the king gathers to himself all the powers and functions that were once diffused in many local communities; and the king himself becomes the godlike incarnation of collective power and communal responsibility.

Henri Frankfort's penetrating exposition of the role of kingship in early civilizations provides a clue to the utopian nature of the city: for, if it was through the king that the functions of the community were concentrated, unified, magnified, and given a sacred status, it was only in the city that the power and glory of this new institution could be fully manifested in monumental works of art. The mystique of kingship, Frankfort suggests, was supported by its immense practical contributions in distributing agricultural plenitude, handling population growth, and creating collective wealth. The king's power to make decisions, to by-pass communal deliberations, to defy or nullify custom brought about vast communal changes, far beyond the scope of village communities. Once amassed in cities, governed by a single head, regimented and controlled under military coercion, a large population could act as one, with a solidarity otherwise possible only in a small community.

If the king represents or, as in Egypt, incarnates divine power and communal life, the city visibly incorporates them: its esthetic form and conscious order testify to an immense concentration of energy no longer needed exclusively for the functions of nutrition and reproduction. The only limits to what might be accomplished in such an organization, while the myth of divine kingship remained in working order, were those of the human imagination. Up to this time, the human community had been widely dispersed in hamlets, villages, country towns: isolated, earthbound, illiterate, tied to ancestral ways. But the city was, from the beginning, related to the newly perceived cosmic order: the sun, the moon, the planets, the lightning, the storm wind. In short, as Fustel de Coulanges and Bachofen pointed out a century ago, the city was primarily a religious phenomenon: it was the home of a god, and even the city wall points to this super-human origin; for Mircea Eliade is probably correct in inferring that its primary function was to hold chaos at bay and ward off inimical spirits.

This cosmic orientation, these mythic-religious claims, this royal preemption of the powers and functions of the community are what transformed the mere village or town into a city: something "out of this world," the home of a god. Much of the contents of the city—houses, shrines, storage bins, ditches, irrigation works—was already in existence in smaller communities: but though these utilities were necessary antecedents of the city, the city itself was transmogrified into an ideal form—a glimpse of eternal order, a visible heaven on earth, a seat of the life abundant—in other words, utopia.

The medieval Christian picture of heaven as a place where the elect find their highest fulfillment in beholding God and singing his praises is only a somewhat etherealized version of the primordial city. With such a magnificent setting as background, the king not merely played god but exercized unqualified power over every member of the community, commanding services, imposing sacrifices, above all enforcing abject obedience on penalty of death. In the city, the good life was achieved only by mystical participation in the god's life and that of his fellow deities, and by vicarious achievement through the person of the king. There lay the original compensation for giving up the petty democratic ways of the village. To inhabit the same city as a god was to be a member of a super-community: a community in which every subject had a place, a function, a duty, a goal, as part of a hierarchic structure representing the cosmos itself.

The city, then, as it emerged from more primitive urban forms, was not just a larger heap of buildings and public ways, of markets and workshops: it was primarily a symbolic representation of the universe itself. Like kingship, the city was "lowered down from heaven" and cut to a heavenly pattern; for even in the relatively late Etruscan and Roman cultures, when a new city was founded, a priest held the plow that traced the outline of the walls, while the main streets were strictly oriented to the points of the compass. In that sense, the archetypal city was what Campanella called his own utopia: a City of the Sun. Such an embodiment of esthetic magnificence, quantitative power, and divine order captivated the mind of even distant villagers who would make pilgrimages to the city on days of religious festival. This probably accounts for the fact that the punishing labors and tyrannous exactions which made this "utopia" possible were so submissively accepted by the whole community.

But still another characteristic utopian trait marked the ancient city, if we may read the earliest records in the Near East with as much confidence as later data from the Peru of the Incas. Not only did the lowliest subject have a direct glimpse of heaven in the setting of the temple and the palace, but with this went a secure supply of food, garnered from the nearby fields, stored under guard in the granary of the citadel, distributed by the temple. The land itself belonged to the god or the king, as it still does ultimately in legal theory to their abstract counterpart, the sovereign state; and the city forecast its literary successor in treating the land and its agricultural produce as a common possession: fair shares, if not equal shares, for all. In return, every member of the community was obliged to perform sacrifices and to devote at least part of the year to laboring for the city's god.

By substituting conscription and communism for the later institutions of the market, wage labor, private property, and money, the utopias of More, Cabet, and Bellamy all reverted to the primitive condition of this aboriginal urban organization: a managed economy under the direction of the king.

V

This brief summary suggests, I realize, a conclusion perhaps even more unacceptable at first glance than the notion that the Neolithic community, seen from the perspective of the Iron Age, once enjoyed the veritable Golden Age that Hesiod described.

If the present interpretation be sound, the ancient city was not only "utopia," but the most impressive and the most enduring of all utopias: one that actually fulfilled at the beginning the principal ideal prescriptions of later fantasies, and in many respects indeed surpassed them. For to an extraordinary extent the archetypal city placed the stamp of divine order and human purpose on all its institutions, transforming ritual into drama, custom and caprice into formal law, and empirical knowledge spotted with superstition into exact astronomical observation and fine mathematical calculation.

While the myth remained operative, a single agent of divine power, the king, unlike a village council of elders, could by spoken command bring about hitherto impossible improvements in the environment and alter human behavior. These were the classic conditions for constructing a utopia. Even when the myth of kingship dissolved, the city passed some of that power on to its citizens.

But one relevant question remains to be asked: At what price was this utopia achieved? What institutional apparatus made it possible to organize and build these vast ideal structures? And, if the ancient city was indeed utopia, what qualities in human nature or what defects in its own constitution caused it to change, almost as soon as it had taken form, into its opposite: a negative utopia, a dystopia or kakotopia? If eutopia became a mere wraith in the mind, a symbol of unattainable desires, of futile dreams, why did its dark shadow, kakotopia or hell, erupt so often in history, in an endless series of exterminations and destructions that centered in the city—a hell that still threatens to become a universal holocaust in our own time?

The answer to the first question may, I believe, provide a clue to the second condition. For the city that first impressed the image of utopia upon the mind was made possible only by another daring invention of kingship: the collective human machine, the platonic model of all later machines.

The machine that accompanied the rise of the city was directly a product of the new myth; but it long escaped recognition, despite a mass of direct and indirect evidence, because no specimen of it could be found in archeological diggings. The reason that this machine so long evaded detection is that, though extremely complicated, it was composed almost entirely of human parts. Fortunately the original model has been handed on intact through a historic institution that is still with us: the army.

Let me explain. In the period when the institution of kingship arose, no ordinary machine, except the bow and arrow, yet existed: even the wagon wheel had not yet been invented. With the small desultory labor force a village could command, and with the simple tools available for digging and cutting, none of the great utilities that were constructed in the Fertile Crescent could have been built. Power machinery was needed to move the vast masses of earth, to cut the huge blocks of stone, to transport heavy materials long distances, to set whole cities on an artificial mound forty feet high. These operations were performed at an incredible speed: without a superb machine at command, no king could have built a pyramid or a ziggurat, still less a whole city, in his own lifetime.

By royal command, the necessary machine was created: a machine that concentrated energy in great assemblages of men, each unit shaped, graded, trained, regimented, articulated, to perform its particular function in a unified working whole. With such a machine, work could be conceived and executed on a scale that otherwise was impossible until the steam engine and the dynamo were invented. The assemblage and the direction of these labor machines was the prerogative of kings and an evidence of their supreme power; for it was only by exacting unflagging effort and mechanical obedience from each of the operative parts of the machine that the whole mechanism could so efficiently function. The division of tasks and the specialization of labor to which Adam Smith imputes so much of the success of the so-called industrial revolution actually were already in evidence in the Pyramid Age, with a graded bureaucracy to supervise the whole process. Every part of the machine was regimented to carry out the king's will: "The command of the palace . . . cannot be altered. The King's word is right; his utterance, like that of a God, cannot be changed."

This new kind of complex power mechanism achieved its maximum efficiency in the era when it was first invented: in the case of the hundred thousand workers who built the Great Pyramid at Giza, that machine could develop ten thousand horse-power; and every part of its colossal job was performed with machine-like precision. The measurements of that pyramid, J. H. Breasted observed, were refined to almost a watchmaker's standard of accuracy—though the giant slabs of stone were hauled on sledges by manpower and there were no derricks or pulleys to hoist the blocks into position. This new mechanical power, this undeviating order, this mathematical refinement are still visible in the remaining artifacts. No earlier creation of man had ever exhibited this magnitude or this perfection.

Most of the dehumanized routines of our later machine technology were incorporated in the archetypal machine, usually in a more naked and brutal state. But the necessary suppression of all human autonomy except that of the king was likewise the imperative condition for operating this giant machine. In other words, the disciplined forces that transformed the humble human community into a gigantic collective work of art turned it into a prison in which the king's agents, his eyes and ears and hands, served as jailers.

Though the lock step discipline of the labor machine was happily alleviated by the art and ritual of the city, this power system was kept in operation by threats and penalties, rather than by rewards. Not for nothing was the king's authority represented by a scepter, for this was only a polite substitute for the mace, that fearful weapon by which the king would kill, with a single blow on the head, anyone who opposed his will. In one of the earliest representations of a king, the Narmer palette, the king holds a mace in his hand above a captive and, in the form of a bull, destroys a city. The price of utopia, if I read the record correctly, was total submission to a central authority, forced labor, lifetime specialization, inflexible regimentation, one-way communication, and readiness for war. In short, a community of frightened men, galvanized into corpselike obedience with the constant aid of the mace, the whip, and the truncheon. An ideal commonwealth indeed!

The archetypal machine, in other words, was an ambivalent triumph of human design. If it vastly widened the scope of human capability and created a visible heaven in the great city, exalting the human spirit as it had never been exalted by man's own works before, it likewise, by the very requirements of the mechanism, debased or wiped out precious human traits that even the humblest village still cherished. What proved equally damaging to the city was that the ability to command such powers produced paranoid fantasies in the rulers themselves: hostility, suspicion, murderous aggression, coupled with collective ambitions that no single city could satisfy.

Nothing is more conspicuous in the religious texts that follow upon the creation of the city and the invention of the human machine than the uncontrolled hostility that the gods display toward each other: in their hatred, their murderous aggression, their absence of moral constraint, their readiness to inflict sadistic punishments, they mirror the boasts and practices of kings. From the beginning the labor machine and the military machine performed interchangeable functions: as an offset to the regression and regimentation necessitated by the labor machine, the destruction of rival cities, the abasement of rival gods, became the chief means of manifesting royal power. If the utopia of the city did not in fact live up to its happy promise, it was because its very success promoted more exorbitant fantasies of unrestrained power. The building of cities was a creative act; but the war machine made a dystopia—total destruction and extermination—far easier to achieve. That is the dark hidden face of the ideal city that kingship had actually built.

VI

When one puts these two archetypal forms, the city and the machine, side by side, one is finally pressed to an all-but-inescapable conclusion: utopia was once indeed a historic fact and became possible, in the first instance, through the regimentation of labor in a totalitarian mechanism, whose rigors were softened by the many captivating qualities of the city itself, which raised the sights on all possible human achievement. Through the greater part of history, it was the image of the city that lingered in the human imagination as the closest approach to paradise that one might hope for on earth—though paradise, the original Persian word reminds us, was not a city but a walled garden, a Neolithic rather than a Bronze Age image.

In their pristine historic forms both the utopian city and the royal machine had only a short career. Fortunately in both cases, beneath the myth, the diverse and divergent realities of communal life remained in operation. Within the actual city, the old cooperative life of the village found a niche for itself; and eventually the family, the neighborhood, the workshop, the guild, the market, drew back to their own province some of the powers and initiatives that the king had claimed for himself and for the dominant minority that served him—the nobles, the priests, the scribes, the officials, the "engineers." The very mixture of vocations and occupations, of languages and cultural backgrounds within the city gave each member of the urban community the advantages of the wider whole, while various material appurtenances and social privileges, once monopolized by the citadel, slowly, over the millennia if not over the centuries, filtered down to the rest of the community. Even the Pharaoh's exclusive monopoly of immortality was broken after the revolutions that ended the Pyramid Age.

Yet the great lesson of the archetypal city, the power of human design to alter natural conditions and customary practices, was never entirely lost. This early success raised the hope, expressed in later utopias—best perhaps by Fourier and William Morris—that similar results could be attained by voluntary effort and free association and mutual aid, rather than by military compulsion, royal or platonic.

As for the Invisible Machine, it remained in existence mainly in its negative form—the army or military machine—for this was the backbone of the coercive power claimed everywhere by the successor of the city, the sovereign state. Obviously, these great collective machines, assembling thousands of working parts, were too powerful and too clumsy to be used on tasks smaller than road-building or canal-cutting. Meanwhile, small machines of wooden or metal parts were invented, with the same properties as their collective human prototype: heightened capacity to perform work with regularity and mechanical precision. Machines like the animal-drawn wagon, the potter's wheel, the loom, and the lathe not only lightened labor but enhanced human autonomy: they could operate without the mediation of priests, bureaucrats, and soldiers. With the invention of the water mill (Third Century B.C.) and the windmill (Seventh Century [?] A.D.) free labor at last achieved a command of energy on a scale that had been possible heretofore only through a regimented assemblage of manpower under a king.

In negative form, the utopian ideal of total control from above, absolute obedience below, never entirely passed out of existence. The will to exercise such control through the military machine incited the great military conquerers from Ashurbanipal to Alexander, from Genghis Khan to Napoleon, as well as many lesser imitators. The negative military form of the Invisible Machine was held in check over the greater part of history by two limiting factors: first its inherent tendency to produce, in the rulers of the machine, delusions of grandeur that intensified all its destructive potentialities and led in fact to repeated collective self-destruction. The other limiting condition was the fact that this authoritarian regime was passively challenged by the archaic, democratic, life-conserving village culture that has always embraced the larger part of mankind. And during the last millennium, the growth of voluntary forms of association, in synagogue, church, guild, university, and the self-governing city, undermined the unconditional, over-riding exercise of "sovereignty" necessary to assemble the Invisible Machine.

Until the sixteenth century, then, when Church and State re-united, in England, France, and Spain, and later in Prussia, as an all-embracing source of sovereign power, the chief conditions for extending the Invisible Machine were lacking. Even the political ideal of total control, as expressed by absolute monarchs like Henry VIII, Philip II, and Louis XIV, and various Italian Dukes, was for some centuries contested by vigorous democratic counter-movements. In its ancient and no longer viable form, kingship by divine right was defeated: but the idea of absolute power and absolute control re-entered the scene as soon as the other components of the Invisible Machine had been translated into more practical modern equivalents and re-assembled.

This last stage was not reached until our own generation; but the first decisive changes started in the sixteenth century.

Since it took three centuries to assemble the new Invisible Machine, and since earlier forms had not yet been identified, the rise of this great mechanical collective for long escaped contemporary observation. Because of the erroneous Victorian belief, still current in history textbooks, that the "industrial revolution" began in the eighteenth century, a vastly more important technological change has been ignored. The thousands of useful mechanical and electronic inventions that have been made, at an accelerating rate, during the last two centuries still conceal the even more significant restoration, in more scientific guise, of the Invisible Machine.

But in retrospect, the sequence is clear. Beginning in the sixteenth century, with the astronomical observations of Copernicus and Kepler, the cult of the sun came back, bringing cosmic order and regularity, already prefigured in the mechanical clock, into every department of life. Though the absolute powers of individual kings were reduced, the powers claimed by their successor, the impersonal sovereign state, were steadily increased, first by reducing the authority of religion as a source of higher knowledge and moral values, then by making all other corporate entities creatures of the sovereign power. "L'état, c'est moi," proclaimed Louis XIV, Le Roi Soleil, in words that even the earliest avatar of Atum-Re would have recognized as a factual statement. But it was only with the French Revolution that the state, under a republican mask, actually achieved in its system of universal conscription the powers that Louis XIV did not dare to exercise completely—but powers which the state now everywhere commands.

With this new mechanical assemblage came the uniformed standing army, whose very uniform was, after the printing press, the first example of mechanized mass production; and that army, in turn, was freshly disciplined everywhere by the same sort of rigorous drill, introduced by William of Orange, that produced the Sumerian or the Macedonian phalanx. In the eighteenth century, this widened mechanical discipline was transferred to the factory. On these foundations the new mechanical order, based on quantitative measurements, indifferent to human qualities or purposes, took form. As outlined by Galileo and Descartes, the new ideology of science, which was finally to become the central component of the Invisible Machine, reduced reality to the calculated, the measurable, the controllable: in other words, the universal world of the machine, both visible and invisible, both utilitarian and ideal.

These transformations came slowly, impeded both by surviving democratic institutions and traditions, and by smaller corporate economic enterprises, in which private property jealously contested the total control of the sovereign state. But the growth of science had meanwhile repaired the shaky ideological premises that had limited the efficiency of the ancient collective machines; and on the new foundations of post-Galilean science utopia again became possible.

Long before all the components of the Invisible Machine were consciously assembled, Francis Bacon, in his *New Atlantis,* was quick not merely to anticipate its benefits but to outline the conditions for its achievement: the application of science to all human affairs, "to the effecting of all things possible." What the temple and the priesthood and astronomical observation did to establish the authority of the king, Solomon's House and its new occupants would do to establish the authority of the machine. Unlike the steam engines and power looms that still engross the historian, the new machine is mainly an assemblage of human parts: scientists, technicians, administrators, physicians, soldiers. Though it has taken more than three hundred years to perfect the parts of this machine, its final organization has taken place within the last twenty years.

In the throes of the Second World War, the archetypal compact between kingship and priesthood was ratified, with a grant of virtually unlimited financial support and opportunity for science on condition that its priesthood would sanction and devote itself to magnifying vastly the powers of the sovereign entity. Within the space of less than a lustrum, the Invisible Machine had finally been re-assembled, with all its original potentialities inordinately inflated. The atom bomb symbolized this union of putative omnipotence with putative omniscience. So effective has been the coalition between these forces, so rapid their extension beyond the field of extermination and destruction, so all-embracing the Invisible Machine's monopoly of the instruments of both production and education, that its implicit goals and its ultimate destination have not yet been subject to any critical examination.

But one thing is already plain: in its new scientific form the Invisible Machine is no longer an agent for creating a visible heaven on earth in the form of the city. The autonomous machine, in its dual capacity as visible universal instrument and invisible object of collective worship, itself has become utopia, and the enlargement of its province has become the final end of life, as the guardians of our New Atlantis now conceive it.

The many genuine improvements that science and technics have introduced into every aspect of existence have been so notable that it is perhaps natural that its grateful beneficiaries should have overlooked the ominous social context in which these changes have taken place, as well as the heavy price we have already paid for them, and the still more forbidding price that is in prospect. Until the last generation it was possible to think of the various components of technology as additive. This meant that each new mechanical invention, each new scientific discovery, each new application to engineering, agriculture, or medicine, could be judged separately on its own performance, estimated eventually in terms of the human good accomplished, and diminished or eliminated if it did not in fact promote human welfare.

This belief has now proved an illusion. Though each new invention or discovery may respond to some general human need, or even awaken a fresh human potentiality, it immediately becomes part of an articulated totalitarian system that, on its own premises, has turned the machine into a god whose power must be increased, whose prosperity is essential to all existence, and whose operations, however irrational or compulsive, cannot be challenged, still less modified.

The only group that has understood the dehumanizing threats of the Invisible Machine are the *avant-garde* artists, who have caricatured it by going to the opposite extreme of disorganization. Their calculated destructions and "happenings" symbolize total decontrol: the rejection of order, continuity, design, significance, and a total inversion of human values which turns criminals into saints and scrambled minds into sages. In such anti-art, the dissolution of our entire civilization into randomness and entropy is prophetically symbolized. In their humorless deaf-and-dumb language, the *avant-garde* artists reach the same goal as scientists and technicians, but by a different route—both seek or at least welcome the displacement and the eventual elimination of man. In short, both the further affirmation of the mechanical utopia and its total rejection would beget dystopia. Wherever human salvation may lie, neither utopia nor dystopia, as now conceived, promises it.

VII

A summary word. Viewed objectively, the classic literature of utopias reveals a singularly barren tract of mind: even Plato's efforts, for all their many stimulating human insights, succeed better as a study in character contrasts, as for example between Socrates and Glaucon, than as an ideal revelation of natural human potentialities. Plato's utopias were by intention too close to archaic history to make history afresh in the future. As for those modern forms of utopia, which under the name of science fiction relate all ideal possibilities to technological innovations, they are so close to the working premises of modern civilization that they hardly have time to be absorbed as fiction before they become incorporated as fact.

If, with all these limitations, a learned body like ours still finds it worthwhile to discuss both myth and utopia, is this not perhaps a covert way of acknowledging that our present scientific methodology, which equates possibility only with chance, is inadequate to deal with every aspect of human experience? Through this respectably academic side-excursion into utopia are we not, with a prudence that touches on cowardice, actually approaching a much more fertile area, now weedy with neglect—the realm embracing potentiality as an aspect of all natural existence, "foreplans of action" (Lloyd Morgan) as a dynamic attribute of living organisms, and design as a necessary constituent of rational human development? These categories constitute the fringe benefits of utopian literature; but they are far more important than the books that embody them. Perhaps after our tour of utopias we shall be ready to explore and reclaim this more important territory, with Aristotle and Whitehead to guide us rather than Plato and Sir Thomas More.

BIBLIOGRAPHY

Mircea Eliade, *Patterns in Comparative Religion* (New York: Sheed & Ward, 1958).

Henri Frankfort, *Kingship and the Gods* (Chicago: University of Chicago Press, 1948).

———, *The Birth of Civilization in the Near East* (Bloomington: University of Indiana Press, 1954).

Leonard T. Hobhouse, *Development and Purpose* (London: Macmillan, 1913).

Carl Kraeling and Robert M. Adams, *City Invincible: A Symposium on Urbanization and Cultural Development in the Ancient Near East* (Chicago: University of Chicago Press, 1960).

Lloyd Morgan, *Life, Mind, and Spirit* (New York: Henry Holt & Co., 1926).

Werner Müller, *Die Heilige Stadt* (Stuttgart: W. Kohlhammer Verlag, 1961).

Lewis Mumford, "Authoritarian and Democratic Technics," *Technology and Culture* (Winter 1964).

———, "Summary Remarks: Prospect," in W. L. Thomas, Jr., (editor), *Man's Role in Changing the Face of the Earth* (Chicago: University of Chicago Press, 1956).

Joseph Rykwert, *The Idea of a Town* (Amsterdam: Aldo van Eyck, n.d. [1964?]).

A. N. Whitehead, *Science and the Modern World* (New York: Macmillan, 1925).

NORTHROP FRYE

Varieties of Literary Utopias

THERE ARE two social conceptions which can be expressed only in terms of myth. One is the social contract, which presents an account of the origins of society. The other is the utopia, which presents an imaginative vision of the *telos* or end at which social life aims. These two myths both begin in an analysis of the present, the society that confronts the mythmaker, and they project this analysis in time or space. The contract projects it into the past, the utopia into the future or some distant place. To Hobbes, a contemporary of the Puritan Revolution, the most important social principle was the maintenance of *de facto* power; hence he constructs a myth of contract turning on the conception of society's surrender of that power. To Locke, a contemporary of the Whig Revolution, the most important social principle was the relation of *de facto* power to legitimate or *de jure* authority; hence he constructs a myth turning on society's delegation of power. The value of such a myth as theory depends on the depth and penetration of the social analysis which inspires it. The social contract, though a genuine myth which, in John Stuart Mill's phrase, passes a fiction off as a fact, is usually regarded as an integral part of social theory. The utopia, on the other hand, although its origin is much the same, belongs primarily to fiction. The reason is that the emphasis in the contract myth falls on the present facts of society which it is supposed to explain. And even to the extent that the contract myth is projected into the past, the past is the area where historical evidence lies; and so the myth preserves at least the gesture of making assertions that can be definitely verified or refuted.

The utopia is a *speculative* myth; it is designed to contain or provide a vision for one's social ideas, not to be a theory connecting social facts together. There have been one or two attempts to take utopian constructions literally by trying to set them up as actual communities, but the histories of these communities make melancholy reading. Life imitates literature up to a point, but hardly up to that point. The utopian writer looks at his own society first and tries to see what, for his purposes, its significant elements are. The utopia itself shows what society would be like if those elements were fully developed. Plato looked at his society and saw its structure as a hierarchy of priests, warriors, artisans, and servants—much the same structure that inspired the caste system of India. The *Republic* shows what a society would be like in which such a hierarchy functioned on the principle of justice, that is, each man doing his own work. More, thinking within a Christian framework of ideas, assumed that the significant elements of society were the natural virtues, justice, temperance, fortitude, prudence. The *Utopia* itself, in its second or constructive book, shows what a society would be like in which the natural virtues were allowed to assume their natural forms. Bacon, on the other hand, anticipates Marx by assuming that the most significant of social factors is technological productivity, and his *New Atlantis* constructs accordingly.

The procedure of constructing a utopia produces two literary qualities which are typical, almost invariable, in the genre. In the first place, the behavior of society is described *ritually*. A ritual is a significant social act, and the utopia-writer is concerned only with the typical actions which are significant of those social elements he is stressing. In utopian stories a frequent device is for someone, generally a first-person narrator, to enter the utopia and be shown around it by a sort of Intourist guide. The story is made up largely of a Socratic dialogue between guide and narrator, in which the narrator asks questions or thinks up objections and the guide answers them. One gets a little weary, in reading a series of such stories, of what seems a pervading smugness of tone. As a rule the guide is completely identified with his society and seldom admits to any discrepancy between the reality and the appearance of what he is describing. But we recognize that this is inevitable given the conventions employed. In the second place, rituals are apparently irrational acts which become *rational* when their significance is explained. In such utopias the guide explains the structure of the society and thereby the significance of the behavior being observed. Hence, the behavior of society is presented as rationally motivated. It is a common objection to utopias that they present human nature as governed more by reason than it is or can be. But this rational emphasis, again, is the result of using certain literary conventions. The utopian romance does not present society as governed by reason; it presents it as governed by ritual habit, or prescribed social behavior, which is explained rationally.

Every society, of course, imposes a good deal of prescribed social behavior on its citizens, much of it being followed unconsciously, anything completely accepted by convention and custom having in it a large automatic element. But even automatic ritual habits are explicable, and so every society can be seen or described to some extent as a product of conscious design. The symbol of conscious design in society is the city, with its abstract pattern of streets and buildings, and with the complex economic cycle of production, distribution, and consumption that it sets up. The utopia is primarily a vision of the orderly city and of a city-dominated society. Plato's Republic is a city-state, Athenian in culture and Spartan in discipline. It was inevitable that the utopia, as a literary genre, should be revived at the time of the Renaissance, the period in which the medieval social order was breaking down again into city-state units or nations governed from a capital city. Again, the utopia, in its typical form, contrasts, implicitly or explicitly, the writer's own society with the more desirable one he describes. The desirable society, or the utopia proper, is essentially the writer's own society with its unconscious ritual habits transposed into their conscious equivalents. The contrast in value between the two societies implies a satire on the writer's own society, and the basis for the satire is the unconsciousness or inconsistency in the social behavior he observes around him. More's *Utopia* begins with a satire on the chaos of sixteenth-century life in England and presents the Utopia itself as a contrast to it. Thus the typical utopia contains, if only by implication, a satire on the *anarchy* inherent in the writer's own society, and the utopia form flourishes best when anarchy seems most a social threat. Since More, utopias have appeared regularly but sporadically in literature, with a great increase around the close of the nineteenth century. This later vogue clearly had much to do with the distrust and dismay aroused by extreme laissez-faire versions of capitalism, which were thought of as manifestations of anarchy.

Most utopia-writers follow either More (and Plato) in stressing the legal structure of their societies, or Bacon in stressing its technological power. The former type of utopia is closer to actual social and political theory; the latter overlaps with what is now called science fiction. Naturally, since the Industrial Revolution a serious utopia can hardly avoid introducing technological themes. And because technology is progressive, getting to the utopia has tended increasingly to be a journey in time rather than space, a vision of the future and not of a society located in some isolated spot on the globe (or outside it: journeys to the moon are a very old form of fiction, and some of them are utopian). The growth of science and technology brings with it a prodigious increase in the legal complications of existence. As soon as medical science identifies the source of a contagious disease in a germ, laws of quarantine go into effect; as soon as technology produces the automobile, an immense amount of legal apparatus is imported into life, and thousands of non-criminal citizens become involved in fines and police-court actions. This means a corresponding increase in the amount of ritual habit necessary to life, and a new ritual habit must be conscious, and so constraining, before it becomes automatic or unconscious. Science and technology, especially the latter, introduce into society the conception of directed social change, change with logical consequences attached to it. These consequences turn on the increase of ritual habit. And as long as ritual habit can still be seen as an imminent possibility, as something we may or may not acquire, there can be an emotional attitude toward it either of acceptance or repugnance. The direction of social change may be thought of as exhilarating, as in most theories of progress, or as horrible, as in pessimistic or apprehensive social theories. Or it may be thought that whether the direction of change is good or bad will depend on the attitude society takes toward it. If the attitude is active and resolute, it may be good; if helpless and ignorant, bad.

A certain amount of claustrophobia enters this argument when it is realized, as it is from about 1850 on, that technology tends to unify the whole world. The conception of an *isolated* utopia like that of More or Plato or Bacon gradually evaporates in the face of this fact. Out of this situation come two kinds of utopian romance: the straight utopia, which visualizes a world-state assumed to be ideal, or at least ideal in comparison with what we have, and the utopian satire or parody, which presents the same kind of social goal in terms of slavery, tyranny, or anarchy. Examples of the former in the literature of the last century include Bellamy's *Looking Backward,* Morris' *News from Nowhere,* and H. G. Wells' *A Modern Utopia.* Wells is one of the few writers who have constructed both serious and satirical utopias. Examples of the utopian satire include Zamiatin's *We,* Aldous Huxley's *Brave New World,* and George Orwell's *1984.* There are other types of utopian satire which we shall mention in a moment, but this particular kind is a product of modern technological society, its growing sense that the whole world is destined to the same social fate with no place to hide, and its increasing realization that technology moves toward the control not merely of nature but of the operations of the mind. We may note that what is a serious utopia to its author, and to many of its readers, could be read as a satire by a reader whose emotional attitudes were different. *Looking Backward* had, in its day, a stimulating and emancipating influence on the social thinking of the time in a way that very few books in the history of literature have ever had. Yet most of us today would tend to read it as a sinister blueprint of tyranny, with its industrial "army," its stentorian propaganda delivered over the "telephone" to the homes of its citizens, and the like.

The nineteenth-century utopia had a close connection with the growth of socialist political thought and shared its tendency to think in global terms. When Engels attacked "utopian" socialism and contrasted it with his own "scientific" kind, his scientific socialism was utopian in the sense in which we are using that term, but what he rejected under the category of "utopian" was the tendency to think in terms of a delimited socialist society, a place of refuge like the phalansteries of Fourier. For Engels, as for Marxist thinkers generally, there was a world-wide historical process going in a certain direction; and humanity had the choice either of seizing and directing this process in a revolutionary act or of drifting into greater anarchy or slavery. The goal, a classless society in which the state had withered away, was utopian; the means adopted to reach this goal were "scientific" and anti-utopian, dismissing the possibility of setting up *a* utopia within a pre-socialist world.

We are concerned here with utopian literature, not with social attitudes; but literature is rooted in the social attitudes of its time. In the literature of the democracies today we notice that utopian satire is very prominent (for example, William Golding's *Lord of the Flies*), but that there is something of a paralysis of utopian thought and imagination. We can hardly understand this unless we realize the extent to which it is the result of a repudiation of Communism. In the United States particularly the attitude toward a definite social ideal as a planned goal is anti-utopian: such an ideal, it is widely felt, can produce in practice only some form of totalitarian state. And whereas the Communist program calls for a revolutionary seizure of the machinery of production, there is a strong popular feeling in the democracies that the utopian goal can be reached only by allowing the machinery of production to function by itself, as an automatic and continuous process. Further, it is often felt that such an automatic process tends to decentralize authority and break down monopolies of political power. This combination of an anti-utopian attitude toward centralized planning and a utopian attitude toward the economic process naturally creates some inconsistencies. When I was recently in Houston, I was told that Houston had no zoning laws: that indicates a strongly anti-utopian sentiment in Houston, yet Houston was building sewers, highways, clover-leaf intersections, and shopping centers in the most uninhibited utopian way.

There is however something of a donkey's carrot in attaching utopian feelings to a machinery of production largely concerned with consumer goods. We can see this if we look at some of the utopian romances of the last century. The technological utopia has one literary disadvantage: its predictions are likely to fall short of what comes true, so that what the writer saw in the glow of vision we see only as a crude version of ordinary life. Thus Edgar Allan Poe has people crossing the Atlantic in balloons at a hundred miles an hour one thousand years after his own time. I could describe the way I get to work in the morning, because it is a form of ritual habit, in the idiom of a utopia, riding on a subway, guiding myself by street signs, and the like, showing how the element of social design conditions my behavior at every point. It might sound utopian if I had written it as a prophecy a century ago, or now to a native of a New Guinea jungle, but it would hardly do so to my present readers. Similarly with the prediction of the radio (called, as noted above, the telephone, which had been invented) in Bellamy's *Looking Backward* (1888). A slightly earlier romance, said to be the original of Bellamy's book, is *The Diothas,* by John MacNie (1883)*. It predicts a general use of a horseless carriage, with a speed of twenty miles an hour (faster downhill). One passage shows very clearly how something commonplace to us could be part of a utopian romance in 1883:

"You see the white line running along the centre of the road," resumed

* I owe my knowledge of *The Diothas,* and much else in this paper, to the admirable collection *The Quest for Utopia, An Anthology of Imaginary Societies* by Glenn Negley and J. Max Patrick (New York: Schuman, 1952).

Utis. "The rule of the road requires that line to be kept on the left, except when passing a vehicle in front. Then the line may be crossed, provided the way on that side is clear."

But while technology has advanced far beyond the wildest utopian dreams even of the last century, the essential quality of human life has hardly improved to the point that it could be called utopian. The real strength and importance of the utopian imagination, both for literature and for life, if it has any at all, must lie elsewhere.

The popular view of the utopia, and the one which in practice is accepted by many if not most utopia-writers, is that a utopia is an ideal or flawless state, not only logically consistent in its structure but permitting as much freedom and happiness for its inhabitants as is possible to human life. Considered as a final or definitive social ideal, the utopia is a static society; and most utopias have built-in safeguards against radical alteration of the structure. This feature gives it a somewhat forbidding quality to a reader not yet committed to it. An imaginary dialogue between a utopia-writer and such a reader might begin somewhat as follows: Reader: "I can see that this society might work, but I wouldn't want to live in it." Writer: "What you mean is that you don't want your present ritual habits disturbed. My utopia would feel different from the inside, where the ritual habits would be customary and so carry with them a sense of freedom rather than constraint." Reader: "Maybe so, but my sense of freedom right now is derived from *not* being involved in your society. If I were, I'd either feel constraint or I'd be too unconscious to be living a fully human life at all." If this argument went on, some compromise might be reached: the writer might realize that freedom really depends on a sense of constraint, and the reader might realize that a utopia should not be read simply as a description of a most perfect state, even if the author believes it to be one. Utopian thought is imaginative, with its roots in literature, and the literary imagination is less concerned with achieving ends than with visualizing possibilities.

There are many reasons why an encouragement of utopian thinking would be of considerable benefit to us. An example would be an attempt to see what the social results of automation might be, or might be made to be; and surely some speculation along this line is almost essential to self-preservation. Again, the intellectual separation of the "two cultures" is said to be a problem of our time, but this separation is inevitable, it is going steadily to increase, not decrease, and it cannot possibly be cured by having humanists read more popular science or scientists read more poetry. The real problem is not the humanist's ignorance of science or vice versa, but the ignorance of both humanist and scientist about the society of which they are both citizens. The quality of an intellectual's social imagination is the quality of his maturity as a thinker, whatever his brilliance in his own line. In the year that George Orwell published *1984,* two other books appeared in the utopian tradition, one by a humanist, Robert Graves' *Watch the North Wind Rise,* the other by a social scientist, B. F. Skinner's *Walden Two.* Neither book was intended very seriously: they reflect the current view that utopian thinking is not serious. It is all the more significant that both books show the infantilism of specialists who see society merely as an extension of their own speciality. The Graves book is about the revival of mother goddess cults in Crete, and its preoccupation with the more lugubrious superstitions of the past makes it almost a caricature of the pedantry of humanism. Skinner's book shows how to develop children's will power by hanging lollipops around their necks and giving them rewards for not eating them: its Philistine vulgarity makes it a caricature of the pedantry of social science. The utopia, the effort at social imagination, is an area in which specialized disciplines can meet and interpenetrate with a mutual respect for each other, concerned with clarifying their common social context.

The word "imaginative" refers to hypothetical constructions, like those of literature or mathematics. The word "imaginary" refers to something that does not exist. Doubtless many writers of utopias think of their state as something that does not exist but which they wish did exist; hence their intention as writers is descriptive rather than constructive. But we cannot possibly discuss the utopia as a literary genre on this negatively existential basis. We have to see it as a species of the constructive literary imagination, and we should expect to find that the more penetrating the utopian writer's mind is, the more clearly he understands that he is communicating a vision to his readers, not sharing a power or fantasy dream with them.

II

Plato's *Republic* begins with an argument between Socrates and Thrasymachus over the nature of justice. Thrasymachus attempts, not very successfully, to show that justice is a verbal and rhetorical conception used for certain social purposes, and that existentially there is no such thing as justice. He has to use words to say this, and the words he uses are derived from, and unconsciously accept the assumptions of, a discussion started by Socrates. So Socrates has little difficulty in demonstrating that in the verbal pattern Thrasymachus is employing justice has its normal place, associated with all other good and real things. Others in the group are not satisfied that an existential situation can be so easily refuted by an essentialist argument, and they attempt to restate Thrasymachus' position. Socrates' argument remains essential to the end, but it takes the form of another kind of verbal pattern, a descriptive model of a state in which justice is the existential principle. The question then arises: what relation has this model to existing society?

If what seems the obvious answer is the right one, Plato's imaginary Republic is the ideal society that we do not live in but ought to be living in. Not many readers would so accept it, for Plato's state has in full measure the forbidding quality that we have noted as a characteristic of utopias. Surely most people today would see in its rigorous autocracy, its unscrupulous use of lies for propaganda, its ruthlessly censored art, and its subordination of all the creative and productive life of the state to a fanatical military caste, all the evils that we call totalitarian. Granted all the Greek fascination with the myth of Lycurgus, the fact that Sparta defeated Athens is hardly enough to make us want to adopt so many of the features of that hideous community. Plato admits that dictatorial tyranny is very like his state-pattern entrusted to the wrong men. But to assume much of a difference between tyranny and Plato's state we should have to believe in the perfectibility of intellectuals, which neither history nor experience gives us much encouragement to do.

We notice, however, that as early as the Fifth Book Socrates has begun to deprecate the question of the practicability of establishing his Republic, on the ground that thought is one thing and action another. And, as the argument goes on there is an increasing emphasis on the analogy of the just state to the wise man's mind. The hierarchy of philosopher, guard, and artisan in the just state corresponds to the hierarchy of reason, will, and appetite in the disciplined individual. And the disciplined individual is the only free individual. The free man is free because his chaotic and lustful desires are hunted down and exterminated, or else compelled to express themselves in ways prescribed by the dictatorship of his reason. He is free because a powerful will is ready to spring into action to help reason do whatever it sees fit, acting as a kind of thought police suppressing every impulse not directly related to its immediate interests. It is true that what frees the individual seems to enslave society, and that something goes all wrong with human freedom when we take an analogy between individual and social order literally. But Plato is really arguing from his social model to the individual, not from the individual to society. The censorship of Homer and the other poets, for example, illustrates how the wise man uses literature, what he accepts and rejects of it in forming his own beliefs, rather than what society ought to do to literature. At the end of the Ninth Book we reach what is the end of the *Republic* for our purposes, as the Tenth Book raises issues beyond our present scope. There it is made clear that the *Republic* exists in the present, not in the future. It is not a dream to be realized in practice; it is an informing power in the mind:

> I understand; you speak of that city of which we are the founders, and which exists in idea only; for I do not think that there is such an one anywhere on earth.
>
> In heaven, I replied, there is laid up a pattern of such a city, and he who desires may behold this, and beholding, govern himself accordingly. But whether there really is or ever will be such an one is of no importance to him; for he will act according to the laws of that city and of no other.
>
> (Jowett tr.)

In Christianity the two myths that polarize social thought, the contract and the utopia, the myth of origin and the myth of *telos*, are given in their purely mythical or undisplaced forms. The myth of contract becomes the myth of creation, and of placing man in the garden of Eden, the ensuing fall being the result of a breach of the contract. Instead of the utopia we have the City of God, a utopian metaphor most elaborately developed in St. Augustine. To this city men, or some men, are admitted at the end of time, but of course human nature is entirely incapable of reaching it in its present state, much less of establishing it. Still, the attainment of the City of God in literature must be classified as a form of utopian fiction, its most famous literary treatment being the *Purgatorio* and *Paradiso* of Dante. The conception of the millennium, the Messianic kingdom to be established on earth, comes closer to the conventional idea of the utopia, but that again does not depend primarily on human effort.

The church, in this scheme of things, is not a utopian society, but it is a more highly ritualized community than ordinary society; and its relation to the latter has some analogies to the relation of Plato's Republic to the individual mind. That is, it acts as an informing power on society, drawing it closer to the pattern of the City of God. Most utopias are conceived as élite societies in which a small group is entrusted with essential responsibilities, and this élite is usually some analogy of a priesthood. For in Utopia, as in India, the priestly caste has reached the highest place. H. G. Wells divides society into the Poietic, or creative, the Kinetic, or executive, the Dull, and the Base. This reads like an uncharitable version of the four Indian castes—particularly uncharitable considering that the only essential doctrine in Wells' utopian religion is the rejection of original sin. Wells' writing in general illustrates the common principle that the belief that man is by nature good does not lead to a very good-natured view of man. In any case his "samurai" belong to the first group, in spite of their warrior name. The utopias of science fiction are generally controlled by scientists, who of course are another form of priestly élite.

Another highly ritualized society, the monastic community, though not intended as a utopia, has some utopian characteristics. Its members spend their whole time within it; individual life takes its pattern from the community; certain activities of the civilized good life, farming, gardening, reclaiming land, copying manuscripts, teaching, form part of its structure. The influence of the monastic community on utopian thought has been enormous. It is strong in More's *Utopia,* and much stronger in Campanella's *City of the Sun,* which is more explicitly conceived on the analogy of the church and monastery. The conception of the ideal society as a secularized reversal of the monastery, the vows of poverty, chastity, and obedience transposed into economic security, monogamous marriage, and personal independence, appears in Rabelais' scheme for the Abbey of Thélème. Something like this re-appears in many nineteenth-century Utopias, not only the literary ones but in the more explicitly political schemes of St. Simon, Fourier, and Comte, of whose writings it seems safe to say that they lack Rabelais' lightness of touch. The government of the monastery, with its mixture of the elective and the dictatorial principles, is still going strong as a social model in Carlyle's *Past and Present.* Utopian satire sometimes introduces celibate groups of fanatics by way of parody, as in *1984* and in Huxley's *Ape and Essence.*

It is obvious from what we have said that a Christian utopia, in the sense of an ideal state to be attained in human life, is impossible: if it were possible it would be the kingdom of heaven, and trying to realize it on earth would be the chief end of man. Hence More does not present his Utopia as a Christian state: it is a state, as we remarked earlier, in which the natural virtues are allowed to assume their natural forms. In that case, what is the point of the *Utopia,* which is certainly a Christian book? Some critics feel that More could have meant it only as a *jeu d'espirit* for an in-group of humanist intellectuals. But that conception makes it something more trivial than anything that More would write or Rabelais and Erasmus much appreciate. The second book of *Utopia* must have been intended quite as seriously as the trenchant social criticism of the first.

We note that the *Utopia,* again, takes the form of a dialogue between a first-person narrator and a guide. The guide is Hythloday, who has been to Utopia, and whose description of it takes up the second book. The narrator is More himself. In the first book the social attitudes of the two men are skillfully contrasted. More is a gradualist, a reformer; he feels that Hythloday should use his experience and knowledge in advising the princes of Europe on the principles of social justice. Hythloday has come back from Utopia a convinced communist and a revolutionary. All Europe's misery, blundering, and hypocrisy spring from its attachment to private property: unless this is renounced nothing good can be done, and as this renunciation is unlikely he sees no hope for Europe. At the end More remarks that although he himself has not been converted to Hythloday's all-out utopianism, there are many things in Utopia that he would hope for rather than expect to see in his own society. The implication seems clear that the ideal state to More, as to Plato, is not a future ideal but a hypothetical one, an informing power and not a goal of action. For More, as for Plato, Utopia is the kind of model of justice and common sense which, once established in the mind, clarifies its standards and values. It does not lead to a desire to abolish sixteenth-century Europe and replace it with Utopia, but it enables one to see Europe, and to work within it, more clearly. As H. G. Wells says of his Utopia, it is good discipline to enter it occasionally.

There is however an element of paradox in More's construct that is absent from Plato's. More's state is not eutopia, the good place, but utopia, nowhere. It is achieved by the natural virtues without revelation, and its eclectic state religion, its toleration (in certain circumstances) of suicide and divorce, its married priesthood, and its epicurean philosophy all mean that it is not, like the Republic, the invisible city whose laws More himself, or his readers, would continually and constantly obey. It has often been pointed out that More died a martyr to some very un-Utopian causes. The point of the paradox is something like this: Europe has revelation, but the natural basis of its society is an extremely rickety structure; and if Europe pretends to greater wisdom than Utopia it ought to have at least something of the Utopian solidity and consistency in the wisdom it shares with Utopia. This paradoxical argument in More re-appears in Montaigne's essay on the cannibals, where it is demonstrated that cannibals have many virtues we have not, and if we disdain to be cannibals we should have at least something of those virtues. Similarly Gulliver returns from the society of rational horses to that of human beings feeling a passionate hatred not of the human race, as careless readers of Swift are apt to say, but of its pride, including its pride in not being horses.

In most utopias the state predominates over the individual: property is usually held in common and the characteristic features of individual life, leisure, privacy, and freedom of movement, are as a rule minimized. Most of this is, once more, simply the result of writing a utopia and accepting its conventions: the utopia is designed to describe a unified society, not individual varieties of existence. Still, the sense of the individual as submerged in a social mass is very strong. But as soon as we adopt the principle of *paradeigma* which Plato sets forth in his Ninth Book, the relation of society to individual is reversed. The ideal state now becomes an element in the liberal education of the individual free man, permitting him a greater liberty of mental perspective than he had before.

The Republic built up by Socrates and entered into by his hearers is derived from their ability to see society on two levels, a lower natural level and an upper ideal level. What gives them the ability to perceive this upper level is education. The vision of the *Republic* is inextricably bound up with a theory of education. The bodily senses perceive the "actual" or objective state of things; the soul, through education, perceives the intelligible world. And though not all utopia-writers are Platonists, nearly all of them make their utopias depend on education for their permanent establishment. It seems clear that the literary convention of an ideal state is really a by-product of a systematic view of education. That is, education, considered as a unified view of reality, grasps society by its intelligible rather than its actual form, and the utopia is a projection of the ability to see society, not as an aggregate of buildings and bodies, but as a structure of arts and sciences. The thought suggests itself that the paralysis in utopian imagination we have mentioned in our society may be connected with a confusion about both the objectives and the inner structure of our educational system.

It is a theory of education, in any case, that connects a utopian myth with a myth of contract. This is abundantly clear in Plato and later in Rousseau, whose *Emile* is the utopian and educational counterpart of his *Contrat social.* In the sixteenth century, Machiavelli's *Prince,* Castiglione's *Courtier,* and More's *Utopia* form a well-unified Renaissance trilogy, the first two providing a contract myth and an educational structure respectively, based on the two central facts of Renaissance society, the prince and the courtier. Other Renaissance works, such as Spenser's *Faerie Queene,* set forth a social ideal and so belong peripherally to the utopian tradition, but are based on an educational myth rather than a utopian one. For Spenser, as he says in his letter to Raleigh, the Classical model was not Plato's *Republic* but Xenophon's *Cyropaedia,* the ideal education of the ideal prince.

Both the contract myth and the utopia myth, we said, derive from an analysis of the mythmaker's own society, or at least if they do not they have little social point. The overtones of the contract myth, unless the writer is much more complacent than anyone I have read, are tragic. All contract theories, whatever their origin or direction, have to account for the necessity of a social condition far below what one could imagine as a desirable, or even possible, ideal. The contract myth thus incorporates an element of what in the corresponding religious myth appears as the fall of man. Tragedy is a form which proceeds toward an epiphany of law, or at least of something inevitable and ineluctable; and a contract myth is by definition a legal one. The *telos* myth is comic in direction: it moves toward the actualizing of something better.

Any serious utopia has to assume some kind of contract theory as the complement of itself, if only to explain what is wrong with the state of things the utopia is going to improve. But the vision of something better has to appeal to some contract behind the contract, something which existing society has lost, forfeited, rejected, or violated, and which the utopia itself is to restore. The ideal or desirable quality in the utopia has to be *recognized,* that is, seen as manifesting something that the reader can understand as a latent or potential element in his own society and his own thinking. Thus Plato's *Republic* takes off from a rather gloomy and cynical contract theory, adapted apparently from the sophists by Glaucon and Adeimantus for the pleasure of hearing Socrates refute it. But the vision of justice which Socrates substitutes for it restores a state of things earlier than anything this contract theory refers to. This antecedent state is associated with the Golden Age in the *Laws* and with the story of Atlantis in the two sequels to the *Republic*, the *Timaeus* and the *Critias*. In the Christian myth, of course, the pre-contract ideal state is that of paradise. We have now to try to isolate the paradisal or Golden Age element in the utopian myth, the seed which it brings to fruition.

III

The utopian writer looks at the ritual habits of his own society and tries to see what society would be like if these ritual habits were made more consistent and more inclusive. But it is possible to think of a good many ritual habits as not so much inconsistent as unnecessary or superstitious. Some social habits express the needs of society; others express its anxieties. And although we tend to attach more emotional importance to our anxieties than to our needs or genuine beliefs, many anxieties are largely or entirely unreal. Plato's conception of the role of women in his community, whatever one thinks of it, was an extraordinary imaginative break from the anxieties of Athens with its almost Oriental seclusion of married women. Every utopian writer has to struggle with the anxieties suggested to him by his own society, trying to distinguish the moral from the conventional, what would be really disastrous from what merely inspires a vague feeling of panic, uneasiness, or ridicule.

So far we have been considering the typical utopia, the rational city or world-state, and the utopian satire which is a product of a specifically modern fear, the Frankenstein myth of the enslavement of man by his own technology and by his perverse desire to build himself an ingenious trap merely for the pleasure of getting caught in it. But another kind of utopian satire is obviously possible, one in which social rituals are seen from the outside, not to make them more consistent but simply to demonstrate their inconsistency, their hypocrisy, or their unreality. Satire of this kind holds up a mirror to society which distorts it, but distorts it consistently. An early example is Bishop Hall's *Mundus Alter et Idem* (1605), much ridiculed by Milton, but perhaps more of an influence on him than he was willing to admit. A more famous one is *Gulliver's Travels,* especially the first part, the voyage to Lilliput. The Lilliputian society is essentially the society of Swift's England, with its rituals looked at satirically. In the voyage to Brobdingnag the ridicule of the gigantic society is softened down, in the portrayal of the king even minimized, the satirical emphasis being thrown on Gulliver's account of his own society. The shift of emphasis indicates the close connection between this kind of satire and utopian fiction, the connection being much closer in the last part, where the rational society of the Houyhnhnms is contrasted with the Yahoos.

In Butler's *Erewhon,* again, we have an early example of the contemporary or technological utopian satire: the Erewhonians are afraid of machines, and their philosophers have worked out elaborate arguments to prove that machines will eventually take over if not suppressed in time. We could in fact trace this theme back to *Gulliver's Travels* itself, where the flying island of Laputa demonstrates some of the perils in combining human mechanical ingenuity with human folly and greed. But most of *Erewhon* adheres to the earlier tradition of the mirror-satire. The Erewhonians, for example, treat disease as a crime and crime as a disease, but they do so with exactly the same rationalizations that the Victorians use in enforcing the opposite procedure.

Following out this line of thought, perhaps what ails ordinary society is not the inconsistency but the multiplicity of its ritual habits. If so, then the real social ideal would be a greatly simplified society, and the quickest way to utopia would be through providing the absolute minimum of social structure and organization. This conception of the ideal society as simplified, even primitive, is of far more literary importance than the utopia itself, which in literature is a relatively minor genre never quite detached from political theory. For the simplified society is the basis of the *pastoral* convention, one of the central conventions of literature at every stage of its development.

In Christianity the city is the form of the myth of *telos,* the New Jerusalem that is the end of the human pilgrimage. But there is no city in the Christian, or Judaeo-Christian, myth of origin: that has only a garden, and the two progenitors of what was clearly intended to be a simple and patriarchal society. In the story which follows, the story of Cain and Abel, Abel is a shepherd and Cain a farmer whose descendants build cities and develop the arts. The murder of

Abel appears to symbolize the blotting out of an idealized pastoral society by a more complex civilization. In Classical mythology the original society appears as the Golden Age, to which we have referred more than once, again a peaceful and primitive society without the complications of later ones. In both our main literary traditions, therefore, the tendency to see the ideal society in terms of a lost simple paradise has a ready origin.

In the Renaissance, when society was so strongly urban and centripetal, focused on the capital city and on the court in the center of it, the pastoral established an alternative ideal which was not strictly utopian, and which we might distinguish by the term Arcadian. The characteristics of this ideal were simplicity and equality: it was a society of shepherds without distinction of class, engaged in a life that permitted the maximum of peace and of leisure. The arts appeared in this society spontaneously, as these shepherds were assumed to have natural musical and poetic gifts. In most utopias the relation of the sexes is hedged around with the strictest regulations, even taboos; in the pastoral, though the Courtly Love theme of frustrated devotion is prominent, it is assumed that making love is a major occupation, requiring much more time and attention than the sheep, and thus more important than the economic productivity of society.

The Arcadia has two ideal characteristics that the utopia hardly if ever has. In the first place, it puts an emphasis on the integration of man with his physical environment. The utopia is a city, and it expresses rather the human ascendancy over nature, the domination of the environment by abstract and conceptual mental patterns. In the pastoral, man is at peace with nature, which implies that he is also at peace with his own nature, the reasonable and the natural being associated. A pastoral society might become stupid or ignorant, but it could hardly go mad. In the second place, the pastoral, by simplifying human desires, throws more stress on the satisfaction of such desires as remain, especially, of course, sexual desire. Thus it can accommodate, as the typical utopia cannot, something of that outlawed and furtive social ideal known as the Land of Cockayne, the fairyland where all desires can be instantly gratified.

This last is an ideal halfway between the paradisal and the pastoral and is seldom taken seriously. The reason is that it does not derive from an analysis of the writer's present society, but is primarily a dream or wish-fulfillment fantasy. In the fourteenth-century poem called *The Land of Cockayne,* roast geese walk around advertising their edibility: the line of descent to the shmoos of "Li'l Abner" is clear enough. The same theme exists in a more reflective and sentimental form, where it tends to be an illusory or vanishing vision, often a childhood memory. This theme is common as a social cliché and in the popular literature which expresses social clichés: the cottage away from it all, happy days on the farm, the great open spaces of the west, and the like. A typical and well-known literary example is James Hilton's *Lost Horizon,* a neo-Kantian kingdom of both ends, so to speak, with its mixture of Oriental wisdom and American plumbing. But though the Land of Cockayne belongs to social mythology more than to the imaginative mythology of literature, it is a genuine ideal, and we shall meet other forms of it.

Spenser's *Faerie Queene,* already alluded to, is an example of the sort of courtier-literature common in the Renaissance, which had for its theme the idealizing of the court or the reigning monarch. This literature was not directly utopian, but its imaginative premises were allied to the utopia. That is, it assumed that for mankind the state of nature is the state of society and of civilization and that, whether man is in his nature good or bad, life can be improved by improving his institutions. The pastoral, though of no importance politically, nevertheless kept open the suggestion that the state of nature and the state of society were different, perhaps opposing states. The pastoral was allied to the spirit of satire which, as in Erasmus' *Praise of Folly* and Cornelius Agrippa's *Vanity of the Arts and Sciences,* called the whole value of civilization into question.

In the eighteenth century these two attitudes both assumed political importance, and met in a head-on collision. The eighteenth-century descendant of the pastoral myth was the conception of the "natural society" in Bolingbroke, and later in Rousseau. Here the natural state of man is thought of as distinct from and, so to speak, underlying the state of society. The state of nature is reasonable, the state of society full of anomalies and pointless inequalities. The conservative or traditional view opposed to this is, in Great Britain, most articulate in Burke, who, following Montesquieu, and in opposition to the principles of the French Revolution, asserted that the state of nature and the state of society were the same thing. The difference between the two views is primarily one of contract theory. For Burke the existing social order in any nation is that nation's real contract: for Rousseau it is essentially a corruption of its contract. The *telos* myths differ accordingly. For Burke improvement is possible only if we preserve the existing structure. This is not a utopian view, but it is not necessarily anti-utopian: it still keeps the utopian premise of the improvability of institutions. For Rousseau the *telos* myth becomes revolutionary: only an overthrow of the existing social order can manifest the natural and reasonable social order that it has disguised.

The fourth book of *Gulliver's Travels* is a pastoral satire representing the conservative opposition to the pastoral conception of a natural society. The Yahoo is the natural man, man as he would be if he were purely an animal, filthy, treacherous, and disgusting. Gulliver has more intelligence than the Yahoos, but what he learns from his sojourn with the Houyhnhnms is that his nature is essentially Yahoo nature. His intelligence, he discovers, is nothing he can take pride in, for human beings back home make "no other use of reason than to improve and multiply those vices whereof their brethren in this country had only the share that nature allotted them." The natural society, if it could be attained at all, could be attained only by some kind of animal like the Houyhnhnm, who possessed a genuine reason not needing the disciplines of state and church. The Houyhnhnms can live in a genuinely pastoral world; human beings have to put up with the curse of civilization.

The terms of this argument naturally changed after the Industrial Revolution, which introduced the conception of revolutionary process into society. This led to the present division of social attitudes mentioned above, between the Marxist utopia as distant end and the common American belief in the utopianizing tendency of the productive process, often taking the form of a belief that utopian standards of living can be reached in America alone. This belief, though rudely shaken by every disruptive historical event at least since the stock market crash of 1929, still inspires an obstinate and resilient confidence. The popular American view and the Communist one, superficially different as they are, have in common the assumption that to increase man's control over his environment is also to increase his control over his destiny. The refusal to accept this assumption is the principle of modern utopian satire.

Whatever utopian thought and imagination has survived this state of affairs in democratic literature has been much more affected by pastoral or Arcadian themes than by the utopian conception of the rational city. Both Plato and More lay stress on limiting the city-state to what would now be called an "optimum" size. And almost anyone today, considering the problems of present-day society, would soon find himself saying "too many people." He could hardly visualize a utopia without assuming some disaster that would reduce the population—at least, those who did not survive might reasonably consider it a disaster. Thus Don Marquis, in *The Almost Perfect State,* speaks of a United States with a total population of five million. The assumption that a more desirable society must be a greatly simplified one marks the influence of the pastoral tradition.

We do find in fact a type of utopian satire based on the theme of cyclical return: contemporary civilization goes to pieces with an appalling crash, and life starts again under primitive conditions like those of some earlier period of history. The best story of this type I know is Richard Jeffries' *After London,* but the theme enters the Robert Graves book referred to earlier and is a common one in science fiction (for example, Walter Miller's *A Canticle for Leibowitz* and some of John Wyndham's stories, especially *Re-Birth*). And even in the nineteenth-century industrial utopias, with their clicking machinery and happy factory crowds and fast-talking interpreters, an occasional one, such as W. H. Hudson's *A Crystal Age,* takes a different tone, and reminds us that ideals of peace, dignity, and quiet are too important to be squeezed into a few intervals of bustling routine.

Of the famous utopias, the one which shows pastoral influence most consistently is William Morris' *News from Nowhere.* This work was, significantly, written as a reaction to Bellamy's *Looking Backward,* and, even more significantly, it scandalized the Communist associates of Morris' magazine, *The Commonweal,* in which it appeared. It was an attempt to visualize the ultimate utopian goal of Communism after the classless society had been reached, and the reader is not asked whether he thinks the social conception practicable, but simply whether or not he likes the picture. The picture is considerably more anarchist than Communist: the local community is the sole source of a completely decentralized authority, and the centralizing economic tendencies have disappeared along with the political ones. There is, in other words, a minimum of industrial and factory production. Morris started out, not with the Marxist question "Who are the workers?" but with the more deeply revolutionary question "What is work?" It is perhaps because Socrates never asked this question, but simply took the agenda of the work done in his own society as the basis of his definition of justice, that Plato's *Republic* is the authoritarian structure it is. Morris was influenced by Carlyle, who, though he tended to imply that all work was good, and unpleasant work particularly beneficial to the moral fiber, still did succeed, in *Sartor Resartus,* in distinguishing work from drudgery as well as from idleness. Ruskin, though also with a good deal of dithering, followed this up, and established the principle that Morris never departed from: work is creative act, the expression of what is creative in the worker. Any work that falls short of this is drudgery, and drudgery is exploitation, producing only the mechanical, the ugly, and the useless. We notice that in Morris we need an esthetic, and hence imaginative, criterion to make any significant social judgment. According to Morris the pleasure in craftsmanship was what kept the medieval workers from revolution: this leads to the unexpected inference that, in an exploiting society, genuine work is the opiate of the people. In the society of the future, however, work has become a direct expression of the controlled energy of conscious life.

In Morris' state "manufacture" has become hand work, and the basis of production is in what are still called the minor or lesser arts, those that are directly related to living conditions. In terms of the societies we know, Morris' ideal is closer to the Scandinavian way of life than to the Russian or the American. To make craftsmanship the basis of industry implies an immense simplification of human wants—this is the pastoral element in Morris' vision. The population has stabilized because people have stopped exploiting their sexual instincts as well as each other's work. England has become a green and pleasant land—something even seems to have happened to the climate—with a great deal of fresh air and exercise. The pastoral theme of the unity of man and physical nature is very prominent. Around the corner, perhaps, looms the specter of endless picnics and jolly community gatherings and similar forms of extroverted cheer; but the sense of this is hardly oppressive even to a cynical reader. There is a certain anti-intellectual quality, perhaps, in the rather childlike inhabitants, their carefree ignorance of history and their neglect of the whole contemplative side of education. It is briefly suggested at the end that perhaps this society will need to mature sufficiently to take account of the more contemplative virtues if it is to escape the danger of losing its inheritance, as Adam did, through an uncritical perverseness of curiosity. In the meantime we are indebted to the most unreligious of the great English writers for one of the most convincing pictures of the state of innocence.

The social ideal is an essential and primary human ideal, but it is not the only one, nor does it necessarily include the others. Human fulfillment has a singular and a dual form as well as a plural one. Marvell's poem "The Garden" speaks of individual and solitary fulfillment in which one is detached from society and reaches a silent incorporation into nature which the poet symbolizes by the word "green." It is further suggested that this solitary apotheosis was the genuine paradisal state, before a blundering God created Eve and turned Eden into a suburban development of the City of God. Yet the creation of Eve, in itself, introduced a sexual fulfillment which, as long as man remained unfallen, had no objective beyond itself. Theoretically, the higher religions recognize and provide for these dreams of lost solitary and sexual paradises; in practice, being socially organized, they tend to be socially obsessed. Christianity is opposed to Communism and other forms of state-worship, but church and family are equally social units. Traditionally, Christianity frowns on the sexual relationship except as a means of producing the family, and on the solitary illumination except as a variety of socially accepted belief. If even religion tends to divide human impulses into the social and the anti-social, we can hardly expect more tolerance from ordinary society, which is a neurotically jealous mistress, suspicious and resentful of any sign of preferring a less gregarious experience.

Yet less socialized ideals continue to hover around the locked gates of their garden, trying to elude the angels of anxiety and censorship. Through the pastoral they achieve some imaginative expression, and it is largely its connection with the pastoral that makes Thoreau's *Walden* so central and so subversive a book in American culture. The theme of the sage who makes a voluntary break with society in order to discover his genuine self in a context of solitude and nature is common in the Orient and has been a major influence on the arts there, but it is rare in the West. Even Wordsworth, though he has much of the theory, speaks, at the opening of the *Prelude* and elsewhere, more as someone on sabbatical leave from society than as someone aloof from it. Thoreau achieves a genuine social detachment, and has the sensitive, loving kinship with nature that characterizes the pastoral at its best. What makes him relevant to a paper on utopias is the social criticism implied in his book. He sets out to show how little a man actually needs for the best life, best in the sense of providing for the greatest possible amount of physical and mental well-being. And while one may quarrel over the details of his experiment in economy, there is no doubt that he makes his main point.

Man obviously needs far less for the best life than he thinks he needs; and civilization as we know it is grounded on the technique of complicating wants. In fact this technique is widely believed, in America, to be the American way of life par excellence. Thoreau says: "the only true America is that country where you are at liberty to pursue such a mode of life as may enable you to do without these, and where the state does not endeavour to compel you to sustain the slavery, and war, and other superfluous expenses which directly or indirectly result from the use of such things." The pastoral revolutionary tradition is still at work in this remark, still pointing to the natural and reasonable society buried beneath the false one. For Thoreau the place of human identity is not the city or even the community, but the home. In constructing his cabin he remarks: "It would be worth the while to build still more deliberately than I did, considering, for instance, what foundation a door, a window, a cellar, a garret, have in the nature of man." Whatever the standards and values are that make a social ideal better than the reality, they cannot appear unless the *essence* of society has been separated from non-essentials. It is its feeling for what is socially essential that makes the pastoral convention central to literature, and no book has expressed this feeling more uncompromisingly than *Walden*.

Walden devotes itself to the theme of individual fulfillment: its social criticism is implicit only and the complications in human existence caused by the sexual instinct are not dealt with at all. The attempt to see the sexual relationship as something in itself, and not merely as a kind of social relationship, is something that gives a strongly pastoral quality to the work of D. H. Lawrence. For him the sexual relation is natural in the sense that it has its closest and most immediate affinities with the physical environment, the world of animals and plants and walks in the country and sunshine and rain. The idyllic sense of this world as helping to protect and insulate true love from the noisy city-world of disembodied consciousness runs through all Lawrence's work from the early *White Peacock* to the late *Lady Chatterley's Lover*. People complain, Lawrence says, that he wants them to be "savages," but the gentian flowering on its coarse stem is not savage. Lawrence has been a major influence on the social attitude which has grown up in the United States since the Second World War, and which may be described as a development of Freudianism. Like the Marxism of which it is, to some extent, a democratic counterpart, it is a revolutionary attitude, but unlike Marxism it imposes no specific social obligations on the person who holds it. The enemy is still the bourgeois, not the bourgeois as capitalist, but the bourgeois as "square," as the representative of repressive morality. Freud himself had little hope that society would ever cease to be a repressive anxiety-structure, but some of the most uninhibited utopian thinking today comes from such Freudians as Norman O. Brown (*Life Against Death*) and Herbert Marcuse (*Eros and Civilization*), who urge us at least to consider the possibility of a non-repressive society.

In literature, some manifestations of this quasi-Freudian movement, like the beatniks, are rigidly conventionalized social ones, but what is relevant to us at present is rather the literature of protest, the theme of vagabondage and the picaresque in Kerouac and Henry Miller, the cult of violence in Mailer, the exploration of drugs and perversions, the struggle for a direct asocial experience which is apparently what the interest in Zen Buddhism symbolizes. The motto of all this is that of the starling in Sterne: "I can't get out": it expresses the claustrophobia of individual and sexual impulses imprisoned by the alien social consciousness that has created civilization. This sounds as though the contemporary literature of protest was intensely anti-utopian, and so in many respects it is. It is, however, for the most part a militant or "Luddite" pastoralism, trying to break the hold of a way of life which has replaced the perspective of the human body with the perspective of its mechanical extensions, the extensions of transportation and social planning and advertising which are now turning on the body and strangling it as the serpents did Laocoon.

The great classical utopias derived their form from city-states and, though imaginary, were thought of as being, like the city-states, exactly locatable in space. Modern utopias derive their form from a uniform pattern of civilization spread over the whole globe, and so are thought of as world-states, taking up all the available space. It is clear that if there is to be any revival of utopian imagination in the near future, it cannot return to the old-style spatial utopias. New utopias would have to derive their form from the shifting and dissolving movement of society that is gradually replacing the fixed locations of life. They would not be rational cities evolved by a philosopher's dialectic: they would be rooted in the body as well as in the mind, in the unconscious as well as the conscious, in forests and deserts as well as in highways and buildings, in bed as well as in the symposium. Do you not agree, asks Socrates in the *Republic,* that the worst of men is the man who expresses in waking reality the character of man in his dreams? But modern utopias will have to pay some attention to the lawless and violent lusts of the dreamer, for their foundations will still be in dreamland. A fixed location in space is "there," and "there" is the only answer to the spatial question "where?" Utopia, in fact and in etymology, is not a place; and when the society it seeks to transcend is everywhere, it can only fit into what is left, the invisible non-spatial point in the center of space. The question "Where is utopia?" is the same as the question "Where is nowhere?" and the only answer to that question is "here."

CRANE BRINTON

Utopia and Democracy

THIS ESSAY is concerned with the problem of the congruity between utopian thinking, and in particular traditional Western utopian thinking, and the whole complex of ideas, sentiments, aspirations, and institutions which, with minimal worry over its inexactness, we may call the democratic way of life. Our main concern here is with the present, while other essays in this volume deal with aspects of the long and rich tradition of that very real land, utopia. We must, however, begin with a brief consideration of the content and continuity of utopian thought.

The utopian starts with the proposition, by no means limited to the utopian thinker, that things (no more exact word is useful here) are bad; next, things must become much better, perhaps perfect, here on earth and soon, or fairly soon; things will not improve to this degree by themselves, by a "natural" growth or development of things-as-they-are; a plan must be developed and put into execution, in a sense, "artificially"; but in this context "artificially" implies—even necessitates—the existence of an enlightened few, or even one enlightened individual, who will think and act in a way the many by themselves will not, cannot, think and act. In short, traditional utopian thought tends to be more or less openly the work of an *élite*—a horrid word which, in view of the death of the word *aristocracy* (and no doubt the thing), has to be used.

Were we here concerned with semantic or taxonomic problems we should have to amplify and modify the above greatly. Utopias deal basically with ideas about human potentialities, and therefore the class utopia has to be a wide and sprawling one. We must, however, at least note that a distinction should be made between utopian thinking which is clearly élitist in its ends, and usually, therefore, in its means of attaining those ends, and utopian thinking which is élitist only regarding its means of attaining an end that may be called anarchic, egalitarian, or democratic. Even though you can argue that Plato in the *Republic* really meant there to be some social mobility (a phrase he would surely have disliked) between his belly-men, his heart-men, and his head-men, it is difficult to maintain that the going Platonic Republic would be a Jeffersonian or any other kind of democracy.

It is broadly true that most utopias before the early nineteenth century, though they are not quite so definitely based on actual inborn, genetically determined caste differences as was Plato's, do not aim at ends that can be called libertarian, egalitarian, or anarchic. But many modern utopias, including the most widely known of all, that of Marx-Engels, do indeed have as a goal the "withering away of the state," the abolition of law, police, armies, the freeing of men from their present, in which they "are everywhere in chains." The means—dictatorship of the proletariat, hidden or open rule of the technocrat, the cultural engineer, the planner, Robert Owen, H. G. Wells, Etienne Cabet, B. F. Skinner—is often, indeed usually, quite definitely the work of an élite.

We cannot here try to explain why the modern, in contrast to the classic, utopia tends toward a democratic end. Certainly the masses in Western society have since the invention of printing been able to assert themselves, been able to produce effective leaders, in a way never before possible. One suspects that the Athenian populace described by Aristophanes was not wholly content with the role of belly-men. But increasingly from the Reformation on the masses have been able to assert themselves; yet, as we shall insist, the intellectual classes who devise literary utopias as distinct from such religiously inspired folk utopias as those of Mother Ann Lee and Joseph Smith have by no means been persuaded that what the awakened masses seem to want is what they ought to want.

For this relation between the utopia-inclined among Western intellectuals and the many non-intellectuals who still make up the majority of any society there can be no clear-cut and simple formula. Most of these intellectuals would describe themselves as good democrats, even as good egalitarians. They certainly abhor such concepts as that of a *Fuehrerprinzip,* and they have never found a good substitute for the word "aristocracy."[1] Certainly a very familiar word can, perhaps must, be used, especially for

American and West European societies, to describe the attitudes of the few toward the many: ambivalence. In fact, that famous slogan from *Animal Farm,* "All animals are equal, but some animals are more equal than others," though with Orwell himself it was the despairing cry of the outraged moralist, can be taken as a simple realistic observation. All Americans of both sexes are nowadays equals in the line waiting to buy tickets or board a bus; they are not equals, do not for the most part even pretend to themselves that they are equals, in any of the innumerable competitions of American life from beauty contests to sports to information quizzes.

This ambivalence is also to be found in the high matters of political and social attitudes and ideals. It is true that the Nazi *Fuehrerprinzip* is offensive to most Westerners; yet of late years even we Americans have taken to using, if not yet quite so obsessively as the totalitarians, those gigantic, blown-up portraits of political leaders. Yet, apart from pockets of resistance to Negro voting, we are all equal before the ballot box. Even in Britain, the various devices which a John Stuart Mill, worried over "the tyranny of the majority," advocated as a nice decent élitist counterweight seem no more than quaint Victorian notions. Especially in politics, there is in the West, though in varying strength in different countries, a deep underlying distrust of the expert. Of course not even in the United States, where that distrust is probably strongest, are the practices derived from an extreme strain of democratic thought—rotation in office, direct election of all officials from dogcatchers to sheriffs and judges to president, initiative, referendum, recall, and the rest—not even in the United States is all this apparatus of turn-of-the-century politics anything more than past history for most of us. Even in Vermont those free farmers freely use the services of the welfare state, county agent, district nurse, state subventions to schools, and, first and foremost, the expert services of the State Highway Department.

Here, too, honesty compels the term: ambivalence. We trust, we even admire, many kinds of experts in many fields, surgeons, engineers, inventors, administrators. "Professor," as S. M. Lipset has shown, holds for most Americans connotations of high status. Even in fields like government, the city manager, the formal planning commissioner, and the expert economist are used and trusted. Yet "bureaucracy" still has overtones in the balance pejorative and is surely much more used in the United States than the noncommittal "civil servant." And there remains an underlying distrust of the expert in just the fields the utopian is most interested in—public morals, public taste, broad problems of public policy in domestic and in international affairs. To this, witness the very complex problem of fluoridation of public water supplies. And since, as we have maintained, there is a strain, usually a very strong strain, of benevolent despotism—cultural engineering, to put the matter most offensively—in modern, perhaps all, utopian thinking, there is in this fact at least a beginning of an explanation for the lack of enthusiasm for utopian thinking in the contemporary free world.

But no more than a beginning. We shall have to go deeper or at least take into account other variables. Since classic utopias—books as well as experimental societies of largely secular and rationalist inspiration—are almost always the work of intellectuals, we may legitimately focus here on the attitudes and ideas of intellectuals. We need not attempt the impossible task of defining with an exactness acceptable to all what is meant by "intellectuals" and "intellectual classes." The terms are now excessively threadbare and loaded down with emotional overtones, but they do seem to apply to something real. We shall here consider as intellectuals, members of the intellectual class or classes, those who are chiefly concerned with the creation or enjoyment of literature, the arts, scholarship, science, teaching, preaching.[2]

First of all, however, we must insist that in no Western society is it realistic to distinguish between a persecuted class of intellectuals and a persecuting class of non-intellectuals, or between an intellectual élite devoted to great art, scholarship, and pure science and a populace wholly uninfluenced by what this élite thinks and does, a populace wholly devoted to its own quite different culture. Though this topic can be touched only tangentially in this essay, a few more words are necessary because the matter is germane to our subject. Even granting that there is a wide gap, perhaps an unusually wide one, in the twentieth century between the tastes of the few and the tastes of the many, that the readers of the *Partisan Review*, the *New York Review of Books*, or *Encounter* and the readers of the pulps and the comics are two almost wholly different groups, it is still true that there is a complex and little understood relation between the tastes, the attitudes, of the few and those of the many. Arnold Toynbee's pleasant concept of *mimesis*, that is, admiring popular imitation of and love for the "creative minority," is probably too rosy a description of relations between the many and the few even in the Age of Pericles; but the relation of mutual scorn and contempt between the two groups described by so much current American—and even French—writing about popular "anti-intellectualism" in our time seems equally unrealistic. Ideas and attitudes do seep down from the few to the many—and back up: without Freud, there would be no noble and always successful psychoanalysts of cinema and T.V., without jazz, a very different "highbrow" music.

The point involved is important, for it would seem that utopias in the classic or, if you prefer, conventional sense are a product of the creative minority. If that minority does not produce them they will not seep down at all into popular consciousness. We must also repeat that, especially in the last two or three centuries, most utopias have been if not rationalist, at least secularist, clearly the work of refined thinkers. This is obviously true of the mechanical "gadget" utopias from Mercier's *L'An Deux Mille Quatre Cent Quarante* to Bellamy's *Looking Backward* as well as of the political and ethical equivalent of such utopias from Owen and Fourier to H. G. Wells or, for that matter, Skinner; but it is also true of utopias like *News from Nowhere* or even *Erewhon,* hostile to the simple rationalist tradition of the eighteenth-century Enlightenment, often of romantic "primitivist" inspiration in which the enemy is the machine. These latter are utopias that might be labeled as basically esthetic in inspiration. All of these, be it repeated, are the work of men of refined minds and tastes, intellectuals, members of the creative minority.

It is certainly true that what may be called utopian movements have in the past originated with uneducated or little educated men of the lower classes. We usually attach to such emotion-charged efforts to remake men in society the label "religious." Modern Christianity has produced a very great number of these movements, usually led by self-educated prophets from the lower classes and not unfairly labeled, as with Jehovah's Witnesses, for example, *proletarian movements.* Mormonism, which certainly has utopian elements, would make a good case-history of such a movement. Obviously, however, the *Book of Mormon* is not a utopia in what we have here called the classic or conventional sense. The society which Joseph Smith's charisma, Brigham Young's gifts as administrator and businessman, and much else built up in Deseret has perhaps been the most successful and long lived of American experimental communities. By contrast, the intellectually more respectable communities, those of Fouriest and Owenite inspiration, for example, soon foundered. The purely religious and not too unorthodox ones lasted longer. Even Shakers and Rappites survived as long as their honest celibacy permitted. It would appear that whatever influence the literary utopias have, they do not work out as social experiments.

The kind of utopia with which this essay is concerned is almost always the work of a member of the intellectual class and usually one who shares and reflects many of the ideas and ideals common to that class, however much he may—or must—reject the existing practices of his society as a whole. We are here at a delicate point in our argument. Briefly, it looks as if the utopian thinker must inevitably reflect the attitudes of his peers, of his class. To get at the problem of why the classic utopia has almost vanished today, we must attempt the difficult task of analyzing in brief space and in very broad lines the state of mind, the *Weltanschauung* of the intellectual classes in our modern Western world.

These classes emerged from the eighteenth century deeply divided—though not quite so deeply as some intellectual historians indicate—over the heritage of what R. R. Palmer has called the "Age of the Democratic Revolutions." The generation of 1800 is a fine example of the generation in revolt. The romantic—and he was a real person, no mere textbook invention—loathed the works of his enlightened rationalist grandfather. Wordsworth could write, of course with no trace of irony, of Voltaire's *Candide* as "that dull product of a scoffer's pen."

Yet intellectual historians today tend to emphasize what the nineteenth century had in common with its predecessor. For in spite of the quarrels of Christian and freethinker, aristocrat and democrat, romantic and classic, idealist and realist, nineteenth-century intellectuals for the most part did accept the central belief in Progress (the initial capital is essential), in a world here below where "things" by their very nature were "evolving" into better things. More important, the typical position of the Western intellectual classes can be said still to involve the whole complex of ideas and attitudes ripened by the eighteenth-century Enlightenment, even though this complex was rejected completely or in part by many distinguished nineteenth-century thinkers. These people "believed in" democracy, however much they might differ in defining it, in methods of achieving it, and above all, in estimating the time-scale for its attainment. And with democracy went many other great words and phrases, imprecise for the naive "social scientist" but accurate summaries of human realities. Such of course was "Progress," but there were many others, "the pursuit"—with "attainment" understood—"of happiness," "liberty, equality, fraternity," "self-determination of peoples," Mazzinian liberal nationalism essential to a true internationalist world order, right on down to those great Wilsonian phrases which end the nineteenth century, "open covenants openly arrived at," "peace without victory," and the folk phrase "the War to end war" which, even for American intellectuals, was hardly irony until 1919.

Central to this democratic faith is the view that a suitable physical and social environment can be devised and put into practice so that what in the West has long been considered evil can be vastly diminished, perhaps eliminated. The formula runs: democracy substitutes for the Judaeo-Christian concept of original sin a concept of the natural goodness and/or reasonableness of man, supplemented by the corollary that evil is a result of bad environment. And bad social environment is generally equated with the broader institutional environment—church, state, class organization, and formal, institutional education—rather than with the more intimate environment of family, early training, neighborhood, and vocation. Furthermore, the necessary changes in the bad environment, though they must be planned and preached by an enlightened minority, will —must, in a democracy—be ratified by the majority of the people and even will, after the necessary universal education, be initiated by the people. Finally, though the new democratic society will be orderly, this order will not depend on compulsion, save perhaps for a very few criminally disposed. In short, liberty, equality, and fraternity were no mere words, but a creed.

The foregoing sampling of great—and most effective—ideas and phrases is, in fact, part of a *diffuse but very real utopia.* No single book sums it up; no single democratic catechism is possible; there is no clear established canon. Western democrats, or, if you prefer, liberals, are not in any narrow sense "people of the book." They have not even a canon in the sense that Communists in the Marx-Engels-Lenin tradition (Stalin no longer added) have one or that German Nazis had one in *Mein Kampf* and its source books. But they are surely "people of the books." The armature of ideas is there, the contribution of many minds over many years. There are indeed classic declarations of principle, the preamble to the American Declaration of Independence, the French Declaration of the Rights of

Man and the Citizen, many others. There is a solid body of formal political philosophy from Locke to Rousseau to J. S. Mill and lesser commentators. Much of this is effectively translated to the many by mass education and the mass media, terms, incidentally, which apply perfectly well to Western culture in the nineteenth century and to a degree even earlier, terms we must not think of as first applicable to our own times.

We must add that this utopia is the only one in our Western history to gain widespread acceptance by the many. We must, of course, qualify that "only"; this diffuse utopia is the first important one to have no real base in a supernatural established religion.[3] This utopia must be realized in this world and not in the next. Democracy is not heaven, nor even pie in the sky. It is not even a projection into a *distant* future. The happiness it wants is not any kind of *nirvana, theoria, mystic ecstasy, transcendence,* but quite simply must include commonplace material comforts and sensual satisfactions. Given the eighteenth-century Enlightenment (itself the culmination of centuries of cultural history), democracy quite naturally has meant in the twentieth century the "revolution of rising expectations" among the many all over the world.

The almost too familiar facts of technological progress in communication, transportation, public health, in short, human ability to achieve satisfaction of perennial needs, are often, in pure and misleading rhetoric, called miracles. But not even the most ignorant really *feel* these things to be true miracles. What the gradual spread of Enlightenment has done is to push the boundaries of the literal miracle, the "other-world," the supernatural, far outside the range of daily life of most human beings. This is not to say that Enlightenment has killed "religion," nor even the Judaeo-Christian contrast of this world and the next. It is to say that we are all materialists of a sort, that we all expect certain material satisfactions, that many human beings hope and expect these satisfactions to be complete, unsullied—utopian.

Now, although most would agree in principle that the masses deserve better things in life, it is also true that for many intellectuals there is more than a trace of disappointment over the quality of the things the masses have gained, and with which they seem quite satisfied, and of which they just want more. If you wanted, and perhaps expected, universal education to lead to mass participation in the best that has been thought and done in our culture, you will not, for instance, be so content with American television programs or with the pulp magazines or the comics as the many seem to be. At the very least, the pace of improvement in taste, morals, good sense, and good behavior, as intellectuals understand these, has among the masses, even in the most hopeful view, been relatively slow over the last two centuries. Many intellectuals hold the opinion that there has been retrogression.

This fact is surely one of the variables that helps explain what has happened to utopian thinking in our time. The intellectual classes who in the last few centuries largely made and spread abroad the diffuse utopia we have called modern Western democracy simply feel that something has gone wrong; they no longer have the confidence in their fellow men and, to be honest, in themselves that is necessary for utopian thinking. Some of the most sensitive of them have turned to the anti-utopia, or dystopia, which is no more than a detailed, imaginatively factual projection of the following: things are bad, and this is the way they'll get worse.

Once more, qualifications are necessary. There are many intellectuals who still hold in chastened form the hopes of the Enlightenment, who believe that at bottom men are reasonably decent creatures, who work with and for the masses. Such faith—and works—are perhaps commoner among scientists, engineers, and technicians than among literary and artistic persons. But such faith and works are not unknown or insignificant even among those who pursue the humanities. The teachers, the preachers, the workers, the main body of the troops, are by no means in the despairing position of some of the leaders. What is true, however, is that ever since the failure of the French Revolution to live up to the hopes they had put in it, many writers, artists, and musicians of great distinction and influence have found the main obstacle to the good society in the bourgeois, the Philistine, the *homme moyen sensuel*, the Babbitts, the masses. Their complaints are many and varied, but they often come down to a belief that, as John Stuart Mill put it, "ordinary human nature is so poor a thing."

We can here do no more than suggest that what the intellectuals object to in our mass society is usually not its "materialism"; indeed most—not, of course, all—literary and artistic intellectuals are not otherworldly, do not use words like "spiritual," "idealistic" at all freely, are themselves often quite happy with their comforts, even with their gadgets. But they do object to the *quality* of what the masses seem to want, their frozen and tasteless foods, their cliché-ridden lives, their love affair (which the intellectuals regard as slavery) with the automobile, their megalopolitan wens, their mere excessive *numbers.* Consider briefly recent popular sociological books—often best sellers—on what the American way of life is like. Nothing really passes muster with these writers, not the automobiles (*The Insolent Chariots*), not business and advertising (*The Waste Makers, The Hidden Persuaders*), not our democratic "career open to talents" (*The Status Seekers*), not the landscape (*God's Own Junkyard*), not, of course, education (*Why Johnny Can't Read, Growing Up Absurd, The Academic Marketplace*—but the list is endless), not even our last *rite de passage* (*The American Way of Death*). And, of course, much unfavorable criticism of the masses is based on more lofty grounds and finds objectionable the "pooled self-esteem" of nationalism, the increasing vulgar "conspicuous consumption" prosperity makes possible, the sound, fury, and intellectual dishonesty of politics, the great lies of advertising.

Some of this censoriousness is perennial and surely a legitimate and normal part of the prophylactic function of an intellectual class, a "clerisy," as Coleridge called it. Some of it is, if not as praiseworthy as the prophylactic activity, at least natural, the equivalent for an intellectual aristocracy of what in a privileged nobility and gentry of birth may be called pride or, less politely, snobbery. But one has the feeling that among many Western intellectuals of recent decades some of this attitude toward the masses is unhealthy, excessive, despairing—"alienating," in short. And these alienated, who may produce dystopias, but not utopias, are surely not reliable support of what we have called the diffuse utopia of Western democracy. But a clerisy has to be such a support for any kind of society.

H. Stuart Hughes makes this point effectively:

> Culturally privileged elites have always resisted the invasion of the vulgar. . . . The novelty appeared only when . . . the intellectual leaders began to identify themselves with democracy or socialism and sought virtue in the cultural pursuits of the common man. From this latter point of departure, a bewildered disappointment could be the only result.
>
> For our contemporary critics have been trying to apply two incompatible standards at the same time. They have clung to the special cultural definitions of a narrow elite—the insistence on a common core of "humanist" reading or artistic enjoyment, on the importance of foreign languages, ancient and modern, and on the elegant manipulation of one's own—maintaining all the while that these are perfectly capable of mass dissemination. They have tried to combine elitism with democracy—things compatible perhaps in a Periclean or Jeffersonian sense of popular

government led by "the best," but, under contemporary conditions, radical opposites.[4]

Another, and by no means independent variable in this situation is the development of modern psychology. We here beg the question of how far modern psychology is a "science." The historian of ideas has, however, to note that in our culture some aspects of every science inevitably spread into the minds of us all. That it spreads in forms that often shock the trained scientist by their distortion, at the very minimum their oversimplification, need not concern us here. The important consideration is that the great sciences of the eighteenth-century Enlightenment, astronomy, physics, chemistry, did *in their dissemination* back up the concept of man as a rational creature. The great frontier science of the nineteenth century, biology, again *in its dissemination*—though in its emphasis on the "struggle for life" it was often used to back up philosophies of the will, sometimes the blind will—did for the most part, especially in its application to sociology and economics, reinforce the notion of man as a rational creature capable of achieving "higher" things. This man as made by Evolution (again the capital letter is necessary) once freed from superstition would recognize that in pursuing his own rational interests he was pursuing the best interests of his fellows, of society, of Nature, and even of God.[5]

Ours is the century in which clearly the findings of psychologists, among whom Freud is *for their dissemination* as important as Newton for the eighteenth and Darwin for the nineteenth century, have called into question the rational nature of man more deeply and widely than did the romantics or the philosophers of the will. The romantics at least thought reason strong enough in man to be feared and attacked; the Freudians consider reason weak and in need of support. Some light on this whole question of the fundamental attitudes of the intellectual classes toward the universe and man's fate in it—we used to call it innocently the "spirit of the age" or the "climate of opinion"—can be afforded by the prevalence not among the professional and usually academic philosophers but among the general educated public of certain specific philosophies not unfairly described as fashionable. Utilitarianism, transcendentalism, positivism, pragmatism, Bergsonism, all fashionable philosophies in the last century, can suggest what we are driving at. In our mid-century, remnants of most philosophies survive, but the only ones that are at all fashionable (in the quite unpejorative sense of the word) are existentialism and, probably much less widely spread in the general educated public, neo-positivism (or logical philosophy, analytical philosophy, or linguistic philosophy). The first, even in its Christian form, is hardly more than a fretful stoicism not very consonant with the utopian spirit and certainly not confident in the instrument of thought as conventionally understood. The second, though rigorously rationalist, or scientific, in its methods, has deliberately confined itself to the narrow range of problems it holds capable of solution, dismissing as insoluble most of the problems that have occupied philosophers since Thales. Both philosophies are convinced that "reason" in the traditional sense of the word is indeed feeble in the majority of mankind and that there is an irreducible irrationality in us all.

How far Freud and his orthodox followers in psychoanalysis hold this irrational "x" to be irreducible is debatable. But, given the social and economic cost of complete analysis, its use to further the utopian spirit in a mass society seems an utterly impossible idea—utopian, in the pejorative sense. What is important for us here is that both existentialism and neopositivism have worked to diminish among educated people belief in the natural goodness and/or reasonableness of man and the consequent possibility of substantial moral progress. It is true that both Christian and freethinking existentialism insist on human freedom, on the ability of men—and the obligation they are under—to use that freedom to fight for the right, the good. But they cannot expect or hope to win the fight. In *The Plague* the hero—if that is the appropriate word—announces that he knows his victories will never be lasting and continues, "But it's no reason for giving up the struggle," though it means "a never-ending defeat." We are a long way from utopia.[6] Neopositivism does indeed trust reason, but only the reason of the educated logician-scientist applied to suitable problems of logic and science. It is a bit distrustful of the social scientist and has, apparently, given up completely on the common man.

The classic utopias, however, even the "esthetic" utopias hostile to conventional scientific rationalism and its technological achievements, are based on the proposition that something within all or most human beings, something not wholly subconscious or unconscious, something that works in and through the cerebral cortex, can be activated to overcome this irrationality. And surely the diffuse utopia we call democracy is fundamentally, even radically, based on belief in the natural reasonableness and/or goodness of man. The not-utopian implications of all this do not appear most clearly in the dystopias, which are in no paradoxical sense at least evidence that the utopian spirit exists, since they are the work of men who are outraged over our failure to pursue a utopian ideal. The not-utopian implications of much of modern science, at least, appear in the work of Sir Charles Galton Darwin, a grandson of the great biologist. Sir Charles, a distinguished physicist trained, perhaps too successfully, to avoid "wishful thinking," published in 1952 a little book entitled *The Next Million Years*. Briefly, the thesis of the book is this: *Homo sapiens* has been on earth at most only a hundred thousand years or so; in that brief span, and particularly in the very few thousand years for which we know much about his actual behavior, he has shown the full range of his capacity, his "human nature"; he cannot do better, cannot live up to the ideals that he has been able to evolve through his highly developed cerebral cortex; in regard to the production of his own offspring, man is a wild animal, so perfection of the species by planned breeding is impossible; to do better will in fact require a brand-new species, and we know that it takes roughly a million years for unaided natural evolution to produce a new species; therefore, the next million years will be like the last few thousand as recorded in history, full of wars, crime, vices, evils of all sorts, as well, of course, as of behavior we should all regard as good, noble, heroic.

This bleak outlook is certainly not representative of attitudes even among our obviously pessimistic and alienated intellectual classes. Few indeed in the West can accept this scientist's version of Nietzsche's Eternal Recurrence, itself a version, or perversion, of an old oriental theme. Most of the intellectuals in the West cling to some belief in moral progress, certainly in moral meliorism, and not merely to a belief that the best that can be done is to regard evil in general as incurable as disease in general, though always possibly curable in specific instances. We still are interested, if not in classical utopias, at least in what may be called the literature of "Whither mankind?"

That literature, surely not wholly outside the utopian tradition (as is Sir Charles Darwin's book), does seem to be based more and more on that element of the utopian tradition we have called "benevolent despotism," or even more pejoratively, "cultural engineering." The prestige of applied science and the engineer, and the always noted gap between the material progress of the last two centuries and the lack of moral progress—if not moral decadence—

of those centuries have clearly strengthened that tendency. The tendency was present from the start of utopian thinking, witness Plato's "Great Lie," at bottom a rather winningly awkward effort in the style of Madison Avenue. Plato, though the term, could he understand it, would surely have offended him deeply, was himself a cultural engineer. As we noted earlier in discussing the problem of means and ends in utopias, the cultural engineer has been a considerable factor in utopian thinking from the start. Indeed, a minimal touch of such an engineer is probably essential to anyone who sits down to write a conventional utopia.

Yet we must insist that there is something—an emotional, an irrational something, if you like—in the concept of cultural engineering that is profoundly disturbing to the good democrat. For some intellectuals, its practice in the world of entertainment and retail business in general can still be attributed to the wickedness of the few who own the instruments of production; and in politics Machiavellian arts, even when practiced by the good for good ends, can still arouse vigorous indignation. In education, the great and final hope of those who want men to behave better permanently and conspicuously, there is still a strong feeling against trying too obviously to seduce, to engineer, the many into high thinking; and not even the conservatives who want to go back to the good old disciplined days quite believe in administering Plato, Shakespeare, and the calculus like castor oil to the unwilling, and also, perhaps, the incapable. As for the many, though they admire the expert in science and technology, they distrust him in government; at the very least, they insist he be controlled by politicians elected by universal suffrage. This statement is surely true in varying degrees in all the West and is by no means true only of what in America is called the Right Wing. We all know the cliché, true as most clichés of this sort are: "I don't know much about music, but I know what I like." In politics, morals, education, all the basic concerns of this essay, John Jones, M. Dupont, the German Michael, and others in the free world go, and perhaps eventually Ivan Ivanovich will go, much further: "I know *enough* about politics, and I know what I want and what's good for me."[7]

The freer and therefore more varied, more multanimous, and, one suspects, more democratic a society, the harder it is to get for the most skilled cultural engineer (the best trained practicing political psychologist), especially in social, political, and ethical fields, the *initial* widespread trust and support he needs. Surely the kind of changes Kemal Ataturk achieved, admittedly from above, undemocratically, in a relatively simple Turkish society could not possibly have been achieved in a Western democracy, certainly not in so short a time and by the same methods. Full and perfect voluntary conditioning among a population of human beings can be achieved only on the unconditioned, and Westerners from infancy on are hopelessly and multifariously conditioned. It is indeed curious that sophisticated modern psychologists should still preserve with all their acceptance of human irrationality an important trace of belief in the *tabula rasa* of Locke. Of course these psychologists today are not really utopians, and the spirit that moves them is the spirit of invention, enterprise, search for the new, the unknown—the scientific spirit. And although the scientific spirit has indeed a relation with the utopian spirit, they are not the same thing, and they have not the same human drives and sentiments behind them. If they had, we should not here be considering any lack of utopias today.

In our free world, then, the applied psychologist who tries to apply himself to politics comes up against a long-standing human sentiment, put by Juvenal in a still uncracked nutshell: *quis custodiet ipsos custodes?* In the balance, the effect of modern psychology *in its dissemination* among the intellectuals and in the reflection of that dissemination among the many has been unfavorable to the utopian spirit and to the production of classical utopias. True, the increased manipulative skills we have learned from this psychology has made possible a variant of the "gadget" utopia well represented by *Walden Two*. But the gadget utopia is rightly suspect to the true utopian as a machine-made imitation, not really in the central utopian tradition. *This tradition requires the moral regeneration of man, and no mere manipulation of unregenerate men.* Moreover, the major conclusion of almost all modern psychology—and in particular of those Freudian principles which have been so thoroughly disseminated into all art and letters of our time—that of the irreducible irrationality of man, has been one of the factors contributing most strongly to the decline of the utopian spirit in our time. The challenge is surely one that can be met, but not by passing it over, not by insisting that man is what the more hopefully enlightened of the eighteenth century—shall we say Condorcet or Godwin?—thought him to be.

To sum up: the complex we have to call modern Western democracy is itself, as a set of ideal purposes, a kind of utopia, the first one in our cultural history to be (a) essentially secularist, relatively devoid of supernatural or other-worldly elements, quite concrete in its promise of material benefits to all men and (b) widely known and accepted among the masses in the sense that the great world religions of the past have been so known and accepted. In the two centuries since in the West democracy became such a complex (I here forbear pressing the parallels or consonances between this democratic complex and other higher religions) and in spite of great and measurable progress in material and in some moral ways, the promises of democracy *as a utopia* have not yet been realized. Condorcet's Tenth Epoch, which began in his own eighteenth century, was not supposed to include an Auschwitz, a Hiroshima, a "Yezhov period," nor even a Great Depression. All this has been an important factor in turning our intellectuals, that is, the group from which the classic utopias of the past have come, away from the utopian attitude. Aldous Huxley, the grandson of T. H. Huxley, who, though he never wrote a formal utopia, clearly accepted much of what we have here called the diffuse utopia of Western democracy, has written one of the most brilliant and despairing anti-utopias of our time.

Some of the cultural attitudes and achievements of the few in the twentieth century—some of the good traits, such as a willingness to experiment, as well as some of the bad ones, such as spiritual hypochondria—have certainly, as they always do, been taken over partially and in other forms by the many. But it may be doubted whether the attitudes of the many in the West—even in that supposedly intellectual land, France—are so despairing of Progress, of better things, moral as well as material, of orthodox democracy as are our intellectuals, and in particular among the intellectuals, our best-known writers and artists. The many actually seem often to enjoy Atlantic City, superhighways, the Beverly Hillbillies, the gladiatorial exercise we call professional football, the form of leather we know as "pizza," and much, much else that makes the despair of their betters.[8] We may put the matter more simply: the masses in the West still believe in Progress, which is after all, a form of belief in utopia.

This essay has been an attempt at a diagnosis not of the whole situation of our society but of the place of utopian thinking in it and especially among its intellectuals. It has not attempted to examine the larger subject of the attitudes of our intellectuals, our clerisy, toward the rest of humanity, and of the rest toward them. It does not claim to be a prognosis nor to suggest a therapy—if a therapy is needed and possible. Still, a few closing words of something more—or less—than analysis may be forgiven. One of the core elements in the classic utopia, a belief in the possibility of cumulative melioristic reform, not hopelessly piecemeal, temporary, mere balancing a step backward by one forward—but, in brief, Progress—is clearly alive among the many in the West and, though not dead, very much weakened among the intellectual few. It may indeed perish from the earth, and for other reasons than its abandonment by the intellectuals. But it will not survive forever in our Western society *without the support of the intellectuals.* It is possible that this core of the democratic utopian drive can once more gain the support of the intellectuals if they will but be a little more patient with ordinary human nature, a little more willing to accept without despair the evidence that man's own cerebral cortex is never fully his master, if they will respect the average man's reluctance to be wholly shepherded even by the kindliest and most intelligent of shepherds, and if they can, without abandoning all they have gained in depth from the revival of the tragic outlook in our own time, from our devotion to science and the "reality-principle" recapture—even in their abandonment of any religious revelation from beyond this universe—something of the hopes of their grandfathers. For liberty, equality, fraternity are not going to survive without some touch of faith, hope, and charity, even—rather, above all—among the intellectuals.

There may be among the intellectuals today a revival, as among some of them there was always a survival, of the utopian spirit. Analysis of so vague if so real a thing as the climate of opinion among any large group of one's contemporaries is difficult. Perhaps the next cultural generation will work its way out of alienation—out of what we must insist is a basic revulsion from much that has happened in the last two centuries—into a new flowering of all the arts, into a new great culture shared with the many. The great anti-utopias of the past generation—*Brave New World, 1984, We*—already begin to date. Many of the new generation have thrown themselves into movements like the Peace Corps, civil rights, disarmament, international, supranational, government, and less heroic but still melioristic tasks like urban renewal, or those M. de Jouvenel writes about in this volume. They do this often to the accompaniment of words of existentialist despair and anger, but their deeds belie their words. Their anger is not directed at poor ordinary human beings. At any rate, they will be in full command in the year

1984, when some of them may hopefully note that Big Brother, too, is dead.

NOTES

1. Note that in an older, frankly aristocratic society words denoting classes of inferior status, probably originally without overtones of scorn, have all been given such overtones—villain, mob, vulgar, and the like. In our time, the process has been reversed, and words like noble, aristocrat, elite, cultured, refined are in many quarters used apologetically, and preferably avoided. I have encountered the really horrid word, meritocrat.

2. We must insist that the "intellectuals" in a culture like ours do not have a monopoly of intelligence, certainly not of applied intelligence, even if intelligence is taken to apply solely or mainly to the effective operation of the cerebral cortex. Some light on this sensitive subject may be thrown by contemporary Russian usage. The word "intelligentsia" which in Tsarist Russia meant almost exactly, overtones and all, what we here mean by "intellectuals" has naturally had to be redefined in Soviet Russia. Not wanting to abandon entirely a word so full of prestige nor yet to admit the existence of such a "class," the "Soviet government has compromised by employing the concept but giving it an extremely broad definition which eliminates the possibility of the intelligentsia being considered as a class apart. The Soviet definition includes not only the intellectuals, in the proper sense of the word, but also two other groups, the professional personnel and the rest of the bureaucracy, civil as well as military. By being attached to the state service class *par excellence,* the intelligentsia, in the old sense of the word, is meant to lose its social identity." Richard Pipes, "Russia's Exigent Intellectuals," *Encounter* (January 1964), p. 81.

3. I must avoid the fascinating and important problem of the actual relations (compromises?) Christianity, Judaism, and, no doubt, Islam have established and are establishing with this heritage of the eighteenth-century Enlightenment. Incidentally, I think it is quite clear that Plato was a "religious" man; thus, the *Republic* cannot be considered an exception to my "only" above.

4. H. Stuart Hughes, "Mass Culture and Social Criticism," *Dædalus* (Spring 1960), p. 388.

5. For an admirable analysis of the rationalist psychological assumptions underlying nineteenth-century English political thought, with all its disavowal of French rationalism and all its claims to be "realistic" about human nature, see the unduly neglected work of Graham Wallas, *Human Nature in Politics* (1908), Chapter I, and *The Great Society* (1914), Chapter VII. Note that Wallas' work comes just as Freud's work was beginning to effect its "transference" in no mere technical Freudian sense into the Western mind.

6. A long way from the classic utopia, at least. I take this quotation from M.

Susan Sorenson, "An Existential Utopia," *Minnesota Review,* Vol. IV (Spring 1964), p. 357. Miss Sorenson maintains that *The Plague* is fairly described as Camus' "existentialist Utopia for a dechristianized society." But an existentialist utopia seems as contradictory as a stoic utopia.

7. This is, I admit, labored, and is of course a "generalization" of a looseness intolerable to many first-rate minds; it is, however, an attempt to get at a human sentiment, or disposition, much less vague than the words used to describe it. Let me here repeat what I noted before: the attitudes of the masses ("people," "common man," "the average individual") toward the expert, or, if you prefer, the gifted and trained intellectual, are most ambivalent. In many ways we all increasingly have to trust the expert, and, as I have noted earlier, we do in many fields, even in politics, so trust him in practice.

8. Their "betters," at least in America, not only would not dare use that term of themselves; deep down most of them don't think they are. We repeat that egalitarianism is no mere abstraction, no mere scarecrow of a word either, but a strong sentiment.

FRANK E. MANUEL

Toward a Psychological History of Utopias

THE WAKING fantasies of utopia are subject to diverse interpretations on as many different levels as ordinary dreams. In one sense they are private worlds whose geography and laws of movement are explicable in terms of their creator's life experience. There are utopias which become so exclusively personal that they border on schizophrenia—*The Description of a New World, called the Blazing World,* by Margaret Cavendish, Duchess of Newcastle, published in 1666, has much in common with the delusions of Dr. Schreber which Sigmund Freud analyzed in a famous paper.[1] Uncounted utopian worlds of this character are being conjured up every day, though few of them are ever set in print. But if one avoids solipsistic manifestations and restricts oneself primarily to those utopias which have won a measure of public acceptance (and become at least *folie à deux*), the maincurrents of utopian feeling, the dreams shared widely enough to be social utopias with a general history, can be identified. Some dreams express so forcefully a poignant longing of masses of men that their words reverberate for centuries.

Thomas More's book is *ex definitione* a utopia, but what else to include under this rubric may be subject to debate. My attitude is latitudinarian and ecumenical. The conception encompasses "extraordinary voyages," moon-travelers' reports, fanciful descriptions of lost islands, ideal constitutions, advice to princes on the most perfect government, novels built around life in a utopian society; the works of men like Owen, Saint-Simon, and Fourier, who surely would have spurned the epithet utopian which Karl Marx, in the wake of Louis Reybaud, thrust upon them, and also of Marx himself, who tried so hard to differentiate his vision from theirs; and finally a group of modern philosophical psychologists and biologists who would be ambivalent about the term, as well as a number of contemporary philosophers of history who have ventured to speculate about the future nature of man. The boundaries need not be demarcated with nice precision. It is moreover not the literary form that establishes the universe of discourse—in the nineteenth and twentieth centuries utopian thought hardly belongs to belles-lettres and is often unbearably prosy and jejune—but the intent to evoke a vision of the life of man in an earthly paradise that would be radically different from the existing order and would presume to render its inhabitants happier in some significant sense of that ambiguous yet unavoidable word.

The utopia should perhaps be distinguished from the religious millennium because it comes to pass not by an act of grace, but through human will and effort. But neither specific reforms of a limited nature nor mere prognostications of the invention of new technological gadgetry need be admitted. Calendar reform as such would not qualify as utopian; but calendar reform that pretended to effect a basic transformation in the human condition might be. Bacon and Campanella, Andreae and Morelly, Fénelon and Condorcet, Restif de la Bretonne and Edward Bellamy, Wells and Hertzka, Wilhelm Reich and Norman Brown, Fromm and Marcuse, Maslow and Julian Huxley, J. B. S. Haldane and Teilhard de Chardin all find a place on the roster of utopia—some, to be sure, against their will.

Surveying the body of writings since the publication of Thomas More's *libellus,* one may ask a few simple questions: what secret wishes of mankind do these works seek to express? how have they described the "happiness" they hope to see realized? what is the temper and character of the life they idealize? what conflicts of psychic desire were they aware of and how did they resolve them? While the responses of the hundreds of utopias written in a Christian Western world since the sixteenth century have something in common, they may also be regarded as psychological documents that significantly reveal the sensibility of the particular historical societies in which they appeared. There may be a perennial utopian theme, but there are also important historical variations of a psychological order in the 450 years under review, and these shall preoccupy us. If the ordinary dream often derives its content from a need denied or a wish repressed and transformed, the utopia may well be a sensitive indicator of where the sharpest anguish of an age lies. In modern utopian thought, there have been a number of marked shifts of direction, reflecting the total changing realities of the world—not alone revolutions in its political and social spheres—and these fluctuations of expression are matters for historical analysis.

The concept *utopia* has from the beginning been used in both a positive and a pejorative sense; it has connoted at the same time an ideal longed-for and a crackpot scheme. The negation of the great dream has always constituted a parallel stream, from the very inception of utopian thought. The anti-utopia was not the invention of Aldous Huxley and Zamiatin: after all, the *Parliament of Women* by Aristophanes was contemporaneous with Plato's *Republic*; More's *Utopia* produced a galaxy of mocking parodies; and even in the body of many a dead-pan utopia, a mischievous little imp occasionally raises its head to debunk. But such intrusions from the real world, the satirical utopia or what has been variously called the dystopia, anti-utopia, or contra-utopia, are excluded from our inquiry. The same applies to the weird, biologically transformed supermen invented for Edward Bulwer-Lytton's *The Coming Race* (1871), and Olaf Stapledon's *Last and First Men* (1930), another subject passed over in order to preserve Thomas More's humanist frame. High seriousness and earnest affirmation of the possibility of human happiness are demanded of all those who approach the blessed isle, as More's poet laureate said in the eulogy appended to the main body of the work:

> "Wherefore not Utopie, but rather rightely
> My name is Eutopie."

The true dreamer, I am told, rarely if ever utters a negative.

In the present sketch the utopias since More have been divided into three ages of unequal duration. The periodization is of course somewhat arbitrary—it is certainly meant to be illustrative rather than definitive—and in a more detailed study subsidiary trends would have to be enlarged upon. The first group might be called utopias of calm felicity, running roughly from More to the age of the French Revolution; the second comprises the dynamic socialist and other historically determinist utopias, which span the greater part of the nineteenth century; and the last are the psychological and philosophical utopias of the twentieth century, for which I borrow from Professor Abraham H. Maslow the term "eupsychia." Throughout this essay the new themes in the utopian dreaming of each period—the most recent fashions in utopia—will be pushed to the fore and highlighted, in full awareness that hackneyed motifs from earlier times are constantly being reiterated in the background.

If a broad definition of utopia is accepted, a headcount would show a vast increase in the number of utopias produced in the last fifty years, but most of them are mere mastication.

Of necessity this *esquisse* will neglect many aspects of life in utopia, such as science, art, and religion, the epigenetic cycle, and death, to concentrate largely on love, work, and aggression—which perhaps immediately defines my orientation.

Utopias of Calm Felicity

The utopian idea, already richly explored in antiquity, was in modern times first embodied in a specific form and baptized by Thomas More, whose Latin work (Louvain, 1516) was translated during the sixteenth century into all the major European languages and has since been republished somewhere on the continent at least once every few decades—there is now even a Chinese version. No other work of this character has enjoyed anything like its popularity, well over a hundred editions. It set the pattern for Western utopia (after Plato, of course). The mainsprings of the good life lay in the wise order, and the solution to the problem of happiness was vested almost exclusively in the "beste state of a Publyque Weale." Through the end of the eighteenth century this stereotype predominated in hundreds of derivative works, for the most part ephemeral, in which typical literary elements were the isolated island, the shipwrecked or adventurous sailor, and the systematic description upon his return home of a government-controlled economy, benign social customs and manners, and a peaceful, tolerant religion. More's way of perceiving things stamped European consciousness so indelibly that his schema was adopted in scores of authentic travel reports as well as imaginary narratives, and it became the framework for many circumstantial accounts of newly-discovered lands. Writers like Garcilaso de la Vega seem to have viewed the reality of the Incan empire, for example, through More's utopian eyes.[2]

In European utopias prior to the nineteenth century, it was assumed that discord in relationships among persons, dissension, conflict, hostility, strife, or sharp competitiveness generated a social climate which brought forth the greatest unhappiness for all men. The panacea lay in the discovery and establishment of social arrangements under which expressions of psychological and physical aggressiveness were virtually eliminated. A supremely good society was feasible because, though by nature man might be capable indiscriminately of both good and evil, appropriate laws and institutions could be devised to cooperate with the loving tendencies in his nature, as well as with his fear of pain and punishment, to create utopia, continuous pleasurable enjoyment subject only to the natural ills of sickness and old age—and even these might be sharply reduced. With proper educational conditioning, mostly through the good example of seniors, it was believed possible to achieve this end so perfectly that transgressions of the established order would be rare.

In most pre-Revolutionary utopias in the Morean tradition, unbridled acquisition of property is identified as the chief, if not the sole, source of all dissension. There is a presumption that with the abolition of monopolies of property and with the establishment of some sort of communism or commonalty the antagonistic spirit, the cause of evil, no longer would find significant expression in society. It would simply vanish. "In this they establish three good qualities of man: equality, the desire for peace, and the contempt for riches, as the world is tortured primarily with the opposites of these," wrote Johann Valentin Andreae in the *Christianopolis* (1619).[3]

A carefully regulated marriage system also contributes to orderliness by reducing to a minimum the possibilities of competition in the gratification of sexual desire. In More's *Utopia* a viewing in the nude of prospective mates in the presence of elderly witnesses avoids the subsequent discovery of secret faults and keeps the marriage secure. Though divorce is possible, it is not encouraged. The social organization thus assures not only a stable order but an absolute one, so that change is confined to the natural seasonal environment, whose capacity for inflicting pain is fairly well controlled by human invention. These Christian utopias have succeeded in imitating among men on earth the constancy and invariance of God's creation. The terrible anxieties of the quest for food and for traditional work on the land or in the guild during a period of social upheaval have been allayed in an established, fixed order. The fear of violent death in war or at the hands of outlaws dispossessed of their inheritance has been assuaged. And the arrogant band of bedecked and bejeweled courtiers, the contumacious new officials of a society witnessing the breakdown of feudal relationships without yet having achieved the relative consensus of the policed nation-state, have been banished from Utopia.

The feelings suffused by this state of commonalty—whether communistic as in Thomas More, or based on small holdings, or even somewhat hierarchized by status in later works—are those of equality and Christian brotherhood. The orgiastic chiliasm of the Anabaptists was merely an exaggerated form of the same temper. "Equality cuts all our vices at their root," say Restif's Megapatagonians.[4] In those spheres of life where emulation was still tolerated, it was carefully contained within bounds in order to avoid envy and hostility—for example, in the choice of magistrates in More's *Utopia,* or of marital partners in Restif de la Bretonne's *Andrographe* (1782), where the whole procedure is regulated with the punctilio of a minuet. In the works written after More there is no consensus on absolute equality, and in late eighteenth-century utopias published in the wake of Rousseau's *Discourse on Inequality* there is a tendency to distinguish between "natural" inequalities, which are allowed some measure of extra reward, and those alien inequalities introduced by "civilization"; but gross inequality is not countenanced. French eighteenth-century utopias might be communistic, as in Morelly's *Code de la nature* (1755), or might idealize a system of private agricultural holdings whose size was strictly controlled or of independent artisan enterprises whose expansion was regulated. In any case, at least the spirit of communal equality prevails, without engrossing or monopoly. The enlightened despot or philosopher-king who emerges "naturally" at the apex of society does not contaminate the general egalitarian atmosphere. Louis XXXVI, the reigning monarch in Sébastien Mercier's *L'An Deux Mille Quatre Cent Quarante* (1770), accompanied by a few companions, walks the streets of the city without pomp or ceremony. When property is allowed, the lands are frequently redistributed and the inheritance laws manipulated to preserve more or less equal holdings. Pierre de Lesconvel's Naudelians are allowed to own no more than twice the land necessary for sustenance.[5] The mode of life is that of an idealized agricultural society, a fantasized early Roman Republic. This small independent farmer's utopia lives on well into the Chartist movement of the nineteenth century—in the writings of James Bronterre O'Brien for example—and it has its partisans even in our own day. (It cropped up again during the Great Depression of the thirties.)

In many pre-revolutionary utopias an exception from the rule of equality is made for those with an inclination toward studies. Philosophers and scientists are preferred as leaders, but their natural superiority is not envied, neither does it always yield them substantially greater material benefits than the work of a farmer or an artisan. Perhaps there is inequality of esteem—occasionally special memorials for scientific benefactors are erected in the marketplace—but in many utopias there is no essential difference of economic condition. There are, to be sure, a few apparent exceptions. The Master of Salomon's House on Bacon's *New Atlantis* is an awesome figure who looks "as if he pitied men." But if Harrington's *Rota: or a Model of a Free State* (1660) is against "Community," it nevertheless holds to its own version of the idea of equality and is still called an "equal Commonwealth."[6] The leaders of the Sevarambians invented by Vairasse do enjoy more women than ordinary citizens, but these extra wives are leftovers or widow ladies. Extraordinary emoluments for outstanding excellence do not undermine the rule of order, more or less equality, and sufficiency for all.

In More a conquering King Utopus had to inaugurate the new system, and the abandonment of his utopian laws and institutions would immediately result in an abrupt weather-change to an atmosphere of depravity, conflict, and misery. The order of happiness is within human capacity but it is not innate. Thus Utopian man is not natural—he has been fashioned by institutions—but the result is not unnatural since the founders of Utopia utilized benign instincts and repressed harmful ones through education and the dictates of the law. In contrast to our contemporary absorption with the problem as a major source of dolorous psychic disturbance, the utopian conception of repression envisages a process that is neither very painful nor very complicated. As a consequence, the social environment in which every new-born utopian first sees the day is uniformly pleasurable and his whole existence will be passed in the same mild emotional climate.

Tranquillity is the highest good. Since only moderate pleasures are deemed to be pleasures at all,[7] there is nothing to disrupt the order of calm felicity, once it has been instituted, as long as the world endures. More's utopia is not even subject to the natural decay that Plato considered inevitable for his Republic.

Labor in moderation is judged to be a good in most utopias, not only to satisfy man's economic needs, but to maintain sound mental hygiene, and both the Biblical curse and the Aristotelian have been lifted. "The Islanders love work and they regard it as a special gift of God's grace," wrote Philipp Balthazar Sinold in *The Happiest Island in the Whole World or the Land of Contentment*.[8]

Though not regarded as a source of great pain, work is nonetheless kept at a minimum in order to allow ample social time for the awakening of other salutary human interests such as learning. While Christian asceticism and the mortification of the flesh are rejected, the spiritual and intellectual life is nevertheless valued above any other. The early utopias are still deeply rooted in the rationalist tradition. More's Utopus made a deliberate and crucial decision when he limited the consumption of commodities to the necessary and the comfortable in order that any surplus labor might be devoted to study. Recognized needs are generally held to the small number necessary for commodious but not luxurious living. The six-hour day was promulgated as adequate under ordinary circumstances; but if it proved excessive for the satisfaction of basic requirements and for building up a reasonable stockpile, Utopians would not go on ceaselessly producing additional commodities—as we do in a society where expansion, not knowledge, is the goal—but would immediately curtail the hours of labor. "What time may possibly be spared from the necessary occupations and affairs of the Commonwealth, all that the Citizens should withdraw from the bodily service to the free liberty of the mind and garnishing of the same."[9]

The psychological assumptions of the pre-nineteenth-century utopias were that man normally sought sensate happiness, that this state of pleasurableness was easily definable, that the condition was derivative from the establishment of an appropriate institutional order, and that this order was not difficult to achieve once its virtues were made known. Man required food, clothing, sexual gratification, some means of protection against foreign enemies, and an educational system to guarantee the transmission of utopia from one generation to another. There were general needs for religious adoration, a bit of good clean fun in the evening, amiable conversation, the respect due to one's age and sexual status, but there were no powerful drives and no stormy passions to upset the equilibrium.

The mood of the system is sameness, the tonus one of Stoic calm, without excitation. Utopia is unchanging; one day is like the next except that natural holidays related to the seasons and nuptial rites punctuate the year with occasional festivities. It is only a rare dystopian—Abbé Gilles Bernard Raguet in the *Nouvelle Atlantide de François Bacon* (1702)—who complains of the boredom of existence. No one would ordinarily want more than a fair share and if normal desires were adequately satisfied there would be no monstrous outbursts of irregularity. Should an infrequent disturbance ruffle the calm of life, it would be handled by a minor police system (which is somehow never described). The natural passions are depicted as mild and gentle, and punishment is merely a bridling of excess. The voracious one, the man of uncontrolled lusts, the hardened criminal, is eliminated, but without wrath or vindictiveness, after he has been persuaded to choose his own doom, as in Mercier's description of the execution of a criminal in *L'An Deux Mille Quatre Cent Quarante*. Indeed, the wretch might have continued to live in obloquy had he been so depraved as to desire it. Shame and public disapproval are the ordinary means of insuring an obedience to the law that soon becomes spontaneous.

There is no need for privacy, no "lurking corners," to use More's phrase, no capricious travel without a social purpose, for in all these might reside new possibilities for inequality in pleasure. The problem of liberty is rarely posed in this phase of utopian literature because the goals are set in a different direction: a quest for serenity, quiet happiness, peace, perhaps virtue, above all order, what Abbate Pietro Chiari called "stabile felicità" and Thomas Floyd, the perfect "caulme of permanent felicitie."[10]

An Epicurean-Stoic could be totally self-fulfilled in this environment; nobody else would be—neither the romantic, nor the voluptuary, nor the hero, nor the entrepreneur, nor the saint, nor the ascetic who inflicted pain upon himself. In this period, the inhabitants of Utopia are all practicing ancient philosophers of varying degrees of moral attainment.

In Bacon's *New Atlantis* the dominant tone set by the inventive scientists, who mix concoctions for physic and man's delectation, offhand seems to be one of movement rather than stability. But I think it could be shown that recent interpreters have gone far beyond the author's original intent when they identify him as the father of modern industrial chemistry eternally in search of novelty. Inquiry into everything that is possible might serve for the prolongation of life and Bacon is not averse to adopting convenient mechanical instruments; but he still thought of science as a body of knowledge that could be acquired in a finite period of time through assiduous cultivation of his method. He would surely not have been in favor of widespread escalating luxury, which could only lead to softness. The rule of the scientists on *New Atlantis* is an example of precedence for the learned, but in this unfinished piece there is no suggestion of a wildly dynamic republic of science, innovating endlessly, such as Condorcet depicted in his *Fragment sur l'Atlantide*, a commentary on Bacon, some two hundred years later.

Perhaps the greatest distinction between the sixteenth- and the eighteenth-century utopias lies in the redreaming of ideal sexual and marital happiness. As the Christian character of utopia began to wear off, the utopian fantasy allowed itself more and more to envision a wider gamut of sexual relationships. Particularly after the discovery of the Blessed Isles of the Southern Seas and the publication of travelers' reports—many, of course, written in Paris garrets—a flood of utopias depicting various exotic forms of marriage inundated Europe. If the utopia was situated in a climatic zone where the bounty of nature was overflowing and little or no labor was required, work regulations, no longer meaningful, gave way to the problems of sexual gratification. Here one can discern two contrary tendencies—sometimes in the same writer. From Restif de la Bretonne, whose vivid portrayals of eighteenth-century sexual life are the best known of his two hundred-odd volumes and who wrote a sexually unrepressed utopia in *Le Dédale français*, come plans that feature maniacally detailed, elaborate, and often terribly repressive, sexual ordinances. In his *Andrographe*, for example, even after marriage free sexual intercourse between couples is prohibited until the age of thirty, at the same time that successful evasion of the girl's vigilant parents is encouraged. Restif reflects the tales he read of esoteric sexual practices among savage peoples, as well as the fears generated by his own extravagant desires. But throughout this rather dull sexual utopia, the ideal of stability and inflexible order is unassailed—if anything, the chains are tightened.

A trend in a different direction, also inspired by Tahiti and the simultaneous de-Christianization of Europe, looks toward complete sexual freedom as an ideal, insists on new, more intricate marriage forms, or at least pleads by implication for the mitigation of existing legal restrictions with their cruel punishments for adultery and homosexuality. In these utopias, Christian monogamy, not rooted in nature, is exposed as both hypocritical and provocative of strife. A freer sexuality, as the utopia purports to demonstrate, does not lead to the disruption of the social order and the exacerbation of hostile emotions among men, but on the contrary contributes to peaceful, amicable relationships among the fortunate islanders. Thus, despite important sexual emendations, the Morean ideal of stability remains intact. The sexual relations described by Diderot in the *Supplément au Voyage de Bougainville* are pleasurable yet innocent, not debauched, without deleterious consequences for moral character or order—essentially More's requirements for honest permissible pleasure. True, in the writing of subtle moralists like Diderot the new sexual pattern is never described without ambivalence, but in many cruder works all manner of sexual combinations are attempted, as for example, the *poli-antropie* described in the *Histoire d'un peuple nouveau dans l'isle de la raison* (1757), where eight men and four women living together without jealousy comprise the rational marital unit, because "woman has received from nature a greater aptitude for and a stronger tendency toward plurality."[11] In some respects the utopia of the Marquis de Sade is still part of this rather naive, eighteenth-century naturalistic vision of freedom from sexual repression; in others it points to the more complex twentieth-century resuscitation of the problem.

The Open-Ended Utopia of the Nineteenth Century

About the time of the French Revolution, or shortly thereafter, depending upon how accurately one presumes to pinpoint the origins of something as intangible as a change in the waking-dream habits of a society, trouble came to the utopia of calm felicity. The disturbing elements were so numerous and varied that the transformation seems overdetermined: a reorganization of industry, though picayune by our standards, in the eyes of contemporaries a revolutionary upheaval that posed unprecedented problems for urban life; a growing awareness among some of the misery of the new industrial working classes, generating a pathos as intense as More's reaction to the first impact of the enclosure movement; a new historical consciousness epitomized in a theory of inevitable, endless progressions; a conception of past—and hence at least the probability of future—biological metamorphoses of the species; a new definition (or a revival of an old one) of human nature that cast doubt upon the hitherto unchallenged Greco-Christian belief in the superiority of man's rational over his passionate and manual-administrative capacities; a further reconsideration of monogamy as the absolute sexual institution; a reappraisal of the need for equality; and, last but not least, the birth of a romantic cult of personality, self-expression, and individuation.

Whereas before the nineteenth century utopias are invariably stable and ahistorical, ideals out of time, they now become dynamic and bound to a long prior historical series. They should henceforth be called euchronias—good place becomes good time. In some respects they hark back to the mystical temporal doctrines of medieval dissidents like the followers of Joachim of Flora and the chiliasts of the Reformation. In *time* we shall have utopia. The early utopia was usually restricted to an island or a similarly isolated environment, and there was a steady counterpoint between the tiny haven of happiness and the greater world outside. By the end of the eighteenth century, historical utopias, typified by Condorcet's canonical depiction of the future of mankind in the Tenth Epoch of his *Esquisse*, can be confined to no narrower limits than the whole globe. The old-fashioned model—or at least some of its elements—may reappear in the nineteenth century: witness Cabet's *Voyage en Icarie* and a host of other dreary utopian novels. But the mainstream of creative utopian thought has moved in another direction, and the fable is often discarded. An introductory philosophy of history now replaces the traditional prefatory literary contrivance.

The goal of the historical progression depicted in nineteenth-century utopias has sometimes been interpreted as static because Christian millenarian images, along with pastoral motifs from the classics, have crept into the writings. In a relatively continuous culture such as the Western one, older utopian fantasies, Greek, Judaic, Christian, Renaissance, and eighteenth-century, are never entirely obliterated, and verbal elements from the past survive with altered meanings. Nietzsche and others less well informed have made sport of the eternal Sabbath of nineteenth-century utopians, calling their blue heaven on earth dull, insipid, and as uneventful as the heavenly Jerusalem of the City of God. And vulgar expositions of Saint-Simon, Fourier, Marx, and Comte make it appear that their ultimate worldly *telos* is fixed and codified. Comparison with the earlier examples of utopia, however, immediately points up their unique quality: virtually all the great nineteenth-century utopias have continued metamorphoses built into their very frame; they are open-ended.

H. G. Wells was in error when he advertised his own dynamic utopia of 1905 as setting a new style in the genre; his was rather among the last of the nineteenth-century utopias—the Saint-Simonians would have found nothing novel in it but peripheral details. Condorcet's Tenth Epoch, the utopian one, is indefinite, by which he meant that ideal transformations in the distant future could not even be imagined until a further higher level of progress had been reached. There is no finish to his dynamic scientific utopia; happiness itself becomes boundlessly progressive with new discoveries. Saint-Simon often talked of a golden age in the future, an image from Hesiod's lexicon, but his disciples understood their Master well when they prognosticated an expansive movement without a cutoff, "moral well-being, social and individual love which grows, grows, grows, always, always."[12] Auguste Comte's portrayal of humanity-to-be in the second volume of the *Système de Politique Positive*—usually forgotten—predicted a complete turning-away from preoccupation with rationalistic science and technology once nourishment for the maintenance of life could be provided without work and inhaled as odors. But this dawn of a world of pure love and play does not inaugurate a static utopia, since Comte foresees a ceaseless extension of the dimensions of human emotiveness and its expression. Marx has few passages that describe the future with customary utopian detail, but the realm of freedom initiated by the passage from prehistory to true history, once man is emancipated from necessity, is dynamic, forever spawning new possibilities for individual self-actualization. In Fourier's phalanstery, a day of life and love is very unlike the yesterday, especially for those whose psychological nature, the butterfly type for instance, drives them to welcome frequent change.

Pre-revolutionary utopians are physically immobile. The Saint-Simonians in utopia, on the other hand, are continually building roads, railways, and canals, the great arteries for the unification of mankind, and they are constantly moving over them, making occasional overnight stops at well-furnished motels. The Fourierist may have a home base in a small phalanstery; but there are armies of bayadera and their male counterparts who are always touring, vast programs of cultural interchange, and great itinerant battalions of young workers for public projects. A little-known German fantasy of 1828, *Die Unterwelt,* conceived of a tremendous subterranean expansion of world-wide communications. Wells' utopians are inveterate world travelers—though a meticulous record is kept of their whereabouts. There is an air of excitement and feverish stimulation in this nineteenth-century utopian world. Perhaps the ne plus ultra of this utopian vision was reached in the concluding sections of William Winwood Reade's bizarre universal history entitled *The Martyrdom of Man* (1872). After him, science fiction could only fill in the boring details. Disease will be extirpated; the causes of decay will be removed; immortality will be invented. And then, the earth being small, mankind will migrate into space, and will cross the airless Saharas which separate planet from planet and sun from sun. The earth will become a Holy Land which will be visited by pilgrims from all quarters of the universe. Finally, men will master the forces of Nature; they will become themselves architects of systems, manufacturers of worlds."[13]

As a consequence of the new commitment to perpetual motion, the problem of ordering a fast-changing world became as intricate in utopia as it is in actuality. The utopia now called itself a "system" by preference. The new mobility altered the whole psychological atmosphere and eternal self-transcendence became a necessity of romantic personality. The utopian problem was how to allow individual dynamism free play and yet prevent it from degenerating into violent anarchy.

The characteristic nineteenth-century solution was epitomized in Auguste Comte's motto, which Brazil adopted as its national slogan: *Order and Progress*. From this viewpoint, a controlled Marxist revolution is still part of a utopia of order; it is merely another way of arranging the dynamic historical process. Up to the nineteenth century, the utopian ideal involved the ordering of life once and for all time. By contrast, the new vision entailed a constant management of run-away historical forces: to tame the future, to know in order to predict and control, to change the world—but always in accordance with its historical destiny.

Many nineteenth-century utopias are organismic and hierarchical, rooted in "scientific" theories of biology and physiology. As the new physiology of popular writers like Bichat, whose ideas both Saint-Simon and Comte took over, dwelt on the fundamental ineradicable differences among men, the egalitarianism of the old utopias was abandoned. Equality, no longer a psychic need, was decried as *égalité turque* by Saint-Simon and condemned as a source of discord because its presumption that human beings were interchangeable counters forced men into the wrong slots, creating social chaos. French nineteenth-century utopians were in quest of an order that emphasized individualism, self-expression, and self-fulfillment. It is perhaps symbolic of the contrast between the two utopian styles that while in More's *Utopia* the identification of people is not an issue, the Saint-Simonian orators had to assure their prospective adepts that under the new system personality would be preserved and their individual names emblazoned upon their costumed breasts. (If the utopia provides what men most keenly miss, the utopian of the earlier period did not fear a loss of personality because he had it, while the nineteenth-century romantic felt endangered by anonymity because his identity had already been threatened by the new industrial society.)

Order now required a complex organization in which the satisfaction of individual uniqueness, not equality, was the paramount key to happiness. Among the Saint-Simonians, utopia was based on three biological types whose Platonic origins are obvious: the rationalist, the emotive, and the motor. To the extent that the egalitarian principle survives, it signifies equality in self-actualization. Saint-Simonian happiness was founded on the fulfillment of natural creative professional capacities and the appeasement of sexual desires in a system that permitted easy divorce under the guidance of priestly love-counselors. More's utopia had also allowed people to choose their crafts freely in accordance with their predilections, but the distinctive occupations were few in number and most young men followed in their fathers' footsteps; the whole problem was unimportant. For the Saint-Simonians, who lived in a more complex world, appropriate choice of occupation as the realization of a "biological" personality was fundamental to the system. An order that was more highly differentiated was denominated the superior order from the time of the Saint-Simonians through the Spencerians.

While the Saint-Simonians constructed hierarchies within professional or sociological categories, Fourier's "passionate series" centered around psychological differences. The bringing together of eight-hundred-odd recognizable psychological types under one roof was a precondition for happiness in a phalanstery; otherwise the variety of relationships necessary for total self-fulfillment in the State of Harmony would be lacking. Since work without love was a psychological burden, a pain to be eradicated from utopia, Fourier developed the mechanism for making labor "attractive," a free expression of the whole self, never divorced from erotic inclinations. You only work with those you love; and you may have as many different work patterns as are congruent with the intricate network of your love relationships. Appropriate provision is made for the specialized psychic needs and desires of each stage of the life-cycle. Since all desires are natural and all have rights to satisfaction, Fourier's utopia operates without any concept of repression. This pathetic little bourgeois salesman may have preserved the idea of unequal returns on investment in the shares of phalanstery, but the poorest man there led a highly stimulated oral and genital existence.

The Christian humanist More had still explicitly distinguished between the lower grosser and the higher spiritual pleasures and he would restrict the former for the sake of the latter. When nineteenth-century utopians appreciated man's passionate nature as at least equal, if not superior, to his reason, the old psychological scale of values was subverted. Where More insisted on continent adequacy, Fourier dreamed of progressively greater pleasurable excitements. The gentle, restrained converse among persons in the older utopias will not suffice the romantics. Fourier widened the dimensions of utopia beyond anything that had been dreamed of before, and in retrospect he emerges as the greatest utopian after More.

How do the French prophets curb the aggressive and hostile tendencies that threaten to endanger the peace of all utopias? The Saint-Simonian system is based on the assumption that once man's natural desire for love and creative self-expression is fulfilled, none but monsters (and they can be disposed of) would have any lust for dominion over others. All energies would be turned toward the endless exploitation of nature on a global scale. Fourier was perhaps more subtle than the Saint-Simonians. He made allowance for certain forms of the aggressive instinct: he fostered emulation among rival work and love groups, which are continually being reshuffled in such a way that competitiveness is at once expressed and tamed, as in the best sporting tradition. To mitigate the pains of an amorous rejection in an order of free love, he employed wise counselors of the opposite sex who had intensely pleasurable techniques at their disposal to console the defeated. The simple Fourierist psychological principle is that harmful aggressiveness is the consequence of frustrated instinct—what he called *égorgement*—and if there are enough salutary outlets there is no eruption in destructive hostility. Fourier devised elaborate mechanisms for the diversion of murderous passions into innocent channels; in phalanstery the potential killer becomes a slaughterer of animals.

Marx's utopia is subject to dispute, since he did not leave a finished blueprint like Owen's *Book of the New Moral World* or Cabet's Fourierist *Voyage en Icarie.* In the *Critique of the Gotha Program* (1875), the slogan "Jeder nach seinen Fähigkeiten, jedem nach seinen Bedürfnissen!" seems to recall the Saint-Simonian belief that there were unique and diverse talents around which society should be organized. (Marx's slogan is, of course, an emendation of the pronouncement in the *Doctrine de Saint-Simon*: "A chacun suivant sa capacité, à chaque capacité suivant ses oeuvres.") Marx's conclusion, "to each according to his needs," is reminiscent of Fourier's language, but its full meaning is rather ambiguous. For Fourier need surely involved sexual and psychological needs, not merely taking from the public granary as much as one wanted to eat. If

Marx was also concerned with this broader definition of need, when he wrote the *Critique of the Gotha Program* he probably referred primarily to means of subsistence.

In general, in Marx's manuscripts of the 1840's the utopian elements had been more fulsomely articulated, and he foresaw a rich and varied sensate life that has distinct Fourierist overtones. He voiced antagonism to the occupational specialization resulting from the division of labor because it entailed a deformation of personality and an impairment of human faculties.[14] In the fifties he explicitly used the term "self-actualization of the individual."[15] Though the concept of alienation is primarily an economic one in Marx, on occasion it does have the psychological sense that some contemporary commentators have made central to his thought. The elimination of alienated labor, whatever its meaning, was part of his utopia. Communism would represent a regaining of personality, the reintegration and the return of man to himself, the transcendence of human self-alienation or self-estrangement. In the ultimate sense, idleness —not work—was the goal of the Marxist utopia, as it was of the Comtean.[16]

In the older utopias—the Germans named the genre "Staatsroman"—the prince or the legislator had been the promulgator of the good economic order and its preserver. In the early nineteenth-century utopias, the state became a sort of superfluous superstructure which ought, and was destined, to wither away. Solve the problem of the organization of labor—or invoke Paul Lafargue's *droit à la paresse*—and you solve the problem of human happiness. If wise Utopus was once the mainspring of the system, the inflated state mechanism of the nineteenth century came to be regarded as an oppressive foreign growth that was probably inimical to the ideal economy. Psychic happiness or misery, the joys of employment and prosperity or the horrors of starvation, flowed directly from the choice of an economy. Society could be "administered" by the central banking system of the Saint-Simonian planners, or it might be a free-functioning grocery-store, an economic anarchy in the Proudhonian manner. In either event, the state was no longer the focal utopian institution—a sharp transfer of the gravitational center from the earlier mode. Society did not have to be ruled and policed, it merely had to be organized and administered. Not until the late nineteenth century, in such state-capitalist utopias as Theodor Hertzka's *Freiland* (Leipzig, 1889), was the state again restored to a directing role in the ideal society.

Contemporary Eupsychias

Mr. Frazier, the founder of Walden Two, exclaimed to his visitors with a gesture of impatience, "No one can seriously doubt that a well-managed community will get along successfully as an economic unit. A child could prove it. The real problems are psychological."[17] One can agree with Professor Skinner's formulation of the contemporary utopian question and yet find his solutions rather derivative, a reasonable amalgam of Morean and Fourierist elements refurbished with some of the newer experimental techniques. The real novelty in twentieth-century utopian fervor is concentrated elsewhere.

While eighteenth- and early nineteenth-century utopian thinking still fitted in neatly with physical science in the shape of the smooth-flowing Newtonian world-machine—it had served as a model for both Saint-Simon and Fourier, who fancied themselves Newtons of the social universe—in the latter part of the nineteenth century two scientific hypotheses about the nature of man appeared to raise almost insurmountable barriers to the prolongation of the utopian dream: the discoveries of Darwin and of Freud. Both were shattering to those men of the nineteenth century who had had visions of a peaceful, orderly, progressive world from which antagonism and aggression were virtually banished and where man's creativity would flower forever.

That Social Darwinism in many of its forms was a gross distortion of Darwin's thought is irrelevant. Phrases such as the "struggle for existence" came to imply that raw tooth-and-nail conflict was imbedded in man's biological nature. Bloody images intruded into the dreams of the utopians. The initial impact of Darwinism called forth a spate of imaginative new worlds representing the activities of a creature who once was man in successive future stages of his biological evolution—Stapledon has eighteen of these periods. Such writings—often in novel form—are for the most part negative, or at best ambivalent, utopias. The loathsome species whose cold aspect and newly acquired physical-scientific powers terrify such residual humans as they encounter hardly belong in a humanist utopia. The supermen of Renan's *Rêves*, for example, maintain their dominion of reason through fear. These biologically transformed beings have generally moved in one evolutionary direction: toward omnipotence and a diminution of human affect. Beast-machines, emotionally impoverished, existing only to exercise power, became a stereotype whose origins in social reality are all too apparent.

Freud's death instinct may have been a relatively late introduction into his system, but the whole of his life work had already established a deep-rooted contradiction between civilization and happiness. The desire for aggression against fathers and brothers was represented as virtually innate and only partially transmutable. In many ways Freud's was the most trenchant and devastating attack on utopian illusions—what he called the lullabies of heaven—that had ever been delivered.

If the two powerful scientific influences of Darwin and of Freud, which found parallel embodiment in great writers like Friedrich Nietzsche, tended to inhibit fresh utopian dreaming—they did not of course stop the flow of incredibly dull novelistic utopias in all European languages that merely re-hashed old social utopian themes, such as Edward Bellamy's *Looking Backward* or Anatole France's *Sur la pierre blanche*—the experience of two world wars, a mass slaughter of innocents, and the murderous aberrations of new social systems in the making even further dampened utopian ardor. The dystopia had its brilliant moment in the works of Zamiatin, Aldous Huxley, and Orwell.

But despite their flood of bitter mockery the utopian energy of man was not irretrievably dissipated. The creature, it seems, could not stop dreaming even as he stood beneath the gallows of the atomic launching pads. Certain of the hopes of old-fashioned Morean and Saint-Simonian utopias had in the meantime become partial political realities, through social legislation, in restricted areas of the world; or they had at least been incorporated as programmatic statements of intent by major institutions. The social encyclicals of Pope John XXIII, the speeches of Khrushchev at Soviet Party Congresses, and the preambles to Democratic Party platforms are a fairly wide-ranging sample of the pentration of early nineteenth-century utopian motifs into the contemporary political arena. Henceforth mankind only had to face the nettlesome problems incident to the implementation of these lofty purposes; a vague consensus about their merit had already been achieved.

Simultaneously with the realization of some reforms that once would have been deemed wildly utopian, in the realm of pure thought Western writers undertook to do battle with both the Darwinian and the Freudian pessimistic denial of the utopian hope, and in the course of their counterattack they developed the two new utopian styles that are peculiar to our age.

Firstly, a group of imaginative life-scientists have transformed the emotional temper of Darwinism. They now assert that a benign spirituality is about to possess the whole of mankind and become a permanent acquisition of the species, that we are on the point of ascending to a higher stage in the autonomous and irreversible evolutionary process. Physical-biological evolution has virtually reached the utmost limits, they say—the size of the brain has hit a plateau since Neanderthal—and the development of man, who now has the power to control his own destiny, must henceforward take place in the realm of mind or spirit. Instead of being associated with tooth-and-nail capitalism, rampant nationalism, and aggressive imperialism, the theory of evolution, in a Kropotkin-like mood, has moved away from dramatization of the individual struggle for survival to envisage a future world peopled by humane, cooperative, totally conscious beings. The German romantic idea of a leap into a higher state of consciousness, a rather metaphysical concept, is replaced by an assertion of psychosocial evolution that purports to have roots in the sciences of anthropology, paleontology, and biology, broadly interpreted of course. Teilhard de Chardin has written of a noösphere, a universal belt of psychosocial forces; Julian Huxley, somewhat less Platonic, prefers the term noösystem. Both of them conceive this new world of consciousness to be stage three in the evolution of matter, which has already passed through a historical transformation from the inorganic into the organic. But for all the scientific learning that buttresses their predictions, within the context of this paper their views can only be looked upon as a dream of reason.

The future expanding order of psychosocial inheritance, they foretell, will result in earlier internalization in the child and in ever more complex psychic awareness in the adult. Through the progressive intimacy and density of the network of human communications throughout the world, a peaceful and universal morality will be achieved. In the course of time the process of natural selection will fortify the new ethical order by showing biological preference for those with superior fitness in adapting to it. The old warfare between nature and culture will be abolished since both will be dominated by rational man.

The Jesuit paleontologist Teilhard de Chardin is emerging as the central prophetic figure of this twentieth-century cosmic historical utopia, with his arms outstretched to embrace humanist English biologists as well as French Marxists, among whom he has recently been assimilated. "Mankind," he wrote in the *Phenomenon of Man*, "the spirit of the earth, the synthesis of individuals and peoples, the paradoxical conciliation of the element with the whole, and of unity with multitude—all these are called Utopian and yet they are biologically necessary. And for them to be incarnated in the world all we may well need is to imagine our power of loving developing until it embraces the total of men and of the earth."[18] J. B. S. Haldane's man of the future will be "more rational and less instinctive than we are, less subject to sexual and parental emotions, to rage on the one hand and the so-called herd instinct on the other."[19] Julian Huxley has a vision of "psycho-social selection" that is unique to man and "decides between alternative courses of cultural evolution." This mechanism, he says, "must be primarily psychological and mental, involving human awareness instead of human genes."[20] Herman J. Muller is perhaps more hortatory than prophetic, but the biological utopia of universal love eugenically controlled is at least a prospect. "The rapid upgrading of our intelligence must be accompanied as closely as possible with a corresponding effort to infuse into the genetic basis of our moral natures the springs of stronger, more genuine fellow-feeling."[21]

These scientists belittle the prophets of doom and those so engrossed in the pettiness of living that they fail to appreciate the grand design of the future happiness of mankind, which, to be sure, is more cerebral than sensate, more spiritual and artistic than physical—in the desexualized Comtean, rather than Fourierist, tradition. Undaunted by the horrors of the twentieth century, Teilhard de Chardin was confident that we were actually witnessing the initial breakthrough into the new age. In a letter written shortly before his death, when the nations of the world, East and West, agreed to cooperate in the scientific investigations of the geophysical year, he playfully yet enthusiastically proclaimed it the first year of the noösphere.

The life-scientists have been joined by a number of eminent philosophers of history, who seem agreed that the next stage of human life either must or is likely to entail a spiritualization of mankind and a movement away from the present absorption with aggressive power and instinctual existence. Arnold Toynbee uses the term "etherialisation" for what Teilhard de Chardin in his private language called "hominisation," and Karl Jaspers, a second "axial period" of spirituality similar to the age of the prophets. For what is the fable of the sleeper on the ledge of a mountainside, which Toynbee has preserved from the first volume to the last, but a historian's utopian dream? One ledge separates the primitive world from the age of civilizations. But this age is drawing to a close, and the rule of circularity that governed the twenty-one known specimens of civilized society in the past is not applicable to the future. Civilization with its inner cyclical dialectic of growth and destruction is about to be transcended. When mankind reaches the next ledge above us new rules will prevail in what Toynbee, a somewhat reluctant utopian, tentatively defined as a spiritual world of brotherhood and communion.

Parallel with this readaptation of Darwinism to serve a utopian ideal of a peaceful, rational, cooperative man, are the efforts of a group of psychologists, anthropologists, and philosophers to grapple with Freud and free him from the rather somber portrait of the future of mankind which he left behind, particularly in his last works. Against the purported elimination of aggressiveness as a consequence of establishing a new order of property relationships (or the abolition of property), which Marx had assumed, Freud consistently aimed his sharpest barbs.[22]

The paltry measure of happiness an individual might attain was dependent upon far more than an ideal social order: it was rather the result of a complex interplay between a man's psychophysiological nature and the particular forms of repression adopted at a given historical time in a specific culture. Some natures were doomed from the outset to suffer under certain cultural regimens, others to flourish; some sought refuge in insanity, while others could be restored through therapy to endure or tolerate what was essentially inimical to them. There are many ways to unhappiness in the Freudian philosophy. Civilization might create higher mental systems which contained the beast, but aggressiveness would inevitably erupt in a thousand guises. If primitive aggressiveness merely assumed different shapes throughout history, if the most that could be done in the name of civilization was to repress and sublimate, then the eudaemonist utopia was sheer nonsense. To the extent that Freud has a utopian ideal it is a Kantian one: the development of all human capacities beyond the instinctual. The preferred historical state of man is the reign of de-emotionalized reason; but this is hardly in prospect.

The first important disciple of Freud's to attempt an adaptation of his discoveries to a more optimistic view of the future of man that would be consonant with the Marxist utopia was Wilhelm Reich. The Marxist and the psychoanalytic movements had once appeared on the European intellectual horizon as profoundly antagonistic orientations. In the twenties, on the eve of the Nazi seizure of power, Reich broke ranks and summoned the German proletariat to abandon their exclusive fixation upon the Marxist sociological interpretation of man's historical destiny and to incorporate much of Freud's psychological theory of genitality into their worldview—"Dialectical Materialism and Psychoanalysis" appeared in *Unter dem Banner des Marxismus* in 1929. But Reich drew revolutionary consequences from the doctrine: instead of a future civilization resting on heightened instinctual repression, he preached an apotheosis of the body in all its parts and a worship of the orgasm. Immediate radical sexual emancipation was for him a prerequisite to the achievement of a victorious social revolution; otherwise the potentially militant masses, enthralled by the repressive psychological forces of the Oedipal family structure, would be inhibited from active political rebellion. The two most important nineteenth-century, pre-Marxist utopian schools, the Saint-Simonian and the Fourierist, had intimately coupled free sexuality with work needs, but this bond had been neglected by the Victorian-Kaiser Wilhelm Marxists. Reich's original *Sexualpolitik,* which of course did more violence to Freud than to Marx, was an authentic return to the older tradition.

Those who have followed Reich's path in the 1940's and 50's, Fromm, Marcuse, and Norman Brown, represent a characteristic resurgence of the Adamite utopia in a mechanized society where relationships are endangered by an atrophy of love. They negate the Freudian negation of the eudaemonist utopia. They reject the underlying dualism of his system and admit no intrinsic reason that the libido cannot enjoy free expression, once mankind is emancipated from the economic and sexual repressions that may have been necessary in lower states of civilization so that culture might be built.

The posthumously published manuscripts of the young Marx are the proof-text for Fromm's great conciliation. Like Hercules at the crossroads, modern man might have embarked upon a new order of free labor in companionship and love—Fromm's restatement of the Fourierist utopia—or he could again allow himself to submit to a pathological sado-masochistic order of society. Man seems to have chosen the second alternative, a competitive power-dominated society in which "alienation as a sickness of the self" is well-nigh universal.[23] He will never be happy until he finds love and security in true democratic socialism. "Man today is confronted with the most fundamental choice; not that between Capitalism and Communism, but that between *robotism* (of both the capitalist and the communist variety), or Humanistic Communitarian Socialism."[24]

Marcuse tackles Freud more directly on the concept of repression. For the purpose of the argument, at least, he accepts the Freudian system in its pure form unadulterated by the neo-Freudians, but to Marcuse's Hegelian-Marxist concept of stadially developing consciousness the idea that civilization must forever be nurtured and sustained by repressed libidinal energies is abhorrent. An era of general non-repressive sublimation will be inaugurated by reactivating early stages of the libido. "The sexual impulses, without losing their erotic energy, transcend their immediate object and eroticize normally non- and anti-erotic relationships between individuals, and between them and their environment. . . . The pleasure principle extends to consciousness. Eros redefines reason in his own terms. Reasonable is what sustains the order of gratification."[25] Fourier never said more. As in Fromm, the abolition of what Marcuse calls "surplus repression" (Marx is not named in *Eros and Civilization,* but he is the absent hero) requires political action as a necessary prolegomenon to the establishment of his new world. As for the general tenor of this utopia without repression, it has none of the wild abandon of spontaneous philosophical anarchism, and Marcuse chides Wilhelm Reich for his failure to distinguish between repressive and non-repressive sublimation. The higher freedom will have its hierarchy à la Saint-Simon, even its general will à la Rousseau. "Repressive reason gives way to a new *rationality of gratification* in which reason and happiness converge. It creates its own division of labor, its own priorities, its own hierarchy. The historical heritage of the performance principle is administration, not of men, but of things: mature civilization depends for its functioning on a multitude of coordinated arrangements. These arrangements in turn must carry recognized and recognizable authority. Hierarchical relationships are not unfree *per se*. . . ."[26]

Norman Brown's utopia also derives from Freud. But he sees no reason for suffering through the later repressive stages of genitality when it would be more human, natural, and indeed pleasurable to stop at the period of greatest self-fulfillment, childhood sexuality. Wilhelm Reich's assumption that the sexuality which culture represses is normal adult genital sexuality is rejected as "simplified and distorted." With a wealth of literary evidence from poets and mystics, Brown demonstrates that Freud's stage of childhood is what mankind has longed for through the ages, that the redemption of the body, the abolition of dualism, the dawn of Schiller's age of play or Fourier's "attractive work" is the final solution to the problem of happiness. Brown contends that Freud himself had sensed this in one of his moods but censored it in another. Brown, too, calls upon the young Marx to bear witness, though his utopia is in general less politically oriented than either Fromm's or Marcuse's. While his argument is not as skillful a dialectical exercise as Marcuse's, he pursues much the same course: Freud is quoted against himself. "The abolition of repression would abolish the unnatural concentrations of libido in certain particular bodily organs—concentrations engineered by the negativity of the morbid death instinct, and constituting the bodily base of the neurotic character disorders in the human ego. . . . The human body would become polymorphously perverse, delighting in that full life of all the body which it now fears."[27]

Maslow's psychological utopia has its roots in a rather different way of wrestling with Freud's concept of aggression; he does not really belong with the group whom Professor Philip Rieff has recently called the Freudo-Marxists. Marx has played less of a role in his thinking than have the anthropological studies of Ruth Benedict and Margaret Mead, which seemed to show that in primitive communities polarities of aggression and mildness were culturally determined and that generally aggressive behavior was by no means universal. From Benedict's manuscripts he drew the concept of "synergy," which allows him to conceive of a society where truly spontaneous, unfrustrated, egotistic behavior would have to express itself in altruistic action—echoes of the eighteenth-century moralists. From a study of what he considers mature self-actualized people, he has come to dream of a totally self-actualized society in which the expression of hostile aggressiveness and the need for its external repression would hardly exist.

Along with the neo-Freudians, Maslow rejects such absolute concepts as the death instinct. He believes that through the discovery of the pure sources of one's own nature there can be a free outpouring of creativity, even the birth of a new way of cognition uncorrupted by the inherited categories of Aristotelian thinking. His seems to be a utopia of the will, emancipated and untrammeled, that somehow achieves direct realization of the traditional love of the great universal religious illuminations of the sixth century before Christ. Often his ideal approaches the yea-saying morality of Nietzsche, freed from its confines of aristocratic exclusivity—its fangs cut—and made available to everyman. Maslow is a psychological utopian not in the sense that he is blind to the economic and social miseries that inspired most past utopias, but that with a utopian's license he moves on to another plane, where, beyond basic needs, he posits requirements for a psychic utopia that are more or less autonomous of any existing political order: the fulfillment of "idiosyncratic potentials, of expression of the self, and of the tendency of the person to grow in his own style and at his own pace."[28]

Of late, one can detect in Maslow's writings a movement away from the definition of self-actualization in romantic terms as the expansive realization of *all* potentialities, and the acceptance of a hierarchy of values in which a kind of religious experience again becomes the highest good to which others must be made subordinate.[29] In this he seems to join those philosophers of history who foresee a new spiritualization of mankind and an end to the sensate culture of our times.

Thus the two alternative utopian visions that have come to the fore in contemporary Western society (in defiance of a numerous population of dystopians) appear to be moving in opposite directions. In one, based upon the hypothesis of a growing spiritualization of mankind, the dross of the body seems to be left behind. In the other, a fantasy of greater rather than diminished sensate gratification is pivotal, and all human activity is libidinized. But the polarization of these two major present-day utopian solutions must give us pause. It has been our contention that in the past the dominant utopian types have been at least relatively uniform, each in its own age. Now we find the persistence of flagrantly divergent tendencies. We could take refuge in a conception of the psychological identity of opposites. Or perhaps these counter-currents are simply two different fantasies for dealing with the gnawing reality of aggression once the problems of work have been resolved in a world of material abundance. In the state of pure, virtually disembodied spirituality there can by definition be no room for aggression; and in the state of totally unrepressed gratification or non-repressive sublimation—however differently they are defined—the two-headed Cerberus of frustration-aggression is silenced forever.

As there is throughout the planet uneven development in the level of economic growth and in the degree of acceptance of the ways of Western civilization, so there are today different utopias coexisting. For a vast proportion of the human beings on earth, the simple static utopias of the period before 1800, with their promise of an orderly society and the assured satisfaction of elementary needs of subsistence, are still pie in the sky. And the wish for eternal peace remains utopian even among those who appear to have abolished at least two of the scourges of mankind, hunger and the plague. For millions of others, the simple nineteenth-century ideal of self-fulfillment epitomized as occupational choice is still a far-off goal, even though they, too, may be free from traditional slavery, starvation, and epidemic disease. Only the most advanced and wealthy segments of Western civilization, where the division of labor is highly perfected, have become so absorbed with their intense and perhaps growing psychic malaise that they deputize special writers to dream for them either of a higher mental system totally possessing mankind, or of a child-like society without instinctual repression, one of complete psychic self-actualization, overflowing with love, and occupied with play. Our affluence even supports commentators on these utopians.

In recent years utopias have in some quarters fallen into ill-repute because of their presumed deleterious political effects when masses of men have been captivated by extravagant visions. But to attack utopias is about as meaningful as to denounce dreaming. No great civilization has lived without them, whether they were reserved for a future life-after-death or brought down to earth. For myself, I am not convinced that they have exerted the catastrophic influence imputed to them. Their release of imaginative energies is innocent, their reflection of the emotional reality of their times authentic. Even if they are judged by an abstract criterion of truth-telling, it may be doubted whether utopians have, in fact, distorted the future any more than historians have the past.

Perhaps our danger lies elsewhere, in the possibility that the utopian quest may become all too matter-of-fact. Moon-flight, for example, is a rather old utopian device—Cyrano de Bergerac's is one of the best known of the sixteenth-century type. Now it is an imminent reality. And this much should be said in preference for the ancient form over the moon-flights of our own time: Cyrano's voyage consumed a far smaller proportion of the national product and the national genius.

References

1. "Yes, answered the Spirits; for every humane Creature can create an Immaterial World fully inhabited by immaterial creatures, and populous of immaterial subjects, such as we are, and all this within the compass of the head or scull; nay, not onely so, but he may create a World of what fashion

and Government he will, and give the Creatures thereof such motions, figures, forms, colours, perceptions, &c as he pleases, and make Whirl-pools, Lights, Pressures and Reactions, &c as he thinks best; nay, he may make a World full of Veins, Muscles, and Nerves, and all these to move by one jolt or stroke: also he may alter that world as often as he pleases, or change it from a natural world to an artificial; he may make a world of Ideas, a world of Atomes, and world of Lights, or whatever his fancy leads him to. . . . You have converted me said the Duchess to the Spirits. I'le take your advice, reject and despise all the worlds without me, and create a world of my own." *The Description of a New World, called the Blazing World, Written by the Thrice Noble, Illustrious, and Excellent Princesse, the Duchess of Newcastle* (London, 1666), pp. 96-98.

See also Sigmund Freud, "Psycho-Analytic Notes on an Autobiographical Account of a Case of Paranoia" (1911), in *Complete Psychological Works,* edited by James Strachey (London, 1958), XII, 1-82.

2. Garcilaso de la Vega [pseudonym, el Inca], *Historia general del Peru* (Cordoba, 1617).

3. Johann Valentin Andreae, *Christianopolis,* translated by F. E. Held (New York, 1916), p. 236.

4. Nicolas Edme Restif de la Bretonne, *La Découverte australe par un Homme-volant, ou Le Dédale français* (Paris, 1781), III, 509.

5. Pierre de Lesconvel, *Nouvelle relation du voyage du prince de Montberaud dans l'isle de Naudely, où sont rapportées toutes les maximes qui forment l'harmonie d'un parfait gouvernement* (Rouen, 1706?; original edition, 1703), p. 83.

6. See also *James Harrington's Oceana* (1656), edited with notes by S. B. Liljegren (Heidelberg: C. Winter, 1924), p. 186: "[If a Commonwealth] be unequal, it tends to strife, and strife to ruine."

7. "They thinke not felicity to rest in all pleasure, but onely in that pleasure that is good and honest." More, *Utopia* (London: printed by B. Alsop and T. Fawcet, 1639 edition), p. 184.

8. *Die glükseligste Insel auf der ganzen Welt, oder das Land der Zufriedenheit, dessen Regierungs-Art, Beschaffenheit, Fruchtbarkeit, Sitten der Einwohner, Religion, Kirchen-Verfassung, und dergleichen, samt der Gelegenheit wie solches Land entdecket worden, ausführlich erzehlert wird von Ludwig Ernst von Faramond* (pseudonym) (Nuremberg, 1749),p. 222. *Relation du voyage de l'isle d'Eutopie* (Delft, 1711) is an example of a Catholic religious utopia of the same type.

9. More, *op. cit.,* p. 144.

10. *L'Uomo d'un altro mondo o sia Memorie d'un Solitario senza nome. Scritte da lui medesimo in due linguaggi, chinese e russiano, e pubblicate nella nostra lingua* (Venice, 1768); Thomas Floyd, *The Picture of a perfit Commonwealth* (London, 1600).

11. *Histoire d'un peuple nouveau dans l'isle de la raison, ou Découverte d'une Isle à 43. Degrés 14. Minutes de Latitude Méridionale, par David Tompson, Capitaine du Vaisseau le Boston, à son retour de la Chine en 1756. Ouvrage traduit de l'Anglois* (London, 1757), p. 134.

12. A canticle by Charles Duveyrier. Bibliothèque Nationale, Ms. n.a.fr. 24609, f. 457v.

13. William Winwood Reade, *The Martyrdom of Man,* 18th edition (London, 1910), p. 515.

14. Engels later expressed the same idea in *Herr Eugen Dühring's Revolution in Science* (Moscow: Foreign Languages Publishing House, 1947), pp. 435-436: "In the division of labour, man also is divided. All other physical and mental faculties are sacrificed to the development of one single activity."

15. Karl Marx, *Grundrisse der Kritik der politischen Ökonomie. Rohentwurf, 1857-1858* (Berlin: Dietz, 1953), p. 505.

16. See Marx's notes on a work on idleness known to Pierre Naville. Naville, *De l'aliénation à la jouissance* (Paris: Librairie Marcel Rivière et Cie, 1957), p. 495.

17. B. F. Skinner, *Walden Two* (1948) (New York: The Macmillan Company, 1962), p. 80.

18. Pierre Teilhard de Chardin, *The Phenomenon of Man* (New York: Harper, 1959), p. 265.

19. J. B. S. Haldane, *Everything has a History* (London: Allen and Unwin, 1951), p. 288.

20. Julian Huxley, "The Emergence of Darwinism," in Sol Tax (ed.), *The Evolution of Life. Its Origins, History and Future* (Chicago: Chicago University Press, 1960), I, 20.

21. Herman J. Muller, "The Guidance of Human Evolution," in Sol Tax (ed.), *The Evolution of Man. Mind, Culture, and Society* (Chicago: Chicago University Press, 1960), II, 456.

22. "In abolishing private property," he wrote in *Civilization and Its Discontents,* "we deprive the human love of aggression of one of its instruments, certainly a strong one, though certainly not the strongest; but we have in no way altered the differences in power and influence which are misused by aggressiveness, nor have we altered anything in its nature. Aggressiveness was not created by property. It reigned almost without limit in primitive times,when property was still very scanty, and it already shows itself in the nursery almost before property has given up its primal, anal form; it forms the basis of every relation of affection and love among people (with the single exception, perhaps, of the mother's relation to her male child). If we do away with personal rights over material wealth, there still remains prerogative in the field of sexual relationships, which is bound to

become the source of the strongest dislike and the most violent hostility among men who in other respects are on an equal footing. If we were to remove this factor, too, by allowing complete freedom of sexual life and thus abolishing the family, the germ-cell of civilization, we cannot, it is true, easily foresee what new paths the development of civilization could take; but one thing we can expect, and that is that this indestructible feature of human nature will follow it there." Sigmund Freud, *Civilization and Its Discontents,* translated by James Strachey (New York: W. W. Norton and Co., Inc., 1962), pp. 60-61.

23. Erich Fromm, *Beyond the Chains of Illusion* (New York: Simon and Schuster, 1962), p. 53.

24. Erich Fromm, *Man for himself; an inquiry into the psychology of ethics* (New York: Rinehart, 1947), p. 363.

25. Herbert Marcuse, *Eros and Civilization* (Boston, 1961), pp. ix, 204.

26. *Ibid.*, p. 205.

27. Norman O. Brown, *Life Against Death. The Psychoanalytical Meaning of History* (New York: Vintage Books, 1959), p. 308.

28. Abraham H. Maslow, *Toward a Psychology of Being* (New York: D. Van Nostrand Co., Inc., 1962), p. 181.

29. Abraham H. Maslow, *Religions, Values, and Peak-Experiences* (Columbus: Ohio State University Press, 1964).

II

UTOPIA IS DEAD

JUDITH SHKLAR

The Political Theory of Utopia: From Melancholy to Nostalgia

WHAT DOES the plaintive question, "why are there no utopias to-day?" mean? Does it merely express the nostalgia of those who were young and socialist in the thirties? Is it just that they resent the lack of sympathy among younger people? Do some of the latter, perhaps, long to re-experience the alleged political excitements of the romanticized thirties, but find that they cannot do so? For it is pre-eminently a question about states of mind and intellectual attitudes, not about social movements. And it says something about the historical obtuseness of those who ask, "why no good radicals?" that they do not usually consider the obvious concomitant of their question, "why no Nazism, no fascism, no imperialism and no bourbonism?" If the absence of utopian feeling mattered only to that relatively small number of intellectuals who are distressed by their inability to dream as they once did, then it might concern a social psychologist, but it would scarcely interest the historian.

There is, however, more to the question than the temporary malaise of a few relics of the inter-war period. The questions "after socialism, what?" and "can we go on without utopias?" were already being asked before 1930, specifically by Karl Mannheim. Here, an entire theory of history and of the historical function of utopian thought was involved.[1] Mannheim's now celebrated proposition was that all the political thought of the past could be divided into two classes, the utopian and the ideological. The former was the "orientation" of those aspiring classes that aimed at the complete or partial overthrow of the social structure prevailing at the time. Ideology, on the other hand, was the typical outlook of the dominant classes, intent upon preserving the established order. It is, of course, more than questionable whether the vast variety of Europe's intellectual past can be squeezed into this Manichean strait-jacket. And, in fact, it was a perfectly deliberate falsification of history on Mannheim's part. As he blandly admitted, the historian's concern with actual differences, contrasts, and nuances was a mere nuisance to one who sought to uncover the "real," though hidden, patterns beneath the actual men and events of the past. As seen through the spectacles of the "sociology of knowledge," history *had* to show successive waves of revolutionary fervor as the chief constant feature of European intellectual and social life. This meant, among other things, that so marginal a figure as the "chiliastic" Thomas Müntzer had to be pushed to the very front ranks of intellectual luminaries. He was the first in a series that included such first-class thinkers as Condorcet and Marx. Karl Kautsky had indeed allowed Sir Thomas More to share with Müntzer the honor of being the first socialist, but he saw More rather as a unique intellectual prophet of the socialist future than as a mere class manifestation.[2] Mannheim, however, rejected Sir Thomas More summarily as a figure of no sociological significance in the "real" history of utopian thought. This entirely Marxian view of the past as dominated by incidents of revolutionary conduct and its reflected thought is of considerable importance, because it is what makes the contemporary absence of such zeal appear so entirely new, unique, and catastrophic and thus gives the question, "why no utopias?" its tense historical urgency. Certainly it had that effect upon Mannheim. If "art, culture and philosophy are nothing but the expression of the central utopia of the age, as shaped by contemporary social and political forces," then indeed the disappearance of utopia might well mean the end of civilization. And since Mannheim assumed that the classless society was at hand, and that no challenging, utopia-inspiring classes would again appear, the new "matter-of-factness" seemed threatening and ominous indeed. The disappearance of "reality-transcending doctrines" brings about "a static state of affairs in which man himself becomes no more than a thing" and in relinquishing utopia men lose the will to shape history and so the ability to understand it. What, above all, is to become of the heirs of Müntzer, Condorcet, and Marx, of the intellectual élite who, until now, have been the producers of utopias? Mannheim's response, natural under the circumstances, was to provide a blueprint of a future society to be run by an intellectual élite trained in the sociology of knowledge, capable of both transforming and controlling history in the interests of freedom, democracy, and rationality.[3]

Since the social role and ideas of the intellectuals are the central concern of the sociology of knowledge, and since Mannheim, unlike Marx, seemed to believe that this élite was of supreme importance in shaping the pattern of history, it is not at all surprising that their notions of utopia should have differed so much. While Mannheim accepted Marxian ideas about ideology, utopia was for him the intellectuals' vehicle of self-expression and it was they, not the voiceless classes, who ultimately shaped the ages. Yet Marx's and Engels' views on utopian thought were historically far more sound in at least one respect. The classical utopia, the critical utopia inspired by universal, rational morality and ideals of justice, the Spartan and ascetic utopia was already dead after the French Revolution. Doomed to impracticability, since the material conditions necessary for its realization had not been prevalent, the classical utopia could be admired even though it had lost its intellectual function with the rise of "scientific socialism." This judgment, according to Marx and Engels, was also applicable to such socialist precursors as Owen, Fourier, and Saint-Simon. Their successors, and indeed all non-Marxist socialists, were, however, utopians in a very different sense. For these rivals *were* in a position to understand the true course and future of bourgeois society and to act accordingly. *They* had the benefit of Marx's theories of surplus value and of dialectical materialism. They could recognize both his "scientific" truths and the necessity for revolutionary activity. Instead they produced "duodecimo editions of the New Jerusalem," preached the brotherhood of man to the bourgeoisie, and ignored the Eleventh Thesis against Feuerbach.[4] Here, "utopian" clearly becomes a mere term of opprobrium for un-Marxian, "unscientific" socialists. One wishes that Marx and Engels might have chosen another epithet. Certainly many useless verbal wrangles over the "true" meaning of the adjective "utopian" might have been avoided. What remains relevant in their views, however, is the serious importance they attached to the classical utopia and their recognition that it was a thing of the past because socialism had replaced it in their own age. To this, one must add that it was not only Marxian socialism, but all forms of socialism and, indeed, all the social belief systems (especially Social Darwinism) which prevailed in the nineteenth century, that joined in this task. Moreover, all of these, in spite of Mannheim's ideosyncratic vocabulary, are now called ideologies. In short, it was ideology that undid utopia after the French Revolution.

To understand why the classical utopia declined, not yesterday, but almost two hundred years ago, demands a more detailed analysis of its character than either Marx, Engels, or Mannheim offered. It also requires a return to that historical way of looking at the past which they despised, because it does not try to uncover "real" patterns, nor to establish laws. Instead of concentrating on paradigmatic, even if obscure, figures which fit a preconceived scheme, it looks at the acknowledged masters of utopian literature: at Sir Thomas More and his successors. Paradoxically, this utopia is a form of political literature that cannot possibly be fitted into either one of Mannheim's categories, for it is in no sense either revolutionary and future directed or designed to support the ruling classes. All the utopian writers who followed More's model were critical in two ways. In one way or another all were critical of some specific social institutions of their own time and place. But far more importantly, utopia was a way of rejecting that notion of "original sin" which regarded natural human virtue and reason as feeble and fatally impaired faculties. Whatever else the classical utopias might say or fail to say, all were attacks on the radical theory of original sin. Utopia is always a picture and a measure of the moral heights man could attain using only his natural powers, "purely by the natural light." As one writer put it, utopia is meant "to confound those who, calling themselves Christians, live worse than animals, although they are specially favored with grace, while pagans, relying on the light of nature manifest more virtue than the Reformed Church claims to uphold."[5] No one doubts the intensity of Sir Thomas More's Christian faith, but the fact remains that his Utopians are not Christians, "define virtue as living according to nature," pursue joy and pleasure and are all the better for it—which is, of course, the main point.[6]

The utopian rejection of original sin was, however, in *no sense* a declaration of historical hopefulness—quite the contrary. Utopia was, as Sir Thomas More put it, something "I wish rather than expect to see followed."[7] It is a vision not of the probable but of the "not-impossible." It was not concerned with the historically likely at all. Utopia is nowhere, not only geographically, but historically as well. It exists neither in the past nor in the future. Indeed, its esthetic and intellectual tension arises precisely from the melancholy contrast between what might be and what will be. And all utopian writers heightened this tension by describing in minute detail the institutions and daily lives of the citizens of utopia while their realization is scarcely mentioned. "Utopus" simply appears one day and creates utopia. This is very much in keeping with the Platonic metaphysics which inspired More and his imitators as late as Fénelon. For them, utopia was a model, an ideal pattern that invited contemplation and judgment but did not entail any other activity. It is a perfection that the mind's eye recognizes as true and which is described as such, and so serves as a standard of moral judgment. As Miss Arendt has said, "in (Platonic contemplation) the beholding of the model, which . . . no longer is to guide any doing, is prolonged and enjoyed for its own sake."[8] As such it is an expression of the craftsman's desire for perfection and permanence. That is why utopia, the moralist's artifact, is of necessity a changeless harmonious whole, in which a shared recognition of truth unites all the citizens. Truth is single and only error is multiple. In utopia, there cannot, by definition, be any room for eccentricity. It is also profoundly radical, as Plato was; for all historical actuality is here brought to judgment before the bar of trans-historical values and is found utterly wanting.

If history can be said to play any part at all in the classical utopia, it does so only in the form of an anguished recollection of antiquity, of the polis and of the Roman Republic of virtuous memory. This is a marked feature also of utopias not indebted to Platonic metaphysics, even those of libertine inspiration. The institutional arrangements of Plato's *Laws,* Plutarch's *Lycurgus,* and Roman history also served as powerful inspirations to the utopian imagination. Thus, to the melancholy contrast between the possible and the probable was added the sad confrontation between a crude and dissolute Europe and the virtue and unity of classical antiquity. It is this, far more than the prevalence of Platonic guardians, perfected and effective education, and rationalist asceticism, ubiquitous as these are, that marks utopia as an intellectualist fantasy. Until relatively recently nothing separated the educated classes from all others more definitely than the possession of laboriously gained classical learning. It might be more correct to say classicism possessed them. They identified themselves more deeply and genuinely with the dead of Athens and Rome than with their own despised and uncouth contemporaries. And inasmuch as utopia was built on classical lines it expressed the values and concerns of the intellectuals. It was to them, not to unlettered lords or peasants, that it was addressed. As such, it was the work of a socially isolated sensibility, again not a hope-inspiring condition. But it survived even the literary and scientific victory of the Moderns over the

Ancients. Nothing seemed to shake the long-absorbed sense of the moral and political superiority of classical man. That is why wistful Spartan utopias were still being written in the second half of the eighteenth century.

Of course, the political utopia, with its rational city-planning, eugenics, education, and institutions, is by no means the only vision of a perfect life. The golden age of popular imagination has always been known, its main joy being food—and lots of it— without any work. Its refined poetic counterpart, the age of innocence, in which men are good without conscious virtue, has an equally long history. The state of innocence can exist, moreover, side by side with a philosophic utopia and illuminate the significance of the latter. Plato's Age of Kronos and Fénelon's Boetica, in which wisdom is spontaneous, are set beside rational, Spartan-style models.[9] The state of innocence is what moral reason must consciously recreate to give form and coherence to what all men can feel and imagine as a part, however remote, of their natural endowment. Both utopias, in different ways, try to represent a timeless "ought" that never "is."

Among the utopias that do not owe anything to classical antiquity at least one deserves mention here: the utopia of pure condemnation. Of this genre Swift is the unchallenged master, with Diderot as a worthy heir. The king of Brobdingnag, the city of giants, of supermen, that is, notes, after he hears Gulliver's account of European civilization, that its natives must be "the most pernicious Race of little odious Vermin that Nature ever suffered to crawl upon the Surface of the Earth." A comparison of his utopian supra-human kingdom with those of Europe could yield no other conclusion. Gulliver, then, tastes the delights of a non-human society of horses, an experience which leaves him, like his author, with an insurmountable loathing for his fellow-Yahoos. Here, utopia serves only to condemn not merely Europe, whether ancient or modern, but the human louse as such. To the extent that Diderot's account of Tahiti slaps only at European civilization, it can be said to be more gentle. However, after observing the superiority of primitive life, his European travelers return home wiser in recognizing the horrors of their religion, customs, and institutions, but in no way capable or hopeful of doing anything about them. The aim, as in Swift, is to expose absurdity and squalor simply for the sake of bringing them into full view.

This all too brief review of classical utopia should suffice to show how little "activism" or revolutionary optimism or future-directed hope there is in this literature. It is neither ideology nor utopia in Mannheim's sense, but then neither is most of the great critical political literature before the end of the eighteenth century. Machiavelli, Bodin, Hobbes, Rousseau: were they "reactionary ideologues" because they were not "revolutionary utopists"? Significantly, it is only during the course of the English Civil War that action-minded utopists appear. However, even the two most notable among them, Harrington and Hartlib, were concerned with constitutional and educational reform, respectively, rather than with full-scale utopias. Nevertheless, for once imminent realization was envisaged. As for poor Winstanley and his little band of Diggers, they have merely been forced to play the English Müntzer in Marxian historiography in search of precursors and paradigms. These were all voices in the wilderness, part of a unique revolutionary situation. It is only as partial exceptions to the rule that they are really illuminating. They seem only to show how unrevolutionary the general course of utopian thought and political thinking was before the age inaugurated by the French Revolution. The end of utopian literature did not mark the end of hope; on the contrary, it coincided with the birth of historical optimism.

Utopia was not the only casualty of the revolution in political thought. Plutarchian great-man historiography and purely critical political philosophy were never the same again either. Nor was it solely a matter of the new theory of historical progress. As Condorcet, one of the first and most astute of its authors, observed, the real novelties of the future were democracy and science, and they demanded entirely new ways of looking at politics. If a democratic society was to understand itself it would need a new history: "the history of man," of all the inconspicuous and voiceless little people who constitute humanity and who have now replaced the star actors on the historical stage. The various historical systems of the nineteenth century, with their "laws"—whether progressive, evolutionist, dialectical, positivist, or not—were all, in spite of their endless deficiencies, efforts to cope with this new history. To write the history of the inarticulate majority, of those groups in society which do not stand out and therefore must be discovered, was a task so new and so difficult that it is scarcely surprising that it should not have succeeded. After all, contemporary sociology is, in a wiser and sadder mood, still plodding laboriously to accomplish it. As for science, Condorcet recognized not only that technology, that is, accumulated and applied knowledge, would transform material and social life, but also that science was not just an acquisition, but an entirely new outlook. With its openmindedness and experimentalism it had to replace older modes of thought which were incompatible with it. As such it was not only the vehicle of progress, but also the sole way in which the new society-in-change could be understood and guided. Scientific thought was inherently a call to action. The new world, as Condorcet saw it, would be so unlike the old that its experiences could be grasped, expressed, and formed only by those who adopted the openness of scientific attitudes.[10] It was this that his systematizing successors, the victims of classical habits of thought, did not appreciate in the slightest. Whatever one may think of Condorcet's own historiography with its simple challenge-and-response ladder of improvement, he, at least, had the great merit of understanding why classical history and critical political theory had to be replaced by more democratic, dynamic, and activist social ideas.

Given the revolutionary changes of nineteenth-century Europe, the preoccupations of the classical utopists were no longer relevant. Original sin and the critical model were not vital interests. Marx, in spite of his protestations, was not the only one to take over the critical functions of the old utopists and to expand them into a relentlessly future-directed activism. All his rivals were just as intent upon action as he was. It was merely that some of them thought, as Saint-Simon had, that philosophers would exercise the most significant and effective authority by ruling over public opinion, rather than by participating directly in political action. Thus "the philosopher places himself at the summit of thought. From there he views the world as it has been and as it must become. *He is not only an observer. He is an actor.* [Italics added.] He is an actor of the first rank in the moral world because it is his opinions on what the world must become which regulate human society."[11] This bit of intellectualist megalomania could be illustrated by endless quotations not only from socialist sources, but also from liberal writings and from the distressed conservative deprecators of both.

The activism of the age was, moreover, not a random one. The future was all plotted out, and beckoning. "The Golden Age lies before us and not behind us, and is not far away."[12] The inevitable had only to be hastened on. Certainly there was no point in contemplating the classical past. However, the impact of the polis was not quite gone. Especially in socialist thought, even if not so openly as in Jacobin rhetoric, the ancient republic was still an inspiration.

The ideal of its unity, of its homogeneous order, colored all their visions of the future. Certainly Marx was no stranger to the nostalgia for that cohesive city or its medieval communal counterpart. It was the liberal Benjamin Constant who noted that efforts to impose the political values of classical antiquity upon the totally dissimilar modern world could lead only to forms of despotism, which, far from being classical, would be entirely new.[13] John Stuart Mill, following him, found this notion, "that all perfection consists in unity," to be precisely the most repellent aspect of Comte's philosophy.[14] Indeed, the engineered community, whose perfect order springs not from a rational perception of truth, but from a pursuit of social unity as a material necessity, provides neither ancient nor modern liberty. The imagery is revealing. Cabet delighted in the vision of factory workers who displayed "so much order and discipline that they looked like an army."[15] Bellamy's "industrial army" speaks for itself.

The form of such works as Cabet's *Voyage to Icaria* and Bellamy's *Looking Backward* should not lead one to think that these pictures of perfected societies are in any sense utopias. Precisely because they affect the external format of the classical utopia they demonstrate most effectively the enormous differences between the old and new ways of thought. The nineteenth-century imaginary society is not "nowhere" historically. It is a future society. And, it too is a summons to action. The purpose of Cabet's expedition to set up Icaria in America was not simply to establish a small island of perfection; it was to be a nucleus from which a world of Icarias would eventually spring. No sooner had Bellamy's work appeared than Bellamy societies, often (and not surprisingly) sponsored by retired army officers, appeared to promote his ideas. Theodore Hertzka's *Freeland* led to similar organized efforts, as its author had hoped it would. He declared frankly that the imaginary society was merely a device to popularize social ideas which he regarded as practical and scientifically sound. This, in itself, suffices to account for the literary feebleness of virtually all nineteenth-century quasi-utopias. There was nothing in them that could not have been better presented in a political manifesto or in a systematic treatise. They were all vulgarizations and were devised solely to reach the largest possible audience. The form of the classical utopia was inseparable from its content. Both were part of a single conception. The social aspirations of the nineteenth century found their literary form in the realistic novel, not in the crude and unstylish fiction of social theorists turned amateur romancers. Even the "utopias" based on scientific, rather than social, predictions were either childish or tedious. Either their fancies displayed no insight into the real potentialities of technology or, if they were well-informed, they were rendered obsolete by the actual developments of technology. Not even the last and most talented of latter-day contrivers of imaginary societies, H. G. Wells, could save the genre. He at least saw that his utopia had nothing in common with the classical works of that name. Now the perfect model is in the future, that is, it has a time and a place and is, indeed, already immanent in the present. It must be world-wide, devoted to science, to progress, to change, and it must allow for individuality. Only the intellectual ruling class of "samurai" is left to remind one of the classical past.[17] As a liberal socialist, Wells was, no doubt, especially aware of the need to root out the remnants of that illiberal, self-absorbed, and closed social order which classicism had left as its least worthy gift to the democratic imagination. However, the novel of the happy future did not prosper in Wells' or in any other hands. For it was simply superfluous. Its message could be presented in many more suitable ways. Certainly it was in no way a continuation of the classical utopian tradition.

It has of late been suggested that the radicalism of the last century was a form of "messianism," of "millennialism," or of a transplanted eschatological consciousness. Psychologically this may be quite true in the sense that for many of the people who participated in radical movements social ideologies fed religious longings that traditional religions could not satisfy. These people may even have been responding to the same urges as the members of the medieval revolutionary millennialist sects. In this sense one may well regard radical ideology as a surrogate for unconventional religiosity. It should, however, not be forgotten that millennialism always involves an element of eternal salvation.[18] And this was entirely absent in the message of even those social prophets who called for new religions as a means of bringing social discipline to Europe. For them it was only a matter of social policy, not of supraterrestrial truth. Marxism and social Darwinism, moreover, did not even involve this degree of "new" religiosity. Whatever they did for the fanaticized consciousness that eagerly responded to them, the intellectual structure of radical doctrines was not a prophetic heresy either in form or in intent. It represented an entirely new chapter in European thought. As Condorcet had clearly seen, it was a matter of new responses to a new social world; and the aspirations, methods of argument, and categories of thought of these historical systems were correspondingly unique, however primordial the human yearnings that they could satisfy might be. One ought not to forget the rational element, the effort of intellectual understanding that is perfectly evident in the writings of Saint-Simon, Marx, Comte, and all the rest. The various political revolutions after 1789 gave more than a semblance of reality to a vision of social history as a perpetual combat between the forces of progress and of conservatism. Conservative and liberal social observers no less than socialists took that view of historical dynamics. Even John Stuart Mill, who recognized that the categories of order and progress were inadequate concepts for a deeper analysis of politics, could see the past as a sequence of struggles between freedom and repression.[19] The theory of class war was by no means the only one that, in a projection of nineteenth-century experience into the past, saw the history of Europe as a series of duels. Some saw it as progress, some as doom, but all perceived the same pattern. Looking back, of course, the century before the First World War appears infinitely more complicated than that, and so do the eras preceding it. However, if it is quite understandable why one should be sensitive to pluralistic social complexities today, it is also not difficult to see why dualistic patterns tended to dominate the historical imagination of the nineteenth century. Nor is it totally irrational that the experience of these rapid changes, so unlike those of the past, should lead men to entertain great expectations of the future. Neither the view of history as a dualistic combat of impersonal social forces nor the confident belief in a better future which would at last bring rest to mankind was a "millennial" fancy, nor was either really akin to the chiliastic religious visions that inspired that apocalyptic sects. If they were not utopias, neither were they New Jerusalem. The desire to stress similarities, to find continuities everywhere, is not always helpful, especially in the history of ideas, where the drawing of distinctions is apt to lead one more nearly to the truth.

The reason that ideology has been represented so often as a type of religiosity is, of course, a response to the terrifying fervor expressed by the members of modern mass-movements. It is the emotional element in Nazism, communism, and other revolutionary movements all over the world that is so reminiscent of many of the old popular heresies. The dynamism of mass parties, however, is really at stake here, not the actual systems of ideas which were produced in such great quantity by nineteenth-century Europe. Ideology, however, when it refers to those systems of ideas which were capable of replacing all the inherited forms of social thought, utopia among them, was clearly more significant intellectually than the brutish "isms" that animate both the leaders and the led of these movements. The latter should not be confused with either ideology, or utopia, or even with the religious extravagances of other ages. Nor is the question, "why no utopias?" really concerned with the organization of mass-parties. Indeed, even in Mannheim's theory, utopia and ideology refer to highly developed modes of thought and not to quasi-instinctive mental reactions. If, unlike Mannheim, one does not identify utopia with the charted mission of the intellectual class, one can recognize that "the end of utopia" involves not sociological, but philosophical, issues. It is the concern of political theory—of the high culture of social thought. What is really at stake is the realization that the disintegration of nineteenth-century ideology has not made it possible simply to return to classical-critical theory, of which utopia was a part. The post-ideological state of mind is not a classical one, any more than an ex-Christian is a pagan. On the contrary, the end of the great ideological systems may well also mark the exhaustion of the last echo of classicism in political theory, even if, occasionally, a nostalgic appreciation for the integral classicism of the more distant past can still be heard.

The occasional contemporary efforts to construct pictures of perfect communities illustrate the point. They are compromises between the old utopia and the newer historical consciousness. Thus, for example, Martin Buber and Paul Goodman argue only for the historical non-impossibility of their plans, not for their inevitability. *Kvuzas,* or perfectly planned cities, are feasible, and certainly their admirers hope for their realization.[20] These are still calls to action, but modest ones. Their scope, moreover, is limited, and their very essence is a revival of that dream of the polis, of the "authentic" small community that truly absorbs and directs the lives of its inhabitants. These relatively mild and moderate proposals, and the more general concern with *real* community life, do show, among other things, the lingering power of classical values. Here the longing for utopia and nostalgia for antiquity are inseparable. And indeed the question, "why is there no utopia?" expresses not only an urge to return to antiquity, but also, and far more importantly, a sense of frustration at our inability to think as creatively as the ancients apparently did.

Classicism, in one form or another, was, as we have seen, an integral part not only of utopia, but also of most political thinking. Hobbes and Bentham in their firm rejection of the conventional classical model were intellectually far more radical than the later ideologists. For in spite of occasional liberal protests, socialist doctrines were by no means the only ones that contrived to perpetuate classical notions throughout the nineteenth century. Long after Platonic mataphysics and the critical-contemplative mode of thought had been abandoned, classical imagery and values retained their hold on the political imagination, and classical methods of description and argument continued to mold the expression of political ideas in a social context in which classicism had ceased to be relevant. In this respect, all the ideologies served to retard political thinking. Their decline now has left political theory without any clear orientation and so with a sense of uneasiness. It is not that political theory is dead, as has often been claimed, but that so much of it consists of an incantation of clichés which seem to have no relation to social experiences whose character is more sensed than expressed. Could it be that classicism, not only as a set of political values and memories, but as a legacy of words, conceptions, and images, acts as a chain upon our imagination? Is it not, perhaps, that language, mental habits, and categories of thought organically related to a social world completely unlike our own are entirely unsuitable for expressing our experiences? May this not be the cause of our inability to articulate what we feel and see, and to bring order into what we know? Certainly a vocabulary and notions dependent upon Greek and Latin can no longer be adequate to discuss our social life-situation. Nor will the continual addition of implausible neologisms composed of more Greek and Latin words help, for they do not affect the structure of thinking. The malaise induced by this state of affairs is responsible for much of the ill-tempered and ill-informed hostility of many humanists toward the natural sciences which do not share these inherited difficulties. It also accounts for many ill-considered efforts to "imitate" science by the metaphorical or analogical use of words drawn from biology or physics. Nor is analytical philosophy of much use, for it does not address itself to concerns which are more nearly felt than spoken and which involve not so much what can be said as the difficulty of saying anything at all. To be sure, nostalgia is the least adequate response of all to these discomforts. And that is just what the question, "why is there no utopia?" does express in this context.

With these considerations, the question, "why is there no utopia today?" has, hopefully, been reduced to its proper proportions, which are not very great. To the extent that it depends on an erroneous and dated view of the European past, it is simply irrelevant. As a psychological problem its interest is great, but of a clinical nature. Lastly, it is only one item in the far more complex range of questions that concern the possibilities of contemporary political philosophy. Here, however, it does at least have genuine significance, even though it does not ask for an answer. For it is more a comment upon an intellectual situation than a real query. That is why a journey, however quick, through the utopian and ideological past seemed a fitting response, since it might show what the question implies, even if it does not offer any solutions.

References

1. Karl Mannheim, *Ideology and Utopia,* tr. by Louis Wirth and Edward Shils (New York: Harvest Books, n.d.), pp. 193, 195-197, 205, 222, 255-257, 263, et passim.
2. Karl Kautsky, *Thomas More and his Utopia,* tr. by H. J. Stenning (New York: Russell, 1959), pp. 1-3, 171.
3. Karl Mannheim, *Freedom, Power and Democratic Planning* (New York: Oxford University Press, 1950).
4. Lewis S. Feuer, ed., *Marx and Engels: Basic Writings* (New York: Anchor Books, 1959), pp. 37-39, 70, 81, 90, 245.
5. Gabriel de Foigny, *Terra Australis Incognita,* in Glenn Negley and J. Max Patrick, *The Quest for Utopia. An Anthology of Imaginary Societies* (New York: Schuman, 1952), p. 402.
6. Sir Thomas More, *Utopia,* tr. and ed. by H. V. S. Ogden (New York: Appleton-Century-Crofts, 1949), pp. 48-49.
7. *Ibid.,* p. 83.
8. Hannah Arendt, *The Human Condition* (Chicago: University of Chicago Press, 1958), p. 303.
9. H. C. Baldry, *Ancient Utopias* (Southampton: University of Southampton, 1956); Fénelon, *The Adventures of Telemachus,* in Negley and Patrick, *op. cit.,* pp. 424-437.
10. A.-N. de Condorcet, *Sketch for the Historical Picture of the Progress of the Human Mind,* tr. by June Barraclough (London: Weidenfeld and Nicolson, 1955), pp. 163-164, 168-170, 184-202.

11. Quoted in Frank E. Manuel, *The New World of Henri de Saint-Simon* (Cambridge: Harvard University Press, 1956), p. 151.

12. Edward Bellamy, quoted in Negley and Patrick, *op. cit.*, p. 80.

13. *Ouevres* (Paris: Bibliothèque de la Pléiade, 1957), pp. 1044-1058.

14. J. S. Mill, *The Positive Philosophy of Auguste Comte* (New York: H. Holt and Co., 1873), p. 128.

15. Etienne Cabet, *Voyage to Icaria,* in M. L. Berneri, *Journey Through Utopia* (London: Routledge & Kegan Paul, 1950), p. 234.

16. Negley and Patrick, *op. cit.*, pp. 77-78, 108, 134-135.

17. H. G. Wells, *A Modern Utopia,* in Negley and Patrick, *op. cit.*, pp. 228-250.

18. On this important point, see Sylvia L. Thrupp, "Introduction," in *Millennial Dreams in Action, Comparative Studies in Society and History* (The Hague: Mouton, 1962), p. 11.

19. J. S. Mill, *Representative Government,* in *Utilitarianism* (London: Everyman's Library, 1944), pp. 186-192, in contrast to the dialectical argument of *On Liberty.*

20. Martin Buber, *Paths in Utopia,* tr. by R. F. C. Hull (London: Routledge & Kegan Paul, 1949), pp. 127-148; Paul Goodman, *Utopian Essays and Critical Proposals* (New York: Vintage Books, 1964), pp. 3-22, 110-118; and Paul and Percival Goodman, *Communitas* (New York: Vintage Books, 1960), passim.

ADAM ULAM

Socialism and Utopia

I

Socialism and utopia. Those two words were once thought to be closely associated, if indeed not synonymous. With all due respect to Sir Thomas More's copyright, creation of utopias is a nineteenth-century phenomenon and so is socialism. To seek salvation on this earth, to achieve human perfectibility in this life would have been almost inconceivable before the onset of rationalism. The wonders and miseries of the industrial age prompted the search for a haven of peace and contentment where science and technology could reign and bestow their benefactions, but from which their fellow travelers, business and competition, would be sternly excluded. Nothing is more productive of intellectual discontent than material progress. The vistas of infinite improvement when seen through the reality of squalor and human degradation lead to an impassioned protest and a reassertion of the golden age, this time thrust into the future.

The organic connection between socialism and utopia becomes more evident when we contemplate the contemporary scene. Seemingly, socialism is the ideology of our age. Regimes which proclaim themselves to be socialist rule one third of mankind. Just as in the nineteenth century no Balkan country could become independent without its leaders doffing their picturesque native costumes, donning frock coats, striped trousers, top hats, and liberalism, and talking in the jargon of John Stuart Mill and Gladstone, so today the independence of Zambia or Algeria is instantaneously followed by the local leaders proclaiming their adherence to an "African" or "Arab" brand of socialism. But in reality socialism as an ideology has become sterile and unexciting. Scratch its Chinese or Russian brand and below the thin veneer of Marxism-Leninism you will find intense nationalism which for purposes of defense and expansion propagates the old slogans and ideas. In the West, socialism as a philosophy rather than a ritual still lingers on. But even there it has in practice coalesced with one or another version of the welfare state. Various Western philosophers, unwilling to relinquish completely their youthful enthusiasms and resentments, are busily rummaging in young Marx trying to clear him of the responsibility for the more deplorable aspects of Leninism and Stalinism. But even that venture proceeds without the zest and faith (the all-important word) of the earlier creators of socialism and utopias.

In fact, it has been the decline of utopian thinking that has seriously damaged the capacity of socialism to stir up emotions of fear or hope. Even in that least utopian of socialisms, in Marxism, it is the vision of the final and frankly utopian phase of social development, of communism, which is responsible for much of its appeal. A society of perfect equality and harmony is the final promise of Marxism, the promise which has enabled it to offset the anarchists' charge that it proposed to displace a multitude of capitalists by one, the state. Yet, how meager has been the residue of this promise. When the then heir of Marx, Nikita Khrushchev, attempted in 1961 to portray the blessings of communism, which the Soviet people are scheduled to enter in 1980, he could think of nothing more imaginative than production of two hundred million tons of steel and free rides on buses and railways. Those are not the kinds of things which stir men's hearts and imaginations.

At the other end of the socialist spectrum a similar disenchantment, "de-utopianism," has stolen in. Wrote Sir William Beveridge in the document which was the foundation of the British Labour Party's victory in 1945, "The suggestion of this Report is that we should find that common objective in determination to make a Britain free of the giant evils of Want, Disease, Ignorance and Squalor."[1] How unassuming in comparison, and prosaic, are the postulates under which the Labour Party won its modest victory in 1964! To close the gap in the balance of payments, to arrest the brain drain, to deprive the upper classes of their still remaining guilty pleasures and pretensions—those are the tasks which British socialism sets before itself. Sir William's manifesto seemed to promise immortality, something which was overlooked even by the most caustic critics of his Report and its adaptation in Labour's program (how else can one interpret the promise to abolish disease?). Mr. Wilson and his colleagues promise to restore solvency and industrial efficiency.

How can one explain this simultaneous decline of socialism and utopia? There are a number of ready answers. We *do* live in a precarious utopia. Those wonderful advances of science which have made possible abolition of so many social evils may also lead to abolition of civilized life. How can one retain a childlike belief in the power of science to work unconditionally beneficent miracles, or in utopias, or in that unhesitating socialism which so stirred our predecessors?

Or, another explanation: we have grown jaded and disillusioned with promises of infinite improvement, of a basic and vast transformation of the conditions of human existence. Freud has left some melancholy observations on this count, and, though most of the psychoanalysts and his lay devotees have adhered to the cause of progress, his warnings hover over this Freudian world of ours. The disillusionment with the dreams of human perfectibility and with the (mostly socialist) utopias of the past has given rise in our times to literary fantasies which can be described as anti-utopias. They range from works like Zamiatin's *We,* an early protest against Soviet society, to more generalized versions of the future horrors of mechanization and collectivism such as *Brave New World* and *1984.* The golden age is once again seen to lie in the past. For all the sufferings and imperfections of the pre-1914 Western civilization, the individual was less trammeled by the state and society. And for all his religious and superstitious fears, the average man was free of *the* fear: that the basis of civilized life, if indeed not its physical continuity, could be utterly destroyed. What are all our advances in comfort, in mechanical contrivances, and in social justice against this fear?

The anti-utopias present a counsel of despair. In the most masochistic of them, *1984,* even the catharsis of total destruction is excluded in order to make the picture of perfect totalitarianism more horrifying. But in a way they are related to a much older and wiser train of anti-utopian thinking: the conservative tradition which considers both economic and scientific progress irrelevant to the problem of human happiness. If the anti-utopian despairs of human progress, then the conservative ranges between resignation and amusement: it really does not make that much difference.

For all their triteness, the sum of all those explanations accounts for the absence of contemporary utopias and for the slackening of socialist fervor in the post-World War II period. But if one wants to find out the organic connection of those two currents of thought, one must go beyond generalities and examine elements in their past.

II

Modern socialism was born out of nostalgia for an idealized past. Hence its frequent similarities to conservatism. Both ideologies share a dislike of business and industrialism (or, as in the case of Marxism, of the *industrialists*); both profess a solicitude for the common man; both have an essentially religious temperament. Some temperamental traits go even deeper: for both the right and the left wing opponent of nineteenth-century capitalism, the Jew was very often the embodiment of forces which were disrupting the allegedly idyllic pre-industrial life. For longer than most historians of socialism like to admit, various socialist sects and movements have preserved a strong undertone of anti-Semitism. *The People's Will,* the Russian revolutionary socialist organization of the late seventies and eighties, was not above occasional anti-Jewish propaganda; and the original attitude of some French Socialists toward the Dreyfus affair bears traces of the same sentiment.

Anti-intellectualism also seems to be a strange charge against the movement which has among its fathers Saint-Simon and Marx. But the history of the early stirrings of the radical and social protest is full of it. The beginnings of Marxism in Russia are very instructive in that respect. There was in the 1890's a very strong movement among various socialist clubs in favor of the proposition that the workers should run their own organizations and that the intelligentsia should stay away from them. Such ideas were propagated by young intellectuals themselves, an incongruity far from startling in a movement whose history is replete with paradoxes.

Those unattractive birthmarks of socialism show how deep are its roots in the opposition to changes wrought by the industrial revolution. That Marxism is so strongly oriented toward technology and science obscures the fact that the sentiments it seeks to exploit are essentially those of anti-industrialism and of hostility to urban civilization. It condemns "the idiocy of rural life," yet it appeals shamelessly to the longing for a purer and uncomplicated agrarian society. Young Engels wrote of the disappearing English craftsman-peasant in words which in their unhistoricism do not yield to the somber lamentations of a utopian socialist—or a conservative:

> True, he was a bad farmer and managed his land inefficiently; nevertheless, he was no proletarian; he had a stake in the country, he was permanently settled and stood one step higher in society than the English workman of today. . . . They did not need to overwork . . . they were, for the most part strong, well built people. . . .[2]

This noble savage was torn from the soil, from his wholesome and productive occupation and then squeezed into a miserable hovel in Manchester or Liverpool, rendered a helpless slave of the Machine and the Market. The same note is struck by William Morris, a quite different type of socialist:

. . . [England] became a country of huge and foul workshops and fouler gambling dens surrounded by an ill-kept poverty-stricken farm pillaged by the masters of the workshops. It is now a garden, where nothing is wasted and nothing is spoilt with the necessary dwellings, sheds and workshops scattered up and down the country all trim and neat and pretty. . . . Like the medievals we like everything trim and clean, and orderly and bright. . . .[3]

The modern historian, unless a hopeless reactionary, presses hurriedly over the obscurantism and sentimentality of much of the early socialist thought. But it does not discredit a theory to point out that its author was not a nice man, or that his private actions, alas, did not square with his public philosophy. The validity of Marxism is not damaged merely by the fact that its father was an irascible man capable of unkind remarks about Jews, Slavs, and Germans. Bakunin's venomous anti-Semitism does not strip him of the right to belong in the pantheon of the fighters for freedom. Herzen's concern for the Russian peasant was not a bit less genuine because of his speculation (financial, not political) on the victory of the slave-owning South in the Civil War. One might argue, in fact, that it is only natural that a great humanitarian's exertions on behalf of mankind leave him less capable of attending to and correcting his personal weaknesses.

It is equally indiscreet and dangerous to push too far the analogy between the emotional basis of socialism and that of such movements as fascism and national socialism. Dislike of the modern city with its hustle and bustle inspired William Morris to write his absurd communist utopia. Not much later, awe and hatred of Vienna, of the anonymity and cosmopolitanism of a great city's life, led an unemployed painter to formulate the first premises of his hideous philosophy. Morris thought that the Parliament buildings could be better employed by having fertilizer stored in them. One remembers the frantic rage into which Lenin would erupt at the mere mention of the word parliamentarism. The gentle dreams of a Kropotkin, or a Blatchford, their complaints that modern industrial organization has stripped life of its spontaneity and charm have found harsh echoes in the Nazis' "blood and soil" and in the corporative state of the Fascists, from which the ignoble motivations of profit and class interest were also to be expelled. But such analogies can hardly be used as the basis for accusations against socialism or individual socialist thinkers. They appealed to the same emotions and often exploited the same fears and superstitions, but their conclusions were different.

However, it would be both squeamish and unreasonable not to acknowledge the common fund of radicalism to which both the extreme right and the extreme left have made their appeal in the struggle against modern industrial civilization. For lack of a better word, this common fund might be called anarchism. It is engendered by an agrarian society undergoing the birthpains of industrialization. The classical model is that of Western Europe during the first half of the nineteenth century. Here we see masses of formerly rural population being transformed into the city proletariat. To the common man, the apparently mysterious forces deprive him of his livelihood on land or in his craft and compel him to sell his labor to the entrepreneur, the hated capitalist. Though economic historians will never tire of pointing out that the workman's miserable standard of living still represented an advance over his previous status, such statistics could hardly be convincing to the victim of progress. His previous mode of existence, or that of his father, appeared to have been "natural"; his present, as an appendage of the machine, monstrously wrong. People who today advocate urban renewal sometimes run into traces of the same psychology: more comfortable dwelling does not seem to compensate for loss of the feeling of neighborhood; the "naturalness" of a broken-down house in the slums is prized perversely over a more comfortable apartment. In a "stable" agrarian society almost everybody could consider himself a proprietor of some kind, even in the humble capacity of tenant. In industrial society, as the *Communist Manifesto* convincingly argued, property for the majority in its meaningful sense, in land or in tools of one's work, was destroyed.

From a similar perspective, preindustrial life must have appeared harmonious and bereft of the catastrophic fluctuations and crises which characterize a commercial and industrial society. Droughts, famines, and the like are forgotten or minimized when contrasted with the instability which in the industrial order is the rule. A new technological invention, constant advances of science, even the improvements in medicine which lengthen life and decrease infant mortality, all lead to periodic overcrowding of the labor market, to loss of jobs, and to complete uncertainty about the future. It is thus understandable how in the earliest types of socialist and reactionary thinking it is the machine which is asserted to be the enemy of the poor and technological progress itself which is said to be responsible for enslaving the masses. A man as intelligent as William Cobbett still could believe that the preindustrial age was one of prosperity and universal contentment and that the population of England had declined as the consequence of industrialization and mechanization. The Luddites were simply the most primitive and direct among those who held the machine a diabolical invention destined to ruin the livelihood of millions and to accumulate all wealth in the hands of a few capitalists.

It was equally easy to idealize the political past. In the preindustrial age the average man was hardly aware of the phenomenon of the state. The system of authority under which he found himself was traditional and thus appeared natural. But even the earliest liberal state becomes a welter of laws and regulations, its very pruning of the archaic and obsolete laws having the appearance of constant legislative revolution. The character of this revolution is only too clearly to bolster the interests of industry and commerce, in brief, of the capitalist. The state, whether it enforces the New Poor Law, calls upon armed force to quell popular uprisings and disturbances, or bestows franchise upon the new commercial classes—including Jews and Dissenters—is thus acting in the interest of the capitalist; it becomes the executive committee of the exploiting class.

The sum of those reactions could not fail to produce a frame of mind which has endured to our own day and which has provided the most fertile soil for radicalism of both left and right. The appeal of anti-industrialism is perennial. Even in the countries most imbued with the industrial ethos, a national disaster or an economic crisis will revive the anti-industrial feeling and will clothe it in new, to be sure, more sophisticated, forms of social protest and theories. In Britain the defeat of Chartism and the triumph of liberalism in politics and economics appeared forever to blot out the old beliefs and superstitions. Karl Marx, whose system and prophecies had been based so much upon the observable tendencies of the English social development of the first half of the nineteenth century, lived to realize, with despair in his heart, how in the first industrial country in the world earlier political turbulence gave way to acquiescence in capitalism, and earlier socialism to tame trade unionism. Yet the slackening of English industrial dynamism led to a rebirth of socialism. Some of its more eccentric varieties, like guild socialism, hearkened back to the anti-industrialism of the left wing of the Chartist movement, repeated the absurd notions of the harmony and stability of the preindustrial age, and sought to impose a quasi-medievalism upon the age of industry and science. Today, such ideas are hardly allowed to protrude from behind the welfare-oriented and bureaucratically-tempered main current of British socialism. No one calls, as the more lyrical of Labour spokesmen did between the two wars, for the creation of a new Jerusalem in England's green and pleasant land. One reason is that a "new Jerusalem" in the opinion of the vast majority of the electorate includes a car for every household—and how can that be reconciled with greenery? But the statesmen and captains of industry of the period of Britain's greatness, who in the past had enjoyed such a good press, have of recent years been increasingly blamed for their alleged heartlessness and devotion to purely material goals. Marx and other critics of triumphant liberalism, so condescendingly tolerated and ignored in their lifetime, have had their revenge.

What stifled the appeal of anti-industrial anarchism in the nineteenth century was a utopia. To be sure, it was not a usual type of nineteenth-century utopia either in its plea or in its format, but a utopia nevertheless. It was the vision of a society where wonders would be achieved by those very evils decried by the anti-industrialists: technology and the love of gain. Wars, superstitions, diseases would be conquered by the progress of science and by the prudent attention of every man to his material advancement. Poverty would be eliminated not by philanthropy or public assistance but by the inevitable progress of science and education. The liberal utopians saw as the greatest obstacles to the realization of their dreams our anti-industrialist friends: the quarrelsome agitators who wanted to perpetuate and exploit popular superstitions, the benevolent prelates, mainly of the Anglican and Catholic persuasion, who justly saw in material progress the frightful threat of secularism, and those disgruntled economists and other intellectuals who in every generation oppose the status quo.

But such was the strength and vigor of the liberal utopia that it even achieved the domination of the intellectual world. There are few examples of an ideology being capable at once of dominating political, economic, and intellectual life of society to the extent that liberalism did in the West during the second half of the nineteenth century. Its victory was nowhere so complete as in England, and even there one can find major dissonances and departures from the canon: for example, social legislation beginning in the forties, first steps toward collectivism which Dicey dates from 1870, and the rising popularity of imperialism, a cardinal sin in the eyes of a strict liberal, which dates from about the same time. But all in all, it is difficult to exaggerate the extent of the triumph of the doctrine.

The reasons for it must be found not only in the prosaic fact that capitalism-liberalism "worked," that is, an increasing number of people felt its benefits. It carried the day largely because it was utopian, because it promised blessings and a universality, which no rational analysis of its premises and the world conditions could really justify. Like every other successful ideology, liberalism scorned an apologetic tone and sociological sophistication. Free enterprise was considered not only socially beneficent but also morally imperative. The future scope of the system was to embrace not only Europe but the whole world. Equally impressive was its lack of historical sense, in which respect it rivaled anti-industrial radicalism: for all the historical sophistication of its theorists, the average devotee blamed all the troubles of the world from its beginning to the end of the eighteenth century on ignorance of the doctrines of Adam Smith, Bentham, and Ricardo.

Liberalism was irrational in its very claims upon human rationality. It expected people to give up those quarrels, prejudices, and beliefs which give zest to life in order to engage in a sober "felicific calculus" of the pros and cons of every action. But in its heyday this rationalism was relieved by a religious and missionary zeal. The cause of political reform or of colonial emancipation was argued by the nineteenth-century liberal entirely without that sense of guilt and hesitation which characterizes his modern descendant's argument. The pre-eminent position of the West was for him not a source of shame, but of pride and of obligation to spread the blessings of industrialism and constitutionalism to Africa and India. He would have scorned the obscurantism of talking about "African personality" and the euphemism of "one-party democracy." Rights and obligations of human beings everywhere were held to be identical; their obvious differences in beliefs and customs were discounted as temporary and subject to erasure by the passage of time.

The source of strength of original liberalism was the same factor which was to lead to its eventual downfall: its unabashed materialism. By the end of the nineteenth century a liberal of the original breed could argue that the gospel of self enrichment has, within a few decades, been productive of greater progress in equality and freedom than that wrought by all the religious and moral preachings since the beginning of our era. How far we, even in this remaining bastion of capitalism, have departed from this passionate and brazen belief in materialism can be indicated by a furor created a few years ago by an incautious remark of a Cabinet member: "What is good for General Motors is good for the country." For a mid-nineteenth-century capitalist the proposition that what was good for business (and his business) was good for the general welfare was so obvious it did not admit of an argument. Not an industrialist but a political reformer and radical wrote:

> As the best men in the working class proceed in their attainment of knowledge, they will cease to enforce their mistaken notions, and this will be called abandoning their caste by those who remain unenlightened; and these men and such other men as have power over multitudes of other men, and have sinister objects to accomplish will misinterpret to the many the actions and opinions of those who have become more enlightened. . . . In the meantime many of the incorrigible leaders and large numbers of their followers who are unteachable will be wearied out with continued and rapidly recurring disappointments, will draw off to be replaced by better men; and not withstanding the times of inactivity and despair which will occasionally occur, the progress of actual improvement in right thinking will go on with increased velocity.[4]

The present generation finds such views almost incomprehensible in their heartlessness. Many a liberal viewed a time "of inactivity and despair" like the great Irish famine of the late forties with perfect composure akin perhaps to the complacency with which the rulers of the Soviet Union must have considered the frightful toll of the forcible collectivization of 1929–1933. But before we place the nineteenth-century liberal and today's Communist (and his apologist) on the same level we must remember that the former's sins were mostly those of omission; *he* did not believe in man-made cataclysms as the means to a better future. But it is from early liberalism that Marxism has inherited its impassioned faith in industrialization and productivity, and its dislike of humanitarian and esthetic objections to progress.

The above arguments[5] would explain much of the character of socialist thought in the nineteenth century. Faced by the domination of liberalism both in politics and in the intellectual sphere, socialism went underground, so to speak. It was reduced to becoming either a conspiracy or a utopian cult. It is fairly late in the century before the socialist argument will achieve intellectual respectability or a socialist movement (as distinguished from a republican or nationalist one with socialist overtones) will frighten statesmen and the middle class. France, especially in 1848, appears to be an exception to this generalization, but even there we see recurrences of the Jacobin tradition rather than socialism in its purer form.

The utopian character of much of socialist thinking represented then a kind of rearguard action which withdrawing radicalism conducted against the triumphant march of industrialism and liberalism. In some ways the retreating had to adopt the same weapons as their enemies. One of them was science. Both Robert Owen and Fourier refuse to yield to anyone in their preference for a small agrarian community free from the evils of industrial life; but it is exactly science which was to make this idyllic community practical. The noble and somewhat demented dreams of both men reach toward something which becomes quite explicit in Saint-Simon: science becomes a religion, a way of making miracles. It is not simply part of the frightening process of modernization; in fact, it shows the way to avoid it. Marx's judgment on them, though ill-humored, is essentially correct:

> They still dream of experimental realisation of their social Utopias, of founding isolated *phalansteres,* of establishing "Home Colonies," or setting up a "Little Icaria"—pocket editions of the New Jerusalem—and to realise all these castles in the air, they are compelled to appeal to the feelings and purses of the bourgeois.[6]

He is equally perceptive in counting Saint-Simon, for whom otherwise he had a considerable respect, among the utopians. The French thinker's cult of science, his advocacy of the managerial élite do not bring him much closer to the realities of the modern industrial state than are Cobbett or Robert Owen. His relationship to modern science and to economic planning is no closer than that of Jules Verne to space travel, or that of H. G. Wells to the exploitation of atomic energy.

But Marx's irritation with the (then) competing brands of socialism was also based on reasons other than their "unscientific" character. For instance, he saw already in 1848 that one could not be a socialist without being utopian unless one accepted capitalism and the industrial ethos of liberalism. For all his earlier flirtation with Blanquism, Marx by then had to tolerate most of capitalism's self-appraisal. Few of its strongest apologists were indeed capable of reaching his height of lyricism on the subject: "The bourgeoisie during its rule of scarce one hundred years, has created more massive and more colossal productive forces than have all the preceding generations together." In *Capital* the praise of the capitalist is even more specific:

> Fanatically bent on making value expand itself, he ruthlessly forces the human race to produce for production's sake: he thus forces the development of the productive forces of society, and creates those very material conditions which alone can form the real basis of a higher form of society, a society in which the full and free development of every individual forms the ruling principle.[7]

This bondage to the ethos of capitalism could not have been easy to endure for a man who had written: "The philosophers have only *interpreted* the world in various ways; the point, however, is to *change* it." In a way, Marx must have envied the utopians the free rein they had given to their fancies and their more straightforward condemnation of the capitalists and the powers that be. His doctrine, as Marx must have realized after Chartism recedes in England, was also condemned to a long period of political impotence. He had mistaken the birthpains of capitalism for its death throes. Not until capitalism has had its full run will *his* socialism come into its own. The inner conflict between the revolutionary and the philosopher of history stayed with Marx for the rest of his life. Until the 1870's, revolutionary opportunities still beckoned enticingly all over Europe; but they were not the "right kind" of revolutionary movements: they were bourgeois nationalist movements or, in the parlance of his successors, "wars of liberation." To cope with the problem, Marx advances the theory of permanent revolution, which his Russian disciples were to develop so successfully in the twentieth century. After the suppression of the Paris Commune, when the revolutionary flame dies down, Marx and Engels seek desperately for a solution of the impasse. As revolutionaries, they grant to the Russian Populists, whose socialism runs against the grain of Marxism, that Russia might skip the phase of capitalism entirely, a horrendous and un-Marxist admission. As philosophers of history, they grant to some countries, notably Great Britain, the option of entering socialism peacefully and through parliamentary means. The situation was as depressing as it was ironic: what there was of the militant revolutionary movement in Europe scorned the whole theoretical ballast of Marxism.

The utopian socialist found himself at the same time in an equally difficult predicament. There was no place in the Europe of railways and factories for the small agrarian communities, havens of repose and isolation from the din of the industrial state. Anti-industrialism finds its expression now in straightforward anarchism—rejection of authority and centralization, an appeal not to nostalgia for the past, but more directly to the class resentments of the present. Anarchists seek the solution of the social problems not in creation of ideal communities; their aim is to preserve the industrial system but without its concomitants, capitalism and the centralized state. This partial capitulation to industrialism will not make anarchism, or its siamese twin, syndicalism, more capable of competing for political power. Anarchism rejects utopia without accepting the reality of modern politics and economics. But it will serve as an invaluable resource for the rebirth of militant Marxism-Communism. It is mainly as a legatee of anarchism that Communism will triumph in Russia and will achieve its greatest influence among the working class of the West. The genius of Lenin consisted exactly in his ability to separate the *revolutionary* part of his program from the scientific and philosophical element of Marxism. Unhampered by historical laws, the Communist will make his appeal to whatever revolutionary potential he will find in society: to the peasant's need for more land, to the worker's dislike of factory discipline, to each national group's desire to preserve its own peculiarities and rights. The supranational, centralistic, and production-oriented aspects of Marxism are muted as long as Communism struggles for power. Once it achieves power, it outdoes the most rapacious type of early capitalism in its insistence on industrialization as the supreme goal of society.

The weakening of the utopian tradition was thus bound to transform the whole nature of socialism and eventually, as argued above, to lead to its decline as an ideology. For without a utopia, or with utopia pushed far, far away in time as in Marxism, socialism had to change its focus of interest. One word which characterizes all utopias is harmony. Even its socialist versions stress that opposition to their beneficent schemes is based on either the ignorance or the selfishness of the defenders of the status quo. They are not almost helpless victims of historical forces which, quite apart from their malice or self-interest, make them behave in an anti-social way. They can be convinced or converted to the new gospel: their *enlightened* self-interest urges them in this direction.

With Marxism, and especially Communism, the key word is struggle. No ideological legerdemain can abolish class struggle, no single revolutionary eruption can overnight transform society and reform human nature. The extreme of this doctrine was formulated by Stalin when he affirmed that the closer one got to socialism the sharper became the character of class struggle, even in a society ruled by socialists. For the dream of a perfect society Communism substitutes the cult of the perfect Party. In it the fighter for socialism will find what he cannot realize on this earth until the distant day of Communism: perfect equality and infallible authority, brotherhood and discipline. A lyrically minded French Communist sang of his "beautiful Party." But lest one think that even in the Party cell he found a haven of repose and harmony, the devotee is sternly reminded that in this most perfect of human institutions there will inevitably and periodically appear the seeds of corruption: revisionism on the one hand and dogmatism and sectarianism on the other. Thus Communism triumphantly reintroduces what all the utopias attempted to expel from terrestrial existence: sin.

III

Nineteenth-century Russia provides an interesting example of the organic tie-up between utopian and socialist thinking. Generations of revolutionaries were brought up on Chernyshevsky's *What Is To Be Done*, undoubtedly the most influential utopian work of all times in terms of its impact upon its own society. Even before that, the Petrashevsky circle provided an example of how readily socialist-utopian ideas found fertile soil in Russia.

The reasons for it are obvious. A Russian *intelligent* lived in an environment almost as fantastic as that of the most extravagant utopia. Serfdom, an utter lack of representative institutions, a judicial system the likes of which have not been seen elsewhere since the end of the Middle Ages, those were only some of the features separating Russia from the increasingly parliamentarian and liberal Europe. The great reforms of the 1860's did not remove the blight of autocracy; hence, in retrospect they must be seen as accentuating the discontent of society (as the term was then being used in Russia) with the government.

From where could salvation come? The thought of merely imitating Western parliamentarism and liberalism filled the Russian radical with horror equal to that experienced by the most reactionary believer in absolutism and orthodoxy. Backwardness, or, to use a currently fashionable term, underdevelopment, creates its own illusions and compensations. This sense of inferiority toward the

West led to a strange amalgam of nationalistic and messianic feeling: just because Russia was backward, so it was her mission to redeem the world from the false gods of materialism and parliamentarism, and to point out a more perfect road to democracy and brotherhood. The Russian radical, helped by a learned German, felt that his utopia, the ideal Community, was already at hand: this was the village commune, with its alleged grass roots democracy the *mir*. All that was needed was to clean this perfection of some encrustations which had grown over the ages: absolutism, the centralized state, and the like. The peasant was seen as a socialist version of the noble savage: an instinctive democrat and communist. The rotten West, in contrast, could present nothing but plutocratic and smug capitalism which through industrialism was destroying the natural order of society. Unlike the peasant, the industrial worker was thought to be very unpromising. The worker everywhere, said Herzen, was slated to become the bourgeois, a horrible fate.

Bad history breeds bad theories which in turn lead to fatal politics. In the service of this ideal and fiction two generations of Russian radicals combatted both autocracy and liberalism. The catastrophic results of the famous Pilgrimage to the people in the mid-seventies did not undermine the Populist's faith in the peasant. The apathy or brutality of the villager was simply added to the list of aberrations which the Russian socialist had to remove so that the natural peasant communism and democracy might emerge. The very superstitions and backwardness of the peasants were to be used in the struggle against Tsarism. A group of young hotheads persuaded peasants of a region in the Ukraine that the Tsar wanted them to rise against the landowners and bureaucrats who were frustrating his benevolent intentions toward the people. A similar rationale was invoked on behalf of terror: only assassination of the leading figures of the regime, or the Tsar himself, could shake the people out of their apathy and could force the government to yield to the just demands of the revolutionaries and convoke the Constituent Assembly which would duly promulgate the era of democracy and socialism for Russia.

The alienation of the Russian intelligentsia was bound to produce some startlingly modern symptoms. In a sense, the radicals realized, though few were honest or clearsighted enough to admit it, that they were fighting not only autocracy and the bureaucratic state but also, and primarily, the inertia and disinterest in politics of a vast majority of their countrymen. The acquiescence of the mass of peasants in their political condition, and the purely materialistic character of their actual aspirations, including the desire of the more enterprising ones to break out of the commune, inspired the intellectual with a distaste comparable to that of a contemporary philosopher when he sees the modern Englishman or American disregarding the injunction of Marx, whether young or middle aged, and persisting in his enslavement to television and the automobile while blissfully unaware of his alienation. Hence a frantic search for a handle, an issue to stir up the "quiet beast," as Proudhon, in an ungracious moment called the people. The anonymous writer (Chernyshevsky or Dobrolyubov?) who wrote to Herzen's *Bell* that a true radical prays for a period of reaction and ought to prefer Nicholas I to Alexander II because only through suffering can people be stirred up to overthrow the whole monstrous system stands between two generations of Russian radicals: one with a generous and utopian faith in the people and the other which longs for struggle and revolutionary cataclysms. The latter will soon find its embodiment in Leninism.

Much of this lusting for violence was unconscious or, as in the case of many a modern intellectual, caused by society's callous indifference to his theories and sufferings. Few radicals were ready to go so far as the very young Tkachev, when he held that a regeneration of Russia required that everybody over twenty-five years of age should be liquidated.[8] But even a more fundamental problem of socialist as well as utopian thinking must be: to what extent can it be genuinely democratic? The Russian radical in the words of Zhelyabov, "wanted to give history a push." Is that impatience entirely consistent with that sympathy for the people at large, with that understanding even of their faults and prejudices and the willingness to cure them through education and example which must be at the basis of the genuine democratic feeling? Certainly Chernyshevsky's "new men," the freshly baked doctors, students, and so forth, are perfectly well aware that they stand above the common herd. "We did not see these men six years ago . . . but it matters little what we think of them now; in a few years, in a very few years, we shall appeal to them, we shall say 'Save us' and whatever they say then will be done by all."[9] When the mistress of a "new man," a reformed prostitute, dies, the bereaved lover's sentiments are described as follows: "It is needless to say that Nastenka was never a match for him, for they were not equals in the intellectual development. As he matured he could do no more than pity her." This was the author and philosopher for whom Plekhanov, Lenin, and many other Russian socialists never ceased to express their admiration and acknowledge their intellectual debt.

For many a Russian radical, as for Dostoevsky's theorist in *The Possessed,* faith in the natural goodness of the common man, never explicitly renounced, was thus to lead to authoritarianism; and their system "beginning from the premise of unlimited freedom concludes in complete despotism." The story of this evolution is writ large in Bolshevism. Russian Marxism grew from and fed upon the earlier Populist tradition, but unlike the latter it was eventually to see in the peasant not a communistic savage, but, in Gorky's words, a "heavy, stupid and semi-Asiatic man of the villages" or, to use a more doctrinal definition, a "petty bourgeois" who had to be destroyed before Russia could enter the promised land of industrialism and socialism.

The history of Russian socialist thought, both in its Populist and Marxian varieties, is then a warning—which does not lose its force because of its commonplace and often repeated character—of the dangers of utopian thinking in politics. In the West, triumphant materialism suppressed, at least for a century, the utopias and nostalgia for the non-existent agrarian past and the *cri de coeur* of the alienated intellectual and esthete masquerading as the social protest. The would-be Lenins of the West saw themselves reduced to leaders of small cults or, worse yet, transformed into parliamentarians and academicians. What happened to many Saint-Simonians is characteristic of the encounter between liberalism, as yet in its full vigor, and socialist utopia: from the devotees of a most extravagant cult, they become bankers, industrialists, and canal builders—in brief, servants and propagators of capitalism.

In Russia the revolt against the utopian tradition in radicalism came later—too late, in fact. In 1909, a group of ex-socialists among the intelligentsia published an avowal of contrition under the title *Vekhi* (Russian for landmarks or signposts). Had the Western intellectuals paid attention to the conclusions of *Vekhi* perhaps there would have been no occasion for a much later compilation of essays under the title *The God That Failed.* "The greatest evil of our society is the spiritual rule by children,"[10] wrote the contrite intellectuals as they deplored the domination of myth and immoderate radicalism in Russian political thinking. And those words still have not lost their relevance. But for the Russian intellectuals it was late in the day. Both the intelligentsia and the institutions they abhorred were to be swept under by the movement which derived its ideology from a work by Lenin—ironically also entitled *What Is To Be Done.*

The Bolshevik triumph was bound to revive the socialist-utopian tradition in the West where liberalism was buried by two wars and the depression. For the first time, utopia was located in an actual country where visitors, if so inclined, could see the future at work. In this actual Icaria one encountered many features of the previous utopias: equality, the all-wise and benevolent autocrat first identified as the Party, and later as a person. Most of all, one encountered planning and full employment which between the two world wars became themselves objects of a utopian cult.

The destruction of the utopian image of the Soviet Union has been taking place in very recent times. It is characterized not only by the disenchantment of the foreign Communists and sympathizers but also by the increasingly apologetic tone of Russian Communism itself. Its strength, just as that of liberalism in its heyday, has been derived from its self-assurance and ruthlessness, its ability to terrorize and shame the opponents of its exposition of Marxism. To a man who said "but this is immoral," Communism answered, "Philistine." Those who dared to point out that things have changed since Marx erected his lofty structure were often shamed out of their doubts by another epithet: "revisionists." The innocent observation "but this is not what Marx had said and what we promised" earned an equally formidable rebuttal, "dogmatists." But today the high priests have increasingly to argue, explain, and even apologize, sure signs of an ideology past its utopian phase.

The organic connection between utopia and socialism appears severed, at least for the moment. It is in the nature of utopia that it must promise not more of the same but an entirely different and marvelous world, and that vision can no longer be sustained by socialism either of the Communist or the democratic variety.

It might be argued that much of the passion, generosity, and naiveté which went earlier into utopian designs goes nowadays into the thinking and writing about international affairs. Some have constructed the vision of a new world order based upon the emergent nations. The current critic of Western civilization and its values (and what is all of utopian thinking and much of socialist thought but a critique of the values and traditions of the West?) is tempted to see the new nations as free from the materialism and power striving of the old. They in turn listen gratefully to the Westerner who has instructed them about the evils of imperialism from which they have suffered and who extols their revolutionary *élan*. But such visions cannot withstand a scrutiny of the facts. The emerging nations are clamoring for automobiles and washing machines. Their brand of socialism upon closer examination is exhibited as nationalism coated by a thin veneer of foreign slogans and symbols.

Have we reached the end of utopianism in radical thought? From other points of view, for example in science, the advances of, say, biology have opened perspectives for the creation of utopias undreamed of by the boldest of science fiction writers. But when it comes to the ordaining of man's social behavior we have grown more sober, and—a horrible word to the utopians—realistic. Much of the evolution of radical thought can be symbolized by the title of books which exhilarated generations of Russian revolutionaries. There was first Herzen's *Who Is Guilty?* Then Chernyshevsky's *What Is To Be Done?* And shortly before his death, Lenin wrote an article entitled *Better Less But Better* (to be sure this was about administration and with no philosophical implications). Perhaps we have reached a moratorium, if not indeed the end of utopias, and perhaps this is not an altogether bad thing.

REFERENCES

1. Sir William Beveridge, *Full Employment in a Free Society* (New York: Norton, 1945), p. 254.
2. Frederick Engels, *The Condition of the Working Class in England in 1844*, in *Karl Marx and Frederick Engels on Britain* (Moscow, 1953), p. 52.
3. William Morris, *News From Nowhere* (Pocket edition; London: Longmans Green & Co., 1912), pp. 84-85.
4. Francis Place, quoted in Graham Wallas, *The Life of Francis Place* (3rd edition; New York: A. A. Knopf, 1919), pp. 383-384.
5. This argument is developed at greater length in my book *The Unfinished Revolution* (New York: Random House, 1960).
6. *A Handbook of Marxism* (New York: International Publishers Co., Inc., 1935) p. 57.
7. Karl Marx, *Capital,* Vol. I (New York: Modern Library, Inc., 1932), p. 648.
8. B. Kozmin, *P. N. Tkachev and the Revolutionary Movement of the 1860's* (Moscow: Novyi Mir, 1922), p. 19.
9. N. Chernyshevsky, *What Is To Be Done* (New York: Vintage Books, 1961), p. 175.
10. *Landmarks, Collection of Essays about the Russian Intelligentsia* (4th printing; Moscow, 1909), p. 43.

III

LIMITATIONS ON UTOPIA

PAUL B. SEARS

Utopia and the Living Landscape

> "Human well-being is an immense resource which can be squandered or marvelously regenerated."
>
> F. Fraser Darling

FROM THE time of Bacon or, to be quite fair, that of Aristotle, scientists have written of the possibilities of a more perfect human society. Of late there has been increasing emphasis upon the "conquest" or "control" of nature as a means to that end. Such a view conceives of man as an external manipulator of the great system of life and environment. Actually he is a part of this ecosystem and must adjust himself to its inexorable processes.

Such an adjustment requires the fullest use of science rather than its rejection. In particular, it calls for the perspective provided by ecology. To proceed with the application of science on the basis of improvisation and expediency while ignoring this broad perspective, and the lessons of history, is to court disaster. What follows is an attempt to indicate something of the viewpoint of the ecologist.

It would be a grave injustice to dismiss utopian thought as mere fantasy, visionary and impractical. To consider it restricted to literary forms that bear its label is to underestimate its wide prevalence at many levels and in all cultures. However expressed, it is essentially a critique of the defects and limitations of society and an expression of hope for something better. For this purpose the artist-thinker must be acutely aware of things as they are, even though he may never mention them in his presentation.

It is beyond this common, implicit starting point that we encounter among utopians and their critics the wide range and divergence which cause confusion. Here, as in mathematics, assumptions determine developments, and results differ according to the choice of working principles.

If interest in utopian literature were confined to it as literature *per se* it could be left there. This is not the case, for it has enjoyed the attention of society, politics, economics, philosophy, and, increasingly, science. Since human society is an enormously complex phenomenon, subject to a wide variety of limiting factors, the choice of assumptions has differed greatly, permitting the vision of trends and possibilities—or lack of them—to range the field of imagination.

However widely projections may differ, it *is* folly to regard them as a useless waste of time. The geologist derives order from the idea that surface processes move toward conditions of maximum uniformity—the peneplain, rare or absent in actual experience. The ecologist solves many of his problems by viewing living communities as working toward an idealized climax condition of dynamic stability, an open steady state. In longer view the physicist looks upon our solar system as moving inevitably toward a condition of maximum entropy—that is, a minimum of energy free to do work. The mathematician, for his part, makes constant use of the idea of limits. All of these formulations are not only useful, but consistent with the rules of experience based on observation.

In classic epistomology, knowledge was divided into moral—that which dealt with man—and natural—that which concerned other phenomena. Science long confined itself to natural knowledge. Today, it transgresses the old boundary, regarding man as part of the world of nature and a proper subject for its attention. As in some ways the most characteristic activity of our time, science is profoundly affecting all phases of life, including literature and philosophy. Consequently, science plays an increasing role in utopian writing, whether optimistic, skeptical, or satiric.

By contrast, the older utopias concerned themselves heavily with moral factors, human behavior being the key problem. In the more appealing instances, an ideal society was pictured as the result of the innate nobility of those who composed it. More often, it was the result of authoritarian enforcement of a strict code in the manner of Lycurgian Sparta. Here we have a theme that persists into the scientific utopias, where human engineering is often invoked to control mass psychology.

The stunning advance of technology has produced a curious mixture of hope and fatalism in the modern mind. To many it is the new *Salvator Mundi,* permitting us to relax traditional controls in the faith that "science" will be equal to any emergency we get ourselves into. Others regard the coming of a completely artificial world as inevitable, saying with a shrug "you can't stop progress" and, by inference, that any attempt to guide change is hopeless. Either attitude is an open invitation to the human engineer.

For the first time in planetary history, a single species, *Homo sapiens,* has become dominant throughout the world. This organism has also become a major natural force, powerfully modifying the landscape in form and substance. Generally this is done for immediate advantage. Often, in terms of sustained benefit, the effect has been disruptive of those very conditions which have made earth habitable. Happily, the power to modify man's physical environment includes the capacity for constructive action. For better or worse, man is now responsible for change and for governing its trend. He is not only a product of evolution, but a chief agent.

As Julian Huxley and others have been at pains to point out, human evolution in the foreseeable future is not likely to involve great physical change. Man will remain man, however much he may improve his body by nurture or selection. What evolution does take place will be in his culture. And from the beginning human cultures have been the chief means of relating man to his environment, physical, biological, and social. These cultures, historically manifold, are now in the painful process of developing a greater range of common traits, if not world-wide uniformity, thanks largely to increasing knowledge and advancing technology.

Behind the material and visible aspects of human behavior patterns lie the intangibles—those beliefs and values which afford sanction. Intuitive, elusive, often distorted when made explicit, they can be modified by force of external conditions and by borrowing. But they can also be modified by individual invention and effective dramatization. Man is as much a shaper as a captive of the culture in which he lives.

How do we test the quality of a culture? Is the pragmatic test of survival enough? When the mammoth, moa, or dinosaur becomes extinct, the loss is complete and irretrievable. With the fall of Carthage, Babylon, Greece, Crete, or Rome, families and tribes may vanish, but elements of culture may survive. Culture, no less than life, may have its own continuities and perhaps may not entirely disappear because of physical extinction. So far as our own species is concerned, utopian thought presupposes the presence of living people and their culture.

Skepticism concerning the permanence of the human race is far older than talk of the population explosion or the atomic bomb. It is reflected in Ragnorok—the Twilight of the Gods—in scriptural adumbration and the assemblage of such credulous groups as the Millerites, whose prophet confided to them the day and hour when all will end. Meanwhile, however dubious we may be of the permanence, not to say ultimate perfectibility, of our race, it may be useful to examine the conditions requisite for the survival of this interesting experiment in which we are involved.

Recently, Philip Handler, the distinguished biochemist, in commenting to a lay audience upon the word "life," noted the remarkable fact that such a word is possible and that its attributes are common to so vast an assemblage of entities, man included. It follows that there are some very general conditions necessary to our species as well as those over which we presume to have dominion, even though we recall the remark of the late L. O. Howard that the last survivor on earth might well be a live insect on a dead weed.

He said this, of course, long before the days of nuclear power, when forecasts still included the phrase "*Deo volente*" in place of today's caveat "barring nuclear holocaust." The substitution at least recognizes our own responsibility. All we can do is to admit its validity and get on with other factors in the situation.

Materials and energy are needed to keep life going. Food, water, and air, suitable and sufficient, supply these needs. At the present time our concern with quality, as reflected in legislation, is in the order named: food, water, air. Yet we can survive longer without food than without water, longer without water than without air. Bad food receives prompt attention when its effects are immediate and drastic, or even when it is unsavory. We endure the flavor of chlorine, or even of phenols along the Ohio, but act promptly when we find that water carries disease. We are at long last rebelling against polluted air, perhaps more because it is unpleasant than because we are certain of what it does to health. We still have much to learn of the cumulative effects of substandard food, water, and air.

Our greatest concern in regard to water and food is with future supplies. With the exception of Alaska and its glacial reservoirs, every state in the Union faces the water problem to some degree. As numbers increase, so does per capita consumption. Meanwhile, we have disrupted those normal processes of the living landscape which control the water supply. Rapid run-off is promoted when we remove natural vegetation, particularly when we replace it with impermeable structures and even when we substitute cultivated crops.

We also drain wet lands which could retard the loss of water. And by using streams as sewers for domestic and industrial waste, we render vast amounts of water either useless or costly to reclaim. In the natural landscape, as we shall note, wastes are recycled and reclaimed far more efficiently.

Although the United States is now producing a surplus of food, millions elsewhere are underfed. Yet even here, there is a divided opinion as to the future. Optimists, particularly those with unbounded faith in the magic of science, assert that we shall be able to feed all comers into the indefinite future. Others, including respected scientists, are more skeptical.

On one point both observation and calculation agree. As pressure upon food supplies increases, food from secondary sources, animal protein, is replaced by that from the primary producers, plant life. This is evident today in crowded lands where the meat supply is inadequate and fuel is scarce; in these areas the staples are rice and thin cakes of meal which can be prepared with a minimum of heat. It is even evident in our own country—for example, a youngster from a prosperous home eats sirloin while a less privileged playmate gets beans and macaroni. There is no promise of a gourmet's utopia for the majority of mankind if demand continues to press upon supply.

This is simply an application of what is known in ecology as the food pyramid. At its base are the organic substances built by green plants using solar energy. At the next higher level are the vegetarian animals and above them, the meat eaters such as ourselves. Just as our best engines are able to use only a fraction of the energy in their fuel, so it is with living organisms using food for energy and structural material. Each successive level in the food pyramid can recover only a small amount of the nutrient value—often as little as ten per cent—present in the layer upon which it feeds.

To counter this somewhat gloomy prospect, the potential of seas and tropical lands is often cited. After all, the oceans, probable cradle of life, cover three fourths of the globe, while the humid tropics, capable of supporting rich forests, are not as a rule heavily populated. Deprived of its natural source and cover by clearing, the rich organic material in tropical soils is rapidly oxidized by heat, and the nutrient minerals are leached by the heavy rainfall. Such lands do not lend themselves to the clean-tilled cultivation practiced in temperate climates, but succeed best by combining trees with suitable under-crops as in the case of coffee. In no sense do they seem to be competitive with the grain belts of the world as a source of mass food production. Meanwhile, their most valuable product may be choice woods, too often being ruthlessly harvested by concessionaires as in the Philippines.

What of the vast and teeming seas? Governments of the world are now intensifying their study of this domain; thus, final judgment must be reserved. So far as our present knowledge goes, areas of heavy food production are limited, being confined generally to cooler waters and regions where upwelling currents bring nutrients to the sunny surface. On the waters as on land, there are unproductive spaces that can fairly be called deserts.

Nations dependent upon marine sources of food—Japan, Britain, and the Scandinavian countries—have long supported ocean research. It is unlikely that many rich sources have been overlooked. News dispatches record increasing conflicts over marginal fishing grounds whose political control is in question. Continental pollution from silt and wastes has already interfered seriously with the yield of shellfish and other marine foods from coastal areas. A curious example of pressure, even on the open seas, has been noted by Hawaiian oceanographers: cubical brown particles found far out from land have turned out to be coffee-grounds cast off from ships.

Until recently, the harvest of fish such as salmon, which spawn far upstream in waters that flow into the ocean, has been an important source of food. Here again yields have been diminishing. Great dams erected to produce power are obstacles to free migration so necessary to the production of such fish. Despite technical measures to overcome this problem, yields have steadily declined. To say the least, it would be interesting to analyze the relative gains, computed on a long-term basis, of the substitution of electrical facilities for biological harvests that were formerly possible.

Meanwhile, there is growing interest in what might be called an extension of water culture onto the land. Since the basic food supply of all marine organisms comes from minute one-celled green plants growing in the surface layers, why not cultivate these in tanks and use them as human food? Actually they can be made to produce a thick culture not unlike pea soup. Mixed with more conventional flours, they can be eaten; but one scientist who has done a great deal of work with them confesses that, undisguised, "they have a high gag coefficient." He foresees their use as poultry food, which leaves matters much as they are.

To recapitulate, we can safely say that people are likely to be around for a long time to come. If the prospect of an earthly utopia continues to recede, it will not be for lack of human beings to create and enjoy it, however they may have to struggle to keep going. The basic problem is not the quantity, but the probable future quality, of human life: all available evidence suggests that the chief threat to the quality of existence is the ungoverned and unprecedented increase in man's numbers.

So far as we know, world population remained fairly stable at about half a billion from late Roman times to the sixteenth century A.D. It appears to have doubled in the next three hundred years, redoubled by 1900, and doubled again in little more than a half-century. A still shorter time for the next doubling is in prospect. The rate of increase is accelerating.

The mathematics of this process are interesting. Under ideal conditions the number that results from repeated doubling is greater than the sum of all previous numbers, as 2 × 2 is greater than 1 plus 2 × 1. It is on this basis that we are sometimes told that there are more people on earth today than the sum of all that have lived in the past. Without pausing to consider other possibilities, one thing is clear: those alive today have come into an environment profoundly changed by their predecessors, and future change can occur only in terms of what is here now.

We are indebted to the geologist not only for his early concern over man's misuse of environment, but for the reminder that minuscule change can be cumulative over the ages. The basic question at any time is the direction in which processes are moving, rather than their high visibility. Deterioration may proceed so slowly that it escapes notice until too late. This has often happened in the case of soil. On the other hand, unfavorable change may accelerate to the point where crisis is plainly signalled, as in the growing pressure upon water supply in many places. It is evident, too, in the rate at which world population continues to increase.

So far as human numbers are concerned, certain purely physical principles apply. The human individual, whatever more he may be, is certainly a dynamic entity, occupying space and moving within it. The space within which he moves, for our practical purposes, is finite, however great. When dynamic particles occupy a finite space, whether that be a flask, island, or continent, any increase in numbers diminishes the mean free path of each. To that extent, its freedom of movement is restricted. And when energy is added to the system, either by warming a flask of gas particles or putting a human population on automotive wheels by the use of fossil fuel, the mean free path is further constricted. If this seems nonsense to the motorist bowling along at sixty miles an hour, he need only recall the millions who are not and brush up on his statistics.

The real paradox comes when we view earlier and simpler stages in human society. Here the increase in numbers, which can take place only where there is an adequate nutrient base, may actually benefit both the group and individual. This comes about by an ecological process, the creation of new niches and specialized roles, thus reducing competition for the time being. Until a saturation point is reached, numbers permit organization to offset what would otherwise be growing pressure. It is this dynamic phase of social evolution rather than warped nostalgia which justifies the concept of a Golden Age as an actual utopia in the past, and which explains its persistence in our thinking.

Historically, however, the saturation point has been a recurring phenomenon. The very success made possible by the original nutrient base, whether Near Eastern, Roman, or Oriental, creates pressure which it can no longer sustain. The utopian trend is checked and reversed. Internally, niches and roles multiply *praeter necessitatem,* while unemployment and poverty increase. Armies of slaves are put to work on vast structures. Armies of soldiers are organized to expand the nutrient base by conquering their neighbors. Such enterprises, along with disease and malnutrition, infanticide, and human sacrifice, contribute to controlling population to some degree.

Only in rare instances and in modern times have techniques of birth control and frugal management of limited resources been used to stem the downward spiral away from utopia. This is notably true in Japan and the small democracies of Western Europe. Even so, an impressive proportion of Scandinavian males spend the major part of their adult lives on the sea.

Save for the small voice of the rural romantics, utopia is the apotheosis of the city. This was true even in the days when the Hebrew prophets were thundering against the vices of urban life. There is no need to elaborate on the city as the center of the leisure arts, political, industrial, and fiscal life, nor upon its allure and prestige. But it is well to recall, too, that the city is the child of agriculture. Cities were impossible until men and women were released from the constant quest for food.

One of the criticisms of city planning, certainly not merited by one of its great founders, Patrick Geddes, is the tendency to think of the city as an isolate from its surrounding country. The country is still its nutrient base, strikingly so in regard to its increasing thirst for water, for which the city's tubular tentacles reach out further and further. Its economic health is tied more closely to that of the rural region than is commonly realized. A recent study in upper New York found that when towns and small cities received as little as fourteen per cent of their income from the country, they prospered. Their neighbors with much less than that amount did not. Again, the great urban depression of 1929 began eight years earlier for the farmer and continued during that time while the flaunting boom of the cities was fed in no small measure at his expense. And it was the disaster of prolonged drought in the Midwest, as well as urban bread lines, that led us to reappraise our whole enterprise.

There can be no effective movement toward utopia without including the entire ecosystem of community and environment. To that end we may profitably examine the operation of the greater biological community of which man is inescapably a part.

The facts are plain enough, though perhaps better known than understood. Certainly their implications are not widely grasped. Man is a parvenu species on a planet some five million times older than he. Imperfect as our knowledge of the past may be, there is no reason to doubt that man's ancestors, and man himself, have survived by meeting the inexorable conditions of environment. Nor do we doubt that conditions, both of life and the physical environment, have been determined by their past history. Carrying this a step further, we can be certain that the future is being shaped by present events and that man is now largely responsible for this.

More briefly, the human species appeared in an environment ready for it, and man for the environment. Though his evolution had been painfully slow, the end result was a remarkable novelty, biologically speaking. His equipment included an erect posture, binocular vision, a rotating head, grasping hands capable of performing an infinite variety of manipulations. Although other animals might excel him in particular respects such as speed, strength, or sensory power, none could match him in versatility—the capacity for an infinite range of experience. To register experience, he possessed a remarkable central nervous system able to recall and recombine the data of his senses. With all of this he possessed speech organs capable of producing a variety of sounds and sound combinations as symbols for communication within and between generations, thus preserving the conscious record of experience and laying the foundations of culture.

The remarkable complex that makes up the human animal can develop to full capacity only with training and use. Nor can it be expected ever to produce a uniform, standard type of individual, even if that were desirable, which it is not. All experience shows that the common life is enriched by variety. One of the evils of overcrowding and consequent restriction of freedom is that it enforces an increasing degree of uniformity. Biologically as well as culturally this is fatal. It was the weakness of Sparta, that utopia of Lycurgus, not to forget some of its subsequent imitators.

The old saying "All Chinese look alike" applies only to the novice. So it is with the impression of seeming monotony or uniformity in such natural communities as forest, swamp, or prairie. So manifold are their plants and animals in typical areas that merely their correct listing generally requires the help of specialists. True, in the earlier stages, when life is invading a newly opened habitat, the kinds of pioneers may be few. But as time goes on, there develops a rich and interwoven complex of organisms, ceaselessly active, yet amazingly resilient to external pressures.

Natural grassland grows in climates where available moisture is not enough to encourage the growth of forest. Here, water is the critical or limiting factor. Periods of drought alternate with groups of more favorable years. Yet whatever the extreme, the prairie, unlike our cultivated croplands, produces something. During any growing season it is a carpet of changing colors and textures as successive waves of flowering and fruiting march by. As groups of dry years occur, the scene is dominated by plants which have been suppressed or invisible during lusher times. Here as in forest, scrub, desert, or tundra, integrity—that is, continuity in space and time—rests upon variety.

Plato with his "drones" was clearer on this point so far as human society is concerned than some of his grimmer successors in utopian writing. Too often the latter have failed to appreciate that spontaneous interplay—to them lost motion—is essential to a flexible and enduring biological and social system. They are like engineers who insist upon too tight a range of tolerance and thus condemn a mechanism to become frozen in the course of operation. The lesson from nature undisturbed by man is quite explicit as to this danger.

How ironical it would be if the human species, richly endowed with so flexible and resourceful a body, failed to preserve that quality in its social organization and thus became fossilized before its time! While genetic science admits the ultimate possibility of breeding humans to specified types, this seems at present a remote contingency, even if it were desirable. On the other hand, there is good reason to believe that people could be conditioned to adjust themselves to a highly artificial, technologically controlled environment such as the city under a plastic bubble which some envision. Such an arrangement, however, would not only congeal the pattern of living, but be vulnerable on two counts. The greater our dependence upon an elaborate chain of technology, the more liable we become to disaster through failure of any link. And the more restricted our range of experience, even though physical needs are met, the greater our loss of flexibility to meet emergency. The too-sheltered child is an example. So is battery-grown poultry. These birds, raised under completely controlled conditions, must be protected against sudden noises or even the presence of a stranger. Otherwise they pile up in a corner and smother each other.

Beginning with Bacon's *New Atlantis,* or perhaps earlier, there has been a significant change of emphasis in the visions of utopia. The older writings, as we have noted earlier, concerned themselves heavily with moral and political factors. Gradually there has been an increasing preoccupation with man's ability to manipulate his environment and rely upon technological devices. At one extreme, this has resulted in the absorbing faith in science as a guarantee against any emergency we may create for ourselves. At the other, there has developed an impressive literature of satire and disillusionment, at least some of whose writers are better versed in science than the uncritical optimists.

Faced with this choice, the biologist can rely only upon the rules of experience. How these apply to the need for flexibility rather than regimentation we have already discussed. They also apply to the model nature provides in the realm of physical process. Here we find that natural communities, whatever their limitations, are relatively effective in their use of impinging energy and available materials. Dependent as they are upon the fixation of a small proportion of solar energy in organic compounds, they move toward a state of dynamic equilibrium. They also work toward an efficient recycling of materials, rather than their dissipation, so evident in our present urban economy.

All communities, including those of man, tend to develop from original simplicity to a state of high organization. In the earlier phases, the physical environment of earth and atmosphere is in stark control. As organization progresses the community itself plays an increasing part in shaping conditions. The climax of this process is manifest in the operations of technological man, with his present enormous geological and biological power. But the consequences of his organized activity differ sharply from those generally observed in what we call natural communities.

These latter operate on a current budget of solar energy, deploying it so as to keep the system itself in operating condition, maintaining or even enhancing the capacity of habitat to sustain life. Through variety and complexity, niches are afforded to organisms, visible and invisible, each of which plays its part in the sustaining activity. Organic materials produced by green plants out of the raw substances of air, water, and earth are broken down, step by step, in elaborate food chains until their components are returned whence they came, once more in usable form.

In the main, this circulation is in place, but moving animals and currents of air and water provide a measure of lateral transport, helping to remedy local deficiencies in nutrient materials such as phosphorus and lime. The whole process is constructive—not perfectly so, it is true, but favorable enough to have made earth habitable for man. Through the ages a reserve of advantage has been built up in this fashion.

As tangible evidence, we have the formation of soil, stabilization of land forms, regulation of the water cycle, renewal of atmospheric oxygen, and the preservation of abundant life with populations adjusted to their means of survival. In the course of geological time, there have been periods of slow accumulation of organic surplus in the form of mineral fuels, thus far essential to modern technology. Nor should we forget the esthetic delight of the natural landscape for all who are not completely insensitive or brutalized.

In the language of physical dynamics this self-repairing, constructive process of nature represents a type of equilibrium that approximates an open steady state. If utopian thought has any proper moral concern for the permanence, beauty, and quality of the human adventure, here is the physical model for our own use of the landscape. Yet we continue to move rapidly further away from it.

Our violence in this respect has no counterpart in nature. We draw upon reserves of fossil energy at a rate infinitely faster than that at which they have accumulated. The same is true of those precious concentrations of mineral ores which we use in fabrication not only of necessities, but often of what are little better than toys for adults. We scalp away the living cover regardless of its beauty or even its utility as a shield against the raw forces of nature. Our wastes are allowed to contaminate earth, air, and water instead of being conserved and converted back to usable form.

The city, prototype of utopia, has become a sprawling monster, devouring space regardless of its best potential and without regard to amenities far more elemental than those of any utopian dream. Our economy, sharply divergent from that of nature, rests upon a tragic confusion of growth with health. For growth in nature is a determinate, self-limiting process, not mere unbridled enlargement. Without control, as in certain hormonal disturbances, it becomes pathological. Perhaps the most immoral expression of this confusion takes the form of rejoicing at unrestricted population increase as the sure guarantee of prosperity.

For nearly a million years humanity has had to play by ear to achieve its destiny, guided only by intuitive dreams of what might be, such dreams as have been expressed by its artists and spiritual leaders. These dreams have ranged the entire gamut of human imagination, from complete peace through non-being to a paradise of physical delights. The Viking, regarding brave death in battle as the climactic earthly experience, would have been contemptuous of our tender concern to sustain life by drawing upon all the resources of science and skill when hope has passed beyond hope.

There is no reason to think that mankind, with all of its diversity, individual and group, will ever agree on what is ultimately most to be desired. Instead we must look upon this very diversity as a potential good enhancing the richness of experience. Today we have the possibility, through a better understanding of the pattern of which we constitute a part, to reverse the present disruptive trend, or at least achieve a setting in which the creative imagination will be free.

JOHN MAYNARD SMITH

Eugenics and Utopia

THERE IS no field of application of science to human affairs more calculated to arouse our prejudices than eugenics. I cannot hope to be free from these prejudices, but in this essay I will try to separate what we ought to do from what we can now do and from what we may in the future be able to do. These problems should be thought about because our ability to alter the future course of human evolution is likely to increase dramatically during the next hundred years.

There are three ways in which we may be able to alter man's biological capacities, which I shall call selectionist eugenics, transformationist eugenics, and biological engineering. Briefly, selectionist eugenics is the application to ourselves of the techniques which, since the Neolithic revolution, we have been applying in the breeding of our domestic animals and plants. In effect, we take measures to ensure that individuals with characteristics we like will contribute more to future generations than individuals with characteristics we dislike. These measures range from the simple to the sophisticated, from the slaughter of runts to the cold storage of spermatozoa for artificial insemination. The development of a science of population genetics has enabled us to estimate with greater accuracy the consequence of any particular interference with the breeding system and to choose between effective and ineffective methods of selection. But it has not altered the fact that this is an extremely slow and inefficient method of altering the genetic properties of a population and one whose speed can be increased only by increasing the intensity of selection; a bigger change is produced in the properties of the next generation if ninety-nine per cent of the males in the present one are selectively slaughtered or sterilized than if one per cent are so treated.

Recent advances in molecular genetics have raised the possibility of a different and far more effective method of genetic change which I shall call transformationist eugenics. At present, if we wish to eliminate an undesirable gene from a population, our only method of doing so is to reduce the breeding chances of those individuals carrying the gene; but now that we know something of the chemistry of heredity, it is possible to think of the direct alteration or transformation of particular genes. Today, this can be done only in micro-organisms, and then in only a very small proportion of the cells exposed to the transforming agent. But it will be surprising if direct gene transformation does not become possible in man and higher animals during the next hundred years. If so, it will increase by many orders of magnitude the speed and economy with which the genetic properties of populations can be changed.

Finally, the continued development of surgical techniques, together with chemical methods of altering development and with tissue and organ culture, will make it possible to produce quite profound alterations in the biological properties of individuals without altering their genetic constitution. This I shall call biological engineering.

Before discussing in greater detail the technical and ethical considerations raised by these methods, there is one general point to be made: man is evolving anyway. That is to say, changes are taking place in the genetic properties of the human population whether we like it or not; and almost every political and social measure we take influences to some degree the nature and direction of these changes.[1] Probably the most important changes at the present time are due not to selective survival or fertility but to changes in the breeding structure consequent on increased population size and increased mobility. At one extreme is the reduction in the frequency of marriages between close relatives, which is likely at least in the short term (that is, for some hundreds of years) to have beneficial effects by reducing the frequency of diseases caused by recessive genes; at the other extreme is the increase in the frequency of inter-racial marriage, although social pressures have both minimized this change and rendered it almost impossible to evaluate its consequences accurately.

But in the literature of eugenics, more attention has been paid to selective effects, and in particular to the differential fertility of social classes and the consequences of improved medical care. The importance of the former subject has probably been exaggerated—the observed differences may not last long enough to have significant evolutionary consequences—but it is comforting in any case that measurements of I.Q. in 1932 and 1947 in Scotland showed a slight but significant rise on the second occasion although the negative correlation between the I.Q. score of children and the size of the family to which they belonged had led to the prediction that the mean I.Q. of the population must decline. Even if, as seems likely, the observed rise was the result of particular environmental rather than genetic factors, at least no measurable genetic decline has occurred.[2]

The effects of improved medical services should perhaps be taken more seriously because these are likely to be long-lasting. The argument is as follows. Improved medical and social care make it possible for people who in the past would have died to survive and have children. In so far as their defects were genetically determined, they are likely to be handed on to their children. Consequently, the frequency of genetically determined defects in the population is likely to increase; and an increasingly large proportion of the population will be engaged in keeping the rest alive. I think we have to accept the fact that there is some truth in this argument, but it is a little difficult to see what we should do about it. To ban the manufacture of glasses and the administration of insulin because these activities permit astigmatics and diabetics to breed seems inhumane. If we are going to administer insulin, there is no rational ground for refusing to undertake the more expensive and time-consuming job of feeding babies who suffer from a genetically determined form of mental defect known as phenylketonuria on a diet free of phenylalanine. And as our knowledge increases, the number of tasks of this kind which we shall feel obliged to undertake will increase. An extreme eugenist might suggest that although we should not ban the administration of insulin we should insist on the sterilization of those who require it. The difficulty with such a policy is that almost every human being possesses at least some characteristics, physical, moral, or intellectual, which we would prefer not to be transmitted to the next generation. The only humane answer at present appears to be that an increasing investment in medical and social care is a price we should be prepared to pay.

But there are two mitigating circumstances. First, as I shall discuss later, there may be a long-term way out of this dilemma. Second, not all the genetic consequences of improved medical services are dysgenic, and it may even be that most are not. To see why this is so, consider the case of malaria and sickle cell anemia.

Briefly, there exists in man a gene S, which in homozygous* condition causes fatal anemia. Yet this gene occurs in high frequency in certain places, particularly in parts of Africa where malaria is or was until recently a common cause of death. The reason for this distribution is that individuals heterozygous for the gene S are resistant to malaria. The frequency of S in Negroes of West African origin now resident in America is lower than those in West Africa, presumably because in the absence of malaria natural selection against homozygotes has not been balanced by selection in favor of heterozygotes; a similar decrease in frequency of S is likely to occur in Africa as malaria is brought under control. This is an evolutionary change consequent on improved medical care (that is, the eradication of malaria), but it is a disirable change since it has reduced the number of children dying of anemia.

The case of sickle cell anemia and malaria is rather a special one, but beneficial evolutionary consequences of improved medical care may be quite common. The greatest change so far produced by medicine (more particularly by preventive medicine) on the pattern of mortality is the reduction in the number of people dying of infectious disease. This has led to a reduction in the selection pressure in favor of disease-resistance and presumably to an increase in susceptibility. As long as we continue to control infectious disease by improved hygiene, innoculation, and so forth, this is probably a good thing. The reason for this is that in evolution, as in other fields, one seldom gets something for nothing. Genes which confer disease resistance are likely to have harmful effects in other ways; this is certainly true of the gene for sickle cell anemia and may be a general rule. If so, absence of selection in favor of disease resistance may be eugenic.

Now that death from infectious disease is rare in industrial countries, the main efforts in medical research are concentrated on diseases such as cancer and rheumatism, which usually affect older people. Cures for cancer (other than leukemia) would not have significant genetic consequences because, although they would prolong the life of many people, they would seldom add to the number of children born to such people. The main dysgenic effects of medical progress arise from cures of defects which are present at birth

* An individual who inherits the same gene, defective or otherwise, from both parents is said to be homozygous; an individual inheriting different genes from his two parents is said to be heterozygous.

or appear before reproductive age, and in whose causation there is a genetic component.

So far, I have considered genetic changes which are happening or are likely to happen as unintended by-products of measures undertaken with other ends in view. I now turn to the possible effects of intentional eugenic measures, first considering measures of selective eugenics which either are already technically possible or are fairly certain to become possible in the near future. Such eugenic measures can be "negative," that is, concerned with the elimination or reduction in frequency of undesirable traits, or "positive," that is concerned with improving the average performance, or the proportion of individuals capable of outstanding performance, of socially desirable tasks.

The probable effectiveness of negative eugenic measures depends first on whether the characteristic in question is genetically determined and, if so, whether it is caused by a dominant* or a recessive gene. For characters caused by dominant genes, negative eugenic measures could be effective but are usually pointless; for characters caused by recessive genes, they are ineffective.[3]

Consider first a character, Achondroplasia (dwarfism with short legs and arms), which is caused by a dominant gene. Since the gene is dominant, we can recognize all carriers of the gene. If we so wished, we could by sterilizing all achondroplastic dwarfs prevent any carriers from passing the gene on to the next generation. This would not completely eliminate the character from the population but would reduce its frequency to the number of cases arising by new mutation in each generation. But why should we wish to do this, since there is little to prevent an achondroplastic dwarf from leading a contented and useful life? If a dominant mutation is lethal or seriously disabling, selection will keep it at a frequency close to the mutation rate without our intervention; if it is not disabling, why should we interfere? Unhappily, there are exceptions to this easy excuse for inactivity. An example is Huntingdon's chorea, which is due to a dominant gene which does not manifest itself until middle life, after the affected person has had children. The condition differs from Achondroplasia in being fatal and very distressing for the sufferer. Additional distress arises if relatives of affected persons foresee, correctly, that they may develop the disease. In such a case,

* A dominant gene is one which produces an effect in single dose, being inherited from one parent only; a recessive gene has no effect unless inherited from both parents, or at least has no serious effect.

there are good grounds for discouraging any person with even one parent or sibling who has developed the disease from having children. I am satisfied that such people should be encouraged to undergo sterilization but doubt that sterilization should be compulsory; the case for compulsory sterilization will be stronger when we learn to recognize heterozygotes before the disease develops.[4]

Now consider a disease such as phenylketonuria, which is due to a gene which is recessive in the sense that only homozygotes suffer from the associated mental defect.[5] Approximately one person in 60,000 in Britain is homozygous for the gene; it follows that one person in 122 is a carrier.[6] Consequently, if we could not recognize the heterozygotes, then the sterilization of homozygotes (in fact, untreated homozygotes normally do not get married or have children) would remove only 1/245 of the mutant genes per generation. Eugenic measures would therefore be ineffective unless applied to heterozygotes, who can in this case be recognized biochemically although they are not mentally defective. But it seems likely that most people are carriers of at least one lethal or deleterious gene, although they cannot at present be recognized as such. It follows that as our ability to recognize heterozygotes increases, we could be led to sterilize almost the whole population on eugenic grounds, which is clearly absurd.

The ability to recognize heterozygotes for such conditions as phenylketonuria makes it possible in principle to eliminate the affected homozygotes by preventing marriage between heterozygotes. (The statement in the previous paragraph that almost everyone is heterozygous for something does not invalidate this conclusion: all that has to be avoided is marriage between two people heterozygous for the *same* gene; and this would rule out only a small fraction of possible marriages.) It is admittedly difficult to see how this can be achieved, but a start might be made by testing relatives of affected persons and partners in prospective marriages between cousins. There is also a sense in which such a measure would be dysgenic. By preventing the birth of affected individuals, it would remove any selection against the mutant gene; and this would lead to an increase in its frequency in the population.[7] To this extent, preventing marriages between heterozygotes could have dysgenic effects similar to the cure of a genetically determined disease.

In earlier discussions of eugenics, suggested measures of positive eugenics took the form of legislation designed to encourage particular classes of persons to have more children. Two examples of such suggestions are increased family allowances for university teachers and a tax on children, the logic behind the latter suggestion being that only the rich would be able to afford children and that wealth is at least an approximate measure of genetic worth.[8] But in recent years increasing attention has been paid to the possibility of artificial insemination. H. J. Muller[9] and, more recently, Julian Huxley[10] have suggested that we should try to persuade married women who have had one child by their husbands to have a second child by a donor of their choice. In view of the sources from which it emanates, if for no other reason, this suggestion merits careful examination.

First, how effective would such a measure be? I shall discuss the effects on a single metrical character; to be concrete I shall consider I.Q. score, since intelligence is the quality most usually prized by people in academic circles who propose eugenic measures. I shall make the following assumptions, which appear to be optimistic:

1) Among women, one per cent could be persuaded on eugenic grounds to have half their children by artificial insemination.
2) The husbands of such women would be a random sample of the population.
3) The mean I.Q. of the donors chosen would be one standard deviation above the population average. (Without intending to be either facetious or offensive, it is fair to ask what would be the relative popularities of Francis Crick and Ringo Starr.)
4) The realized heritability* of I.Q. scores is 0.5.

Given these assumptions, the mean I.Q. score of the next generation (allowing thirty years per generation) would be approximately 0.04 points higher than it would otherwise be. Compared with the rise of approximately two points observed in fifteen years in Scotland—which probably resulted from such things as the spread of radio and television sets—I doubt whether such a rise would be worth the trouble.

Artificial insemination would be less effective in man than in domestic animals because a number of conditions can be satisfied in the latter case but not in the former. These conditions are:

* The realized heritability is defined as the progress under selection divided by the selection differential; that is to say, in the case of I.Q. score, it is the increase in the mean I.Q. score in a generation divided by the difference between the mean I.Q. of the selected parents and that of the population from which they were selected. The realized heritability normally lies between 0 and 1, and the value of 0.5 is fairly typical for a metrical character.

1) It is possible to define the objective of selection—for example, growth rate or milk yield—and to accept deterioration in other characteristics—for example, mobility or intelligence.
2) It is possible to choose the male donors on the basis of this objective and to use progeny testing to ensure that the donors pass the appropriate characters on to their children.
3) It is possible to ensure that most females have most of their offspring by artificial insemination.

I assumed above that only one per cent of women could be persuaded to accept artificial insemination on eugenic grounds. Clearly, the effectiveness of the procedure would be increased if the proportion of women participating were greater. There have been societies in the past in which a large proportion of the women have been persuaded or coerced into a breeding system which had genetic consequences similar to the scheme suggested by Muller and Huxley. For example, among the Nambikuave Indians of central Brazil, a chieftain, nominated by his predecessor but dependent on popular consent, is the only member of the group to have a number of wives.[11] Although this practice does not seem to have been undertaken for genetic reasons, it cannot fail to have genetic consequences.

I do not believe that a larger proportion of the world's population will ever adopt such a system, using either artificial or natural insemination, but this belief may only reveal my prejudices. But it does seem possible that a small racial or religious group might adopt such a practice. If such a group could maintain a fair degree of genetic isolation from the rest of the population and if the great majority of women in the group bore at least one child by a donor of high I.Q. (the argument, of course, will apply to any character), then after a century the mean I.Q. of the group might have risen by one standard deviation, or fifteen points. In other words, a group might arise with an average intelligence similar to that of a group of students selected for a university. This seems hardly sufficient to justify the establishment of a new religion.

But what if artificial selection were continued not for a century but for a millennium? It is unlikely that the mean I.Q. would rise by ten standard deviations. Experience shows that if intense artificial selection for a single character is continued for a number of generations, the genetic response, although rapid at first, tends to slow down and even to stop. It is impossible to predict at what level this "plateau" will be reached.[12] But it seems quite likely that if a human community were to practice artificial selection for intelligence for a thousand years, there would be a rise of several standard deviations in the mean I.Q., and the community might contain several individuals with mental capacities greater than those of anyone alive today.

But as an estimate of what would happen if, for example, a number of groups such as the American Academy of Arts and Sciences were to campaign for artificial insemination on eugenic grounds, a rise of 0.04 points per generation seems optimistic. Nevertheless, it has been argued that artificial insemination is valuable in man because a small rise in mean score would produce a disproportionate increase in the number of people with exceptionally high scores. Thus, if it is assumed that I.Q. score is normally distributed and that a small change in mean I.Q. score does not alter the variance of the score (this need not be true, but it might very well be true),[13] then an increase of one point in mean I.Q. would be accompanied by an increase of twenty per cent in the proportion of people with I.Q.'s above 175. It is argued that although an increase of one point in the mean I.Q. might not be worth bothering about, an increase of twenty per cent in the number of geniuses is well worth striving for.

The argument is weakened by the fact that I.Q. score is not normally distributed; there are many more people with very high and very low scores than would be predicted on the assumption of normality.[14] Thus, if the distribution were normal, an increase of mean I.Q. of one point would lead to an increase in the proportion of people with a score greater than 175 from 3.3 per million to 4 per million. But since the distribution is not normal, the actual increase would be approximately from 77 per million to 85 per million.

But the main weakness of the argument lies in the assumption that an increase in the proportion of people with I.Q. scores above 175 would necessarily, or even probably, be associated with an increase in the number of people of outstanding ability as judged by their achievements. If this were so, it is difficult to explain why some quite small populations, for example Periclean Athens, should in a short time have produced such a number of people who, judged by their achievements, were of outstanding ability, whereas other larger populations, such as Greece during the Byzantine empire, should have produced hardly any. This is not to imply that outstanding achievements do not require unusual genetic endowments or that anyone could have written the *Principia* if he had had Newton's opportunities. What is suggested by a comparison of

Greece in Classical and in Byzantine times is that any reasonably large population is likely to contain people genetically capable of outstanding achievements if social conditions are favorable. The same point is made perhaps more convincingly by referring to the frequent occurrence of simultaneous yet independent discoveries in science. It follows that a small increase in the proportion of people with I.Q. scores above 175 is unlikely to be important.

So far, I have accepted the four assumptions listed above as reasonable approximations. But one of the assumptions—that the husbands of women accepting artificial insemination would be a random sample—is manifestly false for two reasons. First, women accepting artificial insemination on eugenic grounds would hardly be a random sample; and, since mating in man, for intellectual and moral characteristics at least, is not random, their husbands would be likely to resemble them. Second, if the husbands agreed—and the results if they did not would hardly be desirable—they would presumably be above average in humility and unselfishness. It is at least possible to argue that these qualities are more desirable socially than the qualities for which the donors would be chosen. If so, the measure, in so far as it had any effects, would be likely to be dysgenic.

This raises the major difficulty of all suggested measures of positive eugenics, the problem of deciding what we want. It is fairly easy to recognize characteristics—blindness, mental defect, lameness—which we would wish to avoid in our own and in other peoples' children but much more difficult to define characters we wish to encourage, particularly when it is remembered that these characters may be mutually incompatible. Most experience with artificial selection in animals leads to the conclusion that selection in favor of a particular character—for instance, milk yield in cattle or the number of bristles in Drosophila—is effective in altering the selected characters in the desired direction; but the alteration is accompanied by changes in many other characters, changes whose nature cannot be predicted in detail but which are usually undesirable in that they lower fertility or the probability of survival, or impair performance in other ways.[15] This is only a restatement of the point made above when discussing disease resistance, that you rarely get something for nothing. It is a point usually forgotten in discussions of eugenics.

Two other points should be made concerning the problem of deciding what characteristics are desirable. First, it is probable that in man at least some desirable characteristics arise in genetic heterozygotes; if so, it is unreasonable to expect them to breed true. Second, it is far from clear that what we want is a genetically uniform population; indeed, societies seem much more likely to be workable if they contain individuals with a wide range of genetic capabilities.[16]

If our objective is to increase the proportion of genetically gifted people in the population, there is a method which is likely to become feasible in the fairly near future and which would be considerably more effective than artificial insemination. This is to make clonal "copies" of successful people. It has already proved possible to remove the nucleus from a fertilized frog egg and to replace it with the nucleus from one of the cells of a developing embryo; the egg then develops into a frog having the genetic characteristics of the embryo from which the nucleus was taken.[17] It will perhaps soon be possible to remove a fertilized or unfertilized human egg from the oviduct, remove the nucleus, and replace it with a nucleus from, let us say, a germ-line cell of some individual whose genotype we would like to reproduce. Implanted in a uterus, this egg would then develop the same genetically determined characteristics as those of the individual from which the nucleus was taken.

Leaving aside for the moment the desirability of such a "cloning" technique, let us turn to why it would be more effective than artificial insemination. In artificial insemination, only half the genes of the donor are transmitted. Therefore, their effects may be "diluted out" by the genes of the mother; and if the peculiar and desired characteristics of the donor depended on interactions between genes, these are likely to be lost. But in the cloning technique, an exact genetic replica, as in monovular twins, would be obtained.

How strong are the arguments for adopting this measure, supposing that it does become practicable? I do not want to be dogmatic on this point, but two arguments against it should be mentioned. First, the arguments outlined above for believing that human populations have an adequate supply of talented people to meet the problems of the time would, if accepted, show that there is little to be gained by adopting the cloning technique. Second, people "conceived" in this way could have severe and perhaps crippling psychological difficulties. Sons of famous fathers not infrequently suffer because too much is expected of them; much more might be expected of children known to be genetically identical to a famous "ancestor."

I now turn from selectionist to transformationist eugenics, from what we can do to what we may be able to do in the future. I want again to consider the case of sickle cell anemia, although there is a risk that this condition may come to play the same distorting role in evolutionary speculation today that the neck of the giraffe did in the last century. It is known that a person homozygous for the gene S differs from normal people because the hemoglobin in their red blood cells is insoluble and that this difference is due to the substitution of the amino acid valine for glutamic acid at a particular position in the β chain of their hemoglobin. It is reasonably certain that this abnormality is due to the presence of a single abnormal base in a DNA molecule in the chromosomes of blood-forming cells and that this, in turn, is due to the presence of a single abnormal base in a DNA molecule in the fertilized egg from which they developed (strictly speaking, there must have been four abnormal bases, since there were two homologous sets of chromosomes in the egg, each containing an abnormal base pair). When the details of the genetic code have been discovered, which is likely to be soon, it may be possible to specify which base has been substituted for which—for example, that adenine has replaced cytosine at a particular place.

People heterozygous for the gene S can be recognized, since their red blood cells contain about forty per cent of the insoluble hemoglobin and about sixty per cent of normal. A baby suffering from sickle cell anemia will be born only if two heterozygotes marry (except for new mutation or illegitimacy). As was pointed out earlier, the birth of anemic babies could be avoided by preventing the marriage of heterozygotes. It could also be prevented if it proved possible to transform a single base—say adenine to cytosine—in the sperm cells of the father, or in the oocytes of the mother, or in the fertilized egg. This would be an example of negative transformationist eugenics. It would have the immediate effect of preventing the birth of defective children without making it necessary to interfere with the choice of marriage partners and without having the dysgenic effect of causing a gradual increase in the frequency of deleterious genes.

Of the various methods of eugenics which have been or will be discussed in the essay, there seems little doubt that negative transformationist eugenics would be the most desirable. It would require the minimum interference with who marries or has children by whom; its effects would be confined to the limited and generally acceptable objective of preventing the birth of children with specific defects; and, far from having dysgenic effects, transformationist eugenics could provide a means of counteracting the long-term dysgenic effects of some types of medical care.

The drawback, of course, is that such methods are not at present practicable; and it is not yet possible to see how such transformation could be achieved. The major difficulty is the restricted nature of the transformation required. Thus a chemical procedure which transformed all or many of the adenine molecules in a nucleus into cytosine would certainly be fatal; instead, only one particular adenine molecule among the hundreds of thousands present must be transformed. Because of two properties of nucleic acid, namely, homologous pairing and recombination, the problem is not quite so hopeless as it sounds. The first of these two properties makes the following situation possible: if a normal "gene" (DNA molecule) for hemoglobin could be introduced into a cell carrying the mutant S gene, this normal molecule might pair base by base with the abnormal one. The second property raises the possibility that in some circumstances the normal molecule might replace the abnormal one in the chromosome. Something of this kind does occur in the phenomenon of bacterial transformation; unfortunately, it is now confined to bacterial cells, which are much readier to accept nucleic acid molecules than are animal cells, and even then it is possible to transform only a small proportion of the cells exposed to transforming nucleic acid. I find it impossible to say how much my conviction that transformation will become a practicable eugenic tool arises because the wish is father to the thought; but at least it seems rational for the next hundred years or so to attempt to cure or to make life possible for people with congenital diseases without worrying too much about the ultimate dysgenic effects.

Transformationist eugenics has its most obvious area of application in the negative field, in altering genes which give rise to obvious and gross deficiencies. It is possible to visualize positive application in animal breeding; if, for example, resistance to a particular disease, or ability to digest a particular food, could be shown to depend on the presence of a particular enzyme, then a gene determining that enzyme might be incorporated into the genotype of a domestic species. But the major application of transformationist genetics is likely to be in producing genetically changed micro-organisms designed to play particular roles in the manufacture of food and of other complicated chemical substances. It is more difficult to see positive applications to man. The production of individuals of outstanding intelligence will again be taken as an example, although even greater difficulties would arise if the characters chosen were, for instance, artistic ability or moral worth. The difficulty is simply stated: we do not know what changes in the egg's ability to synthesize specific proteins would lead to increased intelligence in the adult developing from the egg; therefore, even if we knew how to bring about specific gene transformations, we would not know what transformations to make. There is no reason to think that the problem is insoluble, but it would appear to be much further from solution than the problem of genetic transformation itself.

This brings me to the third technique available for the alteration of man's nature, that of biological engineering.[18] Here I have in mind the extension of existing medical techniques from the negative to the positive field. Today it is standard practice to attempt to cure many congenital defects by surgical or medical techniques, and there is no reason to doubt that treatment of congenital disease will be supplemented or replaced in the future by methods of treating the fetus so that the developmental process is altered and a normal child is born. But at this moment we do not use or contemplate using such techniques to produce outstanding individuals. For example, it would perhaps be technically possible through surgery to produce a man whose legs were so lengthened that he could run a mile in 3½ minutes. But, sensibly enough, we prefer to let nature take its course and manufacture motor cars and airplanes if we want to move fast. But we do not hesitate to cure a lame child if we can.

It seems, then, that our present practice depends on a concept of normality, however difficult that may be to define. Since we are concerned here with a problem of what we ought to do rather than what is technically feasible, it is perhaps best to regard a characteristic as abnormal if it leads to a loss of function sufficient to cause its possessor to be unhappy. But we should ask also if there are circumstances in which we might wish to produce outstanding individuals. In the field of physical performance this seems unlikely, since it will always be easier to build a machine. There is, however, one exception: we cannot build machines to make us live longer. It is not at present possible to say whether we shall ever be able to produce a large increase in human life expectancy, even though we can already ensure that a larger proportion of people survive to old age. We do not at present know whether senescence is caused by a number of physiologically independent processes—in which case, even if we prevented one of these processes people would still die at much the same age of another—or whether there is one fundamental process of which the various superficial signs of senescence are merely symptoms. If the former assumption is correct, and the evidence suggests to me that it is, then a significant extension of the human life span is likely to prove very difficult.[19] It would also contribute disastrously to the present increase in world population. But should the world population problem prove soluble without war or famine, then an increase in human life span, if it could be associated with an appropriate decrease in human fertility, seems to me very desirable.

Olaf Stapledon, in his book *Last and First Men,* imagined the use of biological engineering to produce super-intelligences. Human neural tissue was permitted to grow and ramify through the corridors of a building and was supplied with sensory information and a motor output. In *Sirius* the same author imagined a dog whose intelligence, by surgical and other means, had been made equal to that of a man. These feats are not at present technically possible, but there is no reason that it should not eventually be possible to bring about a dramatic increase in the size of certain parts of a human or animal brain by influencing development. It is, of course, by no means certain that such a simple procedure would lead to an equivalent increase in intelligence; it might equally well lead to idiocy. But there is one reason to suspect that an appropriate increase in size, together with other comparatively minor changes in structure, might lead to a large increase in intelligence. The evolution of modern man from non-tool-making ancestors has presumably been associated with and dependent on a large increase in intelligence, but has been completed in what is on an evolutionary scale a rather short time—at most a few million years. This suggests that the transformation in the brain which provided the required increase in intelligence may have been growth in size with relatively little increase in structural complexity—there was insufficient time for natural selection to do more. Of course, this process may have reached its limit, and further increase in intelligence may require a major reorganization of structure, which would be difficult to bring about by "engineering" methods.

On balance, it seems quite likely that within a hundred years or so it will be technically feasible to do the kinds of things imagined in Stapledon's books. But even if it is, it is not clear what the consequences would be. To ask oneself the consequence of building such an intelligence is a little like asking an Australopithecine what kind of questions Newton would ask himself and what answers he would give. One way of putting the problem is this: What questions could be asked or answered by a "super-intelligence" composed of neurons which could not be asked and answered by teams of investigators given time and the assistance of computors? It is quite possible that the answer to this question is "none." But I suspect that if our species survives, someone will try it and see.

The subjects discussed in this essay are diverse, so I will attempt to summarize my argument and draw some general conclusions. First, evolutionary changes are constantly occuring in the human species, and most legislative or social measures we take inevitably influence the nature of these changes. Some, but by no means all, of the genetic changes consequent upon improved medical and social services are dysgenic. At present, there is little that we can do to prevent these dysgenic effects, and the proper course for us to adopt is to regard them as part of the price we pay for being civilized. In any case these genetic changes are extremely slow in comparison with technical changes, and it is reasonable to hope that before they have become significant it may be possible to avert or reverse them by techniques of genetic transformation.

Deliberate measures to alter man's biological nature may be negative, designed to prevent or cure mental or physical defect, or positive, designed to produce individuals of unusually high performance in a desired area or to raise the mean level of performance. Techniques available can be classified as selectionist eugenics, transformationist eugenics, and biological engineering. Selectionist eugenics involves altering the relative number of offspring born to particular kinds of individuals or pairs. In most cases, these procedures are likely to be too ineffective to be worth bothering with. But it is worth making an effort to prevent individuals who carry deleterious dominant mutations which manifest themselves late in life from having children and to prevent the carriers of the same recessive lethal or deleterious gene from marrying one another, although the latter measure would have dysgenic effects in the long run. In the positive field, selectionist eugenics is again likely to be relatively ineffective. Probably the most effective procedure, and one which should become technically feasible in the fairly near future, would be some form of cloning.

Transformationist eugenics, involving direct alteration of specific genes in specific ways, is not at the moment possible, but may become so. If it does become possible, its use in negative eugenics would be desirable; but it is less clear what role it could play in positive eugenics.

Biological engineering in the negative field is simply another word for current medical practice. Problems, both technical and ethical, arise in the use of similar techniques to produce individuals of outstanding ability rather than to cure or prevent abnormality. Two major undertakings can be considered. One, a significant increase in the human life span, although dangerous unless the world population problem has been solved, will in the long run be desirable, but it is likely to prove very difficult and perhaps impossible. The other, the production of individuals generally resembling human beings but of outstanding intelligence, may prove relatively easy, although there is no guarantee that this is so; but even if it is technically feasible, it does not seem possible to predict what important results, if any, would ensue.

But these problems of transformationist eugenics, increase of longevity, and super-intelligence still lie in a future which is distant in historical terms even if it is immediate on an evolutionary time scale. Our immediate problem is what should be done with the means now available to us, and, more immediate still, what should geneticists and other biologists recommend be done.

I think the answer to this question is that we should not recommend that anything be done except the simple and limited negative measures suggested above. The reason for this is that I believe recommendations of positive eugenic measures can at the present only distract attention from more urgent and important questions. The most urgent message which biologists have to convey to the public is that if something is not done to arrest the present increase in world population, then that increase will be arrested by war, disease, and starvation. Eugenics can wait, birth control cannot.

References

1. For a discussion of this point, see P. B. Medawar, *The Future of Man* (London: Methuen, 1959).

2. The evidence for a negative correlation between family size and I.Q. is summarized by L. S. Penrose, "Evidence of Heterosis in Man," *Proc. Roy. Soc.*, B. 144 (1955), p. 203. Penrose puts forward a genetic hypothesis which would account for this correlation and yet predict no change in I.Q. with time. His views have been criticized by P. B. Medawar, *op. cit.*, and by K. Mather, "Genetical Demography," *Proc. Roy. Soc.*, B. 159 (1963),

p. 106. For a comparison of the 1932 and 1947 surveys in Scotland, see G. H. Thomson, *The Trend of Scottish Intelligence* (London: University of London Press, 1949).

3. The argument which follows is presented in J. B. S. Haldane, *Heredity and Politics* (London: Allen and Unwin, 1938).

4. Another genetically determined abnormality which, although not caused by a dominant gene, could be reduced in frequency by negative eugenic measures is translocation mongolism. Individuals of either sex heterozygous for a translocation involving chromosome 21 are themselves normal, but one third of their children will be mongolian idiots and one third will be "carriers"; only one third will be normal and likely to have normal children. Such people could be recognized if the chromosomes in a skin or blood sample were examined, and most of them would be found if all relatives of known mongols were examined. But the arguments for sterilization are perhaps less strong than in the case of Huntingdon's chorea because. Mongolian idiots are commonly quite cheerful and contented. In any case, sterilization would not prevent the more common form of mongolism which is due to nondisjunction in the mother.

5. It has recently been found that a homozygous baby, if recognized at birth and subsequently kept on a diet free of phenylalamine, can develop normal intelligence. This does not affect the argument concerning the ineffectiveness of sterilization in the case of diseases caused by recessive genes, but it does illustrate the important point that genetically determined diseases may be curable.

6. This frequency omits cases known to have consanguineous parents. The frequency of carriers has been worked out from the Hardy-Weinberg ratio, assuming random mating.

7. It could be argued that this would not be dysgenic provided that marriage between heterozygotes was prevented. However, it is unlikely that we should succeed in preventing all such marriages. Also, the proportion of marriages contra-indicated on genetic grounds would increase. But it seems likely that long before these effects become serious some technique of negative transformationist eugenics will be available.

8. The idea that financial measures might be used for eugenic purposes was put forward by R. A. Fisher, *The Genetical Theory of Natural Selection* (London: Oxford University Press, 1930). The suggestion of a tax on children was made, perhaps not very seriously, by F. H. C. Crick in Gordon Wolstenholme (ed.), *Man and his Future* (London: Churchill, 1963), p. 276. The suggestion has the virtue of bringing out the necessary contradiction between financial measures suggested on eugenic grounds and those suggested by the humanitarian desire to protect children from the incompetence of their parents. On the same occasion, Crick made the more important point that the time has come to question our present assumption that people have a right to have children.

9. H. J. Muller, *Out of the Night* (New York: Vanguard Press, 1935); and "Genetical Progress by Voluntarily Conducted Germinal Choice," in Gordon Wolstenholme (ed.), *op. cit.*

10. J. S. Huxley, *Eugenics in Evolutionary Perspective* (London: Eugenics Society, 1962).

11. C. Levi-Strauss, *A World on the Wane* (London: Hutchinson, 1961).

12. For the occurrence of "plateaus" in selection experiments, see, for example, K. Mather and B. J. Harrison, "The Manifold Effects of Selection," *Heredity,* Vol. 3 (1949), p. 131; and I. M. Lerner, *Genetic Homeostasis* (New York: John Wiley & Sons, 1954).

13. A small change in mean will not alter the variance if the effects of a different gene on I.Q. are additive and if the frequencies of alleles for high and low intelligence are on the average equal.

14. C. Burt, "Is Intelligence Distributed Normally?" *Br. J. Statist. Psychol.,* Vol. 16 (1963), p. 175.

15. The occurrence of such correlated changes is not in doubt, although their explanation is still a matter of controversy; the subject is discussed in the references given under 12 above.

16. These two points are too important to be dismissed in a brief paragraph; my excuse is that they have been discussed more fully by T. Dohzhansky, *Mankind Evolving* (New Haven: Yale University Press, 1962).

17. T. J. King and R. Briggs, "Serial transplantation of embryonic nuclei," *C.S.H. Symp. Quart. Biol.,* Vol. 27 (1956), p. 271.

18. Some possible developments of biological engineering, or "euphenics," were discussed by J. Lederberg, "Biological Future of Man," in Gordon Wolstenholme (ed.), *op. cit.*

19. For a discussion of this point, see G. C. Williams, "Pleiotrophy, natural selection and the evolution of senescence," *Evolution,* Vol. 11 (1957), p. 398; and J. Maynard Smith, "The Causes of Ageing," *Proc. Roy. Soc.,* B. 157 (1962), p. 115.

JOHN R. PIERCE

Communications Technology and the Future

VIEWS OF the future in which writers have made a strong effort to take science and technology into account have often been anti-utopian. Consider, for example, a type of prediction which goes back as far as Wells' *When the Sleeper Wakes* and forward as far as Aldous Huxley's *Brave New World.* In looking into the future, the writer saw man overwhelmed by machines and by the social structure which seemed to be growing up around the machine and which seemed necessary in a technological civilization. The tyrannies of transportation, of water, of sewers, of communication, no less than the tyrannies of class and of government, seemed to point clearly to a civilization of more compact and more crowded cities and to a domination of every aspect of man's life by the technological civilization which supports him.

When we look at contemporary American life, we find that science, technology, and man himself have played a nasty trick on such prophecies. I shall not pursue at length the divergence of the real world from the world of prophecy; we can all see that sprawling suburbia and wandering population are chief characteristics of the nonstagnant part of our society. Rather, I shall inquire why informed, intelligent, and imaginative prophets went so amiss in their predictions, and I shall ask what science and technology may make possible in the future.

What prophets of utopias and anti-utopias have lacked has been partly a foreknowledge of inherently unpredictable inventions. Among these we may include the vacuum tube and the transistor, which have both had a profound effect on our civilization, as well as the laser, the maser, plastics, antibiotics, and a host of other discoveries and inventions. Any prophet, social or scientific, is bound to miss things of this sort, and to the degree that the unpredictable and the unforeseeable strongly affect the future, a prophet is bound to miss. Partly, however, prophets of the past have underestimated both the adaptability of man and the phenomenally swift and strong impact of inventions and advances which, at their inception, seemed toys of civilization. Outstanding among such inventions and advances have been the telephone, the automobile, the airplane, and the radio and television, which at first showed little promise of the revolutionary effects which they have had.

In contrast with the tiered and domed warrens of humanity foreseen in the nineteenth century and early twentieth century, flexibility in transportation, power, and communication and flexibility of man in using them have created a strikingly different civilization. In our world, highways and the automobile have led a large fraction of our citizens into far corners of our land. Now the airplane is leading a substantial number of Americans not only across the country but across the seas. The automobile, the telephone, and electric power have made it possible for people to live remote from public transportation and from their places of work. Together with bottled gas and septic tanks, these inventions have enabled people of modest means to live at a high level of contemporary comfort far even from standardized suburbs or small communities. Moreover, through radio and television as means of mass communication and through the telephone and automobiles as individual means of communication, men separated in space can keep in as close touch with contemporary events as they care to. Also, our system of marketing has followed the population away from the centers of the cities, so that there is no real need for man to travel to and from a few central points.

What I propose to do in this paper is to examine some new possibilities in the fields of science and technology, and especially in the field of communication, which could perhaps eventually have as great an influence on our lives and on our behavior and on the welfare of mankind as have the developments mentioned above. Some of the things which I will discuss are new; some of them may have a newness for the reader; and some, though old, have aspects which are little recognized and therefore seem novel. The first field which will be examined is that of communication. Here I shall deal with relatively less expensive communication and with technologically and organizationally augmented communication services. Both can have strong effects on our individual lives and on the organization of our lives into a national economy.

The importance of relatively less expensive communication need not be labored. Reduced rates after nine have led to worth-while personal conversations with distant children and relatives and have, incidentally, greatly increased the amount of such communication. General lowering in the cost of communication will make it more practical as well as more convenient to communicate rather than travel, and this may save endless wear and tear on the man of the future. We have become accustomed, but not adapted, to flying repeatedly across the country for a few hours of private conversation, and we may in the future dispense with this drain on our time and our energy.

But it is not merely the decreasing cost which will expand the role that communication plays in our lives. Man is no longer anchored physically to a home or an office; thus, in today's life he may be cut off from important business and personal contacts if he takes full advantage of his mobility. In the present, and increasingly the future, technology can provide a remedy. One part of the remedy is the use of answering services which will take messages or give information when a man is absent from his home or office. Beyond this, personal signalling services are coming into wider use. A man carries with him a small, specialized radio which buzzes when there is a telephone message for him. He can then go to the nearest public telephone and, by dialing a particular number, find out what the message is.

Beyond this personal signalling service lies mobile telephony. Today this is available to a very limited degree for automobiles in some regions of the country. The cost is high and the quality of the service is less than that for stationary telephones. In the future telephones in automobiles may become as common as telephones in homes. Whether or not this will happen turns partly on the problem of the limited availability of radio frequency bandwidths and partly on a hard choice concerning public interest. It would seem that the government, through the Federal Communications Commission, has in the past favored mass communication over individual communication. Thus, the frequencies most suitable for mobile telephony have largely been assigned to ultra high frequency television, although there has been little use of UHF television. The public cannot have mobile telephony unless frequencies are assigned for this use. However, there has also been a technological obstacle to mobile telephony, that of cost. This is an obstacle which can be overcome. Advances such as microminiaturization or integrated circuits will make elaborate electronic equipment cheaper, more reliable, and more compact. Indeed, I for one would not rule out the possibility of a mobile telephone which one could carry in his pocket. But, long before the time when that is practical, the issue will have been settled in connection with mobile telephony in cars. Today, no one can tell whether mass communication or the individual will win out.

Not all the future possibilities of communication will come through a further development and use of already existing services. Some of the communication of the future will be better than or different from what we now have. Present electronic communication (except for broadcasts) is largely between two individuals. It is largely restricted to telegrams and telephone calls. The teletypewriter has a modest usage between business offices of various kinds. One new kind of communication will be conferences held by means of electrical communication, rather than face to face. These will certainly involve voice communication, but probably not by means of hand-held telephones. The conferees will speak and listen as if the people with whom they are conferring were in the room. Certainly, communication beyond voice communication will be necessary in holding a conference. Experiments have been made with telewriting devices, by means of which hand-drawn or handwritten diagrams or text can be made to appear on screens simultaneously in several conference rooms. Perhaps some of the communications in connection with conferences will be carried out by teletypewriter. Facsimile is a more flexible means of communication than either the telewriter or teletypewriter, but it is more expensive. Much more expensive than any of these is television, which is also at present limited in resolution.

Today, experimental and, in a few instances, actual conferences are carried on by means of voice and a variety of other forms of communication: telewriting devices, teletypewriter, facsimile, and television. In a very close tomorrow, there is bound to be a rapidly increasing use of conference facilities involving voice and some sort of record communication. We cannot now see just what course conferences through electronic communication will take, but we can see that the substitution of communication for travel will be made to some degree. But person-to-person as well as group-to-group communication will change with time. All of our communication by electronic means is bound to be extended.

The linking of voice communication and data communication is bound to become more common. Today, in a business conversation I frequently write down particular statements of facts or figures, sometimes of a technical nature and sometimes concerning reservations. Sometimes I dictate such material to a secretary over a telephone. This is a primitive, fallible, and exasperating resort. In the future, I am sure that it will be common in business communication to intersperse typewritten material with remarks, all carried over the same circuit, to a degree dictated by the nature of a particular conversation. And, I can see this extending into the home, in the making of reservations, in the purchasing of advertised goods, in the control of household devices, and in many other ways. Finally, I foresee that as communication becomes less specialized than voice or data communication, it will come to include not only human beings, but computers as well, and here we must make an excursion into some of the present and future capabilities of computers.

Wrong-minded early prophets tended to think of the computer as like a man, only more so. So we might once have thought of an automobile as an imitation of a horse or of an airplane as an imitation of a bird. A horse is wonderful, and an automobile is wonderful, but they are wonderful in different ways. The horse excels in flexibility, self-sufficiency, and intelligence; the automobile is weak in all of these respects. In fact, the automobile could not exist profitably without our elaborate system of highways. However, the automobile is wonderful in speed and endurance. In a like way, a bird is wonderful in flexibility; an airplane is wonderful in speed and endurance.

While a computer has played a good but not championship game of checkers, it has not played a good game of chess, nor has it proved theorems in competition with trained mathematicians. The computer has not excelled at old tasks. What it has done has been to open up the possibility of new tasks, and it has done new and surprising things that are very pertinent to the future. Some of these things one might class as keeping account, in one primitive and limited but very accurate and capacious mind, of all aspects of some simple but knotty problem which was formerly spread ineffectively among a host of human beings and a plethora of records. Thus, the computer can do a superb job in payroll, in accounting, in inventory control, and in reservations services for airlines and railroads. Beyond this, a computer can aid a human being in carrying out fatiguing and vexing chores. Once a group of entries has been reduced to a machine-readable form, it is no trouble for a computer to arrange them in a variety of indexes, according to author, title, important words in the title, or assigned subject headings which have been associated with the title and the author. Computers are widely used in such indexing and will be more extensively used.

In newspapers and libraries, for example, the computer is being exploited as a means for editing texts. Thus, if the original text has been reduced to machine-readable form and recorded on magnetic tape, a separate tape can be prepared which refers to a print-out of the text. Such an editing tape can instruct the computer to make corrections, additions, or deletions. The computer can then make changes; and, beyond that, the computer can justify and hyphenate the text and even arrange it in pages of uniform length.

While the computer has been powerful in dealing with texts, it has been perhaps even more powerful in dealing with a whole spectrum or class of design and production functions. These include the preparation of wiring diagrams, the control of automatic wiring machines, the carrying out of standard sorts of mechanical and electrical design of various structures and of various electrical networks.

In addition, the computer is becoming an aid in more complicated problems, such as the logical design of parts of computers and computer-like systems. This is bound to extend to more and more complex systems. Another profitable use of the computer has been in the manipulation of complex algebraic expressions which are beyond the capability of a human being because of limitations of time and the requirements of accuracy. And, a whole new spectrum of unexpected uses of computers has come about by means of peripheral equipment which can turn strings of numbers into sounds or into motions of the spot on a cathode ray screen, motions which trace out diagrams or pictures.

It was soon realized that a computer is a generalized machine which can simulate the operation of simpler machines. Thus, one can represent the vibrations which constitute a sound wave by a sequence of numbers which specify the amplitude of the wave at evenly spaced intervals. The computer can be programmed to act on these numbers and to produce a new sequence of numbers specifying a new sound wave. This process can be made to simulate what any complicated communication device would do to a sound wave. Thus, it is no longer necessary to build complicated devices in order to try them out. Further, computer simulation can be carried out in a more general way in a much more general class of problems.

If a computer is capable of processing a string of numbers which represent a sound wave, it can also generate a string of numbers which can represent a sound wave. In fact, computers have been used to generate articulate speech from a sequence of phonetic symbols. While the quality is not yet good, it is sure to be improved. Thus, in the future it will be possible for a computer which is queried by means of a sequence of letters or numbers to give a spoken answer from a store of alphabetical information without the crude and complicated expedient of tape-recorded words or sentences. The computer has been pushed beyond, or perhaps to the side of, this difficult process of generating articulate speech to the generation of musical sounds. Here its versatility is without limit. In principle, the computer can generate any sound that any limited number of instruments could generate and, in fact, any sound that can possibly exist. At present, the musician stands in the same relation to the computer as a savage does to a grand piano. Wonderful things could come out of that box if only we knew how to evoke them. The same can be said about the computer and visual arts. Computers have been used not only to solve the equations of motion of a satellite whirling around the earth but to portray in animated motion pictures changes in the attitude of the satellite with the passage of time. They have also been used to mix chance with choice in creating surprising patterns that may well be art.

What will be the effect of the combination of computer and electrical communication in the world of the future? It may lead to a centralization of computers and perhaps to the centralization of men performing some types of functions. We may, for instance, not have even a part-time telephone service representative in every small community. Instead, we may have more centrally located service representatives who, aided by computer-stored information, are available twenty-four hours a day to anyone who cares to call them by telephone.

But the centralization will be that of specialized machines or specialized men. Coupled with communication, the computer will make complicated services more widely available. Project MAC, which is being pursued at MIT, is an example of this. At present, computers are proliferating; many will be found in a large university or a large industrial organization. Project MAC envisions one central computer with peripheral control and display installations in many locations, so that anyone who needs to use a computer can have as much time as he needs in any location that is convenient to him, without the expense, maintenance problems, and inefficiency caused by the clutter of many computers.

Advances such as Project MAC are bound to make computers widely available for teaching in schools where they are not now available. But, beyond that, people will use computers from their homes—ordering, making reservations, or seeking information. In fact, this may extend to banking as well as to other business transactions, so that only actual goods need go through the mails or be carried by anybody. A combination of verbal instructions and button-punching will do the rest.

So far I have written about matters of the technology of communications, but these are insufficient and meaningless unless linked with important developments in transportation. In connection with these, let us first look at the world of the present. Today the country is overrun with automobiles. The greatest effect of the automobile has been a freeing effect. It has enabled man to detach the factory from the city. It has enabled man to detach his home from his place of work. It has enabled him to detach himself from his home in taking wide ranging vacations. But, the automobile has brought with it the problem of congested traffic in cities and in areas which reflect the patterns of past cities. A congestion of automobile traffic can make a city or neighborhood obsolete.

Prophets of a past age foresaw growth of the city, and this has indeed come about. But, the growth is not now chiefly a growth of the center of the city but of its suburban environs. These have flourished when industry has moved into the suburbs and have been beset with a whole new series of problems when the suburbs have been merely dormitories for people who commute to the center of a city. The population of rural areas, the scattered population dependent on farming, has shrunk. The population of inhabited areas has grown. But many of these inhabited areas are a new and unforeseen phenomenon—extensive strips of population, alternately industrial and residential.

The automobile is only a part of the story of present and future transportation. The present would be impossible without the airplane. As yet, the airplane has been geared to the old idea of a centralized city. Transportation to and from an airport is difficult, and the air traveler almost inevitably passes through a congested area either near the airport or on his way to it. The growth of our air transportation is a triumph of a technological good which has succeeded almost without thought or forethought in its application. Air transport is bound to grow, but no one yet knows how it can be fitted into the life of the future. Perhaps this will come about through an improvement in airplanes capable of vertical takeoff and landing so that they become swifter, more enduring, and less obnoxious than the helicopter. A network of local and central airports will also help.

Up to this point I have recited a list of advances in communication and in transportation which can well make possible a world of the future which is different from the world we see about us, or from a world we might imagine if we were to believe that technology inevitably follows man's desires rather than that man's desires frequently follow technological advances. With this sketch of the possible, of the realizable, in mind, I propose to ask, is there a happy vision of the future, a happy world of tomorrow? To me there is a vision which is exciting and desirable indeed.

I do not feel that the Government will grow less obtrusive. Rather, we will increasingly adapt ourselves to an ordered part of existence which is necessary for the general well-being. The Founding Fathers would see our lives as restricted to an intolerable degree by Federal, state, and local authority. But, we have become habituated to a host of licenses, permits, regulations, prohibitions, and directives. We have grown accustomed to these laws of social life, just as we have to the laws of nature. We no longer notice them. But, we would find the poverty and uncertainty of the life of the early years of our republic intolerable. In the same way, we suffer petty annoyances of method in our work which come not from ill will but from the functioning of any large machine. These will persist in the future, but we will not rebel against them.

In the future, government will be larger, business will be larger, life will be more integrated. This is the price that we must pay for technological well-being. But integration will no longer mean centralization. Electrical communication, the computer as a record keeper, and rapid and flexible means of transportation will make possible a civilization which can be highly integrated without being centralized.

In the same way, a certain portion of our lives, of our work, and of our dealing with our obligations to the nation will be more reduced to rule. But within this structure, for those who have something of intellectual importance to offer, the options will be greater, and in our private lives the options will be greater still. The computer will take over "mental" routine as the machine has supplanted specialized physical effort.

It is becoming more and more practical and, indeed, desirable for industries to be scattered widely over the face of the country. Yet in this scattering, with its variety of climate and terrain, there is and will be a greater unity than there ever has been in the past. We will have a population that is less provincial, less concentrated, and more mobile. And, despite great distances, individuals will be able to associate more easily both by electrical communication and by personal travel. The population will be held together by its very mobility, which will increasingly lead people to move to areas of greater temporary opportunity and will bring about more frequent transfer of people from one geographical sector of an industry to another. The population will also be held together through the mass media, whether by printed pages, radio, or television.

Aside from being a unifying influence, the mass media themselves can achieve a new degree of flexibility, a new adaptation to local and group needs. Thus, more local newspapers will become available through improved composing and printing methods. The publication and distribution of books will become simpler and cheaper, and their dissemination wider, through computerized means of going from one initial keyboard operation to a final printing.

What will happen to the arts as society is increasingly integrated and increasingly decentralized? I cannot believe that live, professional theater and opera can be maintained as anything but an input to television distribution. This may not reduce the number of professional performers. Easier transportation may increase rather than diminish highly qualified touring artists and small groups, such as string quartets. But also, good art, in sight and sound, will become more widely available than it has ever been in the world, through the medium of improved recordings.

We may ask, what will happen to the creative artist? Through the computer, the composer will be given something more powerful than any orchestra which now exists and more accessible than the orchestra which was at Haydn's beck and call. What the computer may do to the graphic arts, I do not know. Certainly it will be available to the architect as a means for exploring the visual and structural consequences of various general designs. It will make cheaper and easier the construction of specialized structures and systems out of standard components or by standard mechanized means. In its functioning as an editing and reproducing device, the computer could, as I have said, open more newspapers, more journals, more opportunities for publication of books to the talented writer.

My object in writing this paper has not been to predict a utopia, and I have given one happy view of the future merely to illustrate a possible outcome of probable technology. This is not an inevitable outcome nor is it an outcome which could survive unforeseen inventions or discoveries.

In view of the technology of the present and the future, I could imagine a sad world indeed. Our cities are proud monuments. They are also refuges of the least able and the least mobile elements in our population. It may be that cities are increasingly unnecessary and increasingly uneconomic. Yet it is hard to give the city up when it is in being. A determined effort to preserve the city at any cost might be too onerous a burden for our economy to withstand. There is another aspect of contemporary life that could lead to a gloomy future. Even those without economic training or sociological sophistication have noticed the bustle, the challenge and the productivity of a nation in time of war. There is now to a degree an economic equivalent of war in Federal action in such fields as defense and space. Expenditure without product, and product without use, together with a continuous inflation, have become parts of the functioning of our economic system. Will a diversion of a larger and larger fraction of our national effort to collective enterprises of small utility to the individual in the end leave less and less for the individual in the world of the future?

Another troubling thought is the problem of the underdeveloped nations. Ours is a time of the emergence of more and more nations, each with little skill, little government, and, above all, little economic integration with the technology of the world. New nations are cut off by national pride from the highly integrated economic systems of North America, Europe, the Soviet Union, and Japan. Our prosperity depends increasingly on an integrated, if not a centralized, way of life. Cables and communication satellites and improved transportation could provide links between our economy and the economies of small and underdeveloped nations. But, insistence on national independence and national policies creates barriers that complicate the integration of small nations into a larger life.

The underdeveloped nations may become somewhat more prosperous. It is hard to see a future in which they will not fall further and further behind the larger nations which have well-integrated industrial economies. Nationalism, which Einstein once described as the measles of mankind, now seems to be its plague, and one wonders whether a prosperous technological civilization can indefinitely survive it.

IV

UTOPIA AS PRACTICE

MAREN LOCKWOOD

The Experimental Utopia in America

To SOMEONE living in the nineteenth century, utopia was imminent; it was not an impractical, impossible notion. Utopia could exist: it was expounded as a legitimate hope for the average citizen and it was embodied in more than a hundred experimental communities scattered across the country.[1] Eminent men of letters toyed with the notion. A national convention of "Associationists" took place in New York in April 1844 counting among its officers Charles A. Dana, Horace Greeley, and William H. Channing.[2] One or two of such men, like Hawthorne and Alcott, actually tried the life. On the other hand, superficially it would seem today that utopia is indeed "nowhere." A few communities spot the American landscape, but we pay them scant attention. The concept utopia has dropped out of high-school text books, and, like the New Jerusalem, utopian communities seem to be part of a vague mythology, tried and found wanting. What, one wonders, has happened to the idea of the experimental community since its nineteenth-century golden age?

The intellectual currents of the last century, fed by the notions of the Enlightenment, looked upon the future of mankind with an optimism that is a familiar part of our national self-concept. In the nineteenth century this optimism was not a vaguely hopeful temper of mind so much as a specific belief: man could improve himself socially and morally. For some, this came as a great surge of exultation and a sanguine faith that now men could indeed become like gods. The English poet John Addington Symonds expressed this extreme optimism in a poem that later appeared for a while in the *Methodist Hymn Book:*

> These things shall be! a loftier race
> Than e'er the world has known shall rise
> With flame of freedom in their souls
> And light of science in their eyes.

New arts shall bloom of loftier mould,
And mightier music thrill the skies,
And every life shall be a song,
When all the earth is paradise.[3]

For some, this paradise was not a distant hope, but an immediate expectation. Recent technological discoveries and theoretical reformulations seemed to have increased dramatically the pace of social change. Perhaps society was emerging into some glorious era. There were those who said this social progress lay beyond man's control, part of Spencer's organic and superorganic evolution. Others saw man a willing instrument in the process. They declared he had already made great improvements and asked could he not, with all the confidence of his new-found power, direct his destiny. Could he not begin to remodel society, men's social relationships, their work, their means of support, their very minds?

This was what the utopians asserted. When the idea of the experimental community was imported from Europe through the writings of Fourier and Owen, and through the persuasive lectures of fervent utopians like Arthur Brisbane, it found a warm response. The Yankee practicality that might well discourage such notions even worked in their favor, for the utopians too were, in this sense, practical men. Like those politicians who devised the Constitution, like the pioneers who grappled with their new land, like Franklin experimenting with electricity, they promised a demonstration of the better life. They would detach themselves from the worldly society. Freed of its imperfections, they would create an ideal social system composed of truly moral men.

This widespread expectation of improvement imbued the concept of utopia with much of its nineteenth-century vigor. But its glowing vitality was sustained simultaneously by several other prevalent social themes. These included the deep religious interest of the age, the admiration of individual enterprise and pioneering endeavor, and that prosaic enthusiasm for practical application we have mentioned. Only when such generally acknowledged and approved notions were joined with the exigencies of actual experiment did the peculiarities of utopia appear. Then the communities seemed grotesque fantasies with scarcely a feature to represent the character of their age. Thus the better life might include communalism, celibacy, free love, greatest rewards for the least attractive work, intellectual exercise combined with physical toil, religious devotion, the free expression of natural passion, industry, education, intellectual isolation—a great store of ideas drawn upon in many different combinations by the earnest utopians.

One particular utopia, the Oneida community, produced a remarkable number of exotic variations on general societal practice and combined these in a strangely harmonious and long-lived society. In these specific practices we can trace the influence of the more general social themes and show how they found a very reasonable expression in Oneida's peculiar conception.[4]

Oneida rooted its utopian idealism in religious belief. During the nineteenth century, established doctrine was threatened by radical ideas, and religion was projected into the forefront of change. While the more orthodox churches, such as the Presbyterian and Congregationalist, clung to a creed which accepted human sinfulness as their earthly lot, the radical denominations sought to introduce the vivid solace of the Enlightenment's conception of man. The Puritans had seen man as a depraved soul, who lay beneath the hand of a just but wrathful God and who was powerless to affect his own destiny. This conception gave way to the optimism of the age; the future progress of man was unbounded, and all who put themselves in God's benevolent hands could find earthly redemption. Such interpretations found many varied expressions within the orthodox churches as well as without. They were part of the great shift in the Boston churches from Congregationalism to Unitarianism. They were represented in the heretical wranglings within the divinity schools. And they found their most extreme manifestation among little groups of dissidents who, like the ascetic Shakers and the imperturbable Mormons, voiced their personal sanctity.

This enticing religious development of the theme of progress found one of its strongest statements among the groups of rebellious "Perfectionists" which appeared mostly in the northern and eastern parts of the country. In particular, it underlay the belief system of the Oneida community. Oneida Perfectionism taught that the Second Coming of Christ had occurred in 70 A.D. and that since that date all had been in readiness for the eventual perfection of this earthly life. Far more radical than Channing, who simply saw elements of divinity in man's spiritual nature,[5] it assured the individual of perfection by the simple process of accepting Christ into his soul. Such a spiritual apprehension of perfection in no way guaranteed sinless behavior. That required great personal exertion, and could reach its ultimate state only in "Bible Communism," that is, in community life as practiced at Oneida.

In 1848, John Humphrey Noyes founded the Oneida community in central New York on a piece of land that not long since had belonged to the Indians. There he joined his own gifts (which were material as well as spiritual) to the farming skills of Perfectionist Jonathan Burt and engendered a community that was to survive.

In moving toward if not actually to the frontier, Noyes followed the American utopians' usual practice. With notable exceptions like Brook Farm, most earlier communities had chosen sites west of central New York and Pennsylvania and east of the Mississippi. These newly opened regions provided inexpensive, readily available land. A few communities like New Harmony bought up vast areas, but normally they were satisfied with about a thousand acres.[6] Certainly they needed land; but perhaps even more they needed freedom and seclusion. The conservative East Coast inhibited innovation and experiment. Farther west no single way of life ruled. Just as the missionary churches could alter worship forms and disregard doctrine with impunity,[7] so the utopians could expect to establish their ideal societies unmolested. To this environment Noyes introduced fifty-one charter members of the Oneida Association.[8] Once settled, they must devise some practical way to implement their lofty, idealistic principles.

Many a community floundered in its heroic efforts to earn its living. A majority, of course, turned to farming, the traditional support of utopia. In their own inimitable fashion the communities joined sides in the general conflict between industry and agriculture. Many decried industrialization. They saw it as a mistaken step in the search for improvement, and attempted to discover a better rural route for themselves. Yet this did not prevent them from incorporating elements of the expanding industrial society. The Sylvania Phalanx, for example, while rejecting the destructiveness of modern industry and city life, sought to supplement its agricultural production with the income from the manufacture of shoes. The Shakers exemplified the inventiveness of their age with ingenious gadgets to core apples or wash sheets more efficiently. They did not hesitate to sell these inventions along with their famous herbs in the markets of the commercial world.

Oneida, unlike so many experiments that have since become footnotes in history, looked to new industrial ideas to create a firm economic base. It must be admitted, too, that the early applicants came well-dowered with worldly proof of God's blessing and contributed some $108,000 in the first nine years of the community's existence.[9] With so much capital on hand the Perfectionists could afford to experiment in the best tradition of the American enterprise. Eventually, they developed a whole repertoire of sources of income. They began by canning and selling farm produce and by operating a saw mill and a flour mill; in time, they added the famous Newhouse animal trap, chain manufacture, silk thread production, and handmade traveling bags. In 1857, after years of austere living and constant work, the community finally began to show a profit.[10] From that time its energetic involvement in the American business world brought increasing prosperity and more than a touch of luxury. Accommodated in the great rambling Mansion House, which was set in spacious, tastefully landscaped grounds, the three hundred Perfectionists supplemented the regular creature-comforts with elaborate theatrical properties, musical instruments, a library of at least a thousand volumes, and even a Swedish bath.

The conflict between agriculture and industry in the nineteenth century was not simply a matter of trees as opposed to buildings, or the plough instead of the shuttles of the cotton loom. It included the vital and often unspoken issue of the relationship between the individual and those forces which directed his life. The new industry threatened to turn man into a suppressed mechanical being powerless to influence how he worked, lived, or played. Automation of the individual and alienation from his surroundings surely could not be the better life that the nineteenth century envisioned.

Many of the experimental communities did not state this issue specifically, yet it is a major inspiration behind the frequent experiments in the organization of work and underlies the whole notion of a communal enterprise. The associations frequently announced that all labor was to be paid for equally. Some, like the North American Phalanx, decreed that the more disagreeable the labor, the more reward one would receive for it. Similarly, the Clarkson Domain used Fourier's classification of jobs as "attractive," "useful," or "necessary" and awarded the most work credits to the least agreeable jobs. New Harmony established its well-known Time Store where one paid for goods in "labor notes." All of the communities, more or less, encouraged the member to participate in decisions—at times to the point of spelling their own ruin because everyone demanded the right to shirk unpleasant labor. Vainly their leaders hoped that moral education would encourage the appropriate motivation and solve the problem. But generally, of course, the community had disintegrated before these latter-day retraining programs were begun.

Members of the Oneida community did not hesitate to declare they could find perfection and happiness in work as well as all other aspects of their lives. They encouraged rotation of tasks, for example, moving people from the laundry department out on to the road for the sales department; and they worked together at "bees" to husk corn for canning or to fill a large order for traps. They also instigated formal measures to insure the individual's participation in community affairs. Each day a meeting of the whole community took place in the Big Hall of the Mansion House. Together they examined their joint endeavors. Topics ranged from the amount of butter served at dinner to a talk by Noyes on communism in the Bible, from how best to maintain good relationships with their neighbors to the merits of opening a New York City agency for the community businesses. In spite of some elements of despotism by Noyes, this system assured the survival of a sense of involvement which was being threatened everywhere by the modern industrial age.

The Perfectionists were eminently successful in their experiments in the new industrialism, but neither material progress nor individual involvement was allowed to dominate their interests as it did some of the industrialists of the age. Like the Horatio Alger heroes, who first appeared in the 1860's, they found material prosperity joined to moral earnestness. Yet the enterprising spirit of these commercial efforts and the successful application of talent that they implied were also a direct consequence of Noyes' teachings. To him, intellectual growth was an integral part of the spiritual improvement that ended with perfection. America at large viewed education as a condition for progress. Jefferson had seen it underlying true democracy. Horace Mann was busy revolutionizing the Massachusetts school system. In Boston, members of the "Charitable Mechanic Association" agreed to employ their "mechanic powers" to "assist the necessitous" and "encourage the ingenious."[11] Throughout the country, Lyceum lecturers fed men's curiosity about this new age and sustained their faith in the overwhelming power of knowledge.[12] In the communities, the numerous Owenite and Fourierist groups echoed their masters' belief in learning although, to survive, they often had to forsake intellectual exercise for physical labor.

At Oneida, Noyes had declared that all forms of educational endeavor were necessary to utopia. His *Annual Report* of 1851 found "education [in the general sense] of development under the Spirit of Truth" to be "the central object and inspiration of this Community."[13] The supreme confidence afforded by constant reiteration of the belief in perfection persuaded his followers, individually and collectively, that they could master the modern world's overwhelming discoveries and solve its problems. To achieve this, they must parallel spiritual endeavor with intellectual exercise. The library was assembled and little groups of members set about reading zoology, algebra, French, or phrenology with ingenuous enthusiasm. Eventually some twenty men and women went away at community expense for medical and scientific training at Yale University and musical studies in New York City.

In the context of this sanguine exploration in the new world of science we can understand why the Perfectionists should adopt the belief that maladies of the body as well as the soul could be healed by faith. The notion, which had been a recurrent theme throughout the centuries, lay in the fertile ground between the new religious ideas and the new faith in science. Everywhere the "Mesmerists" investigated the role of hypnotism in this mysterious power of the mind to control the ailments of the body. Later, Mary Baker Eddy's Christian Science would link the notion with Christianity and establish a new church. Eventually, the psychologists would discard for the most part both religion and the trance and teach the mind to heal itself. But mid-nineteenth-century America was still, above all, Bible-reading and religiously-oriented. It was logical, then, that mental healing should be an integral part of Perfectionist doctrine.

While it was always part of Oneida's credo that disease represented some form of lapse from moral perfection, it is also significant that the community did not hesitate to add the resources of science to religion when faith proved inadequate. "Mutual criticism" by one's fellow Perfectionists and the "spiritual bath" of self-scrutiny and self-confession were not entirely successful in quieting the fever of diptheria victims or in stifling children's winter sneezes. Noyes responded by sending his eldest son, Theodore, to train as a physician. Eventually, therefore, Oneida offered a faith that could conquer human ills, but backed it up with secular knowledge.

Throughout the century, the same spirit of exploration and expectation of easy success was found in the widespread interest in diet. Here, whatever his experience, a man could readily experiment with his own notions and glimpse a vision of a panacea for human sickness. Vegetarianism and Graham diets were very popular in the communities. Prairie Home and the Skaneateles Community abjured meat and stimulants. Brook Farm had its Grahamite table. Almost universally the utopias joined with the temperance organizations in their denunciation of alcohol. At Oneida, an austere diet was at first a necessity. Later such limitations remained as an adjunct to spiritual improvement and physical well-being. Though the Mansion House visitor might balk at strawberry-leaf tea, he still ate the vegetarian meals with a hearty appetite.

Such experiments as these in faith healing and diet were, as H. G. Wells said, one "part of a vast system of questionings and repudiations, political doubts, social doubts, hesitating inquiries."[14] When we, in turn, wonder why anyone inside or outside a utopian community should see these as reasonable experiments, we judge from beyond the limited perspective of the nineteenth-century man. His was a time when the sum of knowledge, though vast, could seemingly be collected and analyzed by one person if he be a Spencer or a Hegel. One expected to find scientific, social, philosophical and literary knowledge himself, for belief in the possibility of becoming a cosmopolitan man was not yet shaken by the realization that in knowledge, too, there must be a division of labor. And it was within this context, without today's hindsight, that any potential convert would listen to the words of the founder of Oneida or any other community.

Noyes himself could produce impressive qualifications. Coming from a socially prominent family in Putney, Vermont, he had the kind of education at Dartmouth and later at Andover and Yale which lent his words authority for the intelligent but relatively untaught and uncritical farmers and artisans he selected for Oneida.[15] To these worldly qualifications was added a personal endowment that would inspire confidence in any age. He was not only intellectually superior, but also a physically impressive man, possessing charisma for men and women, adept at promoting an atmosphere at once of fellowship and challenge.

It is easy to say that Noyes' capacity to inspire confidence, combined with the peculiarities of his own psychological makeup, account for the sexual experiments that have brought Oneida lasting fame. But even sexual matters could not escape the scrutiny of the age. Whitman's "Song of Myself" celebrated the body and appealed for an enlarged sense of appreciation. Certainly, the majority preferred Longfellow's gentility to Whitman's sensuousness, but these new ideas, like those of women's rights, were not without influential sympathizers.

In the communities such issues found their usual varied expression. Most frequently they followed the example of the North American Phalanx and incorporated equal rights for women into their constitution. The Northampton Association committed itself to equal pay for both sexes, as well as all occupations. Elsewhere, more extreme views prevailed. Josiah Warren of the Modern Times community was forced to admit that "individual sovereignty" might imply free love. Because outsiders frequently associated sexual experiment with the communities, poor Fanny Wright heard her interracial experiment designed to educate freed slaves designated a "free love colony."[16] At the other extreme were the celibate Rappites and the Shaker "families" whose soulless regimen of mechanical detail drained the sisters' and brothers' lives of humor, joy, and self-expression.

The Oneida community made the most remarkable of the innovations in family life when it introduced "complex marriage" and "stirpiculture." Like the Mormons in their practice of polygamy, the Oneida Perfectionists made complex marriage an integral part of their religious and social system. For Noyes, monogamy was a form of spiritual tyranny wherein "men and women have the power to debar each other from the rights of conscience, and the enjoyment of their religious faith."[17] Exclusive attachment, or the selfish possession of another, unfitted the person aspiring to perfection from practicing a cardinal social-religious ideal, loving his neighbors without discrimination. Further, conventional monogamy in these antebellum years was denigrated by Noyes as a form of slavery. So was excessive childbearing. Women were to be freed from its burdens and the number of children born controlled by the practice of "male continence," a process also carefully detailed by Noyes.[18] Under appropriate controls the delights of "amative" intercourse were to replace the responsibilities of "propagative" intercourse.

This particular version of marriage lasted about thirty years, not so long as that of the Mormons, who lived secluded on the distant frontier, but long enough to allow Oneida to conduct a daring experiment in eugenics. At a period when Charles Darwin and Francis Galton were influencing intellectuals everywhere, Noyes (and Oneida) determined to try out their ideas. With a superior inheritance, the hope of perfection would be even brighter. Stirpiculture was a concerted effort to select those couples whose spiritual and physical qualities most fitted them to reproduce. Members of the community signed an agreement to abide by the decision of a committee as to who should conceive the stirpicults, and between 1869 and 1879 fifty-eight children were born at Oneida.[19]

From sexual matters to educational reform, Oneida explored the *avant-garde* ideas of its time. Obviously neither they nor any other communal experiment embraced every new idea. Some groups sought to improve man's mind, others to change only his environment; some sought individual expression, others immoderate conformity; some saw the ideal society in terms of an advance to modern industrialism, more wanted a retreat to earlier forms of production; and, again, some believed happiness involved activity, personal involvement, and the realization of unknown potential, whereas others grafted a notion of perfection to elements of a Puritan past and saw it as activity without involvement and regulation without the joy of self-determination. At Oneida such ideas were expressed in new interpretations of Christianity, educational reform, varied work routines, joint decision-making, dietary experiments, faith healing, complex marriage, and the stirpiculture experiment. In other communities their different manifestations must have bewildered the fledgling utopian in search of the ideal society. Yet, behind this confusion of practices we see the basic rationality of the nineteenth-century utopia. The community was a logical place to develop several admired social themes, from spiritual improvement to stolid practicality. Some other age would deem the venture foolhardy, but nineteenth-century America justifiably believed in the reality of the utopian vision.

For one reason or another, most communities were fated to disappear by the end of the century.[20] Since then, the supply of replacements has diminished severely. A Bruderhof community flourishes in Connecticut. Koinonia, an interracial group, lives in Christian charity and constant threat of violence in Americus, Georgia. A west coast group may ask a social scientist's help in planning a Pacific island utopia. We admire such valiant fortitude but see these ventures as belonging no more to the intellectual frontier than to the geographical frontier. When we survey the bizarre quasi-religious cults that still manage to find something of the frontier's seclusion in rural California, we feel even more convinced that, today, the utopian community is an anomaly, a curious revival of a dead tradition.[21]

The history of the Oneida community between 1880 and the

present day illustrates the twentieth-century fate of utopia. Struggling to retain its old idealism, Oneida re-explored the social aspects of community life. Radical changes have since eliminated dreams out of keeping with the present age without removing every element of utopia.

The major reconstruction came about at the end of 1880. As John Humphrey Noyes grew older, his command faltered. In 1879 internal troubles flared. These, it seemed, could be solved only by the exchange of complex marriage for ordinary monogamous relationships and, a month or two later, by the withdrawal from common ownership of property. A joint-stock company, the Oneida Community, Limited, was formed. After each member received his portion, he could either depart to the outside world or stay on in the Mansion House and work for a salary in the community industries. Local outsiders who had long been employed in non-supervisory positions continued in their regular jobs with scarcely any change of routine. With Noyes then in retirement in Canada, his place taken by an official Board of Directors, and with disillusionment complete among the younger persons, it seemed that soon there would be nothing more utopian about Oneida than the Victorian Gothic of its great Mansion House.

The final rout of utopia was averted by one of the founder's stirpiculture children, Pierrepont Burt Noyes. In 1899 he led a successful proxy fight to rescue the company from the hands of a party of Perfectionists-turned-Spiritualists. Once in effective control, he scoured the country for able contemporaries who had left, lured them back with his design for a new utopia, and set about remodeling both the business and the idealism so that both might survive. Noyes introduced his new utopian vision to an established organization. Oneida had become a modern business with a management-owned capital investment of over half a million dollars. Without this financial backing Noyes could never have developed for Oneida Community plate a reputation to surpass that of the old community's animal trap. At the end of the nineteenth century, and certainly in the mid-twentieth century, few nascent communities could hope to produce capital on the scale required for financial independence. Noyes' contribution to the business proved more permanent than his vision of utopia. Even so, the new idealism he introduced to Oneida began to fade only in the 1940's.

Before P. B. Noyes took over in 1899, the areas in which perfection was envisioned had, one by one, been rejected; and the patent on their exploration had, in effect, been turned over to someone else. The belief that Oneida could discover ultimate religious truth was effectively quashed at the breakup. So, too, the members lost their sublime faith in complex marriage and the practicality of the stirpiculture experiment. The community never tried to repeat such ventures. Its members, like us, understood too much about the intricacies of man's psychological makeup to argue the superiority of complex marriage. Similarly, neither they nor we could pretend that a new stirpiculture scheme would improve the quality of their descendants. Eugenic change is vastly more complex than the ingenuous Perfectionists realized. In the area of education, too, there was no hope of competition with the universities and research centers of modern America.

Noyes admitted the inevitability of such changes. Under his guidance, Oneida continued to illustrate this process of the dissolution of utopia as it resigns its functions to experts, as it joins the affairs and assumes the ways of the outside society. He saw that, without the excitement and stimulation of the frontier's challenge, isolation would make Oneida a placid but enervating backwater. Consequently, everyone was perfectly free to come and go as he chose. Children attended local public schools before going to college. Those few persons who wished to do so frequented the local churches, and everyone used the stores and recreational facilities of the area round about. In the community itself, individual houses were built on the sites of the old orchard and vineyard so that families with growing children could enjoy more privacy. This restricted residential area, called Kenwood, seemed to borrow from the dominating Mansion House a dignity not found "on the other side of the bridge" in Sherrill.

Oneida was no longer a miniature ideal society. The grandeur of the nineteenth-century utopian spirit was irretrievable. Theologians must inquire into religious truths, the Deweys and Conants search for educational reform, and the new scientific empires direct our technological progress. Intellectual independence was no more possible than economic self-sufficiency. But, in keeping with the growing specialization of the time, Oneida could incorporate a limited number of utopian elements.

The first was a legitimate twentieth-century descendant of the nineteenth-century concept now discovered in the "garden city" idea. Introduced by English planners such as Ebenezer Howard and Patrick Geddes, it is still a central concern for such people as

Percival and Paul Goodman,[22] and it has stimulated the creation of such communities as Greenbelt, near Washington, D.C. Such schemes contrast our segmented lives in supposedly dreary urban environments with the hope of an integrated life in beautiful surroundings where land use is controlled by human as well as economic criteria. These modern utopians see their plans as part of the reconstruction of our present society. For them the rainbow ends at home.

The new Oneida inherited from the old community just such advantages as many a town planner might wish. Tucked away in the rolling hills of central New York, the sales office and Kenwood formed a single unit wherein work and social relationships overlapped. Should such a rural idyl become tedious, Utica and Syracuse were within thirty miles and, for longer trips, the Midland railroad had a stop some five miles from Mansion House.

Another modern theme that lends itself to incorporation in a specialized utopia appears in the disparate threads of the cooperative movement. In the United States the ideas of the Rochdale pioneers have been transferred to a rural setting by the farmers' cooperatives of the western states. The more radical idea of producers' cooperatives is represented in the occasional effort in communal farming.[23] But economic cooperation, which has been less popular here than in Europe, has generally assumed a severely vitiated form. However, Oneida experimented with this idea also. Just as Kenwood was almost a ready-made, miniature garden city, so the company was already a cooperative endeavor. Ex-members and, later, their descendants owned most of the stock. Together with a few "outsiders" who had been brought into management posts, they were, at least until the 1930's, in complete control of the company. This meant that for the officials, for the retired members of management, and for their families the exigencies of the Oneida Community, Limited, were a vital concern. Their daily lives revolved around its operation and they depended on it for a livelihood.

P. B. Noyes used the peculiar situational circumstances that made Oneida a home, a family, and a heritage to extend its objectives beyond mere economic cooperation. He incorporated there an element missing from most of our present-day notions of utopia; a sense of personal involvement that, in its most idealistic form, allows the individual self-realization and gives him the power to influence his own destiny. Under Noyes, a new "team spirit" was devised, and the wrangling of the years following the breakup of the old community. was replaced by a free exchange of ideas, interpersonal frankness, and mutual trust. He created a group of lighthearted, responsible men and women who worked together enthusiastically for the economic and the social good of the whole community.

Such a truly cooperative spirit could not survive if social distinctions were to fracture the unity of the two hundred or more members of management and their families in Kenwood. At Oneida there was, wrote Noyes in 1909, an unwritten constitution which proclaimed a "reasonable equality of wealth; a reasonable equality of opportunity; and a reasonable equality of power."[24] In Kenwood social distinctions were to be minimized. Salaries in management, unlike those in the factory, were to be held down because this would buttress the effort to make Kenwood life simple and unpretentious. Empty status-seeking pleasures, like the urgent acquisition of oriental rugs and antique furniture, were to lose out in favor of creative activities, simple social events, and individual efforts at self-development. Not that life would be Spartan; there would be waiters in the Mansion House dining room and modern conveniences in the separate homes scattered roundabout, but these were physical comforts, not psychological props. Self-respect was to come from the development of the inner man.

This theme of self-realization, so common in the nineteenth-century communities, is also echoed today throughout the larger society but without convincing expression. When a sociologist studying job satisfaction suggests that workers should realize goals of their own, he is concerned with one aspect of the issue.[25] A similar theme appears in the trade unions' gropings toward something more than increased wage rates and better working conditions. From another viewpoint, chiefly that of management, it is recognizable in the occasional, usually abortive, experiment with industrial profit-sharing. In Europe, the problem is conceptualized rather more distinctly as, for instance, by André Philip and the French Personalistic Socialists.[26] Some of their ideas are incorporated in the modern French utopias, the communities of work.[27]

The communities of work, like Oneida under P. B. Noyes, focus on a few aspects of utopia. They devote themselves to the question of self-realization and self-determination of the industrial worker. Oneida, however, was primarily concerned with cooperation and involvement in management. Yet it did make serious efforts to include the factory workers in the modern utopia. Early in the century

P. B. Noyes envisioned the extension of "our society" from "the original two hundred [in Kenwood] to include the entire 2,000 who are working together toward a common end."[28] In effect he achieved this goal. Work hours were reduced, pay scales increased, pensions, profit-sharing, and "war service" wages introduced; a welfare department and recreational facilities were added; and bonuses were awarded to employees who built their own homes. The town of Sherrill became, and still is, a model community with scarcely a dilapidated house to be found. But utopia for the factory employees lacked the involvement that added such zest to the affairs of management. Everything from wages to street names in Sherrill was given to the employees by a highly paternalistic company. And in the plant, cooperation was a one-side affair; although all were able to communicate quite freely, the power to act rested almost entirely in the hands of the company officials.

Noyes' reforms in the Oneida factory are less central to our discussion than the reforms he had instituted in Kenwood. He saw that the old Oneida was outmoded. No community could justify changing every aspect of its members' lives. Instead it must focus on a few areas. Consequently, Noyes offered Kenwood residents an active, congenial social life in a pleasant physical setting and the chance to make a vital contribution to the affairs of both the company and the community. Moreover, echoing his father's admonitions, he urged the exercise of the intellect and cultivation of the inner man.

Although Oneida preserved these few aspects of the utopia, the brilliance of the older vision had faded. The "Great Society" finds few small experiments in action. A different frontier stirs men's imaginations. The themes of improvement, practicality, and individual endeavor can rarely be embodied in a communal enterprise. Throughout the world we discover an amazing array of alternative blueprints for living. Which one of us can decide the best? And who, in the face of so many natural experiments, can hope to devise one better? Toward what should we direct our change when imperfections seem to riddle every society?

We are no longer sure that the future is ours. Nature's complexity is overwhelming. Those very sciences through which we look for understanding have wrought mortal blows to the hope of perfection. The seeds of pragmatism are well rooted in our twentieth-century minds. We see no single truth, but several, no one kingdom of heaven, but several.[29] Protestantism, whose radicals once offered hope of imminent perfection, now finds the questioning theologian tentatively wondering whether utopia is to be found at home. In his recent book, *Honest to God,* the Bishop of Woolwich asks whether "God" and "heaven" should be conceived of as something beyond us, divorced from our secular activities. Perhaps, he suggests, the Christian life might yet be seen as holy worldliness, sacred secularity.[30]

These new conceptions of man's hopes are not without some expectation of human progress for the fragmentation of utopia directs our attention to other types of improvement. We promote new educational schemes, programs for integration, trade union activity, social security programs; a presidential commission studies womanpower; and the Peace Corps is imitated at home and abroad. Our attention is fixed on the existing society, no longer diverted by the notion of the utopian community. Throughout the final decades of the last century, when the frontier had all but disappeared, the experimental and literary utopia remained a popular expression of the reformers' idealism. Some twenty-eight communities were founded between 1880 and 1900,[31] and the visionary schemes of Bellamy and more than forty other writers were greeted enthusiastically.[32] Yet the principles of cooperation and socialism which they advocated never applied immediately to the larger American scene. Only in the twentieth century did such would-be reformers break with the utopian tradition and turn to the slow transformation of that creaking, infinitely complex but apparently viable structure to which they must belong.

The shift of utopia to a national scale has one other significance. As we inevitably delegate the search for improvement to specialized groups like city planners and personnel officers, we risk imposing utopia upon the resident of the garden city or the worker in the Oneida factory. Thus new visions of reform resemble those of the earliest writers on utopia. They thrust utopia on the masses and try to change man from without. Less often, they encourage man to change himself. And yet, ultimately, only he can develop that inner self which Alcott called "the living spirit within the soul."[33]

REFERENCES

1. Frederick A. Bushee, "Communistic Societies in the United States," *Political Science Quarterly,* Vol. XX (1905), p. 625.

2. John Humphrey Noyes, *History of American Socialisms* (New York: Hillary House, 1961), reprint of the 1870 edition, p. 213.

3. John Addington Symonds, "A Vista," in *New and Old; A Volume of Verse* (Boston: James R. Osgood and Company, 1880), pp. 226-227.

4. The information presented here on the Oneida community is part of a larger study which analyzes the community's development from 1848 to the present. Much of the description of the modern Oneida given in the second half of the paper is based upon first-hand interviews with present residents.

5. William E. Channing, "Likeness to God: Discourse at the Ordination of the Rev. F. A. Farley," *Works of William E. Channing* (Boston: America Unitarian Association, 1877), pp. 291-302.

6. Noyes, *op. cit.*, p. 19.

7. Whitney R. Cross, *The Burned-over District; The Social and Intellectual History of Enthusiastic Religion in Western New York, 1800-1850* (Ithaca: Cornell University Press, 1950), pp. 104-109.

8. Data from unpublished manuscript, "Oneida Association Family Register," presently in the library of the Mansion House, Oneida, New York.

9. *Handbook of the Oneida Community, 1875* (Oneida, New York: Office ot the *Oneida Circular* [1875?]), p. 15.

10. *Ibid.*

11. *Constitution of the Massachusetts Charitable Mechanic Association* (Boston: George C. Rand and Avery, 1861), p. 7.

12. Carl Bode, *The American Lyceum: Town Meeting of the Mind* (New York. Oxford University Press, 1956).

13. *Third Annual Report of the Oneida Association* (Oneida Reserve: Leonard and Company, 1851), p. 22.

14. H. G. Wells, *New Worlds for Old* (Chicago: M. A. Donahue and Company, 1907), p. 207.

15. In 1849, the eighty-seven members of the Association included only three ex-ministers and one lawyer among those who might be presumed to have some formal education. "Oneida Association Family Register," *loc. cit.*

16. Bode, *op. cit.*, p. 127.

17. [John Humphrey Noyes], *Slavery and Marriage* (n.p., 1850), p. 12. (Italics omitted).

18. John Humphrey Noyes, *Male Continence,* 1st ed. (Oneida, New York: Office of the *Oneida Circular,* 1872). Between 1848 and 1869 there were probably about a dozen accidental conceptions.

19. Hilda Herrick Noyes and George Wallingford Noyes, "The Oneida Community Experiment in Stirpiculture," *Eugenics, Genetics and the Family,* Vol. 1. Scientific Papers of the Second International Congress of Eugenics, 1921 (Baltimore: Williams and Wilkins Company, 1923), p. 280.

20. Why some failed, while the rare exception like Oneida survived, is beyond the scope of this paper. It has been suggested that the Shakers' celibacy resulted in an inevitable dwindling of their numbers, that many Owenite and Fourierist groups were not selective enough in choosing their members so that incompetents and potential troublemakers proved ultimately disruptive, that some failed to ensure a means of economic survival through times of panic as well as prosperity (What could have been expected of Brook Farm in this respect when Hawthorne was the head of the Finance Committee?). Some could not achieve a successful transfer of power from the original charismatic leader to the inevitable successor.

21. Robert V. Hine, *California's Utopian Communities* (San Marino, California: Huntington Library, 1953), especially Chapter IX.

22. Percival and Paul Goodman, *Communitas: Means of Livelihood and Ways of Life* (Chicago: University of Chicago Press, 1947).

23. Henrik F. Infield, *Utopia and Experiment: Essays in the Sociology of Cooperation* (New York: Frederick A. Praeger, 1955), pp. 66-93.

24. P. B. Noyes, "Basswood Philosophy, III," *Quadrangle,* Vol. II (1909), pp. 10-11.

25. A. Zaleznik, C. R. Christensen, and F. J. Roethlisberger, *The Motivation, Productivity, and Satisfaction of Workers; A Prediction Study* (Boston: Harvard University Graduate School of Business Administration, 1958), pp. 421-422.

26. André Philip, *La democratie industrielle* (Paris: Presses Universitaires de France, 1955).

27. Infield, *op. cit.,* p. 198. Claire Huchet Bishop, *All Things Common* (New York: Harpers, 1950). Albert Meister, *Quelques aspects methodologiques de la recherche sociologique dans les associations volontaires et les groupes cooperatifs* (Unpublished manuscript, Harvard Graduate School of Business Administration, 1960).

28. "Texts of Speeches given at Sixteenth Annual Banquet," *Quadrangle,* Vol. VII (1914), p. 17.

29. Joyce Oramel Hertzler, *The History of Utopian Thought* (New York: Macmillan Company, 1923), pp. 312-314. Arthur E. Morgan, *Nowhere and Somewhere; How History Makes Utopias and How Utopias Makes History* (Chapel Hill: University of North Carolina Press, 1946), p. 184.

30. John A. T. Robinson, *Honest to God* (Philadelphia: Westminister Press, 1963), p. 101.

31. Bushee, *op. cit.,* pp. 663-664.

32. Allyn B. Forbes, "The Literary Quest for Utopia, 1880-1900," *Social Forces,* Vol. VI (1927), pp. 188-189.

33. Edith Roelkler Curtis, *A Season in Utopia: The Story of Brook Farm* (New York: Thomas Nelson and Sons, 1961), p. 137.

FRANÇOIS BLOCH-LAINÉ

The Utility of Utopias for Reformers

"Reformers" may be defined as those who occupy a position between conservatives and revolutionaries. Although doubtless closer to the latter than to the former, they are always doomed to defend themselves on both fronts because they seem at times too bold and at other times too cautious and thus satisfy neither the defenders of the status quo nor the advocates of a basically different social order.

In this uncomfortable position, reformers encounter, among many others, these two contradictory criticisms:

A. For some, they lack sufficient intellectual rigor. Because reformism attempts to adapt institutions to practice and to ratify change by modifying social structures, it seems to abandon itself to a kind of historical determinism. At times, reformers are reproached for relying too much on empiricism and not enough on the creative will. At other times, reformism is suspected of giving free rein—unconsciously or deliberately—to perverse movements, with concepts more clearly formulated than its own, which actually bring about results that the reformers, by a clever dialectic, falsely attribute to determinism. In either case, reformers are advised not to challenge the established order until they have a clear doctrine of their own and not to undertake any initiative unless it leads from a well-known present position to a well-defined future position.

B. To other critics, reformers are, on the contrary, too doctrinaire. Why such haste to give formal sanction to something as yet little known? In attempting to determine prematurely the outcome of a changing situation, they obstruct rather than foster change. Or else, through their preconceived ideas, they exert an improper influence which distorts the natural course of events. They are accused of elaborating artificial constructions that the natural course of events will contradict because the reformers have not taken time to observe real change; thus, the subsequent adjustments will be more difficult to make in the same proportion as the reformers have been mistaken in their predictions.

These two kinds of criticism are made, respectively, by two kinds of conservatives—theoretical or doctrinaire conservatives, on the one hand, and pragmatists, on the other. Although they are in fact mutually contradictory, these two opinions tend to have a cumulative effect more than they cancel each other out; thus, they doubly hinder reformers.

How, then, can reformers escape such a frustrating position? If they do not wish to be held back and finally immobilized by their critics, they must try to lead these latter to other grounds in order to make their criticism less negative.

To be admitted without reservation, these grounds must be distant, separated from each person's daily basis of activity. Insofar as preoccupations connected with the present or the immediate future dictate the attitudes of the interlocutors, we cannot expect that they will feel unconstrained and cooperate in a relaxed and casual manner.

None of our habitual exercises allows for such relaxation. Forecasting of the future is not sufficiently disengaged from present concerns. Nor does the new method which the French philosopher Gaston Berger has called "prospective" constitute a sufficient escape to reach the serenity necessary to a difficult dialogue among partisans. This "prospective" consists in reasoning and in acting not only in terms of what is probable but also in terms of what is possible. Its starting point is the idea that we can determine a voluntary future, a future that, in the words of Gaston Berger, "is never inevitable" provided that we place ourselves resolutely in a *future*-oriented framework to influence the present, rather than remain overly impressed by the past. However, inasmuch as the reasoning here still leads to an action or imposes a judgment on the action, it remains forceably cautious. No matter what the objective one is striving toward, as long as there remains an unduly direct link between thought and action, present implications of the views developed are still too distinct to allow room for pure speculation.

This is why it is advantageous for reformers, though they be realists, to bring conservatives and revolutionaries beyond forecasting of the future and "prospective," in order that they may enter into discussion with them without apprehension.

Discussion of a utopia would offer people of different theoretical approaches a chance to construct, in a manner they find congenial, models that would not be preconditioned by their dogmas. It would make possible a truce between conservatives and revolutionaries, both of whose doctrines tend to congeal between the covers of their sacred books. Intellectuals would meet on new grounds where they could exchange ideas without seriously betraying their own ideological commitments.

The pragmatists are not under such a strain on the theoretical plane. But they also need to say to themselves, "It's just for fun," in order to become serious without anxiety. Their fear of ideologies stems much more from the immediate practical consequences these may entail than from their futile character. Speaking in utopian terms would put them at ease because they would no longer fear that they were adversely affecting pure reality by giving currency to disturbing ideas. They would be told frankly that anyone who engages in a philosophical exercise with courage and honesty ultimately becomes somewhat involved in it. But their fear of a trap would not be the same as if the issue concerned practical measures to be taken.

Finally, the use of a utopia would be good medicine for the reformers themselves, for their behavior would become stronger if they set their sights on distant horizons. And it would relieve them of the most valid reproach against them, namely, that they combine neglect of the ultimate ends with ineptitude in relation to immediate obstacles. In this way reformism would gain the warmer support of those who need to believe and to feel enthusiasm, without frightening off cooler minds that grow colder when faced with enthusiasm.

The strength of revolutionaries is that they promise a better world of tomorrow after the violence of the revolution is over, but this is also their drawback in the eyes of those who do not believe in violence. Reformers oppose revolutionaries in denouncing both the evils they would produce and the tensions they entail. But this is not sufficient. In order to compete with revolutionaries in the area where they make the most converts, one must also make explicit the corresponding hopes of another method and show that one is not renouncing the goal of making the world better just because one refuses to overturn it in a day. If this were not so, reformers could never enlist idealists.

Some may demur and ask, "If one qualifies these hopes as

'utopian,' does one not destroy them at the outset in the minds of reasonable men?"

The idea of "utopia" still tends to have a pejorative connotation for everybody, whatever his temperament, because everyone fancies himself a realist. But in the realm of the arts the benefits of surrealism no longer need to be demonstrated. And in the sciences the most revolutionary discoveries have arisen from nonpositivistic imaginations. In the ethical sphere, too, it is still useful to present good and evil in black and white terms, although human behavior is grey more often than either of these extremes. Why, then, should one exclude from sociology and political economy all notion of the absolute, all imagination, even all surrealism?

But this type of reasoning is not the most convincing. The following clarification may be more effective: *the utopian ideal is not necessarily situated outside of time. Its definition permits the affirmation of "values" that one can hold and respect right away, the setting of "objectives" that can be achieved one by one, and the choice of permanent "scope."* For example:

In regard to values, what kinds of liberty should be safeguarded? What kinds of equality should be established?

In regard to objectives, can the majority of men find joy in their work or must they resign themselves to expect it only in their leisure?

And in regard to scope, should we preserve or abolish the spirit of competition? The profit motive? The national police force?

The further question may be asked, "Why take a detour through utopia to come to these questions, unless it be a ruse to deceive your opponents?" Define liberty as the Liberals do without mincing words: as the recognized capacity of each man to act tomorrow as he is successfuly acting today. Do not wear yourself out in trying to set forth an equality contrary to nature; be content to remedy the worst or least justified inequalities from day to day. Do not construct a far-off perfect society in order to rediscover—to use the examples given above—that man must escape from work when he tries to be happy, that he is lazy when he is not concerned, that he is an egoist when he is not absorbed in a collective passion, and that it is always necessary to make him a little bit afraid for those close to him or for his safety!

Here it is no doubt necessary to justify utopia by strategy rather than by tactics. The realists of whom we have been speaking deny that there is, in the matter, any advantage in creating a great distance between strategic and tactical objectives. Is this because any strategy runs counter to their own, essentially conservative, tactics? There is more to it than this. Many realists are sincerely shortsighted. How can they be convinced that it is better to be farsighted? The argument is always the same. It has served to support "prospective." It is also valid for utopias. It runs as follows:

The distance between tactics and strategy becomes ever greater as change quickens its pace. We know that the faster the movement of troops on a battlefield, the more necessary it is to have a view of the ultimate objectives that is not obscured by the shuffling of the units and the dust they raise. The greater the haste, the more necessary it is for the commander of the operation to stand back a little bit.

Furthermore, even in war, the anticipated victory should always have in its ambition the allure of a utopia. And that not only in order to arouse the soldiers but also to reduce the long-run miscalculation. This may seem paradoxical. In the opposite sense, it is often said that the more modest the claim, the less the inevitable disappointment. But experience shows that one never prepares for victory soon enough, nor with enough serenity and loftiness of mind; one never rises enough above the daily events to conceive a final peace clearly. Victory is never complete; peace is never perfect. But one should strain after them as if they could be. If one does not, one never attains as much as might be possible.

For the economist or the sociologist, acting also as a philosopher who is trying his hand at the method of "prospective," to be concerned with utopia is not a deviation, as an excursion into science fiction might be. Science fiction is not to be condemned in itself, but it is the concern of the novelist, while utopia is still in the domain of the philosopher.

II

How is one to go about constructing a utopia seriously, in such a way that it remains within the sphere of normal concern for the economist and sociologist? To begin with, some things must doubtless be eliminated. For instance, one could begin with the following postulate: *in a century characterized by the irreversible phenomenon of socialization, man's happiness depends on the conditions in which he is integrated into society*. There is no question of searching for happiness outside society, but only of describing the ideal integration. This eliminates utopias of the "pastoral" or anarchistic type.

Such realistic utopianism, which takes the difficulties of life in society for granted and reckons with the constraints it necessarily entails, may seem insufficiently utopian. Serious utopianism, however, deals with things as they are: the nature of man, who is neither angel nor beast—this excludes utopias founded on angelic natures in a universe where everyone would always be good and pure—and the nature of the material world, a hard world where the easy life will not arrive tomorrow—which also excludes utopias characterized by such an abundance of material goods that everyone might soon be satisfied without threatening his neighbor.

Whether or not such realism derives from the idea of original sin and the metaphysics it involves, it leads to rejection also of Marxist utopias, which assume the "withering away of the state," that is, the conception of human organizations functioning successfully without an authority higher than themselves, which, in the well-understood interest of the people, guarantees essential services and exerts a sovereign police power.

This point requires amplification because it relates to the postulate of socialization.

According to their ideas and interests, some people regard socialization as desirable, others resist it, still others accept it as inevitable, more or less reluctantly. The third view is no doubt the most constructive—though it may seem to reflect disillusion. It permits dispassionate treatment of a problem whose solution has everything to gain from objectivity.

In the contemporary world, even as technology creates some surpluses, scarcities in other directions become more obvious, and they necessitate the organization of distribution and even impose the maintenance or reinforcement of certain inequities. As the population grows, usable space, the sources of power, and various natural products become scarce and must, consequently, be economized. The contrast between plenty and scarcity is particularly clear in our most advanced societies where coexistence has become impossible without strict discipline and the pooling of goods which would be wasted if left dispersed in the hands of autonomous individuals. Prosperity does not eliminate all kinds of poverty; it even accentuates some that are critical. The case of land in urban communities is particularly striking. Where men are closely packed in together, individual appropriation and free use of the land tend to become absurdities for practical reasons, regardless of ideologies.

On the other hand, the rise in the standard of living, far from making public services obsolete, increases the need for them. One might have thought that greater financial ease would permit families to free themselves from dependence on the community for furnishing numerous essentials. Indeed, many instruments of comfort and recreation—transportation and sanitation, for example—have become private after having been public for a long time. But consumer studies show that diversification of consumer goods, as people with the lowest incomes can obtain more satisfactions, creates needs that require the community to furnish evermore equipment and services, for instance, in matters of health, culture, and recreation.

Are new forms of servitude arising in areas where liberation was expected? It seems futile to speculate on the notions of wise men about the happiness of others because there is no absolute truth in such matters. The fact is that the pleasures of solitude, such as can be enjoyed in vacations when one has air, water, and sun, can be obtained only through public organizations and substructures. The fact is that individuals, even the rich, must count on powerful community organizations if they are to take advantage of the expensive progress made in medicine. The fact is that the cultural activities most enriching for the individual, no matter how cultivated he is, require the most expensive means of expression, that is, the most public.

A third factor in socialization, beyond new scarcities and new needs, is the shrinking opportunity for individual effort and therefore for individual accomplishment, income, and inheritance. When the most important achievements are those of teams or groups and not of isolated individuals, when the respective contributions of capital and inventive talent in production and commerce are more and more difficult to determine, when monetary upheavals and state interventions, such as those experienced in western Europe, have brought about redistribution of wealth and confusion between credits and debits, the individual can no longer justify his net assets by his own efforts in clear, convincing terms. When most gains and losses are due to circumstances outside the activity of those who benefit or lose, it is clear that the notions of private property and free enterprise, established in the era of the French Revolution, need revision. These notions were themselves developed as a way of breaking with obsolete and inappropriate forms of community life, but reformers of good will and good faith are led today to reconstruct just such a life.

Reformers distrust the Communist dependence on the State, even though Communists claim that it is only temporary: they do not believe that it will disappear. This enduring transition seems to them a needless infringement on liberty, and the anticipated dénouement, a false utopia. They try to conceive of an organized community which would be both less harmful to liberty than that of the present Soviet dictatorship and less impossible of realization than the one the Soviets always promise for the day after tomorrow.

To conceive of a society which would not fall into any of these excesses would be the object of a good and useful utopia. At the present time, a coherent compromise on socialization is without doubt the most opportune intellectual construction for avoiding the possibility that random events should alone fashion the world of tomorrow or that doctrinaires should always vainly oppose one another on the advantages and disadvantages in *theory* of a phenomenon which is a fact.

In order to elaborate a new utopia (for the difficulty of this compromise is sufficient here for it to be indeed a question of a utopia), to progress down the road of ideas in attempting to precede the facts, to conceive of socialization without stumbling over the preliminary approval or rejection of socialism, one could proceed as follows:

Intermediaries are needed between the individual and society; in fact, several mediating elements are needed so that liberty may be protected. How shall the various tasks be distributed among social intermediaries, and how shall man's relation to each of them be established?

In general, there are three kinds of intermediaries or spokesmen: organized communities, private associations, and businesses of all sorts. Most men reside in communities, act through private associations, and work in some kind of business. Their happiness and efficiency depend on the functioning of these various bodies.

What combination of intermediaries is most capable of assuring this happiness and efficiency?

Pessimists will comment that happiness and efficiency are generally antithetical and that if one adds justice as a goal, one makes clearly impossible the perfection one would like to grasp, at least fleetingly. These are mutually contradictory objectives, say the skeptics, and it would be better to declare that one will try to combine them as well as possible from day to day than to give the impression that they can be achieved all together.

A farsighted utopia, however, could take the degree of incompatibility between the objectives into account without being destroyed or becoming useless.

Utopia, according to *Littré*, is "a conception of or an imaginary plan for an ideal government." Once again, it is neither man nor nature that is to be idealized but the organization that would obtain for man the best of himself and of nature combined. Of course, efficiency, happiness, and justice are to some extent contradictory. But it would be no small accomplishment to bring to realization the aspects of each that can be reconciled.

III

What exactly must be reconciled in an acceptable utopia? Let us recognize at the outset that this exercise is inevitably stamped with subjectivity, even partiality. The utopia of utopias would be a model coldly constructed by men without passion, which could be adopted by all their contemporaries because it would suit all opinions, all feelings, all temperaments. But it would be so heartlessly conceived that it would not be alive. Destined for all, it would exist for nobody. In order to avoid the opposite extreme—"to each his own utopia"—all that is necessary is to make enough concessions to objectivity for the model offered to have some chance of gaining an adequate number of supporters. What follows is a broad outline of such an attempt. In terms of operating procedure, the problems posed are not dissimilar to that of squaring the circle. They are just a little less difficult, enough to permit solutions theoretically viable and practicably approachable.

We shall offer three such problems as examples.

A. The first reconciliation to be brought about in an ideal society is that between the autonomy or independence of its elements, on the one hand, and the effective functioning of the whole, on the other. There are two ways for man to exercise his freedom in a disciplined community: either he can remain mobile and independent in order to escape the bondage of the milieu in which he lives or he can participate in its direction in order to exercise a positive influence on the decisions concerning it.

1. To be free is, first of all, not to be a prisoner. Men must be able to change their residence, occupation, religion, political affiliation, and personal association, and this presupposes a range of choice. The justification of democratic pluralism begins with this need to limit the force of particular factors on which one is de-

pendent by the fact that there is a choice. Hence, the necessity to keep separate the three types of social intermediaries listed above, social-political communities, private associations, and business. When business is under the State and there are no more voluntary associations, liberty is inevitably dead. But it is not enough for these three kinds of intermediaries to be distinct. It is also necessary that:

a. within each of them there be room for choice and change. One must be able to move, resign, or make a break and be able to find, without too great difficulty, other places to live, other groups to belong to, and other jobs.

b. It is also necessary that certain requirements be equally available through different intermediaries—for example, housing, medical care, instruction, or leisure-time activity should be obtainable through business, through the local government, or through any association of which one is a member.

This latter demand of a free citizen poses one of the most important questions concerning economic and social organization: how should the several tasks be distributed among the several intermediaries so that both overlaps and gaps can be avoided? How can their efforts be coordinated, their cooperation assured without depriving them of autonomy and without their joint operation becoming so constraining that there is no escape from it?

The best solution seems to be joint operation under strong leadership, but much remains to be done to work out both the procedures of agreement and the powers of such a presiding authority.

2. But is the passive citizen really free, even when he is not subject to bondage, if he remains passive? Is not active responsibility a superior form of liberty?

a. Of what advantage is it to have several masters rather than a single one if they work together and do not listen to you? To assure that they treat you well, it is not enough merely to walk out when they treat you badly, or even to threaten them with doing so. One should also be able to exert some influence on them. If they object that this influence should be measured in terms of loyalty and support in the name of stability, a way must be found to make power proportionate to commitment, without going so far as to make people pay for an uncertain power by complete subjection.

b. Aside from all bargaining, to be really free is to be responsible. Slavery, enforced or voluntary, results from lack of responsibility whether given up or taken. The independent man who is satisfied with the possibility he thinks he has of breaking away from the mooring and the cautious man whose chief concern is not to take personal risks are both slaves without knowing it. In all times there will certainly be some men who prefer chains to danger. What is important is that those men who feel themselves entirely free should always be able to act responsibly when they want to.

The problem of participation dominates all present research on the establishment of a society based on "partnership" to succeed patriarchal society. So much has been said about this, in terms still lacking in precision, that one is tempted to become disgusted already. But it is impossible to get rid of the problem. Any utopia that did not provide for the anxiety it expresses would miss its mark.

B. The second necessary reconciliation is between present welfare and future welfare. The problem is how to establish an equilibrium between men's immediate satisfactions and the sacrifices required by their future or that of their descendents.

Without pushing it too far, one may say that in an attractive utopia—and if it is not attractive, it is pointless—a spirit of pleasure must prevail. The element of subjectivity which it must accommodate, which it cannot renounce without drying up, involves a goodly number of present desires projected into the distance. Authors of utopias, if they want to be effective, should be men who enjoy good living, recognize the needs of their contemporaries through those they experience themselves, and assume them to be enduring. Nothing would be more useless in this respect than "delaying tactics"—those which consist in constantly proposing for tomorrow what is unknown today. Communism and some religions resort to this, each in its own way; but utopias do not have to follow suit. Utopias postulate long-range goals in the realm of time, but they do not on that account have to integrate the time factor. Unlike religions, they do not have to promise in another world joys inaccessible in this one. And, unlike communism, they do not have to make this world the mirror of some perfect society due at a time sufficiently definite to justify long and painful intervening imperfection. Religions do not operate on the same plane as materialist utopias. Communism posits an impure utopia because it draws checks on it, establishing a too direct line between present purgatory and future paradise, both located in the same world.

A real utopia must be free, that is, people must not be made to pay cash for a delivery whose date is undetermined. The proposal should read, "This is how I see your happiness and its conditions in this world," without trying to actualize either the conditions or the result.

This does not mean that utopias should ignore in their elaboration the eternal choice between today and tomorrow. The best solution in relation to personal liberty is, here again, a democracy, which means facing the dilemmas clearly and then following the opinion of the majority. Of course, it is sometimes necessary for despots, official or clandestine, to choose on their own something the masses would reject because they take only the short-term view. But, without giving man more credit than he deserves and because his agreement to the choice made is usually required for its successful operation, consultation—after making available sensible information about the probable results—remains the best means of deciding the present-versus-future conflict. Democratic consultation is also the best way to determine changes dictated by generosity or logic, such as transfers from the rich to the poor, from individuals to the public, from privileged regions to depressed regions.

C. The third reconciliation to be expected of any well-planned utopia tends to another kind of equilibrium. Man fulfills himself through three sorts of activity: education, work, and leisure. In order that he may not miss any opportunities to make the most of himself and his environment and that he may have a well-balanced existence, it is necessary that these three avenues of access to material and abstract goods all allow him an equal opportunity to enrich and develop himself. It is not so much a question of choosing among them, as in the former alternatives, as of making sure that none of them is lacking and that all three combine together to make the maximum opportunity possible.

The revolution in education which accelerated technological progress is producing is well known. Down to the present, the times allotted to education, productivity, and repose in a man's life have been successive rather than simultaneous. They have corresponded to three distinct stages of the life-cycle: childhood and adolescence for education, the mature years for productive work, and old age for repose. Of course, one learns at every age and rests at times during the most active years, but the productive population has been set apart from the young people in school on the one hand and the older people in retirement on the other. This model is in the process of being profoundly modified.

The rapid expansion of knowledge will no longer permit it to be compressed into the early years. Apart from the fact that such cramming can be harmful, it would be more and more futile because of the impossibility of providing oneself with the knowledge needed for a whole lifetime at its outset.

What is being called "continuous education" will in the future be a necessity throughout a professional career, not only for promotion but even in order to remain abreast of developments. Furthermore, the greater life span, even if not yet accompanied by adequate means of combating senility, makes the abrupt termination of active productivity at a predetermined age unnatural. Jobs can be differentiated, in their nature and their intensity, for people in their fifties, sixties, or seventies, so that they will no longer be cut off abruptly by enforced retirement. Conversely, the most active periods should include more intervals of release—like the sabbatical leaves of American universities—so that changes of rhythm can relax the body and recharge the mind. Our utopia could undertake to plan for this profound change and try to anticipate its results.

The optimum goal would be to assure throughout man's life:
—a truly formative education,
—interesting and productive work,
—leisure free from boredom.

Whatever the intermediary organization (community, association, or business) to which the individual might have recourse for education, work, or recreation, the methods and skill of the personnel who constitute and direct it and its means of support will depend on initiatives taken and rules established by the state. Each individual might—more or less—choose his own provider, but an over-all supervision is indispensable if benefits are not to be too haphazard and inequalities in salaries too great. *The utopia to be constructed is that of a distribution center, as nearly perfect as possible, of knowledge, work, and recreation, through the different intermediaries.*

IV

Where, at present, does one find the elements of this utopia that would bring together theoretical thinkers and realists to the great advantage of reformers?

They may be found in two complementary utopias which we

will call, to simplify the matter, the technological utopia and the democratic utopia. The former is more recent than the latter, but their conjunction could renew them both and transform paths already explored into new areas of discovery.

Briefly, according to the technological utopia, automation resulting from rapid progress makes it possible to bring an end to the fragmentation of the job, the multiplication of degrading tasks that have made the majority of workers robots who know nothing of the purpose or the end-product of their labor. Even though jobs have become less and less disagreeable, they do not yet foster the fulfillment of man nor do they ensure the rehabilitation of work. Soon, however, the new technology[1] will offer so many opportunities to "personnel with superior qualifications and education" and will bring about such an upgrading of jobs that everyone will be able to derive from his daily work satisfactions reserved up to now for a privileged minority. When that day comes, business will have become, *ipso facto,* as good an intermediary between the individual and society as other social organisms.

While the technological utopia has as its goal the abolition of degrading specialization, the democratic utopia seeks to abolish oppressive subordination. It would give each man a greater and greater share in the decisions that determine his destiny, so that the individual living in society would have as much responsibility as the isolated individual. With its extension to the economic sphere (from the political sphere where it originated), this utopia takes on a new aspect, as does the technological utopia.

The aim of these two utopias taken together is that society should not diminish man but rather add to his stature—or, at least, that society should increase man's means for fulfillment and should compensate, even beyond that, for the wear and tear he must suffer under its domination.

Despite this agreement on the final objective, however, these two utopias are in some ways antithetical, which makes it all the more necessary to combine them.

The technological view of happiness, reduced to its essence, is nothing more than the perfecting of Aldous Huxley's "best of all possible worlds." It would have each man carry out the function for which he is best qualified by order of an enlightened despot. The organizational chart is merely improved. The individual's lot would match his needs better after the second industrial revolution than after the first. But the conditions in which jobs are created and distributed would be the same if one merely perfected the process. The worker would have a better share in the work, but that would not make him master of his job to any greater extent.

The democratic view of happiness, on the contrary, stresses mastery without much concern for what purpose. It can indeed be suspected of valuing the method of obtaining it at the expense of the quality of the gain itself. The democrats, say their opponents, attach more importance to access to the machine than to its efficient functioning, and their ideal seems to be for everyone to be able to operate it rather than to assure good operation by reserving it to those best qualified. To put it the other way, those who always see the technocratic threat looming behind the new Eldorado of the technicians fear that the optimum use of individual capacities would sacrifice liberty to efficiency. Although they recognize that liberty and efficiency are equally indispensable to happiness and that neither can ever replace the other, they have a different order of priority than the one which inversely they attribute to the technicians.

These opposing points of view provoke most of the never-ending debates over the concurrent ideas of technocracy and democracy. They express either the different temperaments or the different situations of their advocates. However lively these debates may be, they would profit from being raised to a higher plane. The antagonism between technocrats and democrats is a recent development which coincides, in France for instance, with a crisis over the issues and personnel of politics. It lacks the perspective and calmness that could be found on the level of a utopia, if one deliberately sought, at that level, more subtle terms of choice. It is not really a matter of choosing between technocracy and democracy—which would appear if not irreconcilable, at least mutually contradictory—but of determining how each might temper the other in an ideal society that would refuse to sacrifice specialized ability to personal happiness or vice versa.

The principal merit and accomplishment of the new technological utopia is in abandoning the despairing solution considered inevitable as a result of the first industrial revolution: the search for happiness in recreation, considered as the only possible compensation for the unhappiness inherent in work, for most men. As soon as technological progress can raise the intellectual and emotional interest of an increasing number of jobs, such a last-resort solution will no longer be necessary. The exception becomes the rule, over a reasonable time. Above all, it is no longer absurd to propose as a goal to management the multiplication of satisfying jobs up to now reserved for a small minority of highly qualified or especially lucky men.

Sociologists who use the method of "prospective" challenge this optimism with two kinds of argument that shed light on the present discussion. For one thing, they do not think that fragmentation of work will end tomorrow. Even if one extrapolates from the present curve indicating an increase in satisfying jobs, it appears, they say, that an indeterminate period of time must pass before the majority of men succeed in becoming masters of their jobs. "It is probable that for several generations a considerable proportion of jobs will continue to tie workers down, without their being able to express their tastes, their inclinations or their personalities."[2] Furthermore, the same critics doubt that, even if the technical possibility were made open to them, workers would be willing to "contribute their whole mental and professional energies for the benefit of a business in whose technical management and profits they did not share—that is, a business which had not become structurally theirs."[3]

The first of these objections disappears as soon as one speaks in utopian terms, that is, of planned steps toward the future; and, notably in the eyes of realists it pleads more or less in favor of the new technological utopia. In fact, only the general direction matters in utopian terms; the time factor does not enter in—moreover, it escapes precise calculation in the accelerated era in which we live. Therefore, utopian thinking is, in this case, the best way of developing an idea that corresponds to a reality situated outside of time. Any other intellectual framework risks either the neglect of this reality (and of the reasonable hopes it promises) *or* the transformation of it into illusion through too great impatience.

The second criticism also contains a positive conclusion. It does not condemn the new technological utopia in itself. But it makes it appear incomplete, urging that it be united with the new democratic utopia—hence extending from the political into the economic sphere a belief in the possibility of each individual's participation in the conduct of the group of which he is a part. In short, the political revolution of the second half of the eighteenth century made a reality of the citizen as conceived by the *philosophes*—man matured by the spread of education and consequently capable of responsibility, of influencing the community in which he lived. The economic revolution of the second half of the twentieth century, in permitting the worker to mature likewise by putting the machine that had once dominated him at his service, could not fail also to offer him greater responsibility and influence in his place of work.

Under these conditions, the two utopias—technological and democratic—are inseparable. To believe in one or the other obliges one to believe in both, and this very combination provides material for an original utopia particularly suited to the dialectical needs of reformers.

The constructive utopia, of the kind reformers can hope for, is, as David Riesman says, "a rational belief which is in the long-run interest of the holder; it is a belief, not in existing reality, but in a potential reality; it must not violate what we know of nature, including human nature, though it may extrapolate our present technology and must transcend our present social organization."[4]

Again, one may ask whether this extrapolation and transcendence are objectively practicable, whether a utopia in the service of an interest—as in the above definition—is not almost inevitably the expression of a *parti pris,* a preconceived opinion? The author of the definition shows that utopian thought is "neither a mere dream nor a simple description of existing facts." But situated in between the two, and not without ambiguity, is it not necessarily subjective?

This question has real interest only if phrased as follows: "In constructing a utopia by a process of combining opposites so as to gain maximum acceptance in the long run, is one guided only by preferences, is one limited to the development of entirely preconceived ideas?" Objectivity, indeed, does not require a complete vacuum of opinion. If it did, it would be absurd, since the exercise in question is one of imagination based on desires. What is important is to test the desires and to keep the imagination within bounds—that is, to confront a flexible dream with probable reality in order to arrive at a logical compromise. For example, it would not be out of place to accept at the beginning this axiom—which is both a hypothesis and a conviction—"*the future will be a period of technocracy tempered by democracy.*"

After the feudal era and the bourgeois era, power now seems destined to fall to the masters of the technical skills most needed by the community. But once again, the masses who give power to these technicians are in danger of finding themselves dominated by them because they need them. This was the fate of the peasant who found himself subjected to his warrior-protector in the Middle Ages and of the worker who found himself dominated by his bourgeois-liberator in the early modern period. Measures must be taken so that the technician, in a like manner, will not dominate tomorrow those who give him power today.

To put the problem this way does not give us an immediate solution, but it shows what the eventual solution should accomplish. In thus formulating their concerns, the reformers would not deceive anybody. And if those who challenge them are men of as good faith as they themselves, reformers will succeed in gaining the cooperation of many of those whom, at present, they antagonize.

References

1. P. F. Drucker, *The Practice of Management* (New York: Harper & Row, 1954).
2. Georges Friedmann, *Le Travail en miettes* (Paris: Gallimard, 1956).
3. *Ibid.*
4. David Riesman, "Some Observations on Community Plans and Utopia," *Selected Essays from Individualism Reconsidered* (New York: Doubleday & Company, Inc., 1955), p. 70.

BERTRAND DE JOUVENEL

Utopia for Practical Purposes

On the Character of Utopian Writing

THE TERM should not be used as a qualificative. You expound and advocate some political or social blueprint which arouses my incredulity; I feel that your scheme cannot possibly be adopted or that if your system were perchance instaured, it could not possibly maintain itself. These reactions I may properly express by calling your views "chimeric": it is more usual, in such case, to call them "utopian," but this is an unfortunate practice. The term being thus used as an adjective expressing a personal evaluation, the same proposal may be utopia to some minds, while not to others. As we want to join in a discussion of utopias, we need a substantive meaning, such that the extension of the term is the same for all participants.

UTOPIA AS A LITERARY GENRE

Thomas More forged the word to designate a country that does not exist (U-topia) and to suggest a country that would deserve full approval (Eu-topia). Why did he not prefer the latter term? Presumably because he was a theologian to whom the idea of perfection implied the attribute of existence, as we can see in verses where the City is supposed to speak:

> For what Plato's pen hath platted briefly
> In naked words, as in a glass
> The same have I performed fully
> With laws, with men, and treasure fitly
> Wherefore not Utopie, but rather fitly
> My name is Eutopie: a place of felicity.

Eutopie it shall be, if and when brought into being: till then Utopie. A dream: aye but that is a capital point; a dream, while less than reality, is much more than a blueprint. A blueprint does not give you the "feel" of things, as if they existed in fact: a dream does so. If you can endow your "philosophical city" with the semblance of reality, and cause your reader to see it, as if it were actually in operation, this is quite a different achievement from a mere explanation of the principles on which it should rest. This "causing to see" by means of a feigned description is obviously what More aimed at: it is also the essential feature of the utopian genre.

In every utopian tract, the same device is used: the author recounts, as colorfully as his talent allows, a visit to a country which is a land of felicity. The device was obviously suggested to More by the many discoveries made since the Portuguese had ventured into the Atlantic. The great ports of Europe were humming with the tales of seafarers who had witnessed, and more often than not misunderstood, the surprising customs of previously unknown peoples. More used this context: it is in the great port of Antwerp that a mariner, Portuguese-born and supposed to have traveled in the new world with Amerigo Vespucci, describes the society fancied by More.

In the four and a half intervening centuries, "the traveler's account" has remained the mode of exposition characteristic of Utopian tracts. The only change which has occurred is that the journey to a distant place has been gradually superseded by the projection into a time distant in the future, a variant introduced as early as 1770 by Sébastien Mercier (*L'An Deux Mille Quatre Cent Quarante*). Is there any good reason for the great stability of this device? I think there is.

ON THE COMPOSITION OF A UTOPIAN TRACT

An explorer who ventures into an unknown land firstly encounters one person or a small group; he is struck by their appearance and manners; they take him to their own dwellings, he notes the setting of their daily lives and conceives some notion of their occupations and entertainments. It is only later that he is brought to a center, and the journey thither allows him to observe the landscape before he discovers the main monuments. Thus he gains many visual impressions of these strange people before engaging upon conversations which shall explain to him the institutions of this society. That such lecturing should occur only after the traveler has seen for himself, this is essential to any well composed utopian tract: this, for instance, is very well done by William Morris; it is only after he has seen a great deal in the company of a typical Dick that he obtains long explanations from old Hammond.

As the author's purpose is to advocate some institutional scheme, one might regard the lectures wherein this system is exposed as the substantial part of the utopian tract and be tempted to disregard the descriptions as mere ornaments meant only to hold the attention of the fickle reader—ornaments made necessary to sustain the fiction of a journey but indifferent to the main theme. But if so, why did the author burden himself with the fiction of a journey?

Indeed the author has chosen this literary device because the fiction of a journey committed him to lively descriptions, and allowed him to paint pleasing pictures of daily life in utopia, whereby he prepares us to accept the institutional scheme he advocates. See how delightful a world this is, and now listen to the means whereby it is contrived! Such is the mode of persuasion characteristic of and essential to utopian writing, so much so that the designation of "Utopia" should be denied to any exposition of a "New Model" of Society which is bereft of pictures concerning daily life.

WHAT IS REVEALING AND WHAT IS PROBLEMATIC IN A UTOPIA

The pleasing pictures offered by the utopian writer are meant to display the excellent fruit borne by the underlying institutions which he advocates. Now let us consider what this implies. Since the author strives to lure us by way of pictures, he must have painted those which seem to him most alluring. Therefore, he must have represented in his descriptions of every day life in utopia his dream of "life at its best" for a whole people: in other words, the images he uses for our seduction reveal his own dream.

As critical readers, we must doubt that the institutions recommended would in fact produce the way of life depicted. But we cannot doubt that this way of life seems excellent and delightful to the author, else he would not use it to win our acquiescence to his scheme. The pictures, therefore, are the positive element in the utopian tract; they afford us reliable information regarding the author's view of felicitous social existence; the author is a true witness to his own dream. In contrast, we are entitled to regard as unsound the cause-and-effect relationship he affirms between his scheme and his pictures.

I attach great importance to this distinction between what is revealing and what is problematic in utopian tract. It can, I believe, guide us toward a profitable use of utopian procedure.

ON THE HONESTY OF UTOPIAN EXPOSITION

Our pedantic disposition works against reception of utopian writing. "Say it in pictures if you wish to seduce the childish, but we intellectuals must be addressed in abstract terms, and do not expect our attention if you don a colorful costume." Thus do we reject the utopian genre in favor of a mode which seems to us more serious. But is it more honest? Should we not recognize it as a merit of the utopian writer that he lays himself open to a double check?

Firstly, he shows us the felicitous life of the utopians; secondly, he explains by what institutional means this is brought about. This enables me as reader to judge whether his "good life" seems good to me, a first check. If that first test is passed, I can then go on to check whether it seems to me probable that the institutions recommended would result in the "good life" described.

To instance the first check, I quite rapidly make up my mind that I do not want anything like More's Utopia. A passage like the following is decisive: "If any man, of his own head and without leave, walk out of his precinct and bounds, taken without the prince's letters, he is brought again as a fugitive or a runaway with great shame and rebuke, and is sharply punished." The great king Utopus, who is said to have devised the institutions of this excellent republic, must have been quite a martinet, for he has turned the island of Abraxa into a philanthropic penitentiary.

To instance the second check, I turn to *News from Nowhere*. The "new life" described by William Morris obtains my enthusiastic assent. The murky agglomerations have been cleared away, the air and the rivers cleansed; people live in homes scattered in a beautiful landscape, they cherish the beauties of the earth and take pleasure in their work, done unhurriedly, to their own taste, with loving care. Here indeed is an earthly paradise: but how is it contrived? Nothing could be weaker than the explanation given by Morris.

Mind you, I do not say that this dream cannot be actualized but only that the author shows us no plausible way to its achievement. The delightful freedom depicted by Morris is supposed to follow quite naturally from the suppression of "production for profit." It is worth noting that the very same radical change leads in Cabet's *Icarie* to an utterly different organization: a centralized program is carried out by workers assembled in huge factories, where they manufacture standardized goods to be evenly distributed to the population. Men and women receive uniforms denoting their age and occupation. Housewives do not need to worry about the menu: their food allotment for the day is delivered in a niche at their door. The reader can judge for himself whether the radical reform on which Cabet and Morris agree has moved things rather in the direction indicated by the one or in the direction indicated by the other. But anyhow the sharp contrast indicates the ambiguity of abstract formulations.

ON THE AMBIGUITY OF ABSTRACT FORMULATIONS

Both Cabet and Morris, because they give us concrete descriptions, allow us the two checks mentioned above: whether the outcome of their fundamental reform is *likeable,* and whether it is *likely.* No such checks are allowed to us by the author who cannily keeps to abstract formulations. As he does not tell me, in terms of men's actual way of life, what he wants and expects to follow from his proposition, I cannot join issue with him on grounds either of my *dislike* or of my *disbelief.*

Our mind craves pictures. He does not offer them, so I make them up myself. So do his other listeners. The abstract term operates like a drug: it arouses in each his particular dream, by means of which he beguiles himself; and it matters not that these representations are incompatible; the author remains uncommitted. Surely the utopian approach is fairer?

On the Use of the Utopian Approach

Concerned as we are with economic growth, it seems puzzling to us that utopian writers seem unaware of the production problem, easily assuming that for everyone there will be enough, and more than enough, as soon as the institutions have been changed. Why this confidence? Analysis yields three reasons, which it is convenient to designate by the names of the authors who have most clearly revealed them.

Firstly, we have the Seneca-Rousseau theme: our "true" needs are quite limited; there is no difficulty in obtaining their satisfaction from bountiful Nature; we run into difficulties and miseries only because we develop artificial wants. The greater the part assigned to vanity in this development (the theme taken up by Veblen), the more plausible it seems that such artificial wants can be abated by adequate institutions. Note More's device of showering adornments upon children alone, imparting to them the meaning of toys and baubles, which one grows ashamed of and rejects upon reaching years of discretion.

Secondly, we have the belief that quite enormous quantities of labor are wasted upon luxuries for the rich, so that the reversion of all that labor to the production of necessities would exceed requirements. William Morris goes furthest in this direction: in his reformed England there is less production (not only less work).

These first two themes are pervasive and independent of technological progress, upon which, on the contrary, the third theme rests. Robert Owen stresses in his Report to the *County of Lanark* that "scientific or artificial aid to man increases his productive powers, his natural wants remaining the same." And he estimates, in 1820, that the amount of this new productive power "compared to the manual labour of the whole population of Great Britain and Ireland, is at least as *forty to one,* and may be easily made as *100 to 1.*" No fear therefore of having too little: the evil is maldistribution, but even if it be remedied, overproduction is to be feared.

As to the first point, it now seems to us that utopian authors grossly underestimated the difficulty of providing everyone with a decent competence; as to the second, we are aware that they wildly overestimated the productive resources addressed to luxury and which could be recuperated by means of its suppression. The third point is much more intriguing.

THE PUZZLE OF THE "ENERGY SLAVES"

Owen has put his finger upon the great novelty which gives an unprecedented opportunity to procure "the good life." The obtention of so-called "mechanical energy" from inanimate sources has utterly changed the means available to human societies. I have here an estimate by *World Resources Inventory* (the Buckminster Fuller group) according to which the North American population enjoys the services of 185 "energy slaves" per inhabitant, or 460 energy slaves per family. An arresting figure!

But also a misleading statement. What it calls to my mind is that each family *severally* is served by 460 slaves, thus enjoying the same autonomous power as the wealthy Roman of the late Empire, lording it in his *villa* over his own food providers and his own artisans, with many personal servants responsive to his beck and call. With such forces at its service, each family could set its own style of life after its own taste, and this without any scruples or compassion, since its pseudo-slaves would be insentient, incapable of feeling or suffering. The vivid picture thus aroused in my mind bears, as we well know, not the slightest relation to reality.

Firstly, these pseudo-slaves are not distributed among families: I do not mean that they are not distributed evenly or fairly, but that they are not distributed at all, save with some exceptions, mainly those used for individual transport. Chiefly, they are involved in a collective process of production, and it is the fruits of their energy which are made available to us. This brings us to the second point. Take as a basis of reference the pleasant setting and the unhurried pace of a mere bourgeois' life in the eighteenth century. One might think that the great increase in our powers has brought the life of even the most modest worker of our day beyond this line of reference. But it is not so. A problem arises, therefore, of how all this slave-power is being spent. What does it go into? This question involves us in complications: the use of the term "slave-power" implies a versatility in mechanical energy which it has not up to now displayed; at its best in procuring speed, it is not much use in procuring gardens. We tend to get what it can best give us rather than what is most desirable.

But my third objection to the "energy slave" formulation goes even deeper. Our mastery has many traits of a symbiosis: the machines do not serve us unless we service them, and we have to adjust our human organization to our equipment.

THE NEED FOR MODERN UTOPIAN PICTURES

It is a serious fault of the utopian writers that they paid scant attention to the material basis upon which their good life was to be reared; it is an inexplicable fault of ours that we pay no attention to rearing a good life upon our unprecedented material basis. Two hundred and forty years ago Swift derided the "projectors" who, said he, "contrive new rules and methods of agriculture and building, and new instruments and tools for all trades and manufactures; whereby, as they undertake, one man shall do the work of ten." The projectors have indeed honored their promise; and their labors have served us well as we can see when we compare the condition of our people with that of populations of similar density and lagging technology. But who would say that we have made the optimal use of our technological boons? Worse than that, while we are pouring ever increasing intellectual efforts into improving our means, we seem to give no thought to the ends they should serve. Every year we are better armed to achieve what we want. But what do we want?

Finding out what we want should become a major object of our attention. It is a trite saying that we live in an age of very swift change. But there is vast difference between letting changes occur under the impact of technological advances and choosing the changes we want to bring about by our technological means. I see with great pleasure the fashion which impels governments vastly to increase the resources devoted to research, and opposition parties to promise that they would do even more; but also I see with some alarm that we feel bound to carry out what ever technology happens to make possible. It is not clear to me that because we can now build supersonic transport planes we should, therefore, hasten to build them—many other things are more pressing for human convenience. While it was a senile attitude toward technological change to fear and oppose it in every form, we have gone over to a childish attitude: whatever can possibly be done, let's do it! But the very abundance of the opportunities accorded by technological progress bids us to choose, brings us to an adult, responsible attitude of drawing upon the potentialities of technological progress as possibilities to be wisely exploited for the promotion of a sane and happy way of life.

The lack of any clear images of the style of life we are building is a cause of anxiety. This anxiety is revealed in the most characteristic literature of our time—science fiction. This displays what might be called a new Fatalism, a feeling that our ways of life are being determined entirely by technological advances, through no choice of ours. Such a belief is widespread, and fed by many incautious expressions.

This belief is however quite unfounded. It is time that experts represented the many different outcomes which can be obtained by different uses of our many and increasing possibilities. This representation should be in pictures, according to the utopian tradition. For us, television now offers a new technique of exposition. A variety of modes of life which seem achievable can be displayed to the public in order to elicit its preferences: a project of this kind is now being undertaken by means of the French television.

While the great exhibitions of the past century have been exhibitions of means, the exhibitions of the future should be exhibitions of achievable ends. It is probably worth noting that the French television project arose out of discussion of long-term programing by the "1985 group" of the French Plan, in the course of which it became apparent that the far-reaching commitments to be made depend upon the values preferred and that it would be obviously undemocratic to limit the discussion to a small circle. Instead, public participation must be invited, and possible achievements must be pictorialized to make such participation feasible.

COMMON FATE

Why worry about the future way of life if increasing wealth increasingly enables each member of the wealthy society to elaborate his own specific and distinctive manner of life? If that assumption is justified, it is not only useless, it is even dangerous to picture a way of life in advance since this is apt to steer toward convergence upon a single model an evolution which, left to itself, would lead to a far greater variety of styles, corresponding to a diversity of tastes. This is an objection to which I am highly sensitive, as I regard with horror any arrangements apt to herd individuals into a pattern of conformity: such enforced conformity is an odious trait of all but a very few utopias. I would not like to incite the designing of utopias if this were to work toward the narrowing down of individual choices.

But I wonder whether it is a warranted assumption that our social evolution is at present fanning out into an ever richer variety of ways of life? Who would deny that the range of material goods offered is ever-increasing? Who would doubt that different individuals, wandering in self-service stores, can build up an almost endless variety of "packages"? But, in more important respects, can they similarly use their social environment as a "self-service world" from which they can make up highly individualized ways of life? In some respects, this is so; in others, not at all. In quite important respects we can observe a decline in the latitude of deviation from modal conduct (or "Gaborian freedom"[1]), and an increase in what Donald T. Campbell calls "the coefficients of common fate."[2] Therefore, utopian pictures are useful both to insure that the common fate should be that which is preferred and to seek means of securing latitude of deviation.

There are quite fundamental reasons working against individual self-determination. When one considers the increasing income of the average man in a prospering community, one must remember that he is "rich" in quite another way than the rich were in a poorer state of society. According to the best statistical expertise,[3] the average American of 1959 has seven times the income in real terms of his counterpart in 1839. This does not and cannot mean that he is in the same position as the man who in 1839 enjoyed seven times the average income of that time. This rich man of 1839 could use the labor of seven of his contemporaries. If the average American of 1959 gets what is regarded as the equivalent it is because the proceeds of his own work have increased to that extent. What has made such an increase possible? Economies of scale (producing more of the same thing) and technological advances (improving the ways of doing things). The whole process rests upon men's willingness as producers to work together in battalions and to follow the instructions they receive, and upon their willingness as consumers to take those goods and services which are turned out in bulk at declining labor costs per unit. Obviously there would be nothing like the present number of motor cars in the U. S., nor could automobile workers afford them, if each car were built to the specifications of the individual buyer, and if the workers constructed them in the manner of free artisans. Indeed, the great difference in the pace of economic progress during the last decade between Britain and France is probably due to the fact that the British unions are craft and have impeded changes in work rules as the French have not.

We are increasingly integrated both as producers and consumers in a vast organization which need not be collectivist to be empirically collective. We are not forced to fit in, but the inducements to do so are very great indeed. If I choose to travel on horseback rather than by car not only do I forego the advantages of the car, but, moreover, I shall endure many incommodities which did not attend horseback travel in the past. The horseman caught in a rush of cars can serve to symbolize the discomforts of "bucking the trend." It is hardly reasonable to refuse the advantageous bargain offered to us by modern civilization. Realizing that the very process which makes it possible for us to get successively more for less toil clearly commits us to the typical way of life of our fellows, we must make every effort to improve this way of life as best we know.

NO ESCAPE

Our Age of Agglutination has many unpleasant aspects: our environment is ugly and noisy, we are hurried and worried, people speak eagerly of "getting away from it all"—pathetic attempts to do so crowd the roads on weekends and crowd the beaches in vacation periods. It shall be found that there is no escape—quite soon Greece will resemble Coney Island—then it will be realized that what needs to be done is to improve Coney Island. The extraordinarily high value which people set upon the vacation periods gives the measure of their discontent with their daily lives. But surely it is a crying absurdity that the emphasis should be on that small fraction of the year. It is to the workaday world itself that pleasantness must be imparted, failing which, the palliative of escape shall in time make the resorts as unpleasant as the residences.

UTOPIAN PICTURES OF DAILY LIFE

Thus we come to see that what we need is to address ourselves to the ordinary day of the ordinary man. Take this man when he wakes up, follow him through to the time of sleep. Plot, as it were, the sequence of his pleasurable and unpleasurable impressions, and now imagine what "a good day" should be. Picturing this "good day" is the first step into a modern utopia; then you will have to seek the conditions which can bring about this "good day."

Planning for the Good Day

So many are the impressions, feelings, thoughts, crowded into a single ordinary day that if they could be recorded, their account would fill a bulky volume. Of this wealth and variety we should, I believe, take careful notice if we propose to attack meaningfully the problem of human felicity. Instead of starting with some *a priori* doctrine concerning the causes of human happiness or unhappiness, we should pay the closest attention to whatever we find is apt to cloud or light up man's day.

We must beware of taking one part of the picture for the whole. In the course of the day, our man reaches several times in his pocket to pay either directly or through his wife and dependents for the acquisition of goods and services. We may regard the collection of such acquisitions as "the family shopping list." Our man's ability to lengthen the shopping list of the family is surely a very good thing—I have no patience with the austere moralists who belittle this aspect of welfare. On the other hand, it is not serious to take the length of this list as the exclusive measure of welfare. This unfortunately is the present propensity.

From the far-off days of Wilford King and Josiah Stamp through the great works of Colin Clark and Simon Kuznets, I have been an enthusiastic supporter of National Accounting and am, in my own country, deeply involved in its practice. This is a quite admirable tool in the hands of those who understand it—I am sorry that even some economists have to be included among those who do not understand it. In order to wield it effectively, one must never lose sight of the conventions on which it is based. It is a pleasure of the same nature to attend a baseball game or to follow the Olympic Games in Tokyo from one's home, only the second is surely greater; and while the first was possible to the past generation, the second has only been made possible in our day. Yet the first figures in the statistical measure of the standard of life (private consumption) and not the second because the costs thereof are counted as "costs of production" of the firms which provide this entertainment as a part of their advertising. But even if the costs figured, would they be a true measure of the benefit? Conversely, transport expenses on going to work are not distinguished from transport expenses incurred for pleasure. If you buy perfume, that figures, but the stink you may have to endure from the environment does not figure. If ordinary water becomes so polluted that you have to use mineral water, the mineral water figures as an improvement.

These are but anecdotic inconsistencies. Far more serious is the fact that the journey to work may become longer and more tiring, the environment may become murkier, uglier, and more noisy, without any trace of these phenomena as negative components of material welfare. One must conclude that our measurement of consumption, in itself extremely useful, should not be mistaken for a measure of material welfare.[4] This is well understood by specialists of National Accounting, but too often forgotten by others.

Human felicity depends, of course, on many other than material conditions. That some of these conditions are moving unfavorably may be surmised from the rapid increase in the consumption of tranquilizers. Indeed, just as we can point to a successive improvement of the shopping list but some deterioration of the environment, so we can, in the realm of health, point to considerable improvements regarding organic health but notable deterioration in the nervous balance.

Is is hardly necessary to press home points which have been made, often with exaggeration, by denouncers of our industrial civilization. Such is by no means my own mood. The negative features I do not regard as inherent traits of our progress. If I deemed them such, I would regard them as an acceptable price to be paid for unquestionable gains. But my point of view is very different; they are not a necessary price. This is where I am, if you will, utopian in the vulgar sense of the word: I feel convinced that if we put our mind to it, we can quite transform the daily existence of man. Putting our mind to it means that we must begin to consider our man's day in all its aspects, instead of proceeding analytically as we tend to do.

HARMS OF THE ANALYTICAL APPROACH

By proceeding analytically, I mean, for instance, thinking in terms of the reduction of hours on the job without attention to those wasted in transport, thinking in terms of housing without regard for the environment; in general, cutting up the problem of man's existence into discrete problems.

It is a natural outcome of this procedure that each problem is treated in such a way as to give rise to unpleasant by-products, known to economists as "external costs." For instance, you provide a remarkably efficient solution of the problem of cleaning, the detergents; but this solution has the worst conceivable effect upon the water which is spoiled beyond the possibility of recycling by any simple method. The lesson of water is indeed important: because it was a given, it has been treated without respect; because of such treatment, water has become a problem; because it has become a problem, we now set a value on it.

We are enthusiastic about rational calculation but we do not practice it reasonably. It is striking that economists start out by speaking of Land, Labor, and Capital, and then immediately drop out Land as of no account. While any farmer or industrialist knows that he must provide for the upkeep of his plant, the basic "plant" we have received, the Earth, seems to us to call for no stewardship.

In fact, the spirit of our industrial civilization as it now is represents a set-back relative to the spirit of agricultural societies. What I mean is this: societies of hunters took no care of preserving their stock of game. They were predators and depredators. When men settled down to agriculture it became important to provide for the maintenance of fertility. It is only very gradually that the agriculturists mastered that problem. We have not reached that stage in our industrial civilization, which is as yet, or again, a system of predation and depredation of natural resources. At a more advanced stage of our skills, we have returned to a less advanced stage of foresight.

IMMATURITY

Indeed immaturity is a characteristic of our age. The "outboard" might be taken as symbolic of our mood: a toy for grown-ups for moving about rapidly to nowhere with a great deal of noise. If adults can be so childish, and so indifferent to the nuisance they make of themselves, why be surprised that the same "advantages" are offered to children. Let me quote from the *Wall Street Journal* (September 24, 1964): "Mattel scores a hit among youngsters (but not some parents) with V-Rroom motors, which make ordinary bicycles sound like motorcycles. A. C. Gilbert will seek a topper with 'Banshee' roller skates that give off 'an unearthly jet wailing sound.'" Up to our times, it had been assumed that children should gradually be educated out of their natural thoughtlessness: must we now encourage them therein?

Pufendorf observed: "We may conjecture that Divine Providence meant Man to grow up more slowly than animals, so that time enough is given to mellow the natural ferocity of our species. Indeed if Man reached his full vigor soon after birth, he would be more intractable than any animal."[5] It would be hard to deny that our present mores greatly retard the maturity of the human being.

Quételet, in his famous work which has become the cornerstone of modern social science,[6] noted the regularity of criminality and opined that its amount could be reduced only gradually as the outcome of a general improvement of social conditions. Now we know to what degree social conditions have improved in many respects. Therefore, the following figures[7] give food for thought.

Indictable Crime 1957-63

Year	*Total*	*Per cent detected*
1957	545,562	47.2
1958	626,509	45.6
1959	675,626	44.7
1960	743,713	44.5
1961	806,900	44.8
1962	896,424	43.9
1963	978,076	43.1

The speed of the increase is quite striking, and surely significant. As this is a field which I have not studied at all, I am eager to know of any works plotting the evolution of criminality over long periods. I feel that great importance should be attached to this subject. But also I strongly feel that indictable offenses are but the extreme manifestations of a lack of regard for one's fellow men which is displayed in the current boorishness of townsmen. The progress of urbanization does not seem to be attended by a progress of urbanity; and yet, as men are more closely lumped together, it becomes more necessary that they should behave courteously.

THE HAPPY DAY

When a man awakes, he recovers awareness of his surroundings. If he thinks gladly of his family and looks forward to the day's work, he can be called happy, though I would like to add to these criteria a less essential but important component, the pleasantness of his surroundings. There is not much we can do as social reformers, or at least know how to do, toward causing this major blessing of life, a united family. It is quite easy on the other hand to make the physical setting of life one which is delightful. Some people apparently prefer to inhabit towns: how can we pride ourselves on our wealth, as long as we do not make our towns as beautiful as the Renaissance cities of Italy? Most people prefer to open their eyes upon trees, and that can be arranged. I would like our man to walk to his work amidst pleasant scenery. As an economist, I am not, of course, unaware that the quickening pace of reallocation of manpower in itself works toward conurbation and increasing the bustle of the journey to work. But what is the use of utopian thinking, if not to address our intellectual efforts to the countering of sheer "gravity" effects. I find it strange that the very same people who condemn laisser-faire subscribe unthinkingly to the laisser-faire of an economic determinism.

From the journey to work, I naturally pass on to the work itself. We have been engaged in making work more efficient: is it not important to make it more attractive, the great theme broached by Charles Fourier, and which has practically not been followed up at all. Work is currently regarded as the cost of getting what we want, a negative value, the less of it the better. But is this the view which we, intellectuals, take of our work? Do we anxiously watch the clock to see whether we are allowed to knock off? Do we not feel that it is our work which imparts meaning to our life? Do we work to earn our leisure or do we regard our rest as enabling us to do better work? What we most want is to do "good work" and such also is the wish we form for our best friends. Why, then, should our interest in the many take the quite different form of wishing them only to do "less work"? There is reason for that contrast in that we recognize the unpalatable character of many labors. But should we not regard it as our problem to recast our organization of labor so that each man can rejoice in his work as we do? We should not accept it as a datum that the enjoyment of work is a privilege of some few: this is an immoral doctrine, and our concern should be to put our fellow men in that same position which is presently, but not by necessity, a privilege.

I recognize that the interest taken in "the problem of leisure" is well-meant, but I think this is a false track. It is treating men as children to seek means of entertaining them harmlessly. Indeed children themselves sense it as a promotion when they are invited to do something apparently significant. You cannot make men contented through entertainments but only through achievements. It is therefore "the problem of work" which is essential. You cannot have a Good Society if you do not offer to each man a man-sized job, which he can take joy and pride in. This is an immensely difficult problem but quite an essential matter.

IMPLICATIONS FOR DEVELOPING COUNTRIES

If we aim at "the ordinary man's good day" we may find a great change in our priorities, quite possibly that our efforts are misallocated, and that some things which are being done are not worth doing. This would be of great importance for the "developing" countries. While we offer them valuable "know-how," the value of our psychological impact is questionable. As a machinery for the production of happiness our arrangements have a low yield. Consider how much effort and time it would take to reproduce it! If we take our cue from the econometricians, we find that, assuming a 2 per cent per capita rate of growth (slightly higher than the American long-term rate of 1.64 given by R. W. Goldsmith), the Indian people would attain the American standard of life in. . .175 years! This does not take into account the great difference in natural resources. Are there not simpler social machineries with a higher yield in happiness?

With the best intentions in the world, quite a disparaging view has been foisted upon the non-Westerners: it has been pointed out to them how far they trail behind the Joneses. One may question the advantages of looking to a target both so distant and so fast-moving. Is there no smoother path to a good life? Can we confidently assert that our way to a good life is necessary, when it has apparently not proved sufficient?

REFERENCES

1. Dennis and Andrew Gabor, "A Mathematical Theory of Freedom," *Royal Statistical Society* (1954, Part I, Series I).
2. Donald T. Campbell in *Decisions, Values and Groups,* edited by D. Willner (Oxford and New York: Pergamon Press, 1960).
3. Cf. Raymond W. Goldsmith in *Bulletin SEDEIS,* No. 844 (February 10, 1963).
4. B. de Jouvenel, "Niveau de Vie et Volume de la Consommation," *Bulletin SEDEIS,* No. 874 (January 10, 1964).
5. Samuel von Pufendorf, *De jurae naturae et gentium* (London: Scanorum, 1672), Book VIII, Chapter I.
6. L. A. J. Quételet, *Sur l'Homme et la Developpement de ses Facultés, ou Essai de Physique Sociale,* 2 Vol. (Paris, 1835).
7. *The Guardian,* October 15, 1964.

V

UTOPIA THE ETERNAL HUMAN

GEORGE KATEB

Utopia and the Good Life

IN THE modern age, it would seem appropriate that two conditions be assumed as the basis of any seriously projected utopian society: (1) leisure resulting from the greatly diminished need for materially productive labor and (2) abundance. The entire thrust of science and technology is in the direction of freeing men from most kinds of menial work, drudgery, lifeless routine, backbreaking or brutalizing exertion. However the various economic systems of the world eventually use, misuse, or thwart the means of production, coordination, and distribution, a realistic sense of potentiality would indicate that leisure and abundance are attainable for all. Given these assumptions, certain ways of life, certain kinds of character and sensibility, certain varieties of experience are obviously ruled out. Most forms of heroism and endurance, many kinds of resourcefulness and ingenuity, many hallowed attainments and disciplines, and a host of traditional consolations and inducements are incompatible with assured material ease. What then is left? If leisure and abundance foreclose these possibilities, surely they must open the way for others.

In confronting new possibilities, the proper aim would not be to offer a blueprint. Indeed, any serious utopian thinker will be made uncomfortable by the very idea of blueprint, of detailed recommendations concerning all facets of life. The combination of abundance and leisure is inherently dynamic and hence is at war with the traditional utopian fondness for fixed patterns of perfection. Furthermore, even initially, abundance and leisure can promote such a wide range of values, and can be accommodated in such a great number of divergent institutional settings, that the "design of cultures" must proceed in a tentative spirit.

Nevertheless, some speculation about life in utopia can contribute to moral clarity. At its most serious, this speculation is part of a larger intellectual enterprise, that of philosophical anthropology, in which the nature of man—the peculiarly human—and the ends of life are all considered.[1] Short of that degree of seriousness, there is something else: thinking about utopian life in a manner analogous to taking a bird's-eye view of societies in the real world. Thus, the aim of an intelligent traveler is to "get the feel" of a country, to observe novel and salient features, to be watchful for evidences of a coherent style, to make hasty but spirited generalizations and abrupt, occasionally condescending judgments. The aim of some writers is similar: to say what the *tone* of life in utopia would be.

In this paper, we shall refer both to those who further utopian thought by systematic philosophical anthropology, and to those who are content to offer broad suggestions about life in utopia.

Our intention is to make a very rough and quite abstract assessment of these ideas. We shall take up a number of definitions of the good life, starting with a minimal one and finally coming to the most elevated, which turns out to be the oldest and most persistent. Until the last definition is reached, the others are treated as incomplete: if they are not to be rejected altogether, they must not be allowed sole possession of the field. The progression is as follows: the good life as laissez-faire, as the greatest amount of pleasure, as play, as craft, as political action, and, finally, as the life of the mind. These would seem to be the major candidates once leisure and abundance become the *données* of the human condition. Let us acknowledge that the subject of this paper is impossibly grand and large. To talk about the good life is necessary, but it is also presumptuous. To discuss the views of others in a few pages and to judge them (often harshly), as we do, is presumption carried very far indeed.

The presence of abundance and leisure signifies the absence of most of the radical evils of the world. It would be possible to say that the absence of radical evil is the correct definition of utopia and that to go beyond that is to impose on the world, though with the best of motives, a partial or eccentric vision of life. It is not simply the love of blueprints that can damage the sense of utopian possibility. Speculation about the good life and modest talk about the tone of life in utopia are also coercive. The great modern moral idea is that of individuality; it is at the heart of modern humanism, modern liberalism, modern radicalism. There is no understanding utopia apart from these movements of thought: utopia is *their* culmination. Utopia is therefore the culmination of the idea of individuality. But this idea is opposed to philosophical anthropology and to the flights of utopian imagination as strongly as it is opposed to blueprints. Within the limits set by respect for the individuality of others, each person must be free to become what he must or can or wants. The ethics of individuality is the ethics of self-realization: each man is to devote his life to exploiting his inner riches in a society that nurtures and encourages those riches. No style of social life will emerge from this; no tone will be detected. And *a fortiori*, no philosophical anthropology, even the most noble or generous, has any relevance. After the elimination of radical evil, only one task remains: to determine—again in a tentative spirit—what practices and institutions work in support of the principle of self-realization.

Against this extreme individualism two things may be said. First, the relation between social practices and institutions and the self is not simply one of support or encouragement. To put it that way is to imply that there could be selves without society, that society is at most a device for helping the self to do what it could do alone but only very laboriously, and that eventually the self can outgrow society and be realized in a splendid isolation. The plain truth is that without a society there are no selves, that, as Aristotle said, the community is prior to the individual, that the selves to be realized are given their essential qualities by their societies, and that the process of self-realization is a process of continuous involvement with society, as society not only shapes but employs everyone's inner riches. The upshot is that thought about possible styles of life or about the nature of man is necessary to give sense to the idea of individuality. Far from being an oppressive encroachment, social theory (utopian or not) is a basic duty. Second, even the most thoroughgoing theorists of individuality, such as Emerson and Mill, indicate that the flowering of individuality takes place in conjunction with the development of some uniform characteristics and that diverse people will have some common experiences. Society must impose certain standards on all; all good men will impose, in some matters, the same standards on themselves; all cultivated men will share certain preferences; all selves fully realized will attain a common spiritual or philosophical insight or understanding. There is, in short, an essentially human, or humanly perfect, core in the character of all fully developed individuals, while differences of experience and endowment will generate vital differences of tastes, skills, and aspirations which the good society will welcome and reward. Philosophical anthropology, whose purpose is to consider the essentially human or the humanly perfect, is importantly ancillary to the doctrine of self-realization and is therefore an inevitable component of utopian thought.

What ways of life, then, offer themselves as eligible candidates for a utopian society? The readiest answer is that utopia is "the negation of the negation." That is to say, utopia is *au fond* the opposite of the real world: it should be thought of as a society in which radical evil has been abolished *and* human wants are satisfied to the fullest degree possible, a society in which all avoidable pain is eliminated *and* pleasure is maximized. It is in utopia that the utilitarian principle will finally prevail, free from the dilution which that principle suffers in the real world at the hands of inertia, irrationality, and sinister interests.

On the assumption that pleasure is to be understood as pleasurable sensation, utopian life can be defined as a condition of the largest number of pleasurable sensations, or pleasurable sensations of the greatest intensity, or some compromise of the two. (There is no need here to enter into all the details of Bentham's "felicific calculus.") The tone of life in utopia will be hedonist: human wants will multiply as man's technical and scientific ingenuity increases; the restrictions dictated by scarcity or by inequitable distribution will vanish; the regime of guilt, self-hatred, and perverse asceticism will be dismantled. After society has been rid of all forms of wretchedness, utopia will dedicate itself to the science of the pursuit of pleasure in dead earnest.

This ideal immediately encounters a number of serious objections which are to be found in the tradition of utilitarianism itself and also in the tradition of utopianism. Some of these objections are really commonplaces of moral psychology; some stem from a positive revulsion at the thought of a life of unperplexed pleasure.

In John Stuart Mill's *Autobiography* one main point against a life of pleasure is made. Coming as it does from the profoundest champion of the pleasure principle, the point has a special acuteness. In the course of his narration, Mill tells of the mental crisis he endured in his early twenties: of how from his fifteenth year he had consciously sought his own pleasure in being "a reformer of the world," of how after five years of strenuous (though presumably happy) labor in this direction, he ceased to derive pleasure from that labor and became sick of the world.

In this frame of mind it occurred to me to put the question directly to myself: "Suppose that all your objects in life were realized; that all the changes in institutions and opinions which you are looking forward to, could be completely effected at this very instant: would this be a great joy and happiness to you?" And an irrepressible selfconsciousness distinctly answered, "No!"[2]

From this time of despondency Mill drew a number of lessons. The most important was that pleasure could not be attained if it were made the direct object of attainment:

> Those only are happy (I thought) who have their minds fixed on some object other than their own happiness; on the happiness of others, on the improvement of mankind, even on some art or pursuit, followed not as a means, but as itself an ideal end. Aiming thus at something else, they find happiness by the way. The enjoyments of life . . . are sufficient to make it a pleasant thing, when they are taken *en passant,* without being made a principal object. Once make them so, and they are immediately felt to be insufficient. They will not bear a scrutinizing examination.[3]

Mill makes it clear in *Utilitarianism* that he did not think it possible for any life to possess a "continuity of highly pleasurable excitement."[4] But even more, a life deliberately spent in the pursuit of pleasures, intense or not, must conclude in pain, the pain of languor, ennui, and irritability. However, Mill did not go on to fabricate a metaphysic of pain: he never was tempted to speak of pain as the only reality and of pleasure as a pitifully weak distraction from reality. His hope was that reformers would learn the lesson which he had learned from his own bitter experience and would not look on a life of pleasure as something society could unremittingly promote by every conceivable educational and institutional device. Thus corrected, radical reformers could get on with their work. And the ideal result of their work would be a society in which all men would have—in addition to a few occasions of rapturous happiness—"an existence made up of few and transitory pains, many and various pleasures, with a decided predominance of the active over the passive, and having as the foundation of the whole, not to expect more from life than it is capable of bestowing."[5]

The second main point urged against the life of pleasure by those who believe in pleasure is one of the oldest and most pervasive notions in the whole realm of moral thought. That is the view that the elimination of pain is at the same time the elimination of the most intense pleasures. As far back as the Platonic dialogues, especially the *Philebus,* the dependence of deep satisfactions on a prior state of misery, frustration, or longing is maintained. Apart from the pain that is often the necessary price for doing valuable or desirable things, there is the pain that is the necessary preliminary for the experience of real pleasure. If there is no utopia with radical evil, there is no utopia without radical evil. The essence of pleasure is release, relief, restoration, surprise, overcoming. What place have these things in a utopia of leisure and abundance? To refer to Mill's *Autobiography* again: ". . . the question was, whether, if the reformers of society and government could succeed in their objects, and every person in the community were free and in a state of physical comfort, the pleasures of life, being no longer kept up by struggle and privation, would cease to be pleasures."[6]

To the hedonist critique of the hedonist life a few answers have been given. (After all, it is only at rare moments that the social question appears to be the maximizing of pleasure rather than the alleviation of pain.) In the *Philebus,* Socrates settles for the temperate pleasures, independent of pain, which are less intense, and which ". . . attach to colours that we call beautiful, to figures, to most odours, to sounds, and to all experiences in which the want is imperceptible and painless, but its fulfillment is perceptible and painless,"[7] and which also attach to the processes and achievements of learning. John Stuart Mill, in quest of a solution to the problems of hedonism, formulated the doctrine of "the higher pleasures." We shall return to this doctrine later in this paper. For the moment, let it suffice to mention the two major elements of concern over a life of pleasure, as expressed by the partisans of pleasure: the futility of continuously and single-mindedly aiming at pleasure and the close association of intense pleasures with all the usual imperfections of the real world.

Within the body of radical utopian thought there are to be found attacks on the life of pleasure. The burden of these attacks is that the life of pleasure—specifically the pleasures of appetitive satisfaction—is ignominious because animal-like and unhuman. In modern times, the theme is announced by Friedrich Schiller in the Twenty-fourth Letter of *On the Aesthetic Education of Man* (c. 1793). Schiller wrote, "An infinite perpetuation of being and well-being, merely for the sake of being and well-being, is merely an ideal of appetite, and consequently a demand which can be put forward only by an animality that is striving after the absolute."[8] It is not that Schiller preached a gospel of austerity or sought to perpetuate that tradition of utopianism which equates the good life with the life of simplicity or renunciation. Rather, he insisted that there had to be something more to the good life than the complete correction of ordinary life.

The same spirit informs the early manuscripts of Karl Marx. In these fragmentary but occasionally brilliant writings, Marx gave a brief sketch of the historical stage immediately after the successful assault on the old order, a stage which he named "crude" or "raw" communism. It is the stage when the oppressors and the oppressed exchange roles, when the proletariat ceases being the embodiment of appetitive starvation and becomes the embodiment of appetitive indulgence.

> Immediate physical possession seems to it the unique goal of life and existence. The role of the worker is not abolished, but is extended to all men. The relation of private property remains the relation of the community to the world of things. . . . Just as women are to pass from marriage to universal prostitution, so the whole world of wealth (i.e., the objective being of man) is to pass from the relation of exclusive marriage with the private owner to the relation of universal prostitution with the community.[9]

Or as W. H. Auden expresses it in his fine political poem, "Vespers": ". . . some august day of outrage when hellikins cavort through ruined drawing-rooms and fish-wives intervene in the Chamber. . . ."[10]

The subject of crude communism does not appear again in Marx's writings. To be sure, in the *Communist Manifesto* he refers to the *premature* communism of Babeuf and his followers: "The revolutionary literature that accompanied these first movements of the proletariat had necessarily a reactionary character. It inculcated universal asceticism and social leveling in its crudest form."[11] Some of Marx's language here resembles that which he uses in discussing crude communism in his manuscripts of 1844. But his whole intention has changed, and changed permanently: the stress thereafter is on the suffering of the proletariat and the desperate need to rectify it, and on the capacity of a class-conscious proletariat to act coherently so that it might seize and then use power. Marx's comments in his *Critique of the Gotha Program,* for example, indicate an idealism more pedestrian, more purely welfarist than that of the early manuscripts. One has only to notice the derision he turns on the concept of alienation and on its employment by German philosophers in the *Communist Manifesto* to sense an alteration in his moral temper.

Later radicals, however, will not let go of the idea—actually, the disgust—behind Marx's projection of crude communism. There may no longer be visions of the insatiable mob revenging itself on the world by turning all the work of civilization into the stuff of instant sensual gratification. But there is disgust, still; and it is directed at the elevation of the consumer into the ideal type of human being and at the definition of the good society as that in which the ceaseless production of consumer goods answers to the swarming wishes of men in the mass. Aldous Huxley's *Brave New World* (1932) is the classical statement of this disgust, though we must remember that this novel is not the work of a man who (at least at that time) was sympathetic to the ideas of utopianism. Nevertheless, a similar aversion to the consumer ideal is strongly present in the work of genuine radicals like, say, Herbert Marcuse. In *One Dimensional Man,* he laments ". . . the satisfaction of needs which require continuing the rat race of catching up with one's peers and with planned obsolescence, enjoying freedom from using the brain, working with and for the means of destruction."[12] Like the young Marx, Marcuse bases the very humanity of mankind on a way of life far removed from obsessive consumption, even though it is largely artificial and induced rather than animal and desperate.

If the claims of pleasurable sensation and appetitive satisfaction must be moderated and made to share their dominion, where then shall the utopian theorist turn? Again, it is Schiller who announces the theme. In the Fifteenth Letter of *On the Aesthetic Education of Man,* he says: "For, to declare it once and for all, Man plays only when he is in the full sense of the word a man, and *he is only wholly Man when he is playing.*"[13] And in the course of his short book, Schiller expounds the concept of play, connecting it to the esthetic aspects of human life and at last finding in the esthetic the tone of the ideal society. The line of Schiller's thought has been carried forward in two important books of recent times: J. Huizinga's *Homo Ludens* (1944) and Herbert Marcuse's *Eros and Civilization* (1955).

It becomes apparent that the term play is meant to contrast with two others: the necessary and the useful. To the degree that human life is stripped of its concern with necessity and utility, it approaches a condition of liberation or freedom, freedom understood as the ability to play. At the same time the essentially human is allowed a complete disclosure; and of the animal and the practical only the irreducible survives. It also becomes apparent that play in the sense of games and sports is merely a tiny part of the total extent of the concept of play.

Before taking up the various forms of the idea of play, we must notice that material abundance is acknowledged to be a necessary precondition. In the case of Marcuse, contempt for the consumers' paradise is balanced by a faith in the wondrous potentiality of superfluity. At one point he writes:

But the regression to a lower standard of living, which the collapse of the performance principle would bring about, does not militate against progress in freedom. . . . The definition of the standard of living in terms of automobiles, television sets, airplanes, and tractors is that of the performance principle itself.[14]

Elsewhere, however, Marcuse says:

Non-repressive order is essentially an order of *abundance:* the necessary constraint is brought about by "superfluity" rather than need. Only an order of abundance is compatible with freedom.[15]

There is something of a contradiction here. The purport must be that abundance is appropriately human only when it is placed in the service of the play impulse rather than of private gluttonous consumption. The play impulse, in fact, is partly defined by its remoteness from both the satisfaction of elemental appetites and the *unmediated* satisfaction of all appetites.

Now the wish to make play the characteristic activity in the good society must be distinguished from the wish to make the activities of the imperfect world seem like play. That is, the estheticism of utopia must be distinguished from the estheticism of certain noble spirits—such as Nietzsche and his existential followers. This latter estheticism Nietzsche considered to be the tragic view of life, a heroic acceptance of the endless and endlessly repetitious pain and futility of life. His early work, *The Birth of Tragedy* (1872), contains a clear statement of this view:

. . . only as an esthetic phenomenon may existence and the world appear justified: and in this sense it is precisely the function of tragic myth to convince us that even the ugly and unharmonious is an artistic game which the will plays with itself in the eternal fullness of its joy. . . . The Dionysian, with its primordial joy experienced in pain itself, is the common source of music and tragic myth.[16]

Yeats' late poem, "Lapis Lazuli," speaks of "Gaiety transfiguring all that dread"; and of how "All things fall and are built again,/And those that build them again are gay." The speaker in the poem thinks of old Chinese, and says:

. . . I
Delight to imagine them seated there;
There, on the mountain and the sky,
On all the tragic scene they stare.
One asks for mournful melodies;

Accomplished fingers begin to play.
Their eyes mid many wrinkles, their eyes,
Their ancient, glittering eyes, are gay.[17]

Camus' *The Myth of Sisyphus* (1942) preaches the happiness of Sisyphus, the absurdist hero who recovers from metaphysical sickness and moral horror, and meets life with abandon and with something like delight.

There are, of course, numerous versions of the willed transformation of the intolerable, the desire to play at mastering what masters one in the end and to pretend that the given is the chosen. This is the activity of desperate men: some pass beyond good and evil and see only the play of primal and exuberant energy; some fall in love with the surface of things and make beauty into a theodicy; some play the game of life, in and out of it at the same time. This is the play-attitude toward life.

But a utopia of leisure and abundance is built on forgetfulness. What it forgets is history, the record of human suffering; what it tries to forget is mortality. If play, therefore, is the heart of utopian life, it cannot be the play which derives from despair, which flings defiance in the face of unendurable reality. It cannot even be the play that provides the accompaniment to, the relief from, the implicit commentary on normally boring or normally painful existence. In addition to disallowing the play-attitude of extreme existentialism, utopia also disallows play as an ingredient of seriousness. To use the terms employed by C. L. Barber in his *Shakespeare's Festive Comedy:* utopia is to be all holiday, without the contrasts of everyday and doomsday.[18] It is not enough that utopia abolish radical evil and facilitate the maximization of pleasure. Utopia must strive for the creation of a new reality and transform a dependent part (play in the context of seriousness) into an independent whole (life as play).

What then is being offered us when we are offered play as the substance of life? In *Homo Ludens,* Huizinga provides the best formulation of the idea. He says:

> Play lies outside the antithesis of wisdom and folly, and equally outside those of truth and falsehood, good and evil. Although it is a non-material activity it has no moral function. The valuations of vice and virtue do not apply here.[19]

And,

> In play the beauty of the human body in motion reaches its zenith. In its

more developed forms it is saturated with rhythm and harmony, the noblest gifts of aesthetic perception known to man.[20]

Furthermore,

Any game can at any time wholly run away with the players. The contrast between play and seriousness is always fluid. . . . Not being "ordinary" life it stands outside the immediate satisfaction of wants and appetites, indeed it interrupts the appetitive process.[21]

In sum, play is

. . . a free activity . . . absorbing the player intensely and utterly. . . . It proceeds within its own proper boundaries of time and space according to fixed rules and in an orderly manner.[22]

In its highest forms, play shows two basic modes: ". . . a contest *for* something or a representation *of* something."

Huizinga illustrates the concept of play by reference to a wide variety of human activity. Besides sports and games, there are contests of every sort; there are ceremonies, sacraments, rituals, feasts; there is ornamentation, display, fanciful embellishment; there is the fabrication of useless but beautiful things and the creation of new styles; there is a delight in esoteric knowledge, a love of secrets, masks, mimesis, disguises; there is in all the serious fields of human endeavor a play-aspect, a tendency toward virtuosity for its own sake, a tendency to dwell on the forms of the given endeavor, make the endeavor autonomous, and cut it off from its ostensible practical purpose. To the degree that they are specific, Marcuse and Schiller before him speak of the excellence of display, of the desirability of educating men to a love of the surface of things and a heightened awareness of beauty, to intensifying the sensuousness of daily life. Schiller makes much of the peculiarly human capacity to impose form, to keep nature at a distance, to entangle human relationships in a complex but lovely etiquette, to be elegantly artificial. On the other hand, Marcuse sees the prevalence of play and the love of beauty as stemming from a radical change in the instinctual life of man: the end of "surplus repression" and of the compulsive need to produce and compete, a general softening—one might say, a feminization—of human life, and a diffuse erotic relation to all reality, as reality answers in full to one's expectations.[23] One may add that Aldous Huxley's last novel, *Island* (1962), is a very imaginative effort to project a way of life similar in many respects to the one Marcuse conceives.

But the question persists: can play, even in the most extended sense, be anything but one side of life, even a life of leisure and and abundance? There is no doubt that beauty could become immeasurably more pervasive than it is now, that human feelings could be cultivated to the appreciation of beauty much more carefully than is common now, that a larger part of life could be given over to elaborate and hyper-civilized amusements and involvements, that utopian citizens could be encouraged to develop all sorts of pleasurable but eccentric tastes and talents, that a life of continuous shifts in styles and fashions could be economically feasible, that life as a whole could be much more plastic than it is now: that is, the ability to switch roles frequently, to part easily with shreds of one's identity, to move around over the face of the earth, to play out one's fantasies, to "experiment in living," could be enormously enhanced. Do these possibilities, however, add up to a *substantial* life? Or is it all frivolity? Surely a life of leisure and abundance can also be a life of seriousness?

A critique of play, and of much else besides, is found in one of the most impressive philosophical anthropologies of recent times, Hannah Arendt's *The Human Condition*. Its aim is indeed ambitious: to describe the true nature of the various categories of human activity and to assess and compare their contributions to the good life, the life fit for men who aspire to be properly human. The book is marked by a rage for seriousness. And though it is contemptuous of utopian projections, the nature of its concern with the ends of life qualifies it for consideration at this point.

At the outset Miss Arendt makes it clear that she will consider only ". . . those activities that traditionally, as well as according to current opinion, are within the range of every human being."[24] This means that the activities of the mind will not enter into her considerations. Once the contemplative life has been excluded, there remain—to use her categories—labor, work, and action. It turns out that only action, in the sense of political words and deeds, is truly suitable to man.

At the bottom of the scale is labor, or all those activities that have to do with maintaining mere biological existence: the use of the body to produce that which will keep the body alive so that it can produce that which will keep the body alive, and so on. Miss Arendt shares the disgust with unmediated appetite that we have already noticed in the case of Schiller and the young Marx. The laborer is *animal laborans*. She shares with Marcuse a contempt for the consumers' paradise:

. . . the spare time of the *animal laborans* is never spent in anything but consumption, and the more time left to him, the greedier and more craving his appetites. That these appetites become more sophisticated, so that consumption is no longer restricted to the necessities but, on the contrary, mainly concentrates on the superfluities of life, does not change the character of this society, but harbors the grave danger that eventually no object of the world will be safe from consumption and annihilation through consumption.[25]

Above the laborer is the worker, *homo faber.* As the laborer produces for consumption, the worker contrives and fabricates for use. The latter makes things possessed of "permanence, stability, and durability." He constructs the background of human activity and is God-like for doing so:

. . the things of the world have the function of stabilizing human life, and their objectivity lies in the fact that . . . men, their ever-changing nature notwithstanding, can retrieve their sameness, that is, their identity, by being related to the same chair and the same table.[26]

Though the useful is higher than the necessary, both are opposed to the free; and humanity is achieved only in a condition of freedom. Freedom, in turn, is to be understood as free action, political action, action done in the public realm, worldly action done among one's peers. Miss Arendt emphatically rejects the whole idea of play as the perfection of humanity, or as the correct contrasting term to the necessary and the useful. The highest end of human life is glory, the commission of shining deeds. Following Aristotle rather closely, Miss Arendt makes the active political life indispensable to a complete virtue. Far from threatening virtue or, at the least, distracting from the pursuit of virtue, politics offers to virtue its completion. Furthermore, politics is degraded if it is seen as yet another instrumental activity, as the key to the progress of society. She writes:

This specifically human achievement lies altogether outside the category of means and ends; the "work of man" is no end because the means to achieve it—the virtues, or *aretai*—are not qualities which may or may not be actualized, but are themselves "actualities." In other words, the means to achieve the end would already be the end; and this "end," conversely, cannot be considered a means in some other respect, because there is nothing higher to attain than this actuality itself.[27]

Utopia is quite ill at ease when it confronts this system of thought. The only consolation is that the real world fails the system as badly as any utopia. Advanced technology, mass production, and automation constantly diminish the sphere of *homo faber*. The life of craft is now marginal; and when William Morris published *News from Nowhere* (1890), the great utopia of craft, the ideal was already enfeebled. The correct presupposition of modern utopia is a life free from work: anything else is archaism. The source of seriousness in utopia cannot be work. Can it be the highest form of activity, political engagement? The answer must again be no. Just as in the real world, so in any conceivable utopia (apart from the obsolete communitarian type, where utopia is merely played at), the life of direct political action is closed to all but a few men. There must be politics in utopia: but what politics can there be except that of representative government? The societies of millions of inhabitants do not allow for taking turns in office. It may very well be that a plausible case could be made for the proposition that citizenship (in the manner of the city-states) is required for genuine manhood; but, then, utopia as well as the real world must get on as best it can. In the last few pages of her book, Miss Arendt must confess the basic irrelevance of her philosophical anthropology:

> . . . men persist in making, fabricating, and building, although these faculties are more and more restricted to the abilities of the artist, so that the concomitant experiences of worldliness escape more and more the range of ordinary human experience.[28]

Even more important:

> . . . the capacity for action, at least in the sense of the releasing of processes, is still with us, although it has become the exclusive prerogative of scientists.[29]

What is more, the action of scientists is not part of the web of human relationships, does not enter the story of human deeds, does not illuminate human existence:

> In this existentially most important aspect, action, too, has become an experience for the privileged few, and these few who still know what it means to act may well be even fewer than the artists, their experience even rarer than the genuine experience of and love for the world.[30]

What at last is left for the utopian theorist? The claims of sense and appetite must be granted only up to a certain point; the claims of play cannot be taken seriously after a certain point; the making of fine objects and the doing of great deeds can never be common enough to become the prevailing characteristic of any utopian way of life. Must the utopian theorist honor the extreme doctrine of individualism and concede that, after the elimination of radical evil and the provision of material abundance, people must be left alone, more or less to be and do what they want?

One last attempt must be made before yielding to the charms of the idea of laissez-faire. Little acuteness is needed to see that an answer has been waiting to offer itself from the start: the good life is, to use the old solemn language, the contemplative life. To put it less solemnly, the good life is the life spent in the acquisition and use of learning, the self-delighting exercise of intellectual skills, the cultivation of responsiveness to the works of intellectual culture and perceptiveness to the beauty of works of art. There can be no surprise in suggesting that the life appropriate to utopia is the life that the major philosophical traditions of the West advocate. We must allow a commonplace to furnish at least the semblance of a solution of our problem; we must perhaps place all our trust in the life of the mind. And of all the defenses of the life of the mind, that by John Stuart Mill is probably the most relevant to utopianism. Mill is not the first thinker to see in intellectual activity the source of the greatest human happiness; but his manner of arriving at that conclusion is of special interest.

We have already referred to Mill's anxieties concerning the life of pleasure; we now must see how he managed to allay those anxieties. The problem is to find pleasures worthy of humanity, within the reach of all, not liable to cloy and weary when experienced continuously, and as independent as possible from the prior existence of terrible pains and privations. The solution offered by Mill consists in the pleasures given by the operations of the intellect and of the feelings as they blend with the intellect. During the time of his mental crisis, Mill began reading the shorter poems of Wordsworth and found them a "medicine" for his depression:

> . . . they expressed, not mere outward beauty, but states of feeling, under the excitement of beauty. . . . In them I seemed to draw from a source of inward joy, of sympathetic and imaginative pleasure, which could be shared in by all human beings; which had no connexion with struggle or imperfection, but would be made richer by every improvement in the physical or social condition of mankind. From them I seemed to learn what would be the perennial sources of happiness, when all the greater evils of life have been removed.[31]

In this formulation, Mill comes very close to the position stated by Schiller and re-stated by Marcuse. The stress is on the transformation of character under the influence of beauty; a state of passivity and contemplation will encourage the operations of beauty on the soul. But if this seems still a little too precious, Mill's *Utilitarianism* enriches the idea. Mill writes:

A cultivated mind . . . finds sources of inexhaustible interest in all that surrounds it; in the objects of nature, the achievements of art, the imaginations of poetry, the incidents of history, the ways of mankind, past and present, and their prospects in the future.[32]

Mill is not saying that these pleasures crowd out all others or that by themselves they compose a whole life. But he is saying that without them there is no humanity and no permanently desirable pleasure.

It would also be Mill's contention that when he makes the enjoyment of the higher pleasures the greatest aim of the good society he is not legislating for all men or imposing on them a subjective system of values. He assumes that all men want pleasure or happiness. The pleasures of mind and of cultivated feelings are simply those which are most genuinely pleasures. Mill believes that he is asserting a proposition that is empirically verifiable. The test is as follows:

If [of two pleasures] one of the two is, by those who are competently acquainted with both, placed so far above the other that they prefer it, even though knowing it to be attended with a greater amount of discontent and would not resign it for any quantity of the other pleasure which their nature is capable of, we are justified in ascribing to the preferred enjoyment a superiority in quality, so far outweighing quanity as to render it, in comparison, of small account.[33]

In almost all cases, the result of the test is that men able to derive pleasure in the ordinary ways and also from the workings of mind and imagination in themselves and others will prefer the latter if they have to choose and will—apart from comparisons—find the latter intrinsically rewarding and worth whatever it may cost in pain.

There is no doubt that Mill's doctrine of the higher pleasures is open to numerous objections: a large literature has, in fact, grown up around his few words. For our purposes, however, the one point to raise is whether the higher pleasures lie within the capacity of all men. If they do, then one could reasonably advocate that the tone of the good society, its decisive and differentiating characteristic, be as Mill suggested. Mill himself has no doubt that with the right education and social reinforcement all, or nearly all, men can come to experience the higher pleasures. We have already noted the contradictory view of Hannah Arendt's. But this is not a matter that can be settled in the abstract. All we can do here is mention it while realizing that, as Mill was well aware, the weight of history and experience is not on his side. Much would depend on developments in the art of education, in the arts of character formation, perhaps in the science of genetics, if the brute fact of unequal innate endowments is to be shorn of its power to cripple—from the equalitarian utopian point of view—the doctrine of higher pleasures.

Suppose that everything Mill says about the higher pleasures is true, or roughly true. Several significant results would follow.

A high level of mental and intellectual culture would, first of all, determine how far utopia could go in trying to rid the world of pain. If utopia is not to earn all the abuse heaped on it, it must safeguard mind, even at the price of pain. Actually, its mission could be said to be to encourage the growth of intelligence with an intensity surpassing that of the highest civilizations in the real world. At the same time, it is precisely the cultivation of the intellectual and esthetic faculties that makes the best contribution to the endurance of pain: these faculties, ideally, pay with interest for the pain their cultivation necessitates. To advert to the pain inherent in the processes of cultivation is not to accept the view that without suffering and neurosis there would be no artists and thinkers and hence no art and thought to give pleasure. Rather, the toil of discipline and learning must not be forgotten.

Not only is the problem of pain solved in some measure by the doctrine of higher pleasures, but also that of pleasure itself. As we saw, these pleasures, in principle, do not require contrast for their enjoyment and, though intense, are as far removed from animality as it is possible to get. They give meaning to the idea of a life of pleasure and they do so not by threatening human dignity but by establishing it. What is more, an ability to experience the higher pleasures allows the lower pleasures, the unmediated pleasures of sense and appetite, to be restored without peril. It will not do to scorn the joys of consumption and technological progress too much. Where there is cultivation of mind and taste, vulgar creature comforts can be carried ludicrously far, and the senses can be constantly titillated by technological magic without impairment of human dignity. Dostoevsky's Underground Man is, in one of his utterances, a true (but unwilling) philosopher of utopia: he said that "Civilization develops in man nothing but an added capacity for receiving impressions." Advanced technology endlessly multiplies the impressions or sensations that a man may receive. There need be no creativity involved, no esthetic significance; just easy pleasure taken in novelty, gadgetry, silly refinements of useless objects, the flash and roar of progress in transportation and communication; in self-indulgence, satiety, waste, and pretense. Given the presence of educated mind, these delights can be delights and still known for what they are. A utopian society could provide these delights recklessly, and without the motivations of planned obsolescence, maximization of profit, and the stultification of rebellious or disturbing impulses. Thus, by the standard of human felicity, which is the essential utopian standard, the life of mind can plausibly (at least) be described as the best life.

The defense of the life of mind can also be undertaken apart from any strict reference to pleasure and pain. Given the presence of educated mind and feelings, the idea of play takes on added dimensions. There is naturally an intimate connection between play (in its broadest sense) and the active and passive workings of the intellectual and esthetic faculties. Schiller's vision of human improvement is predicated on the play of men whose esthetic faculties have been nurtured in an abundant society. But Schiller makes much of the difference, if not the opposition, between the esthetic and the rational. He conveys the sense that free exuberant action in the fields of beauty is, in some way, an escape from the demands of reason. There is a kind of play, however, which cannot get along without a preponderance of mind: the range of activities included in the notion of "playing at life." We have already referred to the utopian possibility of making life as a whole "more plastic." What we mean to suggest by these phrases is the allowance for a greater relaxation in the definitions of self, role, vocation, than the world customarily allows. Proteus could become the symbol of the tone of utopian life. The aim would be to encourage self-expression to the point where the traditional boundaries between fantasy and reality would become more blurred, to allow individuals to assume various "personae" without fear of social penalty, to allow groups to come together and affect diverse communal relations and then disband, to allow for the greatest possible accumulation of vicarious, mimetic, or semi-genuine experience, to strive to have each self be able to say, in the words of Walt Whitman's "Song of Myself": "I am large, I contain multitudes"; and, finally, in the name of heightened consciousness and amplitude of being to diminish the force of the duality of male and female. And for this "playing at life" to take worthwhile forms and conclude in splendid enrichment of character, the mind and feelings must be cultivated, the capacity to experience the higher pleasures must be developed, the higher faculties must be in control. Otherwise the playing at life would remain just that, and not be, instead, an instrument of self-transcendence.

But play is play: there must be some steadiness, some seriousness in the midst of this release and fluidity. Once again, the cultivation of higher faculties provides the answer. Greater in seriousness than even the making of beautiful objects and the doing of glorious deeds is the life of knowing. There need not be a specific metaphysical theory of the world behind this assertion; on the other hand there need not be a final vision of the world held out as the goal and reward of spending one's life in trying to know. All that is expected is that a prepared mind sustained by civilized feelings will find the engagements of mind to be the worthiest of the possibilities of life. At the end of a long book on the greatness of the active life, Hannah Arendt closes with a beautiful recantation:

> For if no other test but the experience of being active, no other measure but the extent of sheer activity were to be applied to the various activities within the *vita activa*, it might well be that thinking as such would surpass them all. Whoever has any experience in this matter will know how right Cato was when he said: ". . . Never is he more active than when he does nothing, never is he less alone than when he is by himself."[34]

We would compound the intellectualist heresy and say that the man possessed of the higher faculties in their perfection is the model for utopia and already exists outside it; and, perhaps more rashly, we could say that there is no utopia without the liberation of the higher faculties and that there is no need to mean by utopia anything more than the liberation of the higher faculties.

References

1. For a critical and historical discussion of the concept of philosophical anthropology, see Martin Buber, *What is Man?* (1938) in Buber's *Between Man and Man*, trans. by R. G. Smith (Boston: Beacon, 1955).
2. John Stuart Mill, *Autobiography* (New York: Liberal Arts Press, 1957), p. 87.
3. *Ibid.*, p. 92.
4. John Stuart Mill, *Utilitarianism* in *Utilitarianism, Liberty, and Representative Government* (New York: Dutton, 1950), p. 15.
5. *Ibid.*, p. 16.
6. Mill, *Autobiography*, p. 94.
7. Plato, *Philebus* (51B) in R. Hackforth, *Plato's Examination of Pleasure* (New York: Liberal Arts Press, n.d.), p. 100.

8. Friedrich Schiller, *On the Aesthetic Education of Man,* trans. by Reginald Snell (London: Routledge & Kegan Paul, 1954), p. 116.
9. Karl Marx, "Private Property and Communism" in Erich Fromm, *Marx's Concept of Man* (New York: Ungar, 1961), p. 125.
10. W. H. Auden, "Vespers" in *The Shield of Achilles* (New York: Random House, 1955), p. 79. Bunuel's film, *Viridiana,* renders this condition splendidly.
11. Karl Marx and Frederick Engels, *Manifesto of the Communist Party* in Karl Marx and Frederick Engels, *Selected Works* (2 vols.; Moscow: Foreign Languages Publishing House, 1951), p. 58.
12. Herbert Marcuse, *One Dimensional Man* (Boston: Beacon, 1964), p. 241.
13. Schiller, *op. cit.,* p. 80. The dependence of Schiller on Kant's *Critique of Judgment* is discussed by Herbert Marcuse in *Eros and Civilization* (Boston: Beacon, 1955), pp. 172-180.
14. Marcuse, *Eros and Civilization,* p. 153.
15. *Ibid.,* p. 194.
16. Friedrich Nietzsche, *The Birth of Tragedy* (trans. by Clifton Fadiman) in *The Philosophy of Nietzsche* (New York: Modern Library, 1927), pp. 1084-1085.
17. W. B. Yeats, *Collected Poems* (London: Macmillan, 1955), p. 339.
18. C. L. Barber, *Shakespeare's Festive Comedy* (Princeton: Princeton University Press, 1959), chap. 8.
19. J. Huizinga, *Homo Ludens* (Boston: Beacon, 1955), p. 6.
20. *Ibid.,* p. 7.
21. *Ibid.,* pp. 8, 9.
22. *Ibid.,* p. 13.
23. See also Marx's discussion of the emancipation of the senses in "Private Property and Communism," in Erich Fromm, *op. cit.,* esp. pp. 132-133.
24. Hannah Arendt, *The Human Condition* (Chicago: University of Chicago Press, 1958), p. 5. Mention should be made of the stimulating book by Paul and Percival Goodman, *Communitas* (2nd ed.; New York: Vintage, 1960). This book also undertakes a comparative analysis of human activities and styles of life; and it is unashamedly utopian.
25. *Ibid.,* p. 133.
26. *Ibid.,* p. 173.
27. *Ibid.,* p. 207.
28. *Ibid.,* p. 323.
29. *Ibid.*
30. *Ibid.,* p. 324.
31. Mill, *Autobiography,* p. 96.

32. Mill, *Utilitarianism,* p. 17.
33. *Ibid.,* p. 10.
34. Arendt, *op. cit.,* p. 325.

MIRCEA ELIADE

Paradise and Utopia: Mythical Geography and Eschatology

The "Fashion" of Messianism

OVER THE past ten years works on the various millenarianisms and different forms of utopia have increased considerably. And this is true not only of studies on the primitive messianic and prophetic movements—the most well-known being the "cargo-cults"—but also of research on the messianisms of Judeo-Christian origin, from the beginning of our era to the Renaissance and the Reformation, and of works on the religious implications of the geographic discoveries and colonization, principally the colonization of the two Americas. Finally, in recent years several efforts at synthesis have been published: historians, sociologists, and philosophers have tried to compare the different forms of Utopias and millenarianisms, and to articulate them with a view to a final synthesis.

This enormous recent bibliography will not be presented here. Suffice it to recall the several efforts at synthesis: the work of Norman Cohn on the pursuit of the millennium, the works of Lanternari, Guariglia, and Mühlmann on primitive millenarianisms, the research of Alphonse Dupront on the spirit of the Crusades, and the monographs of several American scholars on the eschatological implications of the colonization.[1]

The interest of Western scholars in millenarist movements and utopias is significant; it could even be said that this interest constitutes one of the characteristic traits of contemporary Western thought. The reasons for this interest are manifold. First of all, there is the curiosity aroused by the messianic cults that buffeted "primitive" societies in the last decades of the colonial period. Then, there is the recent research on the importance of prophetic movements in mediaeval Europe, especially the movement of Gioacchino da Fiore and the Gioacchinists in Transalpine Europe. And, finally, there is the rigorous analysis of the religious implications of the colonization of America; for, as we shall see later, the discovery and colonization of the New World took place under the sign of eschatology.

The undertaking of such research and the posing of such problems betray an orientation of thought which tells us a great deal about the spiritual situation of contemporary Western man. Let us point out, to begin with, that contrary to systems of deterministic explanation of history, today we recognize the importance of the religious factor, especially the importance of movements of tension and frenzy—the prophetic, eschatological, millenarist movements. But there is something, in my opinion, still more significant: the interest in the *origins* of the *recent* Western world—that is, in the origins of the United States and the nations of Latin America—reveals among the intellectuals of that continent the desire to turn back and to find their *primordial history*, their "absolute beginnings." This desire to return to one's beginnings, to recover a primordial situation, also denotes the desire to start out again, the nostalgia to relive the beatitude and the creative exaltation of the "beginnings"—in short, the nostalgia for the earthly paradise that the ancestors of the American nations had crossed the Atlantic to find. (Indeed there have rarely been published more books with titles containing the word "paradise" than on the colonization of the Americas. Among works published in recent years, let us point out: *Visão do Paraiso: os motivos edeñicos no descobrimento et colonização do Brasil* (Rio de Janeiro, 1959), by Sergio Buarque de Hollanda; *The Quest for Paradise* (1961), by Charles L. Sanford; *Wilderness and Paradise in Christian Thought* (1962), by George H. Williams, subtitled "From the Garden of Eden and the Sinai desert to the American frontier.")

All this betrays the desire to recover the religious origins, and thus a primordial history, of the recent transatlantic states. But the significance of this phenomenon is still more complex. One may also detect the desire for a renewal of old values and structures, the hope of a radical *renovatio*—just as one might interpret in the most recent experiments in art the will to destroy all means of expression already time-worn by history, but also the hope of beginning the artistic experience *ab initio*.

To return to our subject—Paradise and Utopia—I have chosen

two sorts of illustrations. First of all I shall point out the eschatological and paradisiacal elements in the colonization of North America by the pioneers, and the progressive transformation of the "American Paradise," giving rise to the myth of indefinite progress, to American optimism, and to the cult of youth and novelty. Then I shall consider a Brazilian tribe, the Tupi-Guaranis, who, at the time of the discovery of South America, had already set forth across the Atlantic Ocean in search of a paradise—certain groups still continue the search today.

I. *The Quest for the Earthly Paradise*

Christopher Columbus did not doubt that he had come near the Earthly Paradise. He believed that the fresh water currents he encountered in the Gulf of Paria originated in the four rivers of the Garden of Eden. For Columbus, the search for the Earthly Paradise was not a chimera. The great navigator accorded an eschatological significance to this geographic discovery. The New World represented more than a new continent open to the propagation of the Gospel. The very fact of its discovery had an eschatological implication.

Indeed, Columbus was persuaded that the prophecy concerning the diffusion of the Gospel throughout the whole world had to be realized before the end of the world—which was not far off. In his *Book of Prophecies,* Columbus affirmed that this event, namely, the end of the world, would be preceded by the conquest of the new continent, the conversion of the heathen, and the destruction of the Antichrist. And he assumed a capital role in this grandiose drama, at once historical and cosmic. In addressing Prince John he exclaimed: "God made me the messenger of the new heaven and the new earth, of which He spoke in the Apocalypse by Saint John, after having spoken of it by the mouth of Isaiah; and He showed me the spot where to find it."[2]

It was in this messianic and apocalyptic atmosphere that the transoceanic expeditions and the geographic discoveries that radically shook and transformed Western Europe took place. Throughout Europe people believed in an imminent regeneration of the world, even though the causes and reasons for this regeneration were multiple and often contradictory.

The colonization of the two Americas began under an eschatological sign: people believed that the time had come to renew the Christian world, and the true renewal was the return to the

Earthly Paradise or, at the very least, the beginning again of Sacred History, the reiteration of the prodigious events spoken of in the Bible. It is for this reason that the literature of the period, as well as sermons, memoirs, and correspondence, abounds in paradisiacal and eschatological allusions. In the eyes of the English, for instance, the colonization of America merely prolonged and perfected a Sacred History begun at the outset of the Reformation. Indeed, the push of the pioneers toward the West continued the triumphal march of Wisdom and the True Religion from East to West. For some time already, Protestant theologians had been inclined to identify the West with spiritual and moral progress. Certain theologians had transferred the Ark of the Covenant of Abraham to the English. As the Anglican theologian William Crashaw wrote, "The God of Israel is . . . the God of England." In 1583, Sir Humphrey Gilbert asserted that if England had taken possession "of vast and pleasant territories," it was doubtless thanks to the fact that the word of God, that is, religion, which had begun in the East had gradually advanced toward the West, where, he added, "it is very likely that it will stop."

Solar symbolism. This is a rather frequent motif in English literature of the period. The theologian Thomas Burnet, in his *Archaeologiae* (1692), wrote: "Learning, like the sun, began to take its Course from the *East,* then turned *Westward,* where we have long rejoiced in its light." And Bishop Berkeley, in his famous poem which opens with these lines, "Westward the course of empire takes its way . . . ," makes use of the solar analogy in order to exalt the spiritual role of England.[3]

Moreover, Berkeley was merely conforming to a European tradition already more than two centuries old. Indeed Egyptian hermetism and solar symbolism, revived by Marsilio Ficino and the Italian humanists, had known an extraordinary vogue after the discoveries of Copernicus and Galileo, discoveries that for contemporaries illustrated above all the triumph of the sun and heliocentrism. Recent research has uncovered the religious implications, most often hidden or camouflaged, in the astronomy and the cosmography of the Renaissance. For contemporaries of Copernicus and Galileo, heliocentrism was more than a scientific theory: it marked the victory of solar symbolism over the Middle Ages, that is, the revenge of the hermetic tradition—considered as venerable and primordial, preceding Moses, Orpheus, Zoroaster, Pythagoras, and Plato—over the provincialism of the Mediaeval Church.[4]

The theme of solar symbolism in the Renaissance is too complex for consideration here, but this brief allusion is necessary in order to understand the emphasis placed on solar analogies by authors exalting the religious significance of the colonization of the New World. The first English colonists in America considered themselves chosen by Providence to establish a "City on a Mountain" that would serve as an example of the true Reformation for all Europe. They had followed the path of the sun toward the Far West, continuing and prolonging in a prodigious fashion the traditional passing of religion and culture from East to West. They saw a sign of divine Providence in the fact that America had been hidden to the Europeans until the time of the Reformation. The first pioneers did not doubt that the final drama of moral regeneration and universal salvation would begin with them, since they were the first to follow the sun in its course toward the paradisiacal gardens of the West. As the Anglican poet George Herbert wrote in his *Church Militant:*

> Religion stands tip-toe in our land
> Ready to pass to the American strand.[5]

And this "American strand," as we have seen and shall continually note in what follows, was loaded with paradisiacal qualities. Ulrich Hugwald had prophesized that following the discovery of America humanity would return "to Christ, to Nature, to Paradise."

More than any other modern nation the United States was the product of the Protestant Reformation seeking an Earthly Paradise in which the reform of the Church was to be perfected.[6] The relationship between the Reformation and the recovery of the Earthly Paradise has struck a very great number of authors, from Heinrich Bullinger to Charles Dumoulin. For these theologians, the Reformation hastened the coming of the great age of paradisiacal beatitude. It is significant that the millenarist theme enjoyed its greatest popularity just prior to the colonization of America and Cromwell's revolution. Hence, it is not surprising to note that the most popular religious doctrine in the Colonies was that America had been chosen among all the nations of the earth as the place of the Second Coming of Christ, and the millennium, though essentially of a spiritual nature, would be accompanied by a paradisiacal transformation of the earth, as an outer sign of an inner perfection. As the eminent Puritan, Increase Mather, President of Harvard University from 1685 to 1701, wrote: "when this Kingdom of Christ has filled all the earth, *this Earth will be restored to its Paradise state.*"[7]

The American Paradise. Moreover, certain pioneers already

saw Paradise in the various regions of America. Traveling along the coast of New England in 1614, John Smith compared it to Eden: "heaven and earth never agreed better to frame a place for man's habitation . . . we chanced in a lande, even as God made it." George Alsop presents Maryland as the only place seeming to be the "Earthly Paradise." Its trees, its plants, its fruits, its flowers, he wrote, speak in "Hieroglyphicks of our Adamitical or Primitive situation." Another writer discovered the "future Eden" in Georgia—a region located on the same latitude as Palestine: "That promis'd *Canaan,* which was pointed out by God's own choice, to bless the Labours of a favorite People." For Edward Johnson, Massachusetts was the place "where the Lord will create a new Heaven and a new Earth." Likewise, the Boston Puritan, John Cotton, informed those preparing to set sail from England for Massachusetts that they were granted a privilege of Heaven, thanks to "the grand charter given to *Adam* and his posterity in Paradise."[8]

But this reflects just one aspect of the millenarist experience of the pioneers. For many new immigrants, the New World represented a desert haunted by demonic beings. This, however, did not diminish their eschatological exaltation, for they were told in sermons that the present miseries were but a moral and spiritual trial before arriving at the Earthly Paradise that had been promised to them.[9] The pioneers considered themselves in the situation of the Israelites after the crossing of the Red Sea, just as, in their eyes, their condition in England and Europe had been a sort of Egyptian bondage. After the terrible trial of the desert, they would enter Canaan. As Cotton Mather wrote, "The Wilderness through which we are passing to the Promised Land is all over filled with Fiery flying serpents."[10]

But, later on, a new idea was born; the New Jerusalem would be in part produced by work. Jonathan Edwards (1703–1758) thought that through work New England would be transformed into a sort of "Paradise on Earth." We see how the millenarianism of the pioneers gradually ends in the idea of progress. In the first stage, a relationship was established between paradise and the earthly possibilities presenting themselves in the New World. During the next stage, the eschatological tension was reduced by the omission of the period of decadence and misery that was supposed to precede the "Last Days," and by arriving finally at the idea of a progressive and uninterrupted amelioration.[11]

But before the American idea of progress crystallized, the millenarianism of the pioneers underwent other transformations. The first important crisis in this Puritan eschatology was provoked by the struggle among the European powers for the colonial Empire. Rome and the Catholic nations were identified with the Antichrist—with the destruction on which the coming of the future Kingdom depended.

At one particular time, English colonial literature was dominated by a single theme: the invasion of America by the Antichrist, who threatened to ruin the hope for the glorious triumph of Christ. For John Winthrop, the first duty of New England was to "raise a rampart against the kingdom of the Antichrist that the Jesuits are in the process of establishing in these regions." Other authors affirmed that the New World was a true Paradise before the arrival of the Catholics.

Obviously, the rivalry among the European powers for the domination of the transatlantic empires was in large measure economic in character, but it was exacerbated by an almost manichean eschatology: everything seemed to be reduced to a conflict between Good and Evil. Colonial authors spoke of the threat that the French and the Spanish posed for the English colonies as a "new Babylonian captivity" or "an Egyptian bondage." The French and the Spanish were tyrants, slaves of the Antichrist. Catholic Europe was presented as a fallen world, a Hell, by contrast with the Paradise of the New World. The saying was: "Heaven or Europe," meaning "Heaven or Hell." The trials of the pioneers in the desert of America had as their principal goal the redemption of man from the carnal sins of the pagan Old World.[12]

The return to primitive Christianity. As long as the conflict between Good and Evil took concrete form, in the eyes of the colonists, in the struggle between Protestantism and Catholicism, England remained immune from attack. But after 1640, tension began to arise between the colonists and the mother country. For the perfectionists in the Colonies, the English Reformation was an imperfect reformation. Worse yet, the religious practices of England were considered as the work of the Antichrist. In the colonial apocalyptic imagery, England replaced Rome. The immediate consequence of this substitution was that the colonists—as the chosen people—began to judge their mission in the desert not only as the continuation of a traditional religious activity, but also as something altogether new. Hopeful of being reborn far from the European Hell, the colonists considered that they were about to initiate the final stage of History. In 1647, John Eliot, the apostle to the Indians, announced "The

Daybreaking, if not the Sunrising of the Gospel . . . in New England."[13]

Such language indicates the profound break with the European past. And it must be made clear that this break had already been consumated long before the American Revolution and Independence. In 1646, New England considered itself as a free State and not as a "colony or corporation of England." The reasons for this *prise de conscience* of autonomy were in the first place religious. Cotton Mather expected in New England the return to the early days of Christianity. "In short," he wrote, "the *first* age was the *golden Age;* to return unto that, will make a man a *protestant,* and I may add, a *Puritan.*" This return to the Golden Age of Christianity was to bring about a transfiguration of the earth. As Increase Mather declared, the Restoration of the Early Church would transform the earth into paradise.[14]

The break with England and the European past was accentuated to the extent to which the pioneers prepared for the millennium by returning to the virtue of the Early Church. For the Puritans, the major Christian virtue was simplicity. On the other hand, intelligence, culture, learning, manners, luxury were of the Devil's creation. John Cotton wrote: "The more cultured and intelligent you are, the more ready you are to work for Satan." The superiority complex of the pioneers and the missionaries of the Frontier was already forming. This return to Early Christianity that was supposed to restore paradise to earth also implied a disdain for the erudition of the Jesuits, as well as a criticism of English aristocracy—cultured, elegant, sophisticated, accustomed to power and authority. Extravagance or luxury in clothing became the sin par excellence of the "gentleman." In his book *Simple Cobbler of Aggawam* (1647), Nathanael Ward contrasted the simple life and moral superiority of the colonists to the corrupt mores of England and drew from this contrast proof of the progress toward the paradisiacal state of the early church.[15]

The colonists proclaimed their moral superiority over the English, while recognizing their own inferiority in clothes and culture. According to Charles L. Sanford, the origin of the American superiority complex—manifest in foreign policy as well as in the enthusiastic effort to spread the "American Way of Life" across the whole planet—must be sought in the activity of the Frontier missionaries.[16] A whole religious symbolism flowered about the Frontier, prolonging well into the nineteenth century the eschatology of the pioneers.

The vast forests, the solitude of the infinite plains, the beatitude of the rural life are set in contrast to the sins and vices of the city. A new idea now arises: the American paradise has been infested with demonic forces coming from urban Europe. The critique of the aristocracy, luxury, and culture is now subsumed to the critique of cities and urban life. The great "revivalist" religious movements began on the Frontier and reached the cities only later. And even in the cities, "revivalism" was more popular among the poor than among the rich and educated population. The fundamental idea was that the decline of religion had been caused by urban vices, especially intoxication and luxury, common to the aristocracy of European origin. For, obviously, Hell was—and long remained—"the way of Europe."[17]

The religious origins of "The American Way of Life." But, as we have already pointed out, eschatological millenarianism and the expectation of the Earthly Paradise were subjected in the end to a radical secularization. The myth of progress and the cult of novelty and youth are among the most noteworthy consequences. However, even in drastically secularized form, one detects the religious enthusiasm and the eschatological expectations inspiring the ancestors. For, in short, both the first colonists and the later European immigrants journeyed to America as *the country where they might be born anew,* that is, begin a new life. The "novelty" which still fascinates Americans today is a desire with religious underpinnings. In "novelty," one hopes for a "re-naissance," one seeks a new life.

New England, *New* York, *New* Haven—all these names express not only the nostalgia for the native land left behind, but above all the hope that in these lands and these new cities life will know new dimensions. And not only life: everything in this continent that was considered an earthly paradise must be greater, more beautiful, stronger. In New England, described as resembling the Garden of Eden, partridges were supposedly so big that they could no longer fly, and the turkeys as fat as lambs.[18] This American flair for the grandiose, likewise religious in origin, is shared even more by the most lucid minds.

The hope of being born again to a new life—and the expectation of a future not only better, but beatific—may also be seen in the American cult of youth. According to Charles L. Sanford, since the era of industrialization, Americans have more and more sought their lost innocence in their children. The same author believes that the exaltation of things new, which followed the pioneers to the

Far West, fortified individualism over authority, but also contributed to the American irreverence toward history and tradition.[19]

We shall end here these few considerations of the metamorphosis of the millenarist eschatology of the pioneers. We have seen how, in setting out in search of the Earthly Paradise across the ocean, the first explorers were conscious of playing an important role in the history of Salvation; how America, after being identified with the Earthly Paradise, became the privileged place where the Puritans were to perfect the Reformation, which supposedly had failed in Europe; and how the immigrants believed that they had escaped from the Hell of Europe and expected a new birth in the New World. We have likewise seen to what extent modern America is the result of these messianic hopes, this confidence in the possibility of reaching paradise here on earth, this faith in youth and in the simplicity of the mind and soul.

One might continue the analysis and show how the long resistance of American élites to the industrialization of the country, and their exaltation of the virtues of agriculture, may be explained by the same nostalgia for the Earthly Paradise. Even when urbanization and industrialization had triumphed everywhere, the favorite images and clichés used by the pioneers retained their prestige. In order to prove that urbanization and industrialization did not necessarily imply (as in Europe!) vice, poverty, and the dissolution of mores, owners of factories multiplied their philanthropic activities, constructing churches, schools, and hospitals. At all costs, it had to be made plain that, far from threatening spiritual and religious values, science, technology and industry guaranteed their triumph. A book appearing in 1842 was entitled *The Paradise within the Reach of All Men, by Power of Nature and Machinery*. And one might detect the nostalgia for Paradise, the desire to find again that "Nature" of their ancestors, in the contemporary tendency to leave the metropolis and seek refuge in suburbia—luxurious and peaceful neighborhoods arranged with utmost care in paradisiacal landscapes.

But our concern here is not to present an analysis of the metamorphosis of the American millenarist ideal. What must be emphasized, as other authors have, is that the certainty of the eschatological mission, and especially of attaining once again the perfection of early Christianity and restoring paradise to earth, is not likely to be forgotten easily. It is very probable that the behavior of the average American today, as well as the political and cultural ideology of the United States, still reflects the consequences of the

Puritan certitude of having been called to restore the Earthly Paradise.

II. *The Guaranis in Search of the Lost Paradise*

In 1912, the Brazilian ethnologist Curt Nimuendaju encountered along the coast near São Paulo a group of Guarani Indians who had stopped there in their search for the lost paradise.

They danced tirelessly for several days in the hope that their bodies would become light through continual movement and would be able to fly off to heaven to the home of "Our Grandmother" who awaits her children in the East. Disappointed, but their faith intact, they returned, convinced that, attired in European clothing and nourished with European food, they had grown too heavy for the celestial adventure.[20]

This search for the Lost Paradise was the most recent in a series of migrations undertaken by the Guaranis over many centuries. The first attempt to find the "Beloved Country" dates back to 1515.[21] But it was especially between 1539 and 1549 that a great migration of the Tupinamba group toward the land of the "Great Ancestor" took place. Having set out from the region of Pernambuco, writes Alfred Métraux, these Indians arrived in Peru, "where they met up with certain Spanish conquistadors. These Indians had crossed practically the whole South American continent at its widest point in search of the 'Land of Immortality and Eternal Rest.' To the Spaniards, they related strange stories of half-imaginary cities filled with gold; and their stories, probably tinged with their personal dreams, inflamed the imagination of the Spaniards and determined to a great extent the unfortunate expedition of Pedro de Ursua, the alleged conqueror of the Eldorado. The Spaniards and the Indians sought after the same chimera, the main difference being that the Indians aspired to an eternal felicity, while the Spaniards sought to acquire, at the cost of great suffering, the means to a transient happiness."[22]

Nimuendaju gathered a very rich documentation on these fabled peregrinations of the Guarani tribes searching for the "Land-Without-Evil." Alfred Métraux and Egon Schaden subsequently completed and provided more detailed information.[23] This collective search for paradise lasted over four centuries, and may doubtless be classified among the most singular religious phenomena of the New World. Indeed, the movements described by Nimuendaju in 1912 still continue today; but only one Guarani tribe, the Mbüás, still seeks paradise to the East; the others believe that paradise is found at the center of the earth and at the zenith.[24]

We shall have occasion to return to the different locations and topographies of Paradise. For the moment, let us single out one characteristic of the religion of all the Tupi-Guarani tribes: the considerable role played by shamans and prophets. It was they who, following certain dreams or visions, set in motion and led the expeditions to the Land-without-Evil. Even in the tribes that were not consumed by the passion of the quest for paradise, the shamans succeeded in stirring up the whole population by using certain typically paradisiacal images in recounting their dreams and ecstasies. A sixteenth-century Jesuit wrote concerning the Tupinambas:

> The shamans persuade the Indians not to work, not to go to the fields, promising them that the harvests will grow by themselves, that food instead of being scarce will fill their huts, and that spades will turn over the soil all alone, arrows will hunt for their owners, and will capture numerous enemies. They predict that the old will become young again.[25]

We recognize here the paradisiacal syndrome of the Golden Age. In order to hasten its coming, the Indians renounced all profane activities, and danced night and day, stimulated by their prophets. As we shall see subsequently, dancing is the most effective means of arriving at ecstasy or, at least, of coming closer to divinity.

More than other archaic populations, the Tupi-Guaranis were avid to receive revelations from supernatural Beings through the dreams of the shamans. More than their neighboring tribes, the Tupi-Guaranis did their utmost to maintain permanent contact with the supernatural world, in order to receive in time the instructions indispensable to reaching paradise. Where does this singular religious sensitivity come from—this obsession with paradise, this fear of not understanding the divine messages in time, and consequently facing the risk of perishing in the imminent cosmic catastrophe?

The End of the World. The reply to this question may be found in myths. In the mythology of all the Guarani tribes still surviving in Brazil, there exists the tradition that a fire or a flood completely destroyed a former world—and that the catastrophe will be repeated in a more or less near future. The belief in a future catastrophe is, however, rare among the other Tupi groups.[26] Should this be considered as a Christian influence? Not necessarily. Similar ideas have been attested among many other archaic peoples. And, more important, in certain cases it is difficult to tell if the cosmic catastrophe has taken place in the past or if it will be repeated in the future as well—this is because the grammar of the respective languages does not make a distinction between past and future.[27] Finally, we must recall a Tukuma myth according to which the future catastrophe will be the work of the Civilizing Hero Dyoí. The latter is supposedly offended by the changing of tribal traditions as a result of the contact with white Christians. This belief is partially comparable to that of the Guaranis. Now, it is difficult to conceive that a myth announcing the imminent end of the world because of the cultural influences of the whites should be of Christian origin.

Whatever the case may be, the end of the world is not imagined in the same fashion by the various Guarani tribes. The Mbüás expect an imminent flood, or a fire of cosmic proportions, or a darkness indefinitely prolonged over the earth. For the Nandevas, the catastrophe will be provoked by the explosion of the earth, the latter being conceived as a disk. Finally, the Kaiovás imagine that the end of the world will be brought about by monsters—flying horses and monkeys hunting with flaming arrows.[28] It is important to emphasize that the portrayal of and the quest for paradise are directly related to the fear of the impending catastrophe. The migrations were set in motion by the desire and the hope of reaching the Land-Without-Evil before the apocalypse. Even the names given by the various Guarani tribes to Paradise convey the notion that the latter is the sole place where one is safe from universal destruction. The Nandevas call it *yvý-nomi-mybré,* "the land where one hides"; that is, the place where one can find refuge during the cataclysm. Paradise is also called *yvý-mará-ey,* the "Land-Without-Evil," or simply *yváy,* "Heaven." Paradise is the place where one does not fear—and its inhabitants know neither hunger nor sickness nor death.[29]

We shall return shortly to the structure of paradise and the means to arrive there. But first, we must consider the reasons which, according to the Guaranis, lead inevitably to the end of the world. Contrary to a widespread belief, shared by both Judaism and Christianity, the end of the world is not the consequence of the sins of mankind. For the Guaranis, mankind, as well as the earth itself, is tired of living and aspires to rest. Nimuendaju believes that the ideas of the Apapocuvas on the annihilation of the world are the product of what he calls "Indian pessimism."[30] One of his informers told him: "Today the earth is old, and our race will no longer multiply. We are going to see the dead again, darkness will fall, bats will touch us, all of us who still remain on earth will meet the end."[31] The idea is one of a cosmic fatigue, a universal exhaustion. Nimuendaju also reports the ecstatic experiences of a certain shaman: in a moment of ecstasy in the presence of the supreme God, Nanderuvuvu, he had heard the Earth beg the Lord to put an end to its creations. "I am exhausted," sighed the Earth. "I am stuffed with the cadavers that I have devoured. Let me rest, Father. The waters also implored the Creator to grant them rest, and the trees . . . and thus all of Nature."[32]

One rarely encounters in ethnographic literature such a moving expression of cosmic fatigue and nostalgia for the final rest. It is true that the Indians encountered by Nimuendaju in 1912 were exhausted after three or four centuries of vagabond life and continual dances in search of paradise. Nimuendaju believes that the notion of the end of the world is a native one, and denies the possibility of a potential Christian influence. He considers the pessimism of the Guaranis as one of the results of the Portuguese conquest—the consequence, especially, of the terror unleashed by the slave hunters. Certain scholars have recently questioned the interpretation of Nimuendaju.[33] It might indeed be questioned whether what Nimuendaju calls "Indian pessimism" does not have roots originating in a widespread belief among primitive peoples, which might be summarized as follows: the world is degenerating by virtue of the simple fact that it exists, and it must be periodically regenerated, that is, created again; the end of the world is thus necessary in order that a new creation may take place.[34]

It is probable that a similar belief was shared by the Apapocuva-Guaranis before the Portuguese conquest and the Christian propaganda. The shock of the conquerors must certainly have aggravated and intensified the desire to escape from a world of misery and suffering—but it was not the shock of the Portuguese conquest that created this desire. Like many other archaic populations, the Guaranis longed to live in a pure, fresh, rich, and blessed cosmos. The paradise that they sought is the World restored to its primeval beauty and glory. The "Land-Without-Evil," or the house of Nande ("Our Grandmother") exists here on earth: it is situated on the other side of the ocean or in the center of the earth. It is difficult to reach, but it is located in this world. Although it seems to some extent supernatural—since it entails paradisiacal dimensions (for instance, immortality)—the Land-Without-Evil does not belong to the Beyond. It cannot even be said to be invisible; it is simply very well hidden. One arrives there not—or, more accurately, not only—in soul or spirit, but in flesh and bones. The collective expeditions undertaken in search of paradise had precisely that goal: to reach the Land-Without-Evil before the destruction of the world, to settle down in paradise and enjoy a beatific existence, while the exhausted and unregenerate cosmos awaited its violent end.

The Land-Without-Evil. The paradise of the Guaranis is thus a world at once real and transfigured, where life continues according to the same familiar model, but outside of Time and History, that is, without misery or sickness, without sins or injustice, and without age. This paradise is not of a "spiritual" domain: if today, according to the belief of some tribes, one can get there only after death, that is, as "spirit," in former times men were to arrive there *in concreto.* Paradise thus has a paradoxical character: on the one hand, it stands for the contrary of this world—purity, freedom, beatitude, immortality, and the like; on the other hand, it is concrete, that is, not "spiritual," and is included in this world, since it has a geographic reality and identity. In other words, paradise for the Tupi-Guarani Indians stands for the perfect and pure world of the "Beginning," when it had just been finished by the Creator and when the ancestors of the present tribes lived among the gods and heroes. Indeed, the original myth of paradise spoke only of a sort of Island of the Blessed, in the middle of the ocean, where death was unknown, and which one reached by a rope or other such means. (Let us note in passing that images of rope, or liana, or steps are frequently used to represent the passing from one mode of being to another—from the profane to the sacred world.) In the beginning, one sought the fabulous Island in order to attain immortality by striving to live in spiritual communion with the gods; it was not sought as a refuge from an imminent cosmic catastrophe.[35] The apocalyptic transformation of the myth of paradise took place later, perhaps as a result of Jesuit influence,[36] or simply because the Guaranis, like so many other primitive peoples, found that the world had grown too old and that it must be destroyed and created again.

The fundamental conception of the religion of the Guaranis—the conception from which the certitude that one may reach paradise *in concreto* is derived—is summed up in the term *aguydjé.* This word may be translated as "supreme happiness," "perfection," and "victory." For the Guaranis, *aguydjé* constitutes the goal and the objective of all human existence. To attain *aguydjé* means to know concretely paradisiacal beatitude in a supernatural world. But this supernatural world is accessible before death, and it is accessible to any member of the tribe, provided that he follows the traditional moral and religious code.

Thanks to the recent work of Schaden, we now have fairly detailed information concerning the portrayal of paradise among the various Guarani populations.[37] Thus, for instance, the Nandevas hold two distinct conceptions: one is peculiar to the Nandevas who began migrations long ago and did not reach the Land-Without-Evil; the other belongs exclusively to the Nandevas who did not set out on such journeys. Those who sought after the paradise without finding it—and who ended their wanderings some ten years ago when they arrived at the coast—no longer believe that paradise lies on the other side of the ocean. They situate it as the zenith and believe that it cannot be reached before death.

The other Nandeva populations who did not set out on such journeys to the ocean, believe that the world is doomed to destruction by fire, but the catastrophe is not considered imminent. The place of refuge is paradise, conceived as a sort of Island of the Blessed in the middle of the ocean. Provided that he practice certain rituals, especially dances and songs, man can reach the island in flesh and bones, that is, before dying. But one must know the route—and this knowledge is almost completely lost today. In ancient times, one could find the way because people had confidence in Nanderykey, the Civilizing Hero: the latter came to meet humans and guided them toward the paradisiacal Island. Today, paradise can be reached only "in spirit," after death.

According to information given by a shaman (nanderu) to Egon Schaden, the paradisiacal Island "resembles heaven more than earth." There is a great lake in the center and, in the middle of the lake, a high cross. (The cross very probably represents a Christian influence—but the Island and the lake belong to native mythology. The Island is rich in fruits and the inhabitants do not work, but spend their time dancing. They never die. The Island is not the land of the dead. The souls of the deceased arrive there, but do not settle down there; they continue their journey. In ancient times, it was easy to reach the Island. According to other information, likewise gathered by Schaden, the sea supposedly receded before those who had faith and formed a bridge over which they could pass. On the Island no one died. It was indeed a "holy land."[38]

Still more interesting is the portrayal of paradise among the

Mbüás, the only Guarani group that continues today to look to the coast in search of the Land-Without-Evil. Of all the Guarani populations, the myth of paradise plays the most important role among the Mbüás. This fact is highly significant in that the Mbüás were not at all subject to the influence of the Jesuit missions.[39] The paradise of the Mbüás is not conceived of as a safe shelter from a future cataclysm. It is a fabulous garden, rich in fruits and game, where men continue their earthly existence. One attains paradise by leading a just and pious life in conformity with traditional prescriptions.

The "Road" to the Gods. Among the third Guarani group, the Kaiovás, who, some decades ago, were still journeying to the Atlantic, there exists this peculiarity: the importance of paradise increases in periods of crisis. Then, the Kaiovás dance night and day, without stopping, in order to accelerate the destruction of the world and to obtain the revelation of the route that leads to the Land-Without-Evil. Dance, revelation, road to paradise—these three religious realities stand together; they are characteristic, moreover, of all the Guarani tribes, and not only of the Kaiovás. The image and the myth of the "road"—that is, the passage from this world to the holy world—plays a considerable role. The shaman (nanderu) is a specialist of the "road": it is he who receives supernatural instructions which enable him to guide the tribe in its prodigious wanderings. In the tribal myth of the Nandevas, the Primordial Mother had personally covered the same path when she departed in search of the Father of the Twins. During prayer, or after death, when crossing celestial regions, the soul follows the same mysterious and paradoxical "road," for it is both natural and supernatural.

When asked by Egon Schaden to trace this prestigious "road," the Kaiovás drew the road taken by the shaman in his frequent journeys to heaven.[40] All the Guarani peoples speak of themselves as *tapédja*, that is, "people of pilgrims and travelers." The nocturnal dances are accompanied by prayers, and all these prayers are none other than "roads" leading to the gods. "Without a road," confided one of Schaden's contacts, "one cannot reach the place he desires."[41] Thus, for the Kaiovás, the "road" to the world of the gods symbolizes their whole religious life. Man needs a "road" to communicate with the gods and to reach his destiny. It is only at times of crisis that the quest for this "road" is charged with apocalyptic elements. Then they dance night and day to seek urgently the "road" leading to paradise. They dance frenetically, for the end of the world is near and it is only in paradise that one can be saved. But the rest of the time, in less dramatic periods, the "road" continues to play the central role in the life of the Guaranis. It is only in seeking and following the road that leads to the neighborhood of the gods that a Guarani believes he has fulfilled his mission on earth.

The originality of Guarani Messianism. Let us conclude this brief presentation of Guarani messianism by some more general observations. We note, in the first place, that, in contrast to the prophetic movements of the North American tribes, Guarani messianism is not the consequence of the cultural shock of the European conquerors and the disorganization of social structures.[42] The myth of and the quest for the Land-Without-Evil existed among the Tupi-Guaranis well before the arrival of the Portuguese and the first Christian missionaries. Contact with the conquerors exacerbated the search for paradise, gave it an urgent and tragic—or even pessimistic—character of a despondent flight from an imminent cosmic catastrophe; but it was not the contact with the conquerors that inspired the quest. Moreover, we are not dealing here with tribes in the midst of a crisis of acculturation, like the aborigines of North America, who for two centuries had been periodically buffeted by prophetic and messianic movements. The culture and society of the Guaranis were neither disorganized nor hybridized.

This fact is not unimportant for an understanding of prophetic and messianic phenomena in general. The importance of the historical, social, and economic context in the birth and spread of messianic movements has been widely emphasized, and rightly so. People await the end of the world, or a cosmic renewal, or the Golden Age, especially in times of profound crisis; they herald the imminence of an earthly paradise to defend themselves against the despair provoked by extreme misery, the loss of liberty, and the collapse of all traditional values. The example of the Tupi-Guaranis demonstrates that entire collectivities have been brought to seek paradise, and to search for centuries, without social crises as a stimulus. As we have already indicated, this paradise is not always conceived of as a purely "spiritual" Beyond; it belongs to this world, to a real world transformed by faith. The Guaranis desired to live as their mythical ancestors lived in the beginning of the world—in Judeo-Christian terms, to live as Adam, before the Fall, lived in Paradise. This is not an absurd and peculiar idea. At a certain time in their history, many other primitive peoples believed that it was possible to return periodically to the first days of Creation—that it was possible to live in a dawning and perfect world, such as it had been before it had been consumed by Time and vilified by History.

This article appeared originally as "Paradis et Utopie: Géographie Mythique et Eschatologie," in *Vom Sinn der Utopie, Eranos Jahrbuch 1963* (Zürich: Rhein-Verlag, 1964).

References

1. Cf. Norman Cohn, *The Pursuit of the Millennium* (2nd ed.; New York, 1961); Vittorio Lanternari, *Movimenti religiosi di libertà e di salvezza dei popoli oppressi* (Milan, 1960); Guglielmo Guariglia, *Prophetimus und Heilserwartungsbewegungen als völkerkundliches und religionsgeschichtliches Problem* (Horn, 1959, published 1960); Wilhelm E. Mühlmann, *Chiliasmus und Nativismus* (Berlin, 1961); cf. also Sylvia L. Thrupp (ed.), *Millenial Dreams in Action* (The Hague, 1962); Alphonse Dupront, "Croisades et eschatologie" (*Umanesimo e Esoterismo,* a cura di Enrico Castelli, Padova, 1960, pp. 175–198). On the eschatological implications of the colonization of America, cf. the works of H. Richard Niebuhr, Charles L. Sanford, and George H. Williams cited below.
2. Charles L. Sanford, *The Quest for Paradise* (Urbana, Ill., 1961), p. 40.
3. See the texts cited by Sanford, *op. cit.,* pp. 52 ff. Cf. also George H. Williams, *Wilderness and Paradise in Christian Thought* (New York, 1962), pp. 65 ff.
4. See M. Eliade, "The Quest for Origins in the History of Religions," *History of Religions,* Vol. 4 (1964), pp. 154–169.
5. Quoted by Sanford, *op. cit.,* p. 53.
6. *Ibid.,* p. 74. Cf. also George H. Williams, *Wilderness and Paradise,* pp. 99 ff.; H. Richard Niebuhr, *The Kingdom of God in America* (New York, 1937).
7. Increase Mather, *Discourse on Prayer,* quoted in Sanford, *op. cit.,* pp. 82–83.
8. Texts quoted in Sanford, *op. cit.,* pp. 83–85.
9. Cf. George H. Williams, *Wilderness and Paradise,* pp. 101 ff., 108 ff.
10. Sanford, *op. cit.,* p. 87. Cf. also Williams, *op. cit.,* p. 108.
11. Sanford, *op. cit.,* p. 86.
12. *Ibid.,* pp. 89 ff.
13. Cf. *ibid.,* pp. 96 ff.
14. Texts quoted in Sanford, p. 104.

15. Sanford, *op. cit.*, pp. 105 ff.

16. *Ibid.*, pp. 93 ff.

17. *Ibid.*, pp. 109 ff.

18. Texts quoted in Sanford, *op. cit.*, p. 111.

19. Cf. Sanford, *op. cit.*, pp. 112 ff.

20. Alfred Métraux, "Les Messies de L'Amérique du Sud," *Archives de Sociologie des Religions,* Vol. 4 (1957), pp. 108–112. See p. 151 for text reference.

21. Egon Schaden, "Der Paradiesmythos im Leben der Guarani-Indianer," *Staden-Jahrbuch,* Vol. 3 (São Paolo, 1955), pp. 151–162. See p. 151 for text reference.

22. Alfred Métraux, *op. cit.*, p. 109.

23. Curt Nimuendaju, "Die Sagen von der Erschaffung und Vernichtung der Welt als Grundlagen der Religion der Apapocuva-Guarani," *Zeitschrift für Ethnologie,* Vol. 46 (1914), pp. 284–403; Alfred Métraux, "Migrations historiques des Tupi-Guaranis," *Journal de la Société des Américanistes,* N. S., Vol. 19 (1927), pp. 1–45; Alfred Métraux, "The Guarani," Bureau of American Ethnology, Bulletin 143: *Handbook of South American Indians,* Vol. 3 (1948), pp. 69–94; Métraux, "The Tupinamba," *ibid.*, pp. 95–133; Egon Schaden, "Der Paradiesmythos im Leben der Guarani-Indianer" (cf. note 21); Schaden, *Aspectos fundamentais da cultura guarani* (Universidade de São Paulo, Faculdade de Filosofia, Ciencias e Letras, Boletim No. 188, São Paulo, 1954, pp. 185–204, Ch. X, *O mito do Paraíso na cultura e na vida guarani*); Schaden, "Der Paradiesmythos im Leben der Guarani-Indianer," *XXXth International Congress of Americanists* (Cambridge, 1952), pp. 179–186. Cf. also Maria Isaura Pereira de Queiroz, "L'influence du milieu social interne sur les mouvements messianiques brésiliens," *Archives de Sociologie des Religions,* Vol. 5 (1958), pp. 3–30; Wolfgang H. Lindig, "Wanderungen der Tupi-Guarani und Eschatologie der Apapocuva-Guarani," in Wilhelm E. Mühlmann, *Chiliasmus und Nativismus* (Berlin, 1961), pp. 19–40; Rene Ribeiro, "Brazilian Messianic Movements," Sylvia L. Thrupp (ed.), *op. cit.*, pp. 55–69.

24. Egon Schaden, "Der Paradiesmythos im Leben der Guarani-Indianer," p. 152, and *Aspectos fundamentais,* p. 186.

25. Quoted by A. Métraux, "Les Messies de L'Amérique du Sud," p. 108.

26. Egon Schaden, *Aspectos fundamentais,* p. 187. The belief in a future catastrophe is attested among the Txiriguano (Métraux); Mundurukú (R. P. Albert Kruse, *Anthropos* [1951], p. 922); Tukuna (Nimuendaju, *The Tukuna* [1952], pp. 137–139).

27. Cf. Mircea Eliade, *Myth and Reality* (New York, 1963), pp. 55 ff.

28. Schaden, *Aspectos fundamentais,* p. 187; "Der Paradiesmythos," pp. 152–153; *XXXth International Congress of Americanists,* p. 180.

29. Schaden, *Aspectos fundamentais,* p. 189.

30. Curt Nimuendaju, "Die Sagen von der Erschaffung und Vernichtung der Welt," p. 335.

31. *Ibid.,* p. 339.

32. *Ibid.,* p. 335.

33. See, for instance, Wolfgang H. Lindig, "Wanderungen der Tupi-Guarani," p. 37.

34. Cf. M. Eliade, *Myth and Reality,* Ch. IV, pp. 54 ff.

35. Schaden, *Aspectos fundamentais,* p. 188.

36. In his most recent publications ("Der Paradiesmythos," p. 153, and *XXXth International Congress of Americanists,* p. 181), Egon Schaden estimates that the apocalyptic transformation of the myth of paradise is probably due to Jesuit influence.

37. Egon Schaden, *Aspectos fundamentais,* pp. 189 ff., "Der Paradiesmythos," *Staden-Jahrbuch,* Vol. 3 (1955), pp. 154 ff.

38. Schaden, *Aspectos fundamentais,* p. 192.

39. *Ibid.,* p. 195.

40. *Ibid.,* p. 199.

41. *Ibid.*

42. Cf. Maria Isaura Pereira de Queiroz, "L'Influence du Milieu social interne . . . , pp. 22 ff.

FREDERIK L. POLAK

Utopia and Cultural Renewal

UTOPIA AND its abundant literature have given rise to a score of widely diverging views. Thinking about utopia among scholars, as this book amply demonstrates, tends always to favor opposites and extremes. There is no continuum, only polarization.

A very interesting question is why in the consensus-seeking world of scholars this should be the case. It seems obvious that treacherous subjective elements are creeping in to influence attempts at objective interpretations. But why? Is there something inherently ambivalent or contradictory in the concept of utopia? Or does utopia touch on and attach itself to man's own natural ambivalence? Or have we not yet succeeded in applying objective social-science tools to the analysis of utopia?

This paper will not give final answers to these questions! However, I suggest that this seeming ambivalence, which always attends thinking about utopia, is a reflection of man's changing moods in changing times. The matter is much more complicated than this, however. There is a reciprocal influence between utopian thought and the changing social climate in which it takes place.

Moreover, man is unconsciously much more involved with, not to say indebted to, utopian thought (in its broadest sense) than he —and especially modern emancipated man—is now generally willing to concede, especially as modern connotations of the word "utopian" are steadily deteriorating. At the same time, man's very emancipation owes much both to the utopian forward push and to its very denial or reversal.

Contradictions such as these (and there are others) tend to maneuver us into extreme positions of attack on or defense of utopia. Some will accentuate the newer indication of utopia as unrealistic, illusionary or raising false hope; others will emphasize its original significance of an idealistic, but attainable, future state. Can we disengage ourselves from pride and prejudice?

What is the essence of utopian thought? What is its role, function, and effect?

At least one point is not seriously disputed. Utopian thought always relates to the future, whether near or far away, and a future quite different from present reality. Drastic change is therefore in some way part of it. The conceptualization and visualization of change (a colossal change in itself) is the precondition of actualized social change.

To grasp the significance of this view of the future, we must first turn to the past. In the process we shall see that emerging thought about the future is a significant feature of the historic pattern of man's social and cultural evolution. At some point in an archaic phase of the psycho-physical evolution of life on earth, the unique structure of the human mind emerged. This mental structure was unique in the sense that it had the capacity of dualism. At this point in terrestrial biological evolution, man is the only animal able to pass the frontier of present reality. Man is the only living being who consciously can split reality in two: into the existent and the other. Homo sapiens thus is "split man," who can behave purposefully as a "citizen-of-two-worlds." He can live simultaneously in the here and now and in another world of his own creation. This other world may be quite different from the present one, and even the opposite in many or all respects. The development and refinement of this extraordinary capacity for dualism marks the most significant milestone in the little-understood process of evolution of human culture. It is the key to the progressive bifurcation of nature and nurture. At some point the crude homo faber embarks on his adventurous career as Man the Maker of civilization.

In wrenching itself free from the oppressive grip of the here-now, the human mind was spiritually emancipating itself from spatio-temporal limits of the existing reality and trying to cross the borders of the unknown. It grasped in all directions toward the other, the nonexistent. This other may be seen as having existed previously, to be yet to come, or to be eternally inherent in all time.

Following the evolution of time-consciousness and the mental splitting of the continuous time-flow into "earlier," "later," and "always," the most important step was the separate and definite conception of that which was due "in course of time," some day. Only at this distinctive stage of thought, future-oriented, does the growing difference of degree between man and animal become a fully developed qualitative difference. As soon as the conceptions of "ahead" or "future" are explicitly detached from the undifferentiated time continuum, the real story of man begins.

At that moment the future comes into its own, as a boundless enlargement of the previous limited world view of man. Foresight and forethought enter on the world scene. The future comes to form the central category guiding all incipient cultural activity, and moving the human mind along the age-long road of "progress." Both the idea and reality of a forward-*moving* human civilization are inconceivable without the preceding mental development and advance of forward-*thinking*.

A reality still to come can only be imaginatively built up by mental pictures and communicated in the language of images. This other reality, crystallized in "images of the future," inspires and directs man to reach out above himself, to strive from generation to generation toward another and better time.

A distinction might, of course, be made between a future held to be a universally valid and ultimate embodiment of man's highest ideals, and "the best possible future" for human society as we can conceive it. In Plato we find both conceptions. On the one hand we have the classical platonic ideas which are not only subtle models and mirrors of Plato's own time, Antiquity at its peak, but, even more, universal pre-reflections of an inspired and timeless future for mankind. On the other hand we have his working model of the Politeia as the prototype of an ideal state.

However useful this distinction may be in other respects, I am not concerned with it here. For my purpose both categories can be subsumed under the one heading of man's unequalled capacity to draw a dividing-line between present reality and nonexistent future. And again it is Plato who has given us the sharpest insight, not only into this marvelous working of man's mind, but also into its prodigious and beneficent effects. In his way Plato stresses "split man" as the unique means to evolutionary fulfillment. In the famous dialogue of "Phaedrus," pertaining to the soul of man and its potential to envisage the highest ideas, he has Socrates enunciating the paradox: *"The greatest good comes to mankind through madness, as a divine gift."* . . . Madness, as a divine gift—what does it exactly mean? I am convinced that there is wisdom in these words, also for our time. As Plato's further elucidation shows, such "divine madness" is attached by Socrates to four types of "split personality," to which, from Plato's other writings, a fifth might be added. Such divinely gifted minds are found in: (1) prophets and seers, (2) the poetically bemused, (3) those pre-elected for ritual and religious derangement, (4) those exalted by erotic madness, and (5) those chosen for inspiration or naturally endowed with an affinity for god-sent dreams of therapeutic or predictive significance.

In each of these five cases the relation to the future is a direct and personal one. Prophets are revealing and unveiling the future. Poets tell, in coming back to earth, of their pre-visions of the other world of pure beauty. Religious ecstasy penetrates into the supernatural beyond, or passes temporarily into the absolute, extra-temporal realm of divine truth. Erotic love (in the true platonic sense, so often misunderstood nowadays) leads over, through sublimated passion, to the other, higher world of the spirit, to the immortal soul and the eternal platonic ideas of the good and just. Finally dreams create their own time-dimension, and draw their own time-horizon.

Whatever one is inclined to think of this socratic-platonic dissertation on "divine madness," I myself am convinced that the common essence of these special types of "time-schizophrenia," *viz.* the pull of the future, is of the utmost importance. Prophets, poets, ecstatics, lovers, and dreamers—their flames are kindled in another world by one and the same spark, sprung from the future. Here we meet the prime movers and the forces which drive them toward ever-new forms of civilization and culture.

It becomes clear from Plato's magna opera alone[1] that philosophy at its highest level is intimately integrated with thought about the future. In this sphere, however, philosophy and religion are closely tied, both having their roots in the same dualistic structure of the human mind. It may be well to devote a few paragraphs to this phenomenon, as religion is intertwined with the oldest and most forceful transcendental images of the future—leading over to utopia.

Cosmic speculation and myths, reflecting age-old beliefs concerning the whence and whither, ranging from "in the beginning" to "the last things," merging with the "once upon a time" of the fairy tale and the "and they lived happily forever after" of paradise regained—this is the cradle of any primitive religion. All true religion is essentially prophetic and metahistorical.

If the future were fully known or completely predictable by reason, or by a sixth sense or second sight, the world religions as we know them would never have developed. Religion is partial revelation of the book closed by seven seals. The heart of this revelation is the certainty of coming glory, in some way and at some time, for some people on certain conditions. The core of its prophetic message is contained in a strong positive image of the future.

The Christian faith is born with and vastly expanded by the unveiling of the coming glorious future, previewed in the teaching of the new Messiah. Christianity is indissolubly united with this revelation of God's providential intentions toward man. God is initial Promise and final Fulfillment. A divine future is the a priori premise of God. The idea of time, pregnant with the future, cannot be removed, cannot even be substituted by timeless eternity, without affecting the concept of the Deity. God cannot exist only in the past-present.

This view is in direct contrast with the Freudian conceptions that religion developed in compensation for infantile guilt-complexes and repressed atavistic impulses. Without denying the reinforcing effect of these influences, I hold that we should not look so much back to the unconscious driving forces and motivations from man's prehistoric past, as forward to the propelling force of consciously accepted images of the future. The anthropomorphic gods of cultural history were never stronger than the potential force of the images of the future which they had inspired and which they were firmly pledged to actualize in time.

All religion is concerned with a projected future and can survive only through unconditional belief in this future. Religion, as it has thus far evolved, has been wholly dependent on man's dualistic mental structure. Only by virtue of this time-splitting capacity can man think religiously, that is, futuristically, about infinity, immortality of the soul, reincarnation, or transmigration. It is man's time-schizophrenia which makes possible the concepts of recreation at the apocalyptic end of time, of the perfectability of human life on earth, in heaven, or Beyond, or of the coming Kingdom of God, in consummation of a predetermined plan of eternal harmony for the universe. God acts according to man's projected image after having created man in His own image. In short, religion is based on the condensation and interpretation of eschatological images of the future. The rise and fall of religions corresponds to the vitality or disintegration of their conditioning and controlling images of the future.

Some of these images of the future give only broad outlines of a better world to come; others give more detailed pictures. But never enough! It is typical for man in his ascent that, after splitting off that dimly visaged part of the time flow which is still to come, he wants to know more and more about that future. This leads him to a ceaseless mental probing into the future. A new inventiveness sprouts from this unremitting search. He is now no longer satisfied to know there is such a thing as "later" and eventually "better" in time. He has to discover at all costs how this coming time will work on him personally and—one step further—how he can make it work for him. Here is the origin of all magic and mantic arts, of esoteric priestly knowledge and prophetic divination, of astrology and of science.

In this probing we find the origin of the gradual transition from purely eschatological images of the future to those images which already show utopian traits. In the process, distinctly different attitudes toward the future emerge which assume crucial importance in history, each of which may have either optimistic or pessimistic feeling-tones associated with it. One is the attitude that the future will unfold of itself without man's assistance (*il mondo va da se*). The other is the attitude that man must make his future, determine his own destiny. Most eschatological images of the future, although their final realization may also depend on man's purposeful if foreordained cooperation, are characterized by an underlying *essence*-optimism. In the end all will be well, as was intended from the very beginning. The forces of evil will finally be conquered by divine power.

On the contrary, *influence*-optimism—the conviction that man himself can and must work to make over the barbaric earthly world—is basic for all those images which may be labeled utopian. Here man is given primary responsibility and therefore activated to create a better future. Thus, while *eschatological* images of the future pertain mainly to the last things and the end of historical time, the *utopian* images of the future are mainly concerned with social-humanitarian ideals for the good society and appeal to man specifically in relation to his fellow man.

In reality this distinction often cannot be drawn so sharply, and the two types of images of the future may merge. Eschatological images may have utopian components, and utopian images may have been stimulated by eschatological images and bear their clear imprint. Also, as time goes on, the distinction may blur as man's power over nature grows. In the process the influence-optimism, characteristic of utopian images, may also cast a subtle tint over previous eschatological images, as these come to place a greater weight on man's social being and behavior.

Influence-optimism holds that man cannot become fully man, and attain the summit of human dignity—known in platonic Antiquity and rediscovered in the Renaissance—cannot evolve toward his final maturity in the Kantian sense, if he cannot simultaneously elaborate and refine his mental image of a different and future world. Eschatological or utopian, this image of the future, infusing man with the foreknowledge of happiness and harmony to come, haunts him and challenges him to work for its realization. It is an unborn child seeking to be delivered and promising deliverance to man.

From here we can penetrate to the heart of the matter: As long as feelings of essence- or influence-optimism prevail, the unborn better future is already at work with us. Any positive image of the future which takes hold of the imagination of a society is already interacting with the concrete reality of the past-present.

Would man know more about the future if he studied its pre-reflections in society, the prevailing images and crystallized expectations of the future in various periods of history? In my opinion, yes. Historically, these images of the future not only reflected the shape of things to come; they also *gave* shape to these things and promoted their very coming. Magnetizing images of the future and their inspiring prophets were writing the history of the future. They *made* history by creating this future, by fulfilling their own prophecies. They were like powerful time bombs, exploding in the future, releasing a mighty stream of energy, then flowing back toward the present, which, in its turn, is pushed and pulled to that future.

It is common knowledge that most of our social arrangements and institutions have been foretold long in advance by utopian authors. This is a logical consequence of our main point that the course of history is determined for a considerable part in rough outlines by its preceding and prevailing images of the future, interacting, in complex ways not yet clarified, with the totality of social forces, whenever these images are strongly radiating and resonant in a substantial sector of the society. Even though we do not yet fully understand the nature of this interaction, we get a new perspective on history when we view it as the record of man's ruling images of the future. If we understood better where to look and what to ask, we would see that part of the future is being recorded now in images already operative or in process of creation.

To summarize this view of the role of images of the future in historical development: First and most important is man's emerging time-schizophrenia, his dualistic mental capacity to imagine another and radically different world and time. An élite of spiritual leaders and visionary messengers enter on the scene. They create positive images of a future better than the present. Certain of these images, which happen to combine intellectual insights and esthetic appeal in such a way as to strike emotional resonance with the social and mental needs of the time, arouse great enthusiasm in the masses. Society is then fired by the force of these dominating visions which draw men toward that other and better future. The promises inhering in the visions burst through the historical past-present and break open the hidden present-future. In the process, some of them are seized upon and, as it were, "chosen" by society out of a great many possible futures and harnessed to the present. These images of the future have formed one of the main driving forces of cultural dynamics and have been playing a preponderant role, through their alternating strength and weakness, in the rise and fall of civilizations.

The history of human cultural development abounds with such future-forming images of the future, supplementing and supplanting each other in a continuous golden chain, welded together by the world's greatest prophets, philosophers, poets, humanists, idealists, saints, or scholars. By way of illustration I shall mention here only a few examples of literally world-moving and revolutionizing images of the future.[2]

In the prophetic tradition there is, for example, Iran's prophet Zarathustra, according to whom the history of this world was to come to a climax in the ultimate conquest of the forces of darkness by the God of light. There is, further, the glorious resurrection of Israel by Jahwe, glowingly predicted by the Jewish prophets. Then the coming Kingdom of God, simply and movingly foretold by Jesus and recorded with a wealth of imagery in the Gospels, and the mystically depicted millennium in the Revelation of St. John. There is the presentation of the City of God by Augustine and of the Paradise by Dante. In the intellectual tradition there are conceptions ranging from Plato's ideal State Politeia and his mythical island Atlantis to the Utopia of Thomas More. There is also the new conception of Francis Bacon that natural and technical knowledge equal power, and will rule the future. There are the ideals of human dignity and self-determination of human destiny established in the Renaissance; the proclaimed faith in progress and perfectability by the Age of

Enlightenment and Reason; the utopian projections of Rousseau and Kant; the cry for Liberty, Equality, and Fraternity ringing out through the French Revolution; the belief in the divine and self-evident harmony of individual and general interest evoked by classical liberalism; the firm conviction of the coming classless and stateless society propagated by scientific Marxism. Finally, there is the American Dream, which, living in nameless immigrants and pioneers and activated by the Founding Fathers, formed the spiritual dynamic for the creation of the New World.

A superficial look at the sequence and chronological origins of these examples discloses clearly that at first eschatological images were preponderant, succeeded and later on partly substituted by more earthly utopian images of the future. The demarcation line between these two main categories, however, is not, as said, that sharp. The predicted resurrection of Israel, the promised Holy Land, also contained "utopian" elements, as did the Thousand Year Realm of St. John. Even the evangelic preaching of Jesus in its original interpretation contained clearly utopian concepts concerning the good society. Plato, on the other hand, gives the following "eschatological" answer to the question of whether this utopian city (Politeia) can exist anywhere on earth: "In heaven . . . there is laid up a pattern of it, methinks, which he who derives may behold, and beholding, may take up his abode there. But whether such an one exists, or ever will exist in fact, is no matter; for he will live after the manner of that city, having nothing to do with any other."

In heretic sects and in chiliastic movements from Joachim of Flora in the twelfth century to Thomas Müntzer in the sixteenth century, eschatological images of the future had a strong revival. This millenarian futurism already exhibited an unmistakeable admixture of utopian elements. Chiliastic ideals survived in part of the utopian thought of the Renaissance, which itself contained a revival of platonic and socratic ideals, and found their way into the idealistic and utopian philosophy of Lessing and Kant. Chiliastic and eschatological elements were also still present, in a secularized form, in the utopian, prophetic, and messianic thought of Karl Marx, though he considered himself a declared enemy of utopian socialism.

This mixture of chiliastic and utopian thought fathered two types of offspring who in turn devoured their spiritual progenitors. One strain leads on from Francis Bacon's New Atlantis (from which the Royal Society in England descended in a straight line) toward ideals of technical progress which later blended with the American Creed and finally may lead to an enslaving technocracy.

Another stream has led to the spatio-temporal deformation of ultra-nationalism which substitutes horizontal aspirations of world power for the vertical striving toward the other and better of earlier times. Emerging from the Roman Empire and its successor, the Holy Roman Empire, it moves toward the works of German philosophers like Fichte and Hegel. The colonial empire-builders of the nineteenth century are in this line, as is the Third Reich of Hitler. Within the rising Afro-Asian nations of our time burning images of the future and fiery nationalism have become inseparable. In their necessary search for equality these societies may endanger the very ideals of a coming world order which originally gave them birth.

But even these bumbling, overgrown, fateful descendants or miscreations support the point regarding the impact of images of the future on the actual future. The more we examine history the more we see that the propagation of positive, socially resonant images of the future is a dominating factor in the generation of culture patterns. Cultures slowly climb a staircase of progress, carved out of the future in advance, with the tools of the mind and heart. Cultures are the human expression of the attempt to bridge the gap between the factual environment and another, imagined world. Split man wields the axe which carves the stairway to the future, freeing the world from its cramped perch in the present.

The same process, however, may work in reverse. The weakening, negation, or disintegration of constructive images of the future, and the absence of new positive images to replace antiquated, worn-out conceptions, may spell a period of cultural decline and breakdown. It is possible to trace this process in now extinct ancient world civilizations. Toynbee's concept of challenge and response with regard to the explanation of the rise and fall of civilization is on the right track but is still too vague. The adequacy of the response can be verified by testing the alternating strength and weakness of the images of the future, typical for a specific culture configuration.

Of the thirty civilizations in world history, described by Toynbee, there is, according to his view, a last survivor in the gloomy graveyard of a cultural Stonehenge: our Western civilization. It is a greatly weakened survivor in Toynbee's analysis. I agree, but add: weakened in its cultural core, depleted of one of its main driving forces—its dynamic images of the future.

For thousands of years there was a steady sweep of powerfully propelling images of the future from the early sources of Western civilization. Eschatological, utopian, or mixed, they all pressed forward together. But how does the current move now?

It will probably not be contested that in our time eschatology is no longer an actively operating force in actual history. The evangelical message has been de-mythologized and etherealized. Thus the main force of appealing images of the future now lies in utopian thought in its broadest sense (that is, including chiliastic traces). However, utopianism too has been declining steadily and even come increasingly under attack. There are understandable reasons both for the decline and the attack which cannot be gone into here.[3] *Brave New World* and *1984* are the landmarks of anti-utopia, dividing off the present from all previous time. But this demarcation line is not only a highly significant development of our time; it also holds the key to the shape of things to come. This symptomatic reversal is of a generally underestimated prognostic value.

Western culture today is distorting and destroying those very same images of the future which brought it to its pinnacle. The images of the future are derided, defamed, and dismissed, their ties with the past cut off, their push to the future blocked. Time is centered in the present. Let the future take care of itself. We will cross our bridges when we come to them.

The neurotic personality of our time is no longer schizophrenic by definition. There is a kind of splitting of time into work-time and leisure-time, mainly for escapist ends. The mass media are there to help kill the leisure-time. But this is the very opposite of the idealistic time-splitting among past, present, and future. Where does this repressive mentality leave us? Can we simply forget all about the future, burying our heads and losing ourselves completely in the immediate present? I do think that it is impossible to leave an open space for the future. In culture the abhorrence of the vacuum is as strong and profound as in nature. It is either we ourselves who consciously try to make the future or others who are sure to make the future, both theirs and ours. It is *not* a choice between having or not having any images of the future. It is a choice between good images, worth living and dying for, and bad images, not selected by us but forced upon us. It is a choice between actively devising our own preferred projections of the Promised Land, and the passive choiceless acceptance of a ready-made future, fabricated elsewhere and possibly violating our once most valued ideals.

We may well be approaching, and rapidly, some such fatal stage of development. Let us try to determine our current position, to find true-North and to measure roughly the velocity of the drift. We will examine the strength of the image of the future as an indicator of its regulating power for directing the future course of events in the major areas of the world.

Western Europe, which has held a key position in human civilization of the last few thousand years because, above all, of its unique succession of powerful images of the future, now seems almost exhausted. There are still reverberations from the old idealism, but they grow fainter and fainter. There are attempts at revival and occasional sparks from the still smouldering fire. But the formerly potent images of the future, both eschatological and utopian, if not already in their death-throes, are fading fast. Not only is there no sign of a strong regeneration of these images, but, on the contrary, there is a marked distaste for all idealistic and optimistic thought concerning another and better world. The inverse idea, that we are thrown into the worst of all possible worlds, and one not to be changed, has been making impressive headway.

In North America, largely built up from the European sources of manpower and brainpower, there was at first an astounding renascence of images of the future. As once the Netherlands were literally torn out of the sea and physically and spiritually built up to a Golden Age, so now again step by step the New World was built up straight through rocky mountain ranges, barren wilderness, and arid deserts. Let us not romanticize: of course there was most often an avid desire for material gain. But the beckoning lodestar of the American Dream was also exercising its magnetic force.

By now this too has become past history. This is not the place to assess the validity of this American Dream in today's America. Still it should be persistently asked whether the Dream has indeed retained its old intensity and appeal. Or has it too given way before the forces of anxiety, pessimism, and fatalism? Have these even penetrated into the lion's den of proverbial American optimism? Or has this optimism only shifted its base, altered its objective, and changed its garments? Is the Great Society still to be considered an image of the future, or no more than a short-term program? Extensive socio-psychological research would be necessary to answer these questions, but I fear the answer.

In most of the rest of the world—in what we now call Eastern Europe and in Asia and Africa—there are unquestionably powerful images of the future at work. For the most part indissolubly blended with a nationalistic tidal wave, these pervading images are already changing the face of whole continents, perhaps of the whole world.

To the extent that these new images derive from the thought of Karl Marx they are a product of the same Judeo-Christian heritage which produced the flowering of Western civilization. They are in a way also subject to the same de-eschatologizing and demythologizing process that has undermined the strength of so many former images of the Christian West. However, there has been a little-understood interplay of forces which has made of these secular Marxist images a veritable powerhouse of social energy at the same time that the Christian images have lost their dynamism. There has been, on the other hand, a process of mutual isolation between East and West so that the images have been largely prevented from influencing each other either with their creative or with their destructive potential. As the forces of history tear all isolating curtains down, whether iron or bamboo, we shall see what happens when the images of East and West can really interact in the global context of all the major religious and cultural traditions. Call it a battle for the minds of men, or call it a global dialogue. However it is conceived, these images must interact, and the resulting ideological conflicts will never be resolved on any military battlefield. Conquest of one set of images by the other, or convergence, or a sudden mutation to new unimagined images of the future—whatever is in store will be beyond anything we can now foresee, except that again the potentially strongest, mass-appealing images will come out on top and be builders of the future.

If, in Western society, there ceases to be a place for the image-makers, that is, for philosophers and dreamers, for prophets and poets, for utopian idealists and visionary humanists—and a prominent place at that!—then we risk being, and also deserve to be, swept away in a blaze of new, more vital images of the future, from other parts of the world. The fact that these other images are so often accompanied by a drive for world domination only makes our problem the more pressing, and does not detract from the strength of these new competing images. To answer a drive for power with a counter-drive for power is only a negative answer to an urgent challenge. We must do more than this.

There is still another compelling reason for a *positive* answer, that is, for restoring the constructive images of the future of the West. I refer to the rapidly approaching revolutionary changes that technological innovation, mainly through automation and cybernation, will have wrought in society by the year 2000 or sooner. While automation is no more than a link in an age-old chain of technical evolution, its processes will have far-reaching implications for our conventional social systems, values, and attitudes.

The society of the future will be more radically different from the present than the latter is different from pre-industrial society. The most striking difference will be that the society of the future will carry on preponderantly without productive human labor, but will be based on a robotized economy and a robotized government. I am not here sketching an image of the future, but making a simple extrapolation. The encompassing new problems of this automated society, problems of work and leisure, of a way of life and a right to live fully without working, cannot be met without the timely and adequate forethought of constructive images of the future. Our future society will become sterile and chaotic, our culture will break down and be doomed, as so many civilizations before, if we do not find the right answer to this most formidable challenge of history. To think, dream, and write about this new and almost imminent future is reserved to those few who are gifted with both imagination and the capacity to re-create this awesome prediction into a potentially better future.

Just because today's technology is the offspring of a Baconian image of the future, identified especially in the U.S.A. with ideas of progress as such, it is the more necessary to realize fully that the rapid development toward technocratic machine-society is one more dangerous deformation of a once idealistic image of the future. Left to itself it would ultimately destroy this very future, displacing man and shattering the delicately balanced stability of the social order. Technological change was, of course, at first pushed by Man the Maker, but may itself gradually push man off the scene by means of its self-pushing buttons. More than ever before, a purely technical image of the future now needs a well-equilibrated and up-to-date counterpart, controlling and directing its evolving social processes.

In short, Western culture is threatened by a simultaneous pincer-movement, from without and from within. In meeting the threat of competing images outside and a technology-dominated vacuum within, we have, as a rule, given the wrong answer or none at all. We have indulged in negative anti-utopias aimed at ending all utopias. This is throwing out the baby with the bathwater. Worse still, it encourages the unhampered growth of the imagery of social excrescences. In my opinion, we should give far more attention to constructive counter-utopias, to offset ultra-nationalistic and hyper-technocratic thought about the future. Such deliberate, positive counter-images cannot provide a panacea, nor can they guarantee salvation, but they are an essential prerequisite to continuous progress.

It does not seem very probable, in the context of our cultural evolution, that there will be a mass revival of eschatological images of the future. A counterthrust against modern anti-utopian thought, though difficult, is not impossible. A positive future-consciousness is an absolutely indispensable antidote against the mind-poisoning negativism and threatening ideologies now undermining the foundations of Western culture.

If we do not want, like Toynbee, to depend on miracles, but are disposed to fight for survival, if we strain ourselves to search for a timely and adequate response to the grave challenge of the future, if we really aspire to regain control of human destiny—there is only one way open. A new élite will have to reflect seriously on and completely reorient themselves toward new and galvanizing images of the future. Only images of the future which can depict a drastically changed but viable society can help to write the history of a better future.

To conclude with the words of Thomas More: it is to be desired rather than to be expected. There is no reason at all, however, not to try. Or, again, according to the famous saying of a Dutch Prince of Orange: nul n'est besoin d'espérer pour entreprendre, ni de réussir pour persévérer.

This article was written in consultation with Elise Boulding, Danforth Fellow in the Sociology Department at the University of Michigan, translator of *The Image of the Future,* who is currently working on a paperback condensation of this two-volume work.

References

1. Further elucidation of this point can be found in my paper, "Responsibility for the Future and the Far-Away," given at the Symposium of the International Institute of Philosophy, Paris 1956, and incorporated in its proceedings.
2. A further elucidation will be found in Vol. I of my *The Image of the Future* (Dobbs Ferry, N. Y.: Oceana Publications, 1961).
3. Vol. II of my *The Image of the Future* is devoted to this analysis, which needs further research.

PAUL TILLICH

Critique and Justification of Utopia

A THOROUGHGOING analysis of utopia would involve showing first that it is rooted in the nature of man himself, for it is impossible to understand what it means for man "to have utopia" apart from this fundamental fact. Such an analysis would involve showing further that it is impossible to understand history without utopia, for neither historical consciousness nor action can be meaningful unless utopia is envisaged both at the beginning and at the end of history. And, finally, such an analysis would show that all utopias strive to negate the negative itself in human existence; it is the negative in existence which makes the idea of utopia necessary. These are the three presuppositions for an evaluation of the meaning and characteristics of utopia, and they form the three bases on which this critique and justification will be undertaken.* The evaluation itself will be developed in the following steps:

1) The positive characteristics of utopia
2) The negative characteristics of utopia
3) The transcendence of utopia

Any evaluation of utopia must begin with its *positive meaning*, and the first positive characteristic to be pointed out is its *truth*—utopia is truth. Why is it truth? Because it expresses man's essence, the inner aim of his existence. Utopia shows what man is essentially and what he should have as *telos* of his existence. Every utopia is but one manifestation of what man has as inner aim and what he must have for fulfillment as a person. This definition stresses the social as much as the personal, for it is impossible to understand the

* These presuppositions were developed by Professor Tillich in three preceding lectures of which this was the fourth in the series.

one apart from the other. A socially defined utopia loses its truth if it does not at the same time fulfill the person, just as the individually defined utopia loses its truth if it does not at the same time bring fulfillment to society.

The art of healing serves as a useful illustration of this truth for, as contemporary medical discussions concerning healing have shown, psychological disorders cannot be overcome in the individual and wholeness achieved in the fulfillment of his inner meaning if society at the same time does not provide the surroundings in which health and fulfillment can be maintained. This is revealed in the despairing statement made to me once by a neurologist and analyst. "I have succeeded in healing men," he said, "but I have to send them back to the society from which they come, and I know they will return and beg for my help again." And it is equally true that healing of ills in society and social fulfillment cannot be achieved apart from wholeness in the person. This is the tragedy of the revolutionary movements of the past hundred years, all of which foundered inwardly, and many outwardly, because they expected to heal society without at the same time healing individuals who are the bearers of society. And so they failed. This is what it means to say that the personal and social aspects of utopia cannot be separated. Much of the tragedy of our own situation is rooted in the fact that we do not see it in its unity. If utopia expresses truth about human nature, it then follows that the rejection of utopia, whether cynically or philosophically, is a denial of this truth. Those who reject utopia are therefore lacking in that truth about man which utopia itself expresses. In evaluating utopia, the importance of this truth cannot be overstressed.

The second positive characteristic of utopia is its *fruitfulness*, which stands in closest relationship to its truth. "Fruitfulness" means that utopia opens up possibilities which would have remained lost if not seen by utopian anticipation. Every utopia is an anticipation of human fulfillment, and many things anticipated in utopias have been shown to be real possibilities. Without this anticipatory inventiveness countless possibilities would have remained unrealized. Where no anticipating utopia opens up possibilities we find a stagnant, sterile present—we find a situation in which not only individual but also cultural realization of human possibilities is inhibited and cannot win through to fulfillment. The present, for men who have no utopia, is inevitably constricting; and, similarly, cultures which have no utopia remain imprisoned in the present and quickly fall back into the past, for the present can be fully alive only in tension between past and future. This is the fruitfulness of utopia—its ability to open up possibilities.

And the third positive characteristic of utopia is its *power:* utopia is able to transform the given. Consideration of the great utopian movements of the past will make this immediately evident. Judaism is perhaps the most momentous utopian movement in history, for directly or indirectly it has elevated all mankind to another sphere of existence through its utopia based on the coming Kingdom of God. Bourgeois society with its utopia of the rational state—the "Third Age" of history—has revolutionized, directly or indirectly, the farthest corners of the earth and has thereby called into question and finally made altogether impossible all pre-bourgeois forms of existence. Similarly Marxism through its utopia of the classless society has revolutionized and transformed directly one half of the world and indirectly the other half. These are only three examples that show the power of utopia. In all three cases the question itself concerns something that has no present because it has no place—*ou topos,* "no-place"; but this utopia, which is nowhere, has proved itself the greatest of all powers over the given. The root of its power is the essential—the ontological—discontent of man in every direction of his being. No utopia would have power if it were exclusively economic or exclusively intellectual or exclusively religious. Nor is it true, as a false analysis would have us believe, that it is those who are lowest in society in terms of power of being who are the real bearers of utopia because of their discontent. Rather, the bearers of utopia have been those who in the conflict between security and progress have chosen progress and then enlisted the help of the masses of discontented and used them for their victory, even though in the end the masses perhaps swallowed them up. It is a lesson of history that the bearers of utopia are never those who stand on the lowest rung of the economic ladder, whose discontent is basically economic and nothing more. On the contrary, the bearers of utopia are those who have sufficient power of being to achieve progress. One thinks of the French revolution where the proletariat contributed indispensable assistance but where it was the highly cultivated bourgeoisie who accomplished the revolution. One thinks of the Franciscan revolution where it was the most advanced figures of the order who revolted against the Church. Or one thinks of Marx's analysis of the avant-garde—those at once within the proletariat and yet in part outside who are the real bearers of utopia. This is to say that the power of utopia is *the power of man in his wholeness*—the power of man to push out of the ground of discontent, his ontological discontent, in all directions of being, where the economic plays no greater role than any other factor. The bearers of utopia are those who are able to transform reality, and it is in them that the power of utopia is anchored. So much for the positive meaning of utopia, the "Yes" which we must say to it.

But there is also a *negative meaning*, a "No" which we must say to it, and the first of utopia's negative characteristics is *untruth*. If we previously affirmed the truth of utopia, we must now show its untruth. Both are present together. The untruth of utopia is that it forgets the finitude and estrangement of man, it forgets that man as finite is a union of being and non-being, and it forgets that man under the conditions of existence is always estranged from his true or essential being and that it is therefore impossible to regard his essential being as attainable. One thinks, for example, of the idea of progress, an idea which, to be sure, takes account of man's finitude, at least for this life, yet often grants him development in an after-life. But it forgets that even in an "after-life" finitude would be expressed in every "moment," for the idea of progress belongs not to eternity but to the endless continuation of finitude.

While utopia does presuppose man's essential being, it fails to understand that man has fallen from that essence. "Fallenness" is meant here not in reference to a mythical event of the past but rather as a precise description of man's present condition. The untruth of utopia is its false view of man, and insofar as utopia builds on this untruth in its thought and action it can be dealt with only to the extent that it is shown that the "man" it presupposes is, in fact, *unestranged* man. Here utopia contradicts itself, for it is precisely the utopian contention that estranged man must be led out of his estrangement. But who will do this? Estranged man himself? The question is rather, how can estrangement itself be overcome? And if someone answers, of course not through men themselves but rather through inevitable economic or other processes, then the reply must be made that the understanding of these processes is itself a human act. And if the rejoinder comes, "But freedom is nothing but the knowledge of what is necessary," then we reply that even this knowing stands over against non-knowing, implying the possibility of a decision between them, and this *decision* itself is freedom. The statement "freedom is the knowledge of what is necessary" actually obscures rather than clarifies, for it misconstrues what is called "knowing," namely, the ability to participate in or contradict truth *beyond* necessity, and this ability we presuppose in every moment of our lives. Here is where the untruth of utopia lies. Its untruth is not that it imagines something fantastic in the future; that is unimportant here. What is important is that it actually puts forward a false view of man in contradiction of its own basic presupposition. For almost every utopia is a judgment of the extreme sinfulness of the present or of a social group or people or religion and an attempt to lead out of this situation, but it does not say how this is possible if there is radical estrangement. And this is the heart of utopia's untruth.

Once again we counter a positive characteristic of utopia with a corresponding negative in pointing, secondly, to the *unfruitfulness* of utopia—in addition to and over against its fruitfulness. The fruitfulness of utopia is its discovery of possibilities which can be realized only by pushing forward into the unlimitedness of possibility. The unfruitfulness of utopia is that it describes impossibilities as real possibilities—and fails to see them for what they are, impossibilities, or as oscillation between possibility and impossibility. In so doing, utopia succumbs to pure wishful thinking which, to be sure, has to do with the real (in that it is projected out of and onto real processes) but not with what is essentially human. It is the nature of "wish" to take impossibilities as realities, and this is true from the smallest wishes of children up to the most fantastic wishes of fairy tales. In utopia such wish-projection is self-defeating unrealism, and this is what we call its unfruitfulness. For this reason theologians and political philosophers such as Marx have rightly repudiated this tendency to unrealism in utopian imagination and have made utopia depend on real possibilities, which they show to be real possibilities without overstepping the limits of reality. They have taken care themselves to describe the wishful, unrealistic utopia as a fool's paradise, for those who regard action as something negative and those who have a very distorted view of man will of course visualize utopia in such wishful ways, but such utopias are indeed nothing but a fool's paradise. And this is the origin of the fantastic utopias—they conform not to essential possibilities but rather to a fantastically exaggerated wish for existence which itself has to be overcome. That is the unfruitfulness of utopia in contrast to its fruitfulness.

The third negative characteristic is the *impotence* of utopia in addition to and over against its power. The impotence of utopia is the fact that its negative content of untruth and unfruitfulness leads inevitably to disillusionment. This disillusionment must be discussed metaphysically, not psychologically. It is a disillusionment experienced again and again, and in such a profound way it disrupts man in the deepest levels of his being. Such disillusionment is an inevitable consequence of confusing the ambiguous preliminary with the unambiguous ultimate. However provisionally we live in the future, we actually live always in the preliminary and the ambiguous. But in the movement from present into future what utopia intended as final and therefore fixed as absolute proves contingent in the flux, and this contingency of something regarded as ultimate leads to bitter disillusionment. From this arise two consequences, both very destructive because of utopia's inability to surmount its transitoriness. The first is that those who suffer such disillusionment may become *fanatics against their own past*. This is especially true of those—the intelligentsia above all—who at some time in their life committed themselves to a utopia not as something preliminary but as something ultimate only to learn that not only was it *not* an ultimate, and thus merely preliminary and ambiguous, but in fact was something inherently demonic. This has happened to intelligentsia in America and is a sad and very puzzling fact of American existence—as it is of Western existence generally, and even beyond. This whole class of men represents today one of the most tragic groups in human society and, in a certain respect, one of the most dangerous, because their fanaticism, originally directed against themselves, infects all who have not shared it and whom they therefore take to be secret friends of everything they fanatically oppose. This is one side of the matter and one we must reckon with, though perhaps it is not possible to judge the extent to which this destructiveness characterizes the intellectual and political activity of such men. Yet it is one of the most serious consequences of utopia's impotence.

The other side is that the utopian activists, those who affirm the utopian goal and are able to hold to it despite its contingency and ambiguity, must guard against disillusionment in order to maintain themselves. To do so they resort to *terror*. Terror is an expression of corroding disillusionment in an actualized utopia; disillusionment is staved off through the political effects of terror. And this is the other side we must reckon with, which is just as understandable as the first.

In other words, through disillusionment and through reaction to possible disillusionment the impotence of utopia becomes a demonic force in society. It is just as in the physical realm and above all in the spiritual: "Nature abhors a vacuum." If a demon is driven out and the space remains empty, seven new demons appear to claim it; if a utopia, which is something preliminary, sets itself up as absolute, disillusionment follows. And to the empty place of disillusionment the demons flock; today, especially in Germany, we find ourselves struggling with them.

These are the negative characteristics of utopia, which are just as real as its positive characteristics. But do not think that because the negative meaning is discussed after the positive that the negative is given the last word. The positive endures, but the negative makes its reality felt over against it, and the demand for a way beyond this negativity leads to *the transcendence of utopia.* Every living thing drives beyond itself, transcends itself. The moment in which it no longer does this, in which it remains bound within itself for the sake of internal or external security, the moment in which it no longer makes the experiment of life, in that moment it loses life. Only where life risks itself, stakes itself, and imperils itself in going beyond itself, only there can it be won. The fact that life transcends itself although at the same time it seeks to preserve itself is a universal description, a universal primal law or, as I call it, the ontological structure of being itself. And this structure of life, of wanting to remain within itself and to protect itself while it moves beyond itself, is valid also for utopia. As a consequence utopia is always and necessarily suspended between possibility and impossibility. The decision whether something is possible or impossible has as referent not present reality but something that is on the "other side" of reality, and it is because of this situation that *every utopia is a hovering, a suspension, between possibility and impossibility.* If one now considers what has been said concerning the negative characteristics of utopia, the question arises: Is it not possible to transcend this whole situation in which utopia finds itself? Is it not possible to overcome its negativity in this way not by transcending a little but by a complete and radical transcendence? To transcend a situation radically does not mean to move horizontally—in the sense of always going farther in a horizontal line—but to move vertically, to rise beyond the whole sphere of horizontal transcendence. This question concerns the possibility of transcending the structure of self-preservation and self-transcendence as such, of going beyond it radically in the vertical dimension—or perhaps more accurately, in that dimension where movement is both up and down, out of line and plane. This is a question that can be answered not merely theoretically but historically, from the development of culture itself, from which most utopias come.

If we consider the prophetic line of the Old Testament, we discover in the great prophets a remarkable oscillation or dialectical movement between a partial transcendence, which we can call utopia in the political and social sense, and a radical transcendence that indicates the intrusion of something—the divine—that breaks through the whole horizontal dimension. In the prophetic texts both occur ambiguously together. They are at once political, social, economic, and intellectual—all these elements are present and yet they at the same time go beyond and above everything which can be understood from history itself. They refer realistically to the world and yet they contain an apocalyptic element which transcends the world, and it is this duality, this doubleness, that is so charming in such descriptions, for example, as Isaiah's of the "peaceable kingdom" of animals and men in which the natural and visionary are intermingled and united. But, like all utopias of the vertical dimension, the prophetic utopias themselves were not able to prevent metaphysical disillusionment, a disillusionment as profound and destructive then as now.

In this situation the next stage of radical transcendence occurred, the one we usually call "apocalyptic"—that is, the visionary unveiling (*apokalyptein*, to uncover) of something that is not within history but rather stands against history, "above" or "outside" history, and that makes itself known within history as a new creation. There occurs also a development of this stage in a transcendental way, where all socio-political contents were transcended without, however, negating them. In Christian eschatology, as presented in the New Testament, we find still another stage has been reached: there all social and political contents have been transcended but only the heavenly kingdom itself is described, either in mystical colors or as loving union with the divine. And then there is a final stage, the mystical, where the term "utopia" itself becomes no longer applicable. This is not just the mystical form of Christianity alone but that more inclusive mysticism where fulfillment in the "beyond" completely extinguishes all finite contents. This mysticism, however, is hardly fulfillment at all but rather negation. Now if we view these developments in sequence, we see in the first an oscillation between the political and the transcendental-religious. In the second, the apocalyptic, we see the transcendence of the divine breaking into history but still as something which happens to this world, to transform it though "at the end of the age." In the third we see a transcendental conception in which the earth is "redeemed" or transformed in a more perfect way, yet where in the Christian form something still remains—the symbol "Kingdom of God." And "kingdom" to be sure is a socio-political symbol. Then we see the fourth stage, the mystical, where every political symbol disappears and where everything expressing utopia itself is transcended—not only personality and community but history and form as well.

If we look carefully at these four stages and ask what they have meant for history, we find that the closer they were to the actual political situation the more they manifested both positive and negative characteristics of every utopia: their truth, their fruitfulness, and their power, but at the same time their untruth, their unfruitfulness, and their impotence. We find also that the closer they approached the mystical negation of every utopia, the less real were their socio-political contents and the less was said concerning the essential being of man, but the less threatening was the danger of metaphysical disillusionment, with its ruinous effects.

In response someone might say: Let us then give up every utopia, let us reject not only the prophetic utopia with its secular consequences, and the eschatological, apocalyptic utopia which still maintains relevance to the world and its socio-political realities, and let us renounce even the Christian utopia—lest we miss the transcendent goal of utopia, the mystical union, the mystical fulfillment in the beyond. Perhaps there are people who choose this way as a result of great metaphysical disillusionment in their time, for it is a fact of history, as this discussion has indicated, that this way of escaping disillusionment has been taken.

But if we go this way, if we elevate utopia more and more into the transcendent, out of the horizontal and into the vertical, then there arises the grave danger—and indeed the inevitable danger—that the truth, fruitfulness, and power of utopia will be sacrificed. This can happen in the form of reactionary religious conservatism which in utopian disillusionment not only misunderstands the truth of utopia but denies that truth and, far from affirming the present situation, preaches that denial together with the "fallenness" of the political realm. Such conservatism is a natural ally of a pure transcendental vision of human fulfillment. But those who hold such a view forfeit their influence over history. Even before World War I we found this to be true in Lutheranism where such a conservative transcendental form of utopia resisted every attempt to change reality. We found it also in certain forms of transcendental theology —that theology which in the name of a revelation given from "above" reality denies every realistic effort to better reality. We find it even in the half-religious, half-antireligious stance of certain existentialists who reject the idea of utopia in the name of an idea of absolute freedom of the individual without, however, concern for progress, individual or social. This is what happens if utopia is denied, if it is regarded as untrue, if its fruitfulness is disclaimed and its power thereby undermined. The consequences of this denial, as we know from history, have been extraordinary. A religious transcendentalism that denied utopia has condemned whole peoples to a passivity opposed to all actions which seek to change history and shape reality—and this has been partially the case in Germany. This is why revolutionary-utopian forces have set themselves against transcendentalism with such tremendous power so that now almost everywhere in the world they thrive on this opposition because religions at their center are either quite beyond any utopia, as the great mystical religions of the East, or have a transcendental utopia excluding political activity, as is the case in much of the West. Where this is true, the aggressive utopia is almost irresistible, and in a time of convulsive economic, political, and intellectual upheaval the passive strength of those who must resist such an onslaught has weakened to the extent that the aggressive utopia breaks through in all its revolutionary power. This is a partial analysis of what has happened to a large part of humanity in our own time.

Now, in conclusion, let me attempt briefly to formulate *how we should regard utopia* on the basis of this analysis of its positive and negative meaning and its transcendence. The problem for my generation in Germany came alive when we returned from World War I and found ourselves in the midst of a sharp conflict between a conservative Lutheranism with its transcendental utopia and a worldly utopian socialism with an exclusively immanent utopia.

Socialism had won the revolution because the strength of the conservatives was destroyed or disorganized by the war. Yet the Lutherans, by far the Protestant majority in Germany, rejected with distinct hostility the horizontal utopia of the socialists and accused them of having a false view of man—of being utopia in the sense of utopian untruth. At this time the problem of the relation of politics and religion ceased to be abstract for us and became highly concrete because of this postwar situation. From our experience in the war and our own reflection we were certain of two things: First, that a utopia of simple progress failed to take seriously the finitude and estrangement of the human situation and thus would lead inevitably to metaphysical disillusionment; and, second, that a religion in which utopia is exclusively transcendent cannot be an expression of the New Being, of which the Christian message is witness. These were the two firm convictions which impelled us to act, and in the power of these negations we then tried to understand what the truth, fruitfulness, and power of utopia could mean if we did not fall prey to its untruth, unfruitfulness, and impotence and the metaphysical disillusionment resulting from this impotence. We answered that in the horizontal dimension something *can* happen, something new, something realizable here and now, under present circumstances and conditions, with their unique possibilities. We determined to press forward in order to become aware of our possibilities and convert them into reality. We believed it to be an "hour of fulfillment" of possibilities which earlier had been unable to come to fulfillment. Thus we affirmed the idea of utopia. We felt that man's essential being cried out for a new order and that this new order could be born at that historical moment for a definite historical period. That was one side, and that is why we opposed the transcendental theology of Lutheranism.

On the other side, we fully understood the new order we sought was a preliminary one and therefore ambiguous and not to be taken as absolute. But then came those things of such horrible consequence—terror, and fanaticism turned against itself. Both show that every utopia, when actualized, stands as a transitory reality and is therefore preliminary and ambiguous. We were told that if we dared express such an idea—for which we often used the Greek word *kairos* (the "right time," the hour of fulfillment which has come, which previously had not been and which subsequently would no longer be)—we would weaken the revolutionary forces of the socialist utopia by undermining the faith of those who fought for it. I have always maintained that the power of a movement, particularly a utopian movement, depends on its ability to demand an unconditional faith; and, if it is not granted such faith, then it is unable to actualize itself. The possibility that such faith will be undermined presents perhaps the most serious problem for the concept of *kairos,* one for which there is no adequate solution.

But there is a possible solution, if not a perfect one. Under certain conditions every finite reality which is idolatrously regarded as absolute will inspire fanaticism. This is always a possibility because men will quickly commit themselves to any cause that promises certainty in their existence, and such total commitment produces an abundance of combative forces—the will to martyrdom, the readiness to surrender autonomy, and above all what one might call "ideocracy," total submission to the absolute authority of an idea endowed with divine sanction, even to the extent of becoming a substitute for God, no longer subject to doubt and therefore commanding unconditional adherence. This total commitment is always a possibility, and its power over men should never be underestimated. These are indeed powerful forces, but our question is this: Shall we let such forces, which inspire such fanatic, such idolatrous commitment, go unchallenged? Shall we let them have their way? If we do, they may for a time get the best of us, but then the moment comes in which the aggressive utopia shows it is nothing more than a finite form masquerading as an infinite, an absolute one; and at that moment it collides with other finite forms and is itself shattered in the collision.

This seems to me to be an unavoidable conclusion, and we must choose whether to renounce the forces of fanaticism altogether or, despite the risk, to demand an unconditional commitment to them in the hour of need. In committing ourselves, however, we recognize that we are not committed to something absolute but to something preliminary and ambiguous. It is therefore not of divine inviolability but something we ourselves judge and, if need be, even reject; yet in the moment of action we are enabled to affirm it with an unqualified "Yes." This is true not only in the life of society but in our own lives, every moment, whenever we surrender ourselves to a thing or person—as in every love relationship. If we commit ourselves idolatrously, then metaphysical disillusionment is inevitable. Then the finite person or thing that has been made absolute collides with our own finite and is shattered in the collision. If, however, we say "Yes" to something whose finitude we admit, then the truth of utopia is on our side and this truth will ultimately triumph. I know how difficult it is; I know that from the heated debates in those years between the world wars in which we were repeatedly accused by the utopian side of undermining the forces of battle by appealing to this principle of final criticism. I believe history has proved us right.

This is one answer we gave then, and it is an answer I give today even though the concrete situation itself has changed drastically. The second answer concerns the relation of the immanent and transcendental utopias—or better, since these terms bear such misleading connotations, between the horizontal and vertical utopias. This answer is *the idea of two orders,* one in the horizontal plane, the order of finitude with its possibilities and impossibilities, its risks, its successes and failures; and another, a "vertical order" (the term now used symbolically), an order which secular and religious utopias have expressed in symbols such as "Kingdom of God," "Kingdom of heaven," "Kingdom of justice," and "the consummation." We must always bear in mind that in discussing such symbols we cannot in the least depict literally what they may mean; we only know that no objective concept can yield a meaningful statement about them. But we do have knowledge of these two "orders" because both participate reciprocally in one another. The vertical order participates in the horizontal order—that is, the Kingdom of God actualizes itself in historical events. It both actualizes itself and at the same time is resisted, suppressed, vanquished. Yet it is this fighting Kingdom of God in history that cannot disillusion because it does not confer utopian finality to any place or time in history; rather it always makes itself known again and again in ever new actualizations, so that the truth of utopia is always borne out. This reciprocal participation of the two orders is the solution to the problem of utopia. A Kingdom of God that is not involved in historical events, in utopian actualization in time, is not the Kingdom of God at all but at best only a mystical annihilation of everything that can be "kingdom"—namely, richness, fullness, manifoldness, individuality. And, similarly, a Kingdom of God that is nothing but the historical process produces a utopia of endless progress or convulsive revolution whose catastrophic collapse eventuates in metaphysical disillusionment.

In the doctrine of the two orders we have both historical reality and transhistorical fulfillment: We have the vertical, where alone fulfillment is to be found, yet precisely where we are unable to see it but can only point to it; and the horizontal, actualization in space and time but for that very reason never full actualization but always partial, fragmentary, in this hour, in that form. This is our double answer, and even in making it I would like to say that every manifestation since the end of World War I, when these ideas were conceived, has borne out this answer, and it seems to me today to be still the solution. Whether one can speak at all today in the sense of a *kairos,* as it was unquestionably possible to speak after World War I in Germany—and in such a way as even to be heard beyond the borders of Germany—no one indeed can judge, for we are already emerging from that period into a new one. But my own deep feeling is that ours is a period in which the *kairos,* the right time for utopian realization, lies far before us, invisible, while only a void, an unfulfilled space, a vacuum, surrounds us. But it should be taken as no more than a personal opinion if I have found the situation after both world wars in Germany comparable with that in America. That is not important. What is important are the principles to be derived from the present situation as from that one, insofar always as we are able to describe our situation. What is important is the *idea* of utopia that overcomes utopia in its untruth and sustains it in its truth. Or, as I can perhaps say in summation of the whole discussion: *It is the spirit of utopia that conquers utopia.*

This article appeared originally as "Kritik und Rechtfertigung der Utopie," in *Politische Bedeutung der Utopie im Leben der Völker* (Berlin: Gebrüder Weiss, 1951).

Notes on Contributors

François Bloch-Lainé, born in 1912 in Paris, is Inspector Général des Finances and Directeur Général de la Caisse des Dépôts in France. He is former Directeur du Cabinet of Robert Schuman and Directeur du Trésor. Among his publications are *L'Emploi des Loisirs Ouvriers et l'Éducation Populaire* (1935), *La Zone Franc* (1954), *Le Trésor Public* (1961), and *Pour une Réforme de l'Entreprise* (1963).

Crane Brinton, born in 1898 in Winsted, Connecticut, is McLean Professor of Ancient and Modern History at Harvard University. He was Chairman of the Society of Fellows at Harvard from 1942–64. His publications include *The Jacobins* (1930), *English Political Thought in the 19th Century* (1933), *Decade of Revolution* (1934), *Anatomy of Revolution* (1938), *The United States and Britain* (1945), *Ideas and Men* (1950), and *History of Western Morals* (1959).

Mircea Eliade, born in 1907 in Bucharest, Romania, is presently Sewell L. Avery Distinguished Service Professor for History of Religions at the University of Chicago. Among the books he has written are *The Myth of the Eternal Return* (1955), *Patterns in Comparative Religion* (1958), *Yoga: Immortality and Freedom* (1958), *Shamanism: Archaic Techniques of Ecstasy* (1964), and *The Two and the One* (1965).

Northrop Frye, born in 1912 in Sherbrooke, Quebec Province, is Professor of English and Principal of Victoria College in the University of Toronto. He has also taught at Harvard, Princeton, Columbia, and other universities. Included among his publications are *Fearful Symmetry: A Study of William Blake* (1947), *Anatomy of Criticism* (1957), and *Fables of Identity* (1963). His essay "Myth, Fiction, and Displacement" appeared in the Summer 1961 issue of *Dædalus.*

Bertrand de Jouvenel, born in 1903 in Paris, is President of Société d'Études et de Documentation Economique, Industrielle et Sociale and Director of Études FUTURIBLES. His publications include *Du Contrat Social* (1947), *On Power; Its Nature and the History of its Growth* (1949), *Sovereignty; An Inquiry into the Political Good*

(1957), *The Pure Theory of Politics* (1963), and *L'Art de la Conjecture* (1964). He is also a regular contributor to *SEDEIS*, a journal of economic studies.

GEORGE KATEB, born in 1931 in Brooklyn, New York, is Associate Professor of Political Science at Amherst College. He recently published a book entitled *Utopia and Its Enemies* and has contributed articles and reviews to many periodicals including the *Political Science Quarterly, Zeitschrift für Politik, Symposium, Commentary,* and the *New York Review of Books.*

MAREN LOCKWOOD, born in 1933 in England, is Assistant Professor in the Department of Sociology at the State University of New York at Buffalo. She has just completed a book on the Oneida Community to be called *The Almost Perfect Society.*

FRANK E. MANUEL, born in 1910 in Boston, Massachusetts, is Professor of History at New York University. His publications include *The New World of Henri Saint-Simon* (1956), *The Eighteenth Century Confronts the Gods* (1959), *The Prophets of Paris* (1962), *Isaac Newton, Historian* (1963), and *Shapes of Philosophical History* (1965). His essay "Two Styles of Philosophical History" appeared in the Spring 1962 issue of *Dædalus.*

LEWIS MUMFORD, born in 1895 in Flushing, Long Island, is an eminent author who has taught at Stanford University, the University of Pennsylvania, and Massachusetts Institute of Technology. His extensive publications include *The Story of Utopias* (1922), *Technics and Civilization* (1934), *Art and Technics* (1952), *The Transformation of Man* (1956), and *The City in History,* which received the National Book Award in 1961. Mr. Mumford's article in this book received one of the 1965 Kaufmann International Design Awards of the Institute of International Education.

JOHN R. PIERCE, born in 1910 in Des Moines, Iowa, is Executive Director of Research for the Communications Principles and Systems Divisions of Bell Telephone Laboratories. His technical publications include *Theory and Design of Electron Beams* (1949, with revision in 1954), *Traveling Wave Tubes* (1950), *Electrons, Waves and Messages* (1956), *Symbols, Signals and Noise* (1961), and *Electrons and Waves* (1964). In addition, he has written articles on popular science and short stories.

FREDERIK L. POLAK, born in Amsterdam in 1907, is a Senator in the Netherlands and President of the Netherlands Television University. Among the books he has written are *Value Judgments in the Social Sciences* (1949), *The Image of the Future* (1955), *Hopeful Future Perspectives* (1957), *Automation* (1959), and *How Do We Conquer the Future?* (1964).

PAUL B. SEARS, born in 1891 in Bucyrus, Ohio, is Professor of Conservation and Botany emeritus at Yale University. Among the books he has written are *Deserts on the March* (1935), *This Is Our World* (1937), *Who Are These Americans* (1939), *Life and Environment* (1940), *Charles Darwin* (1950), and *Where There Is Life* (1962). He has also published numerous technical and general papers on ecology and natural resources.

JUDITH N. SHKLAR, born in 1928 in Riga, Latvia, is Lecturer on Government at Harvard University. Her publications include *After Utopia* (1957) and *Legalism* (1964). She has contributed articles to learned journals on Bergson, Harrington, Rousseau, and others.

JOHN MAYNARD SMITH, born in 1920 in London, is Professor of Biology at the University of London. Among his publications are *The Theory of Evolution* (1958) and papers on evolution, population genetics, and the physiology of aging which have appeared in various periodicals. He studied genetics under J. B. S. Haldane at University College, London.

PAUL TILLICH, born in 1886 in Starzeddel, Kreis Guben, Prussia, died in Chicago in 1965. He was most recently John Nuveen Professor of Theology at the University of Chicago. Among his major publications are *The Interpretation of History* (1936), *The Protestant Era* (1948), *The Shaking of the Foundations* (1948), *Systematic Theology*, 3 Vols. (1951, 1959, 1963), *The Courage To Be* (1952), *Theology of Culture* (1959), and *Love, Power and Justice* (1960).

ADAM B. ULAM, born in 1922 in Lwow, Poland, is Professor of Government at Harvard University and Research Fellow at the Russian Research Center at Harvard University. Among the books he has published are *Titoism and the Cominform* (1952), *The Unfinished Revolution* (1960), and *The New Face of Soviet Totalitarianism* (1963).

INDEX

Abundance, 239, 246–250
Academic Marketplace, The, 59
Activism, 108–109
After London, 44
Agrarianism, 74, 119–123, 126, 127–128, 132, 186
Agrippa, Cornelius, 42
Air pollution, 140, 148
Alcott, Bronson, 183, 198
Alexander, 3
Almost Perfect State, The, 44
Alsop, George, 265
American Way of Death, The, 59
Anabaptists, xiii
Anarchy, 27, 44, 51, 121, 128, 205
L'An Deux Mille Quatre Cent Quarante, 54, 74, 77, 220
Andreae, J. V., 70, 73
Animal Farm, 52
Anthropology, philosophical, 240–251
Antichrist, 266–267
Anti-Dühring, ix
Anti-Semitism, 119, 120. *See also* Naziism
Anti-utopia. *See* Dystopias
Ape and Essence, 35
Arendt, Hannah, 105, 250–251, 252, 254, 257
Aristophanes, 71
Aristotle, ix, 7–9, 10, 24, 137, 241, 251
Army: in ancient civilizations, 16–23, 33; in *Looking Backward,* 29; modern utopias abolish, 51. *See also* War
Art, 23, 40, 41, 102, 175, 178–179
Artificial insemination, 150, 156–160
Associationists, 183
Athens, 51; Plato and, 4, 6, 11, 27, 33; role of women in, 39
Atlantis, 4, 11, 39
Atom bomb, 22
Auden, W. H., 245
Authoritarianism, 3, 138; in Greek utopias, 4–6, 9, 10, 11, 33, 45; in ancient civilizations, 12–14, 15–21; effect of technology on, 29; in nineteenth century Russia, 132; in future, 177
Automation, 31, 214, 252, 293–294
Azaïs, Hippolyte, xiv

Babeuf, François, 245
Bacon, Francis, 21, 70; and technology, 26, 27, 28, 75, 77, 137, 147; prophetic tradition, 288, 289
Bakunin, M. A., 120
Barber, C. L., 248
Bellamy, Edward, x, 6, 54, 70, 87; and the city, 3; limitations of his utopia, 9, 14; and world state, 28; his influence, 29; predictions fall short of reality, 30; Morris' reaction to, 44; and social unity, 109
Benedict, Ruth, 93
Bentham, Jeremy, 103, 124, 242
Berger, Gaston, 202
Bergson, Henri, 7, 60
Berkeley, Bishop, 263
Better Less But Better, 134
Beveridge, Sir William, 117
Bichat, M. F. X., 82
Biology, 60, 69, 71, 83, 86, 134
Birth of Tragedy, The, 247
Blanquism, 126
Bloch, Ernst, xi
Bodin, Jean, 107
Bolingbroke, Henry, Viscount, 42
Bourgeois era, 217–218
Brave New World, x, 29, 65, 66, 118, 169, 246, 291
Brazil, 262, 270–277
Breasted, J. H., 16

INDEX

Brisbane, Arthur, 184
Brook Farm, 183, 186
Brown, Norman O., 48, 70, 91, 92–93
Buarque de Hollanda, Sergio, 261
Buber, Martin, 112
Bullinger, Heinrich, 264
Bulwer-Lytton, Edward, 71
Burke, Edmund, 42–43
Burnet, Thomas, 263
Burt, Jonathan, 186
Butler, Samuel, 40, 54

Cabet, Etienne, 14, 51, 80, 84, 109, 222, 223
Calendar reform, 70
Campanella, Tommaso, 35, 70
Campbell, Donald T., 227
Camus, Albert, 61, 248
Candide, 55
Canticle for Leibowitz, A, 44
Capitalism, 27, 91, 130; its relation to liberalism, 122–125, 132; Marx and, 126–127; and anarchism, 128
Carlyle, Thomas, 35, 45
Castiglione, Baldassare, 38
Cavendish, Margaret, 69
Censorship, 5–6, 33, 34
Chance, 9
Change: discouraged in utopias, 7, 31, 76; and nineteenth-century utopias, 80–85; necessity for, 209–210
Channing, William Ellery, 185
Channing, William Henry, 183
Chartist movement, 74, 122–123, 127
Chernyshevsky, N., 129, 131, 134
Chiari, Pietro Abbate, 77
Chiliasts, 79, 289, 291
Christianity: place of utopias in, 34–36; city and, 40–41, 46; and existentialism, 61; and utopias of tranquility, 73, 74; in nineteenth-century utopias, 80; and More, 104. *See also* Religion
Christianopolis, 73
Christian Science, 189
City, the, 144–145, 220; in Greece, 3–12; in Egypt and Mesopotamia, 12–18; and king, 18–22; in literature, 27; in Christianity, 40–41; in Renaissance, 41; presents problems, 149; future decentralization, 176, 177–178, 179. *See also* City planning; Urbanism
City Invincible, 12
City of the Sun, 35, 70
City planning, 4, 106, 112, 193, 194–195, 233
Clark, Colin, 229
Clarkson Domain, 187
Classes: in Greek utopias, 5–6, 9, 51; in nineteenth century, 29, 111; and pastoral ideal, 41; communism and, 44; Mannheim on, 102; and education, 105; resentments, 128–129; in Kenwood, 196. *See also* Democracy; Egalitarianism; Elitism
Cobbett, William, 122, 126
Cohn, Norman, 260
Colonization, 260–269
Columbus, Christopher, 262
Coming Race, The, 71
Commonweal, The, 44
Communism, 14, 46, 56, 245; its effect on utopian thought, 29–30; Morris and, 44; in Morean utopias, 73, 74; Fromm on, 91–92; emotional element in, 111; utopian aspects, 117; and anarchism, 128; and sin, 129; and state, 208; and future, 211. *See also* Karl Marx; Marxism
Communist Manifesto, ix, 121, 245
Computer, use of, 173–176, 177–178
Comte, Auguste, 80, 82, 89; influence of monastic community on, 35; and science and technology, 81; and labor, 85; and social unity, 109; and rationality, 111
Condorcet, M. J. A. N. de, 64, 65, 70; and global utopia, 80; Mannheim on, 102; on democracy and science, 107–108, 110–111
Conservatism, 118, 119, 201–203
Constant, Benjamin, 109
Consumer ideal, 246–247, 250–251
Contract myth, 25, 34, 38–39, 42–43
Cooperative movement, 195
Copernicus, 20, 263
Cotton, John, 265, 267
Council of Europe, xi
County of Lanark, 224
Courtier, 38
Crashaw, William, 263
Crete, 5, 11
Crime, 232–233
Critias, 11, 39
Crossman, Richard, 4
Crusades, 260
Crystal Age, A, 44
Cybernation, 293–294
Cyropaedia, 38

Dana, Charles A., 183
Dante, 34, 288
Darwin, Charles, 60, 62, 191
Darwin, Sir Charles Galton, 62
Darwinism, 86–90, 100, 103
Das Prinzip Hoffnung, xi
Declaration of Independence, 56
Declaration of the Rights of Man, 56–57
Democracy, 4, 29–30, 43–44, 50–68, 107, 213–218
Democratic Party, 87
Depression of 1930's, 74, 145
Descartes, René, 21
Diderot, Denis, 78–79, 106
Diothas, The, 30
Discourse on Inequality, 74
Dostoevsky, Fyodor, 132, 255
Dreyfus affair, 119
Dumoulin, Charles, 264
Dupront, Alphonse, 260
Duveau, Georges, x
Dystopias, x, 9, 15, 23, 291; army and, 18; intellectuals and, 58, 59, 62, 65, 66; parallel utopias, 71; in nineteenth century, 87; arise from disillusionment, 118; and science and technology, 169. *See also* specific titles

Ecology, 137–149
Economy, 35, 214–217; in ancient cities, 14; in literature, 27; and democracies, 30; Morris and, 44; in nineteenth-century utopias, 85; current confusion, 149; production problem, 223–224; colonization and, 266
Eddy, Mary Baker, 189
Education, 210; and utopian myth and contract myth, 37–38; and pastoral ideal, 45; intellectual criticism of, 57–58, 59; and cultural engineering, 63; in utopias of tranquility, 76; liberalism and, 123; in experimental communities, 188–189, 192, 194; continuous, 212–213
Edwards, Jonathan, 265
Egalitarianism, 50–67, 74–75, 77, 79, 82–83
Egypt, 11, 12–18
Eliade, Mircea, 13
Eliot, John, 266
Elitism, 50–67, 102–103
Emerson, Ralph Waldo, 241
Emile, 38
Enclosure movement, 79
Engels, Friedrich, ix, 29, 51, 56, 103, 104, 119, 127
England, 117, 122–124, 266–267
Enlightenment, 57, 58, 60, 185
Erasmus, 42
Erewhon, 40, 54
Eros and Civilization, 48, 92, 246
Eschatology, 260–269, 270–277, 285–295, 303
Esquisse, 80
Études sur les réformateurs ou socialistes modernes, ix
Eugenics, 89; in Plato's utopia, 6; Sir Charles Galton Darwin on, 62; in political utopias, 106; future possibilities, 147, 150–166; in experimental communities, 191–192, 193, 194
Eupsychia, 71, 86–95
Eutopia, 15
Existentialism, 61, 247, 248

Faerie Queene, 38, 42
Fascism, ix, 4, 120–121
Fénelon, François, 70, 105, 106
Feudalism, 217
Feuerbach, P. J. A., 103
Fichte, J. G., 290
Ficino, Marsilio, 263
Fiore, Gioacchino da, 260
Floyd, Thomas, 77
Food supply, 5, 14, 73, 140–143, 148, 189–190
Foreign policy, 267
Fourier, François, 19, 54, 55, 69, 80, 89; limited socialism, 29, 103; influence of monastic community on, 35; dynamic utopia, 81, 83–84, 85; theory of work, 83–84, 91, 93, 187, 233; influence on Skinner, 86; and science, 126
France, Anatole, 87
Frankfort, Henri, 12
Freedom, 31, 33–34, 77, 111, 208–210
Freiland, 85, 109
French Revolution, 21, 42, 79, 103, 107, 288, 298
Freud, Sigmund, 48, 54, 60, 61, 64, 69
Freudianism, 48, 86–87, 90–94, 118
Fromm, Erich, 70, 91–92, 93
Frontier, American, 267–268
Frye, Northrop, viii
Fuller, Buckminster, 224

Fustel de Coulanges, Numa Denis, 13
Future-orientation of utopias, 281–295

Galileo, 21, 263
Galton, Francis, 191
Geddes, Patrick, 145, 194
Geist der Utopie, xi
Geography, 260–269
Germany, 304–309
Gilbert, Sir Humphrey, 263
God's Own Junkyard, 59
God That Failed, The, 132
Godwin, William, 64
Golding, William, 29
Goldsmith, R. W., 234
Goodman, Paul, 112, 195
Goodman, Percival, 195
Gorky, Maxim, 132
Graham diets, 190
Graves, Robert, 32, 44
Greece, 3–11
Greeley, Horace, 183
Growing Up Absurd, 59
Guaranis, 262, 270–277
Guariglia, Guglielmo, 260
Gulliver's Travels, 37, 40, 106

Haldane, J. B. S., 70, 89
Hall, Bishop, 39–40
Handler, Philip, 140
Harrington, James, 75, 107
Hartlib, Samuel, 107
Hawthorne, Nathaniel, 183
Hedonism, 211–212, 242–257
Hegel, Georg W. F., 290
Heliocentrism, 20, 263–264
Henricus ab Ahlefeld, ix
Herbert, George, 264
Hertzka, Theodor, 70, 85 109
Herzen, Alexander, 120, 130, 131, 134
Hesiod, 4, 15, 80
Hidden Persuaders, The, 59
Hilton, James, 42
Hippodamus, ix, 9
Hitler, Adolf, 4, 120, 290
Hobbes, Thomas, 25, 107, 113
Homer, 34
Homo Ludens, 246, 248–249
Housing, 210
Howard, Ebenezer, 194
Howard, L. O., 140
Hudson, W. H., 44
Hughes, H. Stuart, 59–60
Hugwald, Ulrich, 264
Huizinga, J., 246, 248–249
Human Condition, The, 250
Huxley, Aldous, x, 29, 35, 65, 71, 87, 118, 169, 214, 246, 249
Huxley, Julian, 70, 88, 89, 139, 156, 157
Huxley, T. H., 65

Ideology and Utopia, x
Image of the Future, xi
Imperialism, 124
Incan empire, 72
Income, 228
Individuality, 240–241
Industrialism: Morris and, 44–45; after French Revolution, 79; and conservatives and socialists, 116–117, 119–128, 130; and experimental communities, 186–188, 192; and search for paradise, 268–269
Industrial Revolution, 28, 43, 119
Inheritance laws, 74
Innocence, state of. *See* Paradise.
Insolent Chariots, The, 59
Intellectuals: and the masses, 51–52, 53–67, 108; and political theory, 101–114; in nineteenth-century Russia, 119, 129, 130–131, 132; and liberalism, 123–124; and experimental communities, 183–198; and the good life, 253–257
International conferences on utopias, xiii
International Institute of Philosophy, xiii
Irish famine, 125
Island, x, 249

Jacobsen, Thorkild, 12
Jaspers, Karl, 89
Jefferson, Thomas, 188
Jeffries, Richard, 44
Jehovah's Witnesses, 54
Joachim of Flora, 79, 289
John XXIII, Pope, 87
Johnson, Edward, 265
Justice, 32–33, 36, 39

Kant, Immanuel, 289
Kapital, Das, 127
Kautsky, Karl, 102
Kemal Ataturk, 64
Kepler, Johannes, 20
Kerouac, Jack, 48
Khrushchev, Nikita, 87, 117

Index

King, role of, 12–14, 15–18, 19–22, 74, 75, 85
King, Wilford, 229
Koinonia, 192
Kraeling, Carl, 12
Kropotkin, Peter, 120
Kuznets, Simon, 229
Kvuzas, 112

Labor: in Plato's utopia, 5; in Bellamy, 6; in ancient civilizations, 14, 15–23; nature of, 44–45; in utopias of tranquility, 75–76; Fourier's theory of, 83–84, 91, 93, 187; Marx on, 85; and western civilization, 95; in experimental communities, 187–188, 197; and production, 224; and leisure, 233–234; Arendt on, 250; and search for paradise, 265
Labour Party, 117
Lady Chatterley's Lover, 48
Lafargue, Paul, 85
Land of Cockayne, 41–42
Lanternari, Vittorio, 260
Last and First Men, 71, 164
Law, 27–28
Lawrence, D. H., 47–48
Laws, 4, 6, 11, 39, 105
Lee, Mother Ann, 51
Leisure, 210, 212, 213, 234, 239, 240, 248–250
Lenin, V. I., 56, 120, 128, 132, 133, 134
Lesconvel, Pierre de, 74
Lessing, Gotthold Ephraim, 289
Liberalism, 122–126, 129, 132, 133
Life Against Death, 48
Lipset, S. M., 52
Literature, utopia in, 3–10, 25–49, 51–52, 55, 62, 70–94, 109–110, 118, 219–226. *See also* individual authors, individual titles, and Dystopias
Littré, 209
Locke, John, 25, 57, 64
Longfellow, H. W., 190
Looking Backward. See Edward Bellamy
Lord of the Flies, 29
Lost Horizon, 42
Louis XIV, King, 20–21
Luddites, 48, 122
Lutheranism, 304–305
Lyceum lectures, 188
Lycurgus, 105

Machiavelli, Niccolo, 38, 107
Machine, human, 11, 15–23
MacNie, John, 30
Mailer, Norman, 48
Mann, Horace, 188
Mannheim, Karl, x, 101–104, 107, 112
Marcuse, Herbert, 70, 91, 92, 93, 253; on repression, 48; on consumer ideal, 246–247, 250; on display, 249
Marquis, Don, 44
Marriage: in Greek utopias, 6, 9; monastic influence on, 35; in utopias of tranquility, 73, 74, 78–79; in nineteenth century, 79, 83; in experimental communities, 190–192, 193, 194. *See also* Sexual mores
Martin, Roland, 12
Martyrdom of Man, The, 81–82
Marvell, Andrew, 46
Marx, Karl, ix, 56, 69, 80, 104, 109, 119, 131, 292, 298; and technology, 26; and anarchy, 51; dynamic utopia, 81, 300; *Critique of the Gotha Program,* 84–85; and Freudianism, 90–93; Mannheim on, 102; an activist, 108; his rationality, 111; and England, 122; on Owen and Fourier and St. Simon, 126–127; on life of pleasure, 245, 246, 250; his messianism, 289
Marxism, 7, 48, 298; and nineteenth-century utopias, 29; distant ends, 43, 117, 206; not prophetic, 110; beginnings, 119–120; anarchism and, 128; in nineteenth-century Russia, 129–134; prophetic, 289
Maslow, Abraham H., 70, 71, 93–94
Mass media, 178, 179
Mass movements, 111–112
Materialism, 124–125, 130, 132
Mather, Cotton, 265, 267
Mather, Increase, 264, 267
Mead, Margaret, 93
Medicine: improved care, 151, 152–154, 207, 210; mental healing, 189, 190
Mein Kampf, 56
Mercier, Sébastien, 54, 74, 77, 220
Mesmerism, 189
Mesopotamia, 11, 12–18
Messianism, 130, 260-269
Métraux, Alfred, 270
Mill, John Stuart, 25; and élitism, 52, 57; on human nature, 58; on unity, 109; on class war, 111; on individ-

uality, 241; on hedonism, 242–243, 244; on the life of the mind, 253–255
Millenarianism, 80, 110, 260–269, 289
Miller, Henry, 48
Miller, Walter, 44
Millerites, 140
Milton, John, 40
Modern Times community, 191
Modern Utopia, A. See H. G. Wells
Mohl, Robert von, ix
Monasticism, 35
Montaigne, Michel de, 37
Montesquieu, 42
More, Thomas, vii, xii, 69, 70, 71, 79, 84, 116, 295; his utopia, 3, 8, 9, 14, 24, 26, 27, 35, 36–39, 222; his use of term, 8, 219–220; effect of technology on, 28; size of city, 44; and utopia of tranquility, 72–79; and marriage, 73; and personality, 82, 83; influence on Skinner, 86; influence on politics, 87; Mannheim on, 102, 103; political theory, 104–105; and production, 224; in prophetic tradition, 288
Morelly, 70, 74
Morgan, Lloyd, 23
Mormonism, 54, 185, 191
Morris, William, 19, 54, 221, 222, 223; sees world state, 28; pastoral influence, 44–46, 120; and production, 224; on craft, 252
Moses, 263
Mucchielli, Roger, xi
Mühlmann, Wilhelm E., 260
Muller, Herman J., 89, 156, 157
Mumford, Lewis, ix
Mundus Alter et Idem, 39–40
Müntzer, Thomas, 102, 289
Mussolini, Benito, 4
Mysticism, 79, 303–305
Myth of Sisyphus, The, 248
Mythe de la cité idéale, le, xi

National Accounting, 229–230
Nationalism, 179–180, 290, 292
Naziism, 52, 56, 87, 111, 120–121, 290
Neo-positivism, 61
New Atlantis. See Francis Bacon
New Harmony, 186, 187
News from Nowhere. See William Morris
Newton, Sir Isaac, 60, 86
Next Million Years, The, 62
Nietzsche, Friedrich, 6, 80, 93, 247
Nimuendaju, Curt, 270, 272–273
1984, 29, 35, 118, 291
North American Phalanx, 187, 191
Northampton Association, 191
Noyes, John Humphrey, 186, 188–189, 190–191, 193
Noyes, Pierrepont Burt, 193–197

O'Brien, James Bronterre, 74
One Dimensional Man, 246
Oneida Community, 6, 185–198
Original Sin, 104, 108
Orpheus, 263
Ortega y Gasset, x
Orwell, George, 29, 32, 35, 52, 66, 87, 118
Owen, Robert, 54, 55, 69, 84, 103; and élite, 51; and science, 126; experimental communities, 184; and production, 224

Palmer, R. R., 55
Paradise: the search for, 106; in utopian myth, 34, 39–49; and colonization of New World, 260–269; and Guaranis, 270–277
Paradiso, 34
Parliament of Women, 71
Pasch, Georg, ix
Past and Present, 35
Pastoral influence, viii, 40–49, 80, 205
Peace Corps, 198
Peloponnesian War, 11
People's Will, The, 119
Perfectionism, 185–198
Personality, cult of, 79, 82
Petrashevsky, 129
Phaleas, ix, 9
Philip, André, 196
Plague, The, 61
Plato, vii, ix, 49, 71, 72, 106, 146, 263; sees utopia in terms of city, 3–7, 8–9, 27, 44; gives utopia historic foundation, 11, 23–24, 26; isolated utopia, 28; his Republic exists, 32–34, 36; and education, 37–38; and contract theory, 39; and social mobility, 51; as cultural engineer, 63; and natural decay, 75; influence on nineteenth-century utopias, 83; on pleasure and pain, 243–244; his conception of future, 283–284, 288, 289

Play, 246–257
Plekhanov, Georgi V., 132
Plutarch, 105
Poe, Edgar Allan, 30
Polak, Frederik, xi
Police, 76–77
Politics: and Aristotle, 8; and nineteenth-century utopias, 29–30, 35, 87; and pastoral, 42–44; and utopia and democracy, 50–67, 214–217, 252; effect of utopias on, 95; and theory of utopias, 101–114; and utopia and socialism, 116–134; in Germany, 304–309
Politics. See Aristotle
Popper, Karl, x
Population control: in ancient civilization, 12; present, 44; and Morris, 45; and food and water, 140, 141; and future, 143–144, 149, 166; problems with growth, 206–207. *See also* Eugenics
Positivism, 60
Possessed, The, 132
Pragmatism, 60
Prairie Home, 190
Praise of Folly, 42
Prince, 38
Progress: belief in, 55–56, 62, 65–66; religious development of idea, 185; and North American colonization, 262–269
Proletarian movements, 54
Propaganda, 6, 23, 29
Property, 5, 9, 14, 21, 37, 73, 74, 207
Proudhon, Pierre, 131
Psychology: its dissemination, 60–64; and dreams of utopia, xii, 69–71, 76, 83, 84–85, 86–95
Pufendorf, Samuel von, 232
Purgatorio, 34
Pythagoras, 263

Quételet, L. A. J., 232

Rabelais, François, 35
Ragnorok, 140
Raguet, Abbé Gilles Bernard, 76
Rappites, 55, 191
Rationalism, 117
Reade, William Winwood, 81–82
Re-Birth, 44
Reformation, 261, 263, 266
Reformism, 129, 201–218
Reich, Wilhelm, 70, 90–91, 92
Religion: and More, 9; foundation of Egyptian and Mesopotamian civilizations, 12, 13–14, 17–18; authority reduced, 19; place of utopias in, viii, 34–36, 38; inspires utopias, 52, 54–55, 57; utopias distinguished from millennium, 70; in utopias of tranquility, 76; and ideology, 110–112; and socialism and conservatism, 119; and experimental communities, 184–186, 189, 192, 194; and colonization of North America, 260–269; and Guarani search for paradise, 270–277; and future, 281–295; and critique and justification of utopia, 296–309
Renaissance, 27, 289
Renan, Ernest, 86
Republic. See Plato
Restif de la Bretonne, Nicolas Edme, 70, 74, 78
Revisionism, 133
Revivalism, 268
Revolutionism: and utopias, 102–103, 107, 108; emotional element in, 111; Marx and, 127; in nineteenth-century Russia, 129–134; and reformism, 201–203
Reybaud, Louis, ix, 69
Ricardo, David, 124
Rieff, Philip, 93
Riesman, David, 217
Rituals: in utopian literature, 26–27, 28, 30, 31, 39–40; in church, 35
Rochdale pioneers, 195
Rousseau, J. J., 57, 92, 107, 289; and education, 38; and natural society, 42–43; and equality, 74; and production, 223
Ruskin, John, 45
Russell, Bertrand, 4
Russia, 4, 45, 125, 128, 129–134, 208
Ruyer, Raymond, x

Sade, Marquis de, 79
St. Augustine, 34, 288
St. John, 288, 289
St. Simon, Claude Henri, xiv, 69, 86, 91, 92, 103, 119; influence of monastic community, 35; dynamic utopia, 80-81; and egalitarianism, 82–83; and aggression, 84; influence on politics, 87, 108; rationality, 111; and science, 126
Sanford, Charles L., 261, 267, 268

Sartor Resartus, 45
Satire, 28–29, 35, 39–40, 42-44. *See also* Dystopias
Scandinavia, 45
Schaden, Egon, 270, 275–276
Schiller, Friedrich, 244, 246, 249, 250, 253, 256
Science and technology, 6, 11; role of, 21–24; Bacon and, 26, 27, 77; in utopias, 27–29; literary disadvantages, 30–31; man trapped by, 39, 40; and modern utopias, 51; dissemination of, 60; innovation not necessarily utopian, 70; and utopia of tranquility, 74–75; and nineteenth-century utopias, 80–81, 82, 83, 116, 126; Freudianism and, 80–87, 90–94; Darwinism and, 86–90; Condorcet on, 107–108; Marxism oriented to, 119; effect on industrialism, 122–123; and ecology, 137–149; and eugenics, 150–166; and communications, 169–180; and experimental communities, 184, 189, 191; and democracy, 213–218; and production, 224, 228; and leisure, 239; coming changes, 293–294
Science fiction, 28, 35, 81, 134, 205; theme of cyclical return, 44; anxiety in, 226
Self-sufficiency, 5, 9, 12, 28, 81
Sexual mores, 5; and pastoral, 41, 45, 46, 47; and civilization, 48; and utopias of tranquility, 73, 76, 78–79; in nineteenth-century utopias, 79, 83, 84; Eupsychias, 91, 92, 93, 94; in experimental communities, 190–192, 193, 194. *See also* Marriage
Sexualpolitik, 91
Shakers, 55, 185, 186, 191
Sinold, Philipp Balthazar, 75
Sirius, 164
Skaneateles Community, 190
Skinner, B. F., 10, 32, 51, 54, 86
Smith, Adam, 124
Smith, John, 264–265
Smith, Joseph, 51, 54
Socialism: and nineteenth-century utopias, 29–30, 103; intellectuals and, 59; and utopian political theory, 101–114; decline of, 116–134; and realistic utopian thought, 205–207; in Germany, 304–306
Socrates, 5, 6, 9, 37, 39
Solar symbolism, 263–264
Solon, 11
Sorel, Georges, ix
Sparta, 4, 5, 6, 11, 27, 33, 138, 146
Spencer, Herbert, 184
Spenser, Edmund, 38, 42
Spiritualism, 193
Stalin, Joseph, 4, 56, 129
Stamp, Josiah, 229
Stapledon, Olaf, 71, 86, 164
Status Seekers, The, 59
Sterilization. *See* Eugenics
Sterne, Laurence, 48
Stirpiculture, 191–192, 193, 194
Sun, cult of, 20, 263–264
Swift, Jonathan, 37, 40, 43, 106, 225
Sydney, Sir Philip, viii
Sylvania Phalanx, 186
Symonds, John Addington, 183–184
Syndicalism, 128

Teilhard de Chardin, Pierre, 70, 88–89
Temperance movement, 190
Thoreau, H. D., 46–47
Timaeus, vii, 5, 7, 11, 39
Tkachev, P. N., 131
Totalitarianism. *See* Authoritarianism
Toynbee, Arnold, xii, 53, 89, 90, 290, 295
Trade unionism, 122, 196, 197
Tranquility, utopias of, 72–79
Transcendentalism, 60
Transportation and communication, 81–82, 169–180, 207
Tupi-Guaranis, 262, 270–277

Unterwelt, Die, 81
Urbanism, 79, 119, 120, 233, 269. *See also* City
Urban renewal, 121
Ursua, Pedro de, 270
Utilitarianism, 60
Utopia. *See* Thomas More
Utopie et les utopies, L', x

Vanity of the Arts and Sciences, 42
Veblen, Thorstein, 223
Vega, Garcilaso de la, 72
Vegetarianism, 190
Vekhi, 132
Verne, Jules, 126
Vespucci, Amerigo, 220
Voltaire, François, 55
Voluntarism, 19, 20, 209–210
Voting, 52

Voyage en Icarie, 80, 84, 109, 223

Walden, 46–47
Walden Two, 10, 32, 64, 86,
War: and Greek utopias, 5, 6, 7, 8, 9; and ancient civilizations, 12, 17; and utopias of tranquility, 73; economic equivalent of, 179
Ward, Nathanael, 267
Warren, Josiah, 191
Waste Makers, The, 59
Watch the North Wind Rise, 32
Water, 140–142, 145, 146, 148, 231
We, 29, 66, 71, 87, 118
Wells, H. G., 10, 36, 54, 70, 110, 126, 169; sees world state, 28; his class divisions, 35, 51; and change, 80, 81; on diet and faith healing experiments, 190
What Is To Be Done? (Chernyshevsky), 129, 134
What Is To Be Done? (Lenin), 133
When the Sleeper Wakes, 169
Whitehead, Alfred North, 24
White Peacock, 48
Whitman, Walt, 7, 190, 256
Who Is Guilty?, 134
Why Johnny Can't Read, 59
Williams, George H., 261
Wilson, Harold, 117
Winthrop, John, 266
Women, 39, 191
Wordsworth, William, 46, 55, 253
Work. *See* Labor
Wright, Fannie, 191
Wyndham, John, 44

Xenophon, 38

Yeats, W. B., 247–248
Young, Brigham, 54
Youth, cult of, 268

Zamiatin, 29, 66, 71, 87, 118
Zarathustra, 288
Zen Buddhism, 48
Zhelyabov, 131
Zoroaster, 263